# Parallel Lives Vol. 2

# Parallel Lives Vol. 2

## by Plutarch

©2012 SMK Books

Wilder Publications, LLC.
PO Box 3005
Radford VA 24143-3005

ISBN 10: 1-5154-2816-8
ISBN 13: 978-1-5154-2816-9

# Table of Contents:

# Life of Pelopidas.

I. Cato the elder, speaking to some persons who were praising a man of reckless daring and audacity in war, observed that there is a difference between a man's setting a high value on courage, and setting a low value on his own life—and rightly. For a daring soldier in the army of Antigonus, but of broken and ill health, being asked by the king the reason of his paleness, confessed that he was suffering from some secret disorder. When then the king, anxious for him, charged his physicians to use the greatest care in their treatment, if a cure were possible, at length this brave fellow, being restored to health, was no longer fond of peril and furious in battle, so that Antigonus reproved him, and expressed surprise at the change. The man made no secret of his reason, but answered: "My, king, you have made me less warlike by freeing me from those miseries on account of which I used to hold my life cheap." And the Sybarite seems to have spoken to the same effect about the Spartans, when he said that "they do no great thing by dying in the wars in order to escape from such labours and such a mode of life as theirs." However, no wonder if the Sybarites, effete with luxurious debauchery, thought men mad who despised death for love of honour and noble emulation; whereas the Lacedæmonians were enabled by their valour both to live and to die with pleasure, as the elegy shows, which runs thus:

"'Twas not that life or death itself was good, That these heroic spirits shed their blood: This was their aim, and this their latest cry, 'Let us preserve our honour, live or die.'"

For neither is avoidance of death blameable, if a man does not cling to his life from dishonourable motives; nor is exposure to peril honourable, if it springs from carelessness of life. For this reason Homer always brings the most daring and warlike heroes into battle well and beautifully armed, and the Greek lawgivers punish the man who throws away his shield, but not him who throws away his sword or spear, showing that it is each man's duty to take more care that he does not receive hurt himself, than to hurt the enemy, especially if he be the chief of an army or city.

II. For if, as Iphikrates defined it, the light troops resemble the hands, the cavalry the feet, the main body the breast and trunk, and the general the head, then it would appear that he, if he runs into danger and shows personal daring, risks not only his own life, but that of all those whose safety depends upon him; and vice versâ. Wherefore Kallikratidas, although otherwise a great man, yet did not make a good answer to the soothsayer; for when he begged him to beware of death, which was presaged by the sacrifices, he replied that Sparta had more men besides himself. No doubt, in fighting either by sea or land Kallikratidas only counted for one, but as a general, he combined in his own person the strength of all the rest, so that he by whose death so many perished, was indeed more than one. A better answer was that of old Antigonus, who, as he was about to begin a sea-fight off Andros, some one having said that the enemy's fleet was the more numerous, asked, "And for how many do you count me?"—setting a high value, as is due, upon a skilful and brave leader, whose first duty is to keep safe him who preserves all the rest.

So Timotheus said well, when Chares was displaying to the Athenians the wounds on his body, and his shield pierced by a dart. "Now I," said he, "when I was besieging Samos, was quite ashamed if an arrow fell near me, thinking that I was exposing myself more boyishly than was fitting for the general and leader of so important a force." In cases where the personal risk of the general is of great moment to his army, then he must fight and expose himself without stint, and disregard those who say that a general should die of old age, or at any rate, when an old man. But where the gain is small in case of success, while failure ruins everything, no one demands that the work of the common soldier be performed at the risk of the general's life.

These prefatory remarks occurred to me in writing the Lives of Pelopidas and Marcellus, great men who fell in a manner scarce worthy of themselves: for being both of them most stout in battle, and having each illustrated his country by splendid campaigns, against, too, the most terrible antagonists—the one, as we read, having routed Hannibal, who before was invincible, and the other having in a pitched battle conquered the Lacedæmonians, the ruling state by sea and land—yet they without any consideration endangered themselves and flung away their lives just at the time when there was special need for such men to live and command. And on this account I have drawn a parallel between their lives, tracing out the points of resemblance between them.

III. The family of Pelopidas, the son of Hippokles, was an honourable one at Thebes, as likewise was that of Epameinondas. Bred in great affluence, and having early succeeded to a splendid inheritance, he showed eagerness to relieve the deserving poor, that he might prove that he had become the master, not the servant of his riches. In most cases, Aristotle observes, men either do not use their wealth through narrow-mindedness, or else abuse it through extravagance, and the one class are always the slaves of their pleasures, the other of their gains.

Now, while all other persons gratefully made use of Pelopidas's liberality and kindness, Epameinondas alone could not be induced to share his wealth; he thereupon shared the other's poverty, priding himself on simplicity of dress and plainness of food, endurance of fatigue, and thoroughness in the performance of military service; like Kapaneus, in Euripides, who "had plenty of wealth, but was far from proud on account of his wealth," for he felt ashamed to be seen using more bodily luxuries than the poorest Theban citizen. Epameinondas, whose poverty was hereditary, made it lighter and more easily borne by the practice of philosophy, and by choosing from the beginning a single life; while Pelopidas made a brilliant marriage and had children born to him, yet, in spite of this, diminished his fortune by disregard of money-making and by giving up all his time to the service of his country. And when his friends blamed him, and said that he was treating lightly a necessary of life, the possession of money, "Necessary, indeed," he answered, "for Nikodemus here," pointing to a man who was a cripple and blind.

IV. They were both alike in nobleness of spirit, save that Pelopidas took more pleasure in bodily exercise, and Epameinondas in learning, and that the one in his leisure time frequented the palæstra and the hunting field, while the other would listen to and discuss philosophy. And though they have both many titles to glory, yet judicious persons think nothing so much to their credit as that their friendship should have remained from beginning to end unimpaired through so many important crises, campaigns, and administrations. For any one who considers the administrations of Aristeides and Themistokles, and Kimon and Perikles, and Nikias and Alkibiades, how full they were of mutual enmity, distrust, and jealousy, and then contrasts them with the kindness and respect shown by Pelopidas to Epameinondas, will pronounce with truth these men to have really been colleagues in government and war rather than those who were constantly struggling to get the better of one another instead of the enemy. The true cause of this was their virtue, guided by which they sought no glory or gain for themselves from their deeds, from which envious rivalry always results, but both, inflamed by a noble desire to see their country reach its climax of power and renown in their own time, used one another's successes for this purpose as if they were their own. Not but what most people think that their closest friendship arose from the campaign of Mantinea, which they made with a contingent sent from Thebes to serve with the Lacedæmonians, who were then their friends and allies. Stationed together in the ranks, and fighting against the Arcadians, when the wing of the Lacedæmonian army in which they were gave way, and many took to flight, they closed up together and beat off their assailants. Pelopidas, having received seven wounds in front, fell down upon a heap of slain, friends and enemies together; but Epameinondas, though he thought him desperately hurt, ran forward and stood in defence of his body and arms, risking his life alone against a multitude, determined to die rather than leave Pelopidas lying there. He too was in evil plight, with a spear wound in the breast, and a sword-cut on the arm, when Agesipolis, the Spartan king, came to the rescue from the other wing, and most unexpectedly saved the lives of both.

V. After this, the Spartans behaved towards Thebes outwardly as friends and allies, but really viewed with suspicion the spirit and strength of that state. They especially disliked the club presided over by Ismenias and Androkleides, of which Pelopidas was a member, as being of democratic and revolutionary principles. Consequently Archias and Leontidas and Philippus, men of the aristocratic party, wealthy and unscrupulous, persuaded Phœbidas, a Laconian who was passing through the town with an armed force, to seize the Kadmeia by surprise, and, banishing the party that opposed them, establish an aristocratic oligarchy which would be subservient to Sparta.

He was persuaded to do this, and attacked the unsuspecting Thebans during the feast of Thesmophoria. When he gained possession of the height, Ismenias was seized and conveyed to Lacedæmon, and there not long afterwards made away with. Pelopidas, Pherenikus, and Androkleides, with many others, went into exile and were outlawed by proclamation. Epameinondas stayed at home disregarded, not being thought to be a man of action, because of his philosophical habits, nor a man of any power, because of his poverty.

VI. When the Lacedæmonians removed Phœbidas from his command and fined him a hundred thousand drachmas, but nevertheless held the Kadmeia with a garrison, all the other Greeks wondered at their inconsistency, in punishing the doer but approving of the deed; but the Thebans, who had lost their old constitution and were now held in bondage by the party of Archias and Leontidas, had lost all hope of release from their tyrants, who they perceived were merely acting as a guard to the Spartan supremacy in Greece, and therefore could not be put a stop to, unless their enterprise by sea and land could also be checked. However, Leontidas and his party, learning that the exiles were living at Athens, and were popular with the people there, and respected by the upper classes, began to plot against them, and by sending thither men who were unknown to the exiles, they killed Androkleides by stratagem, but failed with the others. There came also despatches from

Lacedæmon to the Athenians, ordering them not to take them in nor to meddle in the matter, but to banish the exiles, on the ground that they had been proclaimed to be public enemies by their allies. But the Athenians, who besides their natural and innate kindness were returning a debt of gratitude to the Thebans, who had been main instruments in the re-establishment of their government, and had decreed that if an Athenian should march in arms against the tyrants through Bœotia, no Bœotian should see or hear him, did the Theban exiles no harm.

VII. Now Pelopidas, although one of the youngest of the exiles, yet used to encourage each of them separately, and would make speeches to them all, pointing out that it was both dishonourable and wicked for them to endure to see their country enslaved and garrisoned by foreigners, and, caring only to save their own lives, to shelter themselves behind decrees of the Athenians, and to pay servile court to the orators who had influence with the people. Rather was it, he urged, their duty to run the greatest risk, taking pattern by the courage and patriotism of Thrasybulus, so that, as he once, starting from Thebes, drove out the thirty tyrants from Athens, they also in their turn, starting from Athens, might set Thebes free. When then he prevailed with these arguments, they sent secretly to Thebes to communicate their determination to such of their friends as were left there. They agreed, and Charon, who was the leading man among them, offered his house for their reception, and Phillidas proceeded to act as secretary to the polemarchs, Archias and Philippus. Epameinondas had long been instilling feelings of patriotism into the youth of Thebes; for in the gymnasia he would bid them lay hold of the Lacedæmonians and wrestle with them, and then seeing them pluming themselves on their success, he would upbraid them, telling them that they ought rather to feel ashamed at being, through their own cowardice, in bondage to men whom they so greatly excelled in strength.

VIII. When a day was fixed on for the attempt, the exiles determined that Pherenikus, with the main body, should remain in the Thriasian plain, while a few of the youngest men ran the risk of entering the city; and if anything were to befall these men, the others would take care that neither their parents nor their children should want for necessaries. First Pelopidas volunteered for the attempt, then Mellon and Damokleides and Theopompus, men of the first families, faithful friends to one another, and ever rivals in glory and bravery. Having made up a party of twelve in all, and embraced those who were to stay, and sent a messenger before them to Charon, they set out, dressed in short cloaks, with hounds and carrying stakes for hunting nets, so that no one whom they met on the road might suspect them, but that they might seem to be merely ranging about the country and hunting. When their messenger reached Charon, and told him that they were on their way, Charon did not, even now that the danger was close to him, falter in his determination, but acted like an honourable man, and received them into his house. But one Hipposthenides, not a bad man, but one who loved his country and favoured the exiles, yet proved wanting in that audacity which this emergency, a hazardous one indeed, and the attempt they had in hand, required.

Apparently the importance of the issue with which he was dealing turned him dizzy; he with difficulty grasped the idea that, trusting in the desperate hopes of exiles, these men were in some fashion about to attempt to overthrow the Lacedæmonian government in Thebes, and the power of Sparta. He went quietly home, and sent one of his friends to Mellon and Pelopidas, bidding them put off their design for the present, to go back to Athens, and await a better opportunity. Chlidon was the name of the messenger, and he hurriedly went to his own house, and, leading out his horse, asked for his bridle. His wife was at her wit's end, as she had it not to give him, but she said that she had lent it to a neighbour. Hereupon there was a quarrel, and words of ill omen were used, for his wife said that she wished it might be a bad journey for him, and for those that sent him; so that Chlidon, having wasted a great part of the day in this squabble, and also drawing a bad augury from what had happened, gave up his journey altogether, and betook himself to something else. So near was this greatest and most glorious of his adventures of missing its opportunity at its very outset.

IX. Now Pelopidas and his party changed their clothes with country people, and separating, came into the city by different ways while it was still daylight. There was a strong wind, and the weather was snowy, so that they were the less noticed, as most people had betaken themselves to their houses on account of the storm; but those who were in the plot met them as they entered, and brought them to Charon's house. With the exiles, they amounted to forty-eight in all.

As to their oppressors, Phillidas the secretary, who had been working with the exiles and knew all their plans, having long before invited Archias and his friends to a wine party to meet certain courtesans, intended to endeavour to hand them over to their assailants in as enervated and intoxicated a condition as possible. However before they were very far gone in liquor a rumour was brought to their ears, which, although true, was without confirmation and very vague, to the effect that the exiles were concealed in the city. Though Phillidas endeavoured to change the subject, still Archias sent one of his servants to Charon, ordering him to come instantly. Now it was evening, and Pelopidas and his party were preparing themselves, in the house, and had already got their corslets on, and had girt on their swords. Suddenly, a knock was heard at the door. One of them ran out, and hearing the servant say that Charon had been sent for by the polemarchs, he in great trepidation brought the news to the rest. At once it occurred to all that the plot had been betrayed, and that they all were lost, without even having done anything worthy of their courage. Yet they agreed that Charon should comply with the summons and that he should unsuspiciously present himself before the Spartan chiefs. He was a man of courage, and slow to lose heart, but now he was panic-stricken and terrified lest when so many brave citizens lost their lives, some suspicion of treachery might rest on himself. So, just when he was going, he brought his son from the women's apartments, a boy still, but in beauty and strength surpassing all of his own age, and handed him over to Pelopidas's party, bidding them treat him as an enemy and show no mercy, if they should find him guilty of any deceit or treachery. Many of them shed tears at the feeling shown by Charon, and his noble spirit, and all felt shame, that he should think any of them so base and so affected by their present danger, as to suspect him or even to blame him, and they begged him not to mix up his son with them, but put him out of the way of the coming stroke, that he might be saved and escape from the tyrants, and some day return and avenge his father and his friends. But Charon refused to take away his son, for what life, he asked, or what place of safety could be more honourable to him than an easy death with his father and so many friends? After praying and embracing them all, and bidding them be of good cheer, he went away, taking great pains to adopt a look and tone of voice as different as possible to that of a conspirator.

X. When he came to the door, Archias and Philippus met him and said, "Charon, I have heard that some people have come here, and are concealed in the city, and that some of the citizens are in league with them." Charon was at first disconcerted, but then enquired who these persons might be, and who they were that gave them shelter. Seeing then that Archias knew nothing for certain, he perceived that the news did not come from any one who knew the truth. "Take care," said he, "that this be not a mere idle rumour that is alarming you. However, I will make due enquiries; for we ought not to disregard anything." Phillidas, who was present, expressed his approval of this, and carrying Archias back again plied him with liquor, prolonging his debauch by holding out the expectation of the women.

Now when Charon returned to his house, he found the conspirators there prepared to fight, not expecting to survive or to win the day, but to die gloriously and kill as many of their enemies as possible. He told Pelopidas's party the truth, and made up some story about Archias to satisfy the others. This storm was just blown over when Fortune sent a second upon them. A messenger came from Athens, from Archias the hierophant to his namesake Archias the Spartan, whose guest and friend he was, bearing a letter which contained no vague and conjectural suspicion, but a detailed account of all that was being done, as was afterwards discovered. Now the messenger, when brought before Archias who was drunk, gave him the letter, and said, "He who sent you this letter bade you read it instantly, for he said it was written about most serious matters." Archias laughing, said, "Serious matters to-morrow." He took the letter and placed it under the pillow on which he rested, and again listened to Phillidas about what they were talking of before. This story, handed down in the form of a proverb, is current among the Greeks even now.

XI. As the hour for the attempt seemed now to have arrived, they sallied forth, in two bodies: the one, under Pelopidas and Damokleides, to attack Leontidas and Hypates, who lived near one another, while the other, under Charon and Mellon, went to Archias and Philippus, with women's gowns over their steel corslets, and their faces concealed by thick wreaths of fir and pine wood; and so when first they entered the door of the dining-room they caused great applause and disturbance, as the guests imagined that the long-expected ladies had at length come. They looked carefully round the party, and having ascertained who each of the guests were, they drew their swords, and made for Archias and Philippus. When they thus betrayed themselves, Phillidas persuaded some few of the guests to remain quiet, but the rest, who rose and tried to assist the polemarchs, were easily disposed of on account of their drunken condition.

The task of Pelopidas and his party was a harder one; for they went to attack Leontidas, a sober and brave man, and, finding his house shut up, for he was already asleep, they knocked for some time without rousing any one. At length the servant heard them and came and drew back the bolt of the door; then, as soon as the leaves of the door yielded they burst in in a body, and upsetting the servant made for the bedchamber. Leontidas, guessing from the noise and confusion what was going on, started up and seized his dagger, but he forgot to put out the light, and make the men fall upon each other in the darkness. In full view of them, in a blaze of light, he met them at his chamber door, and with a blow of his dagger struck down Kephisodorus, the first man who entered. As he fell dead Leontidas grappled with the next, Pelopidas. The struggle was a fierce one and rendered difficult by the narrow passage and the corpse of Kephisodorus lying in it, but at length Pelopidas gained the upper hand, and having despatched him, immediately went with his party to attack Hypates. And in the same way they broke into his house, but he heard them sooner, and fled away to the neighbours, but was pursued and slain.

XII. Having accomplished this, and joined Mellon's party, they sent word to the remaining exiles in Attica, and called together the citizens to complete their deliverance, and as they came, gave them arms, taking down the trophies which hung in the public colonnades, and breaking into the workshops of spear-makers and sword-cutlers. And Epameinondas and Gorgidas, with their party, came to help them, armed; for they had collected together no small number of the younger men and the strongest of the elder ones. By this time the whole city was roused, and there was great confusion, lights flitting about, and people running to one another's houses, but the people had not yet assembled, but being alarmed at what had happened, and knowing nothing for certain, they waited for daylight. And here the generals of the Lacedæmonian garrison seem to have missed an opportunity in not at once sallying out and attacking them, for the garrison itself consisted of 1500 men, and many people kept running to them for refuge from the city; however, alarmed at the shouts and fires and mass of people assembling from all parts, they remained quiet, holding the Kadmeia only. At daybreak arrived the exiles from Attica, fully armed, and the public assembly met. Epameinondas and Gorgidas led forward the band of Pelopidas, surrounded by the priests, who crowned them with wreaths, and called upon the citizens to fight for their country and their gods. The whole assembly, with shouts and applause, rose at the sight, and received them as their benefactors and saviours.

XIII. After this, Pelopidas, who was chosen Bœotarch, with Mellon and Charon as colleagues, at once blockaded the citadel, and made assaults upon it on all sides, being eager to drive out the Lacedæmonians and recover the Kadmeia before an army should come upon them from Sparta. And so little time had he to spare, that the garrison, when going home after their capitulation, met at Megara Kleombrotus, marching with a great force against Thebes. Of the three men who had been governors of Thebes, the Spartans condemned two, Herippidas and Arkissus, to death, and the third, Lysanorides, was heavily fined and banished.

This adventure was called by the Greeks the "sister" of that of Thrasybulus, as it resembled it in the bravery and personal risk of its chief actors, and was, like the other, favoured by fortune. It is difficult to mention any other persons, who with fewer numbers and scantier means than these, conquered men more numerous and powerful than themselves, by sheer daring and ability, or who conferred greater blessings on their own countries; and that which made this more remarkable was the change which it effected. The war which destroyed the prestige of Sparta, and put an end to her empire by sea and land, began in that night, in which Pelopidas, without having made himself master of any fort, stronghold, or citadel, but merely coming to a private house with eleven others, loosed and broke to pieces, if we may use a true metaphor, the chains of Lacedæmonian supremacy, which seemed fixed and immovable.

XIV. Now when a great Lacedæmonian army invaded Bœotia, the Athenians manifested great alarm. They repudiated their alliance with the Thebans, and impeached those who had shown Bœotian sympathies; some of these men were put to death, others fined and banished. The case of the Thebans seemed desperate, as no one offered to help them; but Pelopidas, who with Gorgidas was Bœotarch, contrived to alienate the Athenians from Sparta by the following plot. Sphodrias, a Spartan, of great renown in the wars, but somewhat flighty and prone to wild enterprises and reckless ambition, had been left near Thespiæ with an army, to receive and assist those Thebans who were now sent into exile because they favoured the Lacedæmonians. Pelopidas sent secretly to this man a merchant, a friend of his own, who gave him a bribe, and also made proposals which fascinated him more than the money, that he should attempt some enterprise on a great scale, and surprise Peiræus by a sudden attack when the Athenians were off their guard: for the Lacedæmonians would be better pleased with the capture of Athens than with anything else, and the Thebans would not assist them, for they were at variance with them and regarded them as traitors. At length Sphodrias was prevailed upon to agree to this, and, with his soldiery, invaded Attica by night. He got as far as Eleusis, but there the soldiers lost heart, and the attempt was detected. So, having involved the Spartans in a war of no slight importance, he retired to Thespiæ.

XV. Upon this the Athenians again most eagerly allied themselves with the Thebans, and, aspiring to supremacy at sea, sent embassies round to the other maritime states, and brought over to their own side those who were willing to revolt from the Spartans. Meanwhile the Thebans, alone in their country of Bœotia, constantly skirmishing with the Lacedæmonians, and not fighting any great battles with them, but organising themselves with the greatest care and discipline, began to pluck up spirit, gaining skill from practice, and becoming confident from the result of these encounters. This was why they say that Antalkidas the Spartan, when King Agesilaus was being carried home wounded from Bœotia, said to him, "Indeed, you are receiving nice lessons from the Thebans, now that you have taught them how to fight against their will." But their real teacher was not Agesilaus, but those who, seizing fit opportunities, and with due management, skilfully used to let them loose upon their enemies, as men train young mastiffs, and then when they had tasted victory and self-confidence brought them safely back. Of these leaders Pelopidas received the chief credit. From the year in which he was first elected general they never ceased to re-elect him, and he was always either in command of the Sacred Band or most commonly acting as Bœotarch until his death. There took place also about Platæa and Thespiæ defeats and routs of the Lacedæmonians, in which Phœbidas, who seized the Kadmeia, perished; and Pelopidas routed a number of them near Tanagra, and slew Panthoides the governor. Still, although these skirmishes raised the spirits and confidence of the victors, yet they did not cast down the pride of the vanquished; for they were not regular battles, but the Thebans won their successes by well-timed charges and harassing the enemy by alternate retreat and advance.

However, the affair at Tegyra, which in a manner was preliminary to that at Leuktra, won Pelopidas a great reputation; for there was no question of any other general having assisted in the design of the battle, nor of the enemy being thoroughly routed. The city of Orchomenus had taken the Spartan side, and had received two moras of Spartan troops for its protection. He always had his eye upon this place, and watched his opportunity. Hearing that the garrison had made an expedition into Lokris, he marched, hoping to catch Orchomenus defenceless, taking with him the Sacred Band and a few cavalry. When he came to the city he found that the garrison had been relieved by fresh troops from Sparta, and so he led off his men homewards through Tegyra, the only way that he could, by a circuitous route at the foot of the mountains; for the river Melas, which from its very source spreads into morasses and quagmires, made the direct way impassable.

Near the marshes stands a temple of Apollo of Tegyra and an oracle, which is now forsaken; it has not been long so, but flourished up to the Persian War, when Echekrates was priest. There the myths say that the god was born; and the neighbouring mountain is called Delos, and there the overflowings of the river Melas cease, while behind the temple there flow two springs remarkable for the sweetness, coldness, and volume of their waters, which we up to this day call, the one "The Palm," and the other "The Olive," as though the goddess had not been delivered between two trees, but two fountains. Indeed, close by is the Ptoüm, whence they say that she was driven in terror by the sudden apparition of a wild boar, and with regard to the legends of Tityos and Pytho, the localities are in like manner associated with the birth of the god. I omit the greater part of these proofs, for our ancestral religion tells us that this god is not to be ranked among those divinities who were born as men, like Herakles and Dionysus, and by their merits were translated from this earthly and suffering body, but he is one of the eternal ones who know no birth, if one may form any conjecture upon such matters from the writings of our wisest and most ancient writers.

XVII. At Tegyra, then, Pelopidas and the Thebans retiring from Orchomenus met the Lacedæmonians marching back from Lokris, in the opposite direction. When they were first descried coming out from the narrow gorges of the hills, some one ran to Pelopidas, and cried out, "We have fallen into the midst of the enemy!" "Why so," asked he, "more than they into the midst of us?" He at once ordered his cavalry to the front to charge the enemy first, and closed up his infantry, three hundred in number, into a compact body, trusting that wherever he attacked the enemy he should break through, although they outnumbered him. They consisted of two moras of Lacedæmonians: now Ephorus says that a mora consists of 500 men, but Kallisthenes says 700, and some other authorities, and amongst them Polybius, put it at 900.

Gorgoleon and Theopompus, the polemarchs in command of the Spartans, moved confidently to the attack of the Thebans; and the onset was directed on both sides, with great fury, specially at the persons of the leaders. The two polemarchs dashed against Pelopidas, and both fell; then the slaughter of their immediate followers produced a panic in the whole force, and it gave way to the Thebans, opening a lane through the centre as if for them to pass through. But when Pelopidas led his men into the passage thus offered, and assailed those who stood their ground, passing through it with great slaughter, then all fled in hopeless rout.

The pursuit was not pressed far, for the Thebans feared the vicinity of Orchomenus and of the Spartan reinforcement there; but as far as winning the victory, and forcing their way through the beaten enemy, they were completely successful; so after setting up a trophy and spoiling the dead they returned home in high spirits. For in all the wars which had previously taken place, both with Greeks and barbarians, it never before had happened that Lacedæmonians should be conquered by an inferior force, nor yet even when the numbers on each side were equal. Wherefore they were invincible in their own estimation, and established an ascendant over the minds of their opponents, for they were wont to engage with men who did not themselves think that with equal force they could be a match for the same number of Spartans. But this battle first proved to the rest of Greece that it is not only the Eurotas, and the country between Babuke and Knacion that nurtures brave and warlike men, but that wherever the youth of a nation fears disgrace and is willing to risk life for honour, and shrinks from shame more than from danger, these form the troops most terrible to their foes.

XVIII. The Sacred Band, they say, was first formed by Gorgidas, of 300 picked men, whom the city drilled and lodged in the Kadmeia when on service, wherefore they were called the "city" regiment; for people then generally called the citadel the "city." Some say that this force was composed of intimate friends, and indeed there is current a saying of Pammenes, that Homer's Nestor is not a good general when he bids the Greeks assemble by their tribes and clans:

"That tribe to tribe, and clan to clan give aid,"

whereas he ought to have placed side by side men who loved each other, for men care little in time of danger for men of the same tribe or clan, whereas the bond of affection is one that cannot be broken, as men will stand fast in battle from the strength of their affection for others, and from feeling shame at showing themselves cowards before them. Nor is this to be wondered at, seeing that men stand more in awe of the objects of their love when they are absent than they do of others when present, as was the case with that man who begged and entreated one of the enemy to stab him in the breast as he lay wounded, "in order," said he, "that my friend may not see me lying dead with a wound in the back, and be ashamed of me." And Iolaus, the favourite of Herakles, is said to have taken part in his labours and to have accompanied him; and Aristotle says that even in his own time lovers would make their vows at the tomb of Iolaus.

It is probable, therefore, that the Sacred Band was so named, because Plato also speaks of a lover as a friend inspired from Heaven. Up to the battle of Chæronea it is said to have continued invincible, and when Philip stood after the battle viewing the slain, in that part of the field where the Three Hundred lay dead in their armour, heaped upon one another, having met the spears of his phalanx face to face, he wondered at the sight, and learning that it was the Band of Lovers, burst into tears, and said, "Perish those who suspect those men of doing or enduring anything base."

XIX. As to these intimacies between friends, it was not, as the poets say, the disaster of Laius which first introduced the custom into Thebes, but their lawgivers, wishing to soften and improve the natural violence and ferocity of their passions, used music largely in their education, both in sport and earnest, giving the flute especial honour, and by mixing the youth together in the palæstra, produced many glorious examples of mutual affection. Rightly too did they establish in their city that goddess who is said to be the daughter of Ares and Aphrodite, Harmonia; since, wherever warlike power is duly blended with eloquence and refinement, there all things tend to the formation of a harmonious and perfect commonwealth.

Now, as to the Sacred Band, Gorgidas originally placed them in the first rank, and so spread them all along the first line of battle, and did not by this means render their valour so conspicuous, nor did he use them in a mass for any attack, but their courage was weakened by so large an infusion of inferior soldiery; but Pelopidas, after the splendid display of their valour under his own eye at Tegyra, never separated or scattered them, but would stand the brunt of battle, using them as one body. For as horses driven in a chariot go faster than those going loose, not because they more easily cleave the air when galloping in a solid body, but because their rivalry and racing with one another kindles, their spirit, so he imagined that brave men, inciting each other to an emulation in adventure, would prove most useful and forward when acting in one body.

XX. When the Lacedæmonians made peace with all the other Greeks and attacked the Thebans alone, and Kleombrotus, their king, invaded Bœotia with ten thousand hoplites and a thousand cavalry, the danger was not that they should be reduced to their former condition, but absolute destruction plainly threatened their city, and such terror prevailed as never before had been in Bœotia. Pelopidas, when leaving his house, as his wife wept at parting with him and begged him to be careful of his life, answered, "My dear, this is very good advice for private soldiers, but we who are commanders must think about saving the lives of others." When he reached the camp, he found the Bœotarchs differing in opinion, and he at once gave his voice for the plan of Epameinondas, who voted for battle. He was not named Bœotarch, but he was in command of the Sacred Band, and enjoyed great confidence, as was only just a man should who had given such proofs of patriotism.

When, then, they had determined to face the enemy, and taken up a position at Leuktra opposite to the Spartan army, Pelopidas saw a vision in his sleep which greatly disturbed him. In the plain of Leuktra there are the tombs of the daughters of Skedasus, whom they call Leuktridæ because of the place of their burial; for there it was that they were buried after they had been violated by some Spartan strangers. When this base and impious deed was done, their father, as he could get no satisfaction from the Lacedæmonians, invoked curses upon the Spartan race, and slew himself at the tombs of his daughters. Oracles and legends always had warned the Spartans to beware of the vengeance of Leuktra, though most of them did not understand it, and were not clear as to the place, since a small sea-side town in Laconia is also called Leuktron, and there is a place of the same name near Megalopolis in Arcadia, and, also, this crime was committed a long time before the battle.

XXI. So now Pelopidas, when asleep in the camp, seemed to see the maidens weeping over their tombs and invoking curses on the Spartans, and Skedasus, who bade him sacrifice a red virgin to the maidens, if he wished to conquer his enemies. And as this command seemed to him shocking and impious, he started up and consulted the prophets and the generals. Some of them forbade him to neglect or disobey the warning, quoting the famous old instances of Menækeus the son of Kreon and Makaria the daughter of Herakles, and, in later times, Pherekydes the philosopher, who was killed by the Lacedæmonians, and whose skin, according to some oracle, is still kept by their kings, and Leonidas, who following the oracle did in some sort offer himself as a victim on behalf of Greece; and futhermore they spoke of those persons whom Themistokles sacrificed to Dionysus before the sea-fight at Salamis. All these are verified by the success which followed them. And again, Agesilaus when starting from the same place that Agamemnon did to fight the same enemies, was asked by the god, during a vision at Aulis, to give him his daughter as a sacrifice; but he did not give her, but by his softheartedness ruined the expedition, which ingloriously failed. Others spoke on the other side, urging that so barbarous and impious a sacrifice could not be pleasing to any of the powers above, for, they said, it is not the Typhons and giants of legend that rule in heaven, but the father of all gods and men. To believe that there are deities that delight in the blood and slaughter of mankind is probably a foolish fancy; but if there be such, it is our duty to disregard them and treat them as powerless, for these strange and shocking desires can only take their origin and exist in feeble and depraved minds.

XXII. While the chiefs of the army were engaged in this discussion, and Pelopidas especially was at a loss what to do, a filly escaped from some horses at pasture, and running through the ranks stopped opposite them. They admired her coat shining with the brightest red, and the mettled courage of her neigh, but Theokritus the prophet, comprehending what was meant, called to Pelopidas: "Happy man! Here is your victim; let us not expect any other virgin, but take the gift the gods provide you." Hereupon they caught the filly and led it to the tombs of the maidens. Here, after prayer, they hung garlands on the tombs, and made the sacrifice with joy, explaining to the whole army the vision of Pelopidas and their reasons for the sacrifice.

XXIII. In the battle, Epameinondas brought his main body slantingly towards the left, in order that the Spartan right might be drawn as far as possible away from the other Greeks, and that by falling violently on Kleombrotus with his whole force on that wing, he might overpower and crush him. The enemy, perceiving what was being done, began to alter their own formation, extending their right, with the intention of outflanking and enveloping Epameinondas. At this moment Pelopidas charged with the Three Hundred in serried ranks. He caught the Lacedæmonians in a moment of confusion, when they were not standing ready to make an attack, for Kleombrotus had not time either to extend his right, or to bring the troops back again and close up the ranks. Yet the Spartans, skilled as they were to the highest pitch in war, had been specially educated and practised in changing their formation without disorder or confusion; each man used any other as his right-hand or rear-rank man, and wherever danger threatened they would meet it, forming and fighting simultaneously. But now, when the main Theban phalanx under Epameinondas, projecting before all the rest of the line, bore down upon them, and when Pelopidas, by a charge of inconceivable speed and daring was already amongst their ranks, their spirit and discipline was so shaken that the rout and slaughter of the Spartans was such as had never been before. In this victory and success as much glory belonged to Pelopidas, though not one of the generals, and only in command of a few men, as to Epameinondas, who was Bœotarch and leader of the whole force.

XXIV. In the invasion of Peloponnesus they were both Bœotarchs, and they brought over to their side most of the nations there, for they detached from the Lacedæmonian alliance Elis, Argos, the whole of Arcadia, and most part of Laconia itself. It was mid-winter, a few days only remained of the last month, and with the new year the law was that the commands should be delivered up and new generals chosen. Death was the penalty in case of disobedience, and all the other Bœotarchs, fearing this law and wishing to avoid the severe weather, wished to withdraw the army homewards, but Pelopidas first, supported by Epameinondas, encouraged his fellow citizens, and crossed the Eurotas. He took many of their towns and wasted all their country up to the sea-coast, with an army of 70,000 Greeks, of whom the Thebans formed less than a twelfth part. But the great reputation which these men enjoyed made the rest follow them without any formal vote or decree to do so; for the first and most fundamental law is that which makes men in need of help follow him who can save them; and even if, like men sailing on a calm sea or anchored close to port, they sometimes murmur at and brave their pilot, yet in time of danger and storm they look up to him and place all their hopes in him, so the Argives and Eleans and Arcadians would at the council-board dispute the Theban claims to supremacy, but in war and at critical moments they of their own accord obeyed the Theban generals. In this campaign, Arcadia was consolidated into one state; they also separated Messenia, which had been annexed by the Spartans, and bringing back the Messenian exiles established them in the old capital, Ithome. On their homeward march through Kenchreæ they gained a victory over the Athenians, who attempted to harass them and hinder their march through the narrow isthmus of Corinth.

XXV. After these exploits all men were full of admiration and wonder at their courage and success, but at home the envious feelings of their countrymen and political opponents, which grew along with the growth of their renown, prepared a most scurvy reception for them. On their return they were both tried for their lives, on the ground that whereas the law is that during the first month of the year, which they call Boukation, the Bœotarchs must lay down their office, they had held it for four additional months, during which they had been settling the affairs of Messenia, Laconia, and Arcadia. Pelopidas was tried first, and so incurred the greater danger, but both were acquitted.

Epameinondas, who thought that true courage and magnanimity was best shown by forbearance in political strife, bore this contemptible attack with patience, but Pelopidas, who was of a hotter temper, and whose friends encouraged him to revenge, chose this for its opportunity. Menekleides the orator had been one of the conspirators who came with Pelopidas and Mellon to Charon's house. As, after the revolution, he did not obtain equal rights with the rest, being a man of great ability in speaking, but reckless and ill-conditioned, he took to using his powers to slander and assail the men in power, and was not silenced even by the result of that trial. He got Epameinondas turned out of his office of Bœotarch, and for a long time succeeded in lessening his influence in the state; but Pelopidas he could not misrepresent to the people, so he endeavoured to make a quarrel between him and Charon. He used the usual method of detractors, who if they themselves be inferior to the object of their spite, try at any rate to prove that he is inferior to some one else; and having the ear of the people, he was ever singing the praises of Charon, and uttering panegyrics on his skill and his success. He endeavoured to set up a memorial of the cavalry battle at Platæa, before the battle of Leuktra, in which the Thebans under Charon were victorious, in the following manner. Androkydes of Kyzikus had been entrusted by the state with the task of painting a picture of some other battle, and had been engaged on it at Thebes. When the war broke out, this picture, nearly completed, was left in the hands of the Thebans; and Menekleides persuaded them to put it up publicly and to write on it the name of Charon, in order to throw the glory of Pelopidas and Epameinondas into the shade; a silly exhibition of ill-feeling indeed, to compare one poor skirmish, in which Gerandas, an obscure Spartan, and some forty men fell, with the great and important services of the others.

Pelopidas indicted this proposal as illegal, arguing that it was not the custom of the Thebans to show honour to individuals, but to keep alive the name of a victory for the glory of the country at large. He bestowed unmeasured praise upon Charon throughout the trial, and proved Menekleides to be a malignant slanderer. He was fined a large sum, and not being able to pay it, subsequently endeavoured to bring about a revolution in the state; by which one gains some insight into his character.

XXVI. Alexander, the tyrant of Pheræ, was at this time at open war with many states of Thessaly, and threatened the independence of all. Ambassadors from these states were sent to Thebes, begging for a military force and a general to be despatched to their assistance. Pelopidas, since Epameinondas was busy settling the affairs of Peloponnesus, offered himself to the Thessalians, as he could not bear that his talents and skill should lie idle, and he thought that where Epameinondas was, no second general could be needed. So he marched with a sufficient army into Thessaly, took Larissa, and, when Alexander begged for terms of peace, endeavoured to convert him into a mild and law-abiding ruler. But he, a wild, desperate, cruel barbarian, when he was accused of insolent and grasping practices, and Pelopidas used harsh and angry language, went off in a rage, with his body-guard. Pelopidas, having relieved the Thessalians from fear of the tyrant, and reconciled them one to another, proceeded to Macedonia. Here Ptolemy was at war with Alexander the king of Macedonia, and each of them had sent for him to act as arbitrator and judge between them, thinking that he would right whichever of them should prove to have been wronged. He came, and settled their dispute, and after bringing back the exiled party, took Philip, the king's brother, and thirty other sons of the noblest families as hostages, and kept them at Thebes, to show the Greeks how far the Theban policy extended, merely through its reputation for power and for justice.

This was that Philip who afterwards endeavoured to enslave Greece; at that time he was but a lad, and lived in the house of Pammenes. On this account he was thought to be an imitator of Epameinondas, and perhaps he did take to heart that great man's energy in war, which was one of his virtues, but as to the spirit of self-restraint, justice, magnanimity and mildness, which formed the true greatness of his character, of this Philip neither by nature or education had the least idea.

XXVII. After these events, the Thessalians again complained of Alexander of Pheræ for attacking their cities, and Pelopidas and Ismenias were sent as ambassadors to them. Pelopidas, however, brought no army with him, as no war was expected, and was forced to make use of the native Thessalians in this emergency. As affairs in Macedonia had again fallen into disorder (for Ptolemy had assassinated the king, and was in possession of the sovereignty, while the friends of the deceased invited Pelopidas to interfere), he wished to do something; and having no troops of his own, he hired some local mercenaries and marched off at once against Ptolemy. When they drew near to each other, Ptolemy by bribes induced the mercenaries to desert to himself, but, fearing the mere name and prestige of Pelopidas, he went out to him as though he were the more powerful of the two, and after greeting him and begging him to be his friend, he agreed to hold the kingdom in trust for the brothers of the deceased king, and to form a defensive and offensive alliance with Thebes. For the fulfilment of these conditions he gave as hostages his own son Philoxenus and fifty of his companions, whom Pelopidas sent to Thebes, but as he was angry at the desertion of his mercenaries, and learned that their property, wives and children were for the most part placed in Pharsalus, so that by capturing that place he could make them pay the penalty of their crime, he got together a force of Thessalians and came to Pharsalus. When he was just arrived, Alexander the tyrant appeared with his army. Pelopidas and his friends supposed that he had come to establish his innocence, and went to meet him, knowing him to be profligate and bloodthirsty, yet fearing no harm, because of the name of Thebes and their own personal prestige. But he, when he saw them approaching him unarmed and alone, at once secured them and took Pharsalus, striking fear and terror into all his subjects; for they expected that after an act of such daring lawlessness he would spare no one, but treat them as one who had made up his mind to lose his own life.

XXVIII. The Thebans when they heard of this were greatly moved, and at once despatched an army to the rescue, but on account of some quarrel with Epameinondas they appointed others to the command. The tyrant took Pelopidas to Pheræ, and at first allowed any who chose to converse with him, supposing that he would be cast down and humbled by his misfortunes; but when the people of Pheræ came to lament over him, Pelopidas bade them be of good courage, as now if ever the tyrant would have to pay the penalty of his crimes: and he sent a message to the tyrant himself, saying that he was a strange man, to torture and murder his wretched and innocent citizens every day, and to spare him, who he knew would be sure to wreak vengeance on him if he should escape. The tyrant, admiring his spirit and fearlessness, said, "What! does Pelopidas wish to die?" The other, hearing of this answered, "Yes, that you may become even more hateful to heaven than you are now, and so may die sooner."

Hereupon he prevented the people from having access to him, but Thêbê, the daughter of Jason, and Alexander's wife, having heard from the guards of Pelopidas of his daring and nobleness, desired to see the man and converse with him. When she was come she did not, woman-like, at once perceive the greatness of his mind in the position in which he was, but judging from his short-cut hair, his dress and his food, that he was treated ill and not as became such a man, she wept. Pelopidas, not knowing at first who she was, was surprised at this, but, when he knew her, addressed her by her father's name, for he was a companion and friend of Jason. When she said, "I pity your wife," "So do I pity you," answered he, "that without being a prisoner you stay with Alexander." This speech somehow touched the lady, for she was grieved at the ferocity and licentiousness of the tyrant, who, besides his other atrocities, had debauched her youngest brother. She constantly visited Pelopidas, and, talking to him of her sufferings, became filled with courage, and with hatred of Alexander.

XXIX. The Theban generals invaded Thessaly, but through incompetence or misfortune effected nothing, and had to retreat in disgrace. The state fined them ten thousand drachmas, but sent Epameinondas with the army. There was at once a great fluttering of hope among the cities of Thessaly at the reputation of that general, and the cause of the tyrant tottered to its fall, such fear fell upon his officers and friends, and such a longing to subvert his government upon his subjects, who viewed the future with hope, as now they expected to see the tyrant meet with his deserts. However, Epameinondas, disregarding his own glory in comparison with the safety of Pelopidas, and fearing that if Alexander were driven to despair by seeing his kingdom falling to pieces, he might turn upon him like a wild beast, conducted the war remissly. By degrees and after slow preparation he surrounded the tyrant and confined him to one spot, so as to be able to check any attack that he might venture on, and yet not to excite his savage and ferocious nature; for he had heard of his cruelty and disregard of what is right, and how he would bury men alive, and dress them in the skins of wild boars and bears and then set dogs at them and hunt them with spears, making this his sport, and how he surrounded two peaceful cities, Melibœa and Skottusa, with his body-guard when the inhabitants were at their public assembly, and slew them all from the youth upwards, and how he had consecrated and crowned the spear with which he killed his uncle Polyphron, and used to address prayers to it and call it the Slayer. Once when he saw a tragedian performing Euripides' tragedy, the 'Troades,' he went suddenly out of the theatre, and sent a message to him to be of good courage, and not act worse for this, for he had not left the house because he disliked his acting, but because he felt ashamed that the citizens should see him weeping at the woes of Hekuba and Andromache, though he never had pitied any of the people whom he had put to death himself. But he, terrified by the prestige and reputation of Epameinondas for strategy,

"Let fall his feathers like a craven cock,"

and quickly sent an embassy to him to make peace. Epameinondas scorned to make a treaty of peace and friendship between the Thebans and such a man, but agreed to an armistice for thirty days, and taking Pelopidas and Ismenias returned home.

XXX. When the Thebans heard that ambassadors were being sent from Athens and Sparta to the Great King to make an alliance with him, they also sent Pelopidas, a step most advantageous to his reputation. As he went on his journey through the Persian provinces he excited the greatest admiration, for the fame of his victories over the Lacedæmonians had spread trumpet-tongued through Asia, and from the time of his first success at Leuktra it had begun to reach far and wide, some new exploit being ever added to it, till it reached to the furthest peoples. Next, when he reached the court, he was an object of wonder and interest to the satraps, generals, and officers there. "This is the man," they said, "who destroyed the Lacedæmonian dominion over sea and land, and who reduced to the little state at the foot of Taygetus by the Eurotas, that Sparta which a little while before went to war under Agesilaus with the Great King himself about Susa and Ecbatana." At this Artaxerxes himself was pleased, and admired Pelopidas and showed him great honour, as he wished it to appear that he was courted and sought after by the most powerful Greeks. After an interview, in which he found that he spoke with sounder sense than the Athenians, and greater simplicity than the Spartans, he esteemed him still more, and after the fashion of monarchs, did not conceal his regard, but let the other ambassadors see plainly that he was highest in favour. Of all the Greeks he showed Antalkidas the greatest honour, when he took off his own wreath of flowers at table and dipping it in scent, gave it him to put on. He attempted no such refinements with Pelopidas, but gave him presents, more splendid and valuable than was customary, and assented to his proposals that all Greek states should be independent, that Messenia should be reconstituted, and that the Thebans should be accounted the king's old friends.

With these answers, and none of the presents except such as were pledges of friendship and good will, he returned, to the great discredit of the other ambassadors. The Athenians condemned and executed Timagoras, and if it was for the amount of presents which he received, rightly enough; for he not only took silver and gold, but a costly bed and slaves to make it, as if Greeks did not know how, and also eighty cows and their herdsmen, on the pretence of wanting cow's milk for some weakness that he suffered from; and at last he went down to the sea-coast carried in a palanquin, and four talents were given by the king to his bearers—still, it does not seem to have been his venality which especially disgusted the Athenians. At any rate, Epikrates, called the "Bearded," once brought a motion before the assembly that instead of electing nine archons yearly they should send nine poor citizens as ambassadors to the Great King, that they might be enriched by him, at which there was great laughter. But it was because of the success of the Thebans that they were so vexed, not reflecting on the power of Pelopidas's name, and how far it outweighed all their rhetoric in the estimation of one who always inclined to the stronger side.

XXXI. On his return, Pelopidas was welcomed with no little gratitude because he had re-established Messenia, and obtained freedom for all other Greeks. But Alexander of Pheræ had relapsed into his old courses, and had ravaged the territory of many cities of Thessaly. The Phthiot Achæans and Magnetes formed a league to oppose him, and hearing of Pelopidas's return, these cities sent to Thebes begging for a force to help them and for him as its general. The Thebans willingly decreed this, but when all was ready and the general was about to march, the sun was eclipsed and darkness fell upon the city. Pelopidas, seeing that all men were disheartened at this, thought that it was useless to force frightened men full of presage of evil, to march with him, nor did he like to risk the lives of six thousand citizens, but he offered his own services to the Thessalians, and took with him three hundred horsemen, volunteers and men of other states. With this force he started, though forbidden by the prophets and against the will of his fellow citizens, who all held that a great portent had been shown in heaven about some celebrated man. However, he was all the fiercer against Alexander, remembering his own sufferings, and hoping from his conversations with Thêbê, that by this time his own family would have turned against him. He was also much encouraged by the glory of the action, that, at a time when the Lacedæmonians were sending out generals and governors to help Dionysius the Sicilian tyrant, and when the Athenians had Alexander in their pay, and had even set up a bronze statue of him as a public benefactor, he might show the Greeks that it was the Thebans alone who took up arms in defence of the oppressed, and who put an end to the violent and illegal rule of despots in Greece.

XXXII. When he had come to Pharsalus and collected his army there, he marched straight to attack Alexander. But he, seeing that Pelopidas's force of Thebans was small, while he had more than double his numbers of Thessalian hoplites, met him near the shrine of Thetis. When some one said to Pelopidas that the tyrant was coming on with a great force, he answered. "So much the better, for we shall conquer more."

Between the two armies, near the place called Kynoskephalæ, or the Dog's Heads, were some high and isolated hills. Each party tried to occupy these with their infantry, but Pelopidas, knowing his cavalry to be numerous and good, sent it to charge that of the enemy. The enemy's horse was routed, and pursued over the plain, but meanwhile Alexander had secured the hills, and when the Thessalian infantry came afterwards, and tried to force their way up the hill into that strong position, he was able to cut down the foremost, while the rest suffered from his missiles and could do nothing. Pelopidas now recalled the cavalry, and sent it to attack the enemy's position in flank, while he himself took his shield and ran to join the infantry in their fight on the hill. Pushing his way through their ranks till he reached the front he infused such strength and ardour into them, that the enemy thought that they attacked with new bodies as well as new spirit. They repulsed one or two assaults, but seeing that the infantry resolutely came on, and also that the cavalry had returned from its pursuit and was threatening their flank, they made an orderly retreat. Pelopidas, when he gained the height, saw below him the whole of the enemy not yet beaten, but confused and shaken. He stood still and looked around him, seeking Alexander himself. When he saw him, on the right, rallying and encouraging his mercenaries, he could no longer restrain his rage, but kindling at the sight, and, reckless of his own person and of his duties as a general, rushed far beyond the rest, shouting and challenging the tyrant to fight. He would not await the attack, but took refuge in the ranks of his body-guard. Pelopidas attacked these troops and cut them down, wounding several mortally, but they from a distance struck him through his armour with their spears, till the Thessalians in great anxiety charged down the hill to the rescue. But he had by this time fallen.

The cavalry now charged and routed the whole body, and pursuing them to a great distance, strewed the country with corpses, for they cut down more than three thousand of them.

XXXIII. It was no wonder that the Thebans who were there grieved at the death of Pelopidas, and called him their father, their saviour, their teacher in all that was best and noblest; but the Thessalians and their allies, who decreed greater honours than had ever been shown to any brave man, proved their gratitude to him, even more by their sorrow. It is said that the men who were at the fight did not lay aside their armour, nor unbridle their horses, nor even bind up their wounds, when they heard of his death, but warm as they were from victory, in their arms, flocked round the corpse, piling up near it, as a trophy, the arms of their slain enemies. They cut off the manes of their horses, and their own hair, and many went off to their tents, lit no fire, and ate no supper, but there was such silence and despondency in the whole camp as would have befitted men who had been defeated and enslaved by the tyrant, not who had just won a great and glorious victory over him.

As soon as the sad news reached the cities of Thessaly, the chief men, youths, children and priests came forth in procession to receive his body, and carried trophies and wreaths and golden armour in its honour. When the body was about to be brought home, the chiefs of the Thessalians begged the Thebans to allow them to bury him, and one of them spoke as follows: "Allies, we beg of you a favour which will prove to be an honour and a comfort to us in this our great misfortune. We Thessalians shall never again escort Pelopidas, nor render him the honours which he deserved; but if we may have his body to touch, and ourselves adorn it and bury it, we shall then be able to show you that we Thessalians truly feel this misfortune more than even you Thebans. For you have only lost a good general, while we have lost that, and our liberty too, since how can we ever have the heart to ask you for another general, after not giving you your Pelopidas back."

This proposal the Thebans agreed to.

XXXIV. No funeral was more splendid than this, not indeed in the estimation of those who think that splendour lies in ivory and gold and purple, as Philistius celebrates and praises the funeral of Dionysius, where his tyranny concluded like the pompous finale of some great tragedy. Alexander the Great, when Hephæstion died, not only cut off the manes of the horses and mules, but actually took down the battlements from the walls, that cities might seem in mourning, presenting a shorn and woeful look in contrast to their former appearance.

But these were the commands of tyrants; they were done under compulsion, and caused a feeling of dislike to the person honoured, and of absolute hatred against those who enforced them, but showed no gratitude or desire to honour the dead. They were mere displays of barbaric pride and boastful extravagance, which wastes its superfluity on vain and useless objects; whereas, here was a private citizen who died in a foreign land, without his wife, his children or his friends, and, without any one asking for it or compelling them to it, he was escorted to his grave, buried and crowned with garlands by so many provinces and cities, vying with one another in showing him honour, that he seems to have enjoyed the most blessed fate possible. For as Æsop says, the death of the fortunate is not grievous, but blessed, since it secures their felicity, and puts it out of Fortune's power. That Spartan spoke well, who, when Diagoras, the Olympic victor, was looking at his sons being in their turn crowned as victors at Olympia, with his grandchildren about him, embraced him and said, "Die, Diagoras; for you cannot rise to Olympus and be a god there." Yet I do not suppose that any one would compare all the Olympian and Pythian prizes together with one of Pelopidas's achievements, of which he performed many, and lived the most part of his life esteemed and looked up to, and at last, in his thirteenth Bœotarchy, when fighting gloriously against a tyrant, he died in defence of the liberties of Thessaly.

XXXV. His death caused great sorrow to his allies, but likewise benefited them; for the Thebans as soon as they heard of the death of Pelopidas did not delay for a moment to avenge his fall, but hastily marched with an army of seven thousand hoplites and seven hundred cavalry, under Malkitus and Diogeiton, against Alexander. Finding that he was weakened and shorn of much of his power, they compelled him to restore to the Thessalians their cities, which he held, to liberate the Achæans in Magnesia and Phthiotis, to withdraw his garrisons from those countries, and to swear to the Thebans, that he would attack, and assist them to attack, any enemy they might choose.

The Thebans were satisfied with these terms; but I will now recount how, shortly afterwards, Heaven exacted retribution from him for the death of Pelopidas. Thêbê his wife, as we have said before, had been taught by Pelopidas not to fear the outward pomp and body-guard of the tyrant, since she was within all his defences. She, dreading his suspicious nature, and hating his cruelty, made a plot with her three brothers, Tisiphonus, Pytholaus, and Lykophron, which she carried out in the following manner. The night patrol of the guard watched in the house, but their bedchamber was upstairs, and before the door there was a dog chained as a guard, very savage with every one except themselves and one of their servants who fed it. Now when Thêbê determined to make the attempt, she got her brothers concealed near at hand during the day in one of the rooms, and when she came, as usual, alone to Alexander's chamber, she found him asleep. In a little time she came out again, and ordered the servant to take away the dog, as the despot wished to sleep undisturbed. Fearing that the stairs would make a noise when the young men mounted, she covered them with wool, and then brought up her brothers, with their swords drawn. Leaving them outside she herself went in, and taking down the sword that hung over his head, showed it to them as a proof that he was in their power and asleep. The young men now were terrified, and hesitated to act; but she reproached them bitterly, and swore that she would herself awaken Alexander and tell him the whole plot. Between shame and terror she got them in and placed them round the bed, herself holding the light. One of them seized his feet, another held his head back by the hair, and the third despatched him with a stab of his sword, a death, perhaps, easier than he deserved. He was the first, or perhaps the only despot ever assassinated by his own wife. His body after death was dragged about and trodden under foot by the people of Pheræ, a recompense which his villanies deserved.

# Life of Marcellus.

I. Poseidonius tells us that Marcus Claudius, who was five times consul of the Roman people, was the son of Marcus, and was the first of his family to receive the name of Marcellus, which means warlike. Indeed, by his experience he became a thorough soldier; his body was strong, and his arm powerful. He was fond of war, and bore himself with a lordly arrogance in battle, though otherwise he was of a quiet and amiable disposition, fond of Greek culture and literature, to the extent of respecting and admiring those who knew it, though he from his want of leisure could not make such progress as he wished. For the Roman chiefs of that period were, if any men ever were, condemned, in the words of Homer,

"From youth to age, disastrous wars to wage."

In their youth they fought the Carthaginians on the Sicilian coast; in middle age they fought the Gauls in defence of Italy itself; when advanced in years they again contended with Hannibal and the Carthaginians, not, as common men do, obtaining any relief from constant service because of their old age, but ever urged by their courage and nobility of soul to accept the command in new campaigns.

II. Marcellus was practised in all forms of battle, but was especially skilful in single combat, so that he never declined any man's challenge, and slew all who challenged him. In Sicily he saved the life of his brother Otacilius when in great peril, by holding his shield over him and killing his assailants. For this conduct, young as he was, he received crowns and rewards from the generals, and as he grew in reputation was elected curule ædile by the people, and augur by the priests. This is a kind of priestly office, to which the law especially assigns the observance of auguries drawn from the flight of birds. During his tenure of the office of ædile, he was obliged, much against his will, to commence a law-suit. He had a son of his own name, in the bloom of youth, of great beauty, and equally with it admired by his countrymen for his modesty and education. Capitolinus, Marcellus's colleague, a licentious and reckless man, made disgraceful proposals to this lad. He first repelled his attacks alone, but on a second attempt told his father, and Marcellus, being much enraged, summoned the man before the Senate. He attempted many quibbles and subterfuges, and appealed to the tribunes of the people to support him, but as they refused his application he betook himself to pleading denial of the charge. There being no witnesses of what he had said, the Senate decided to send for the boy, and when they saw how he blushed and wept with a modesty mingled with unquenchable rage, they, without requiring any other proof, found Capitolinus guilty, and condemned him to pay a fine, with which Marcellus had silver libation vessels made, and consecrated them to the gods.

III. After twenty-two years the first Punic War came to an end, and the Romans turned their attention to Gaulish troubles. The Insubrians, a Celtic tribe dwelling in Italy at the foot of the Alps, powerful by themselves, were collecting other forces, and enrolling all those Gauls who fought for hire, called Gæsatæ.

It was a wonderful and fortunate circumstance that this Celtic war did not break out at the same time as that with Carthage, but that the Gauls, like the gladiator who waits to fight with the survivor of a pair of combatants, had remained quiet during the whole of that war, and now stepped forward and challenged the victors when they were at leisure. Yet the war caused much terror, because it would take place on their own frontier against their neighbour states, and because of the ancient reputation of the Gauls, whom the Romans seem to fear more than any other nation. They once lost their city at their hands, and afterwards passed a law that the priests should be exempt from all military service, except in case of another war with Gaul. Their alarm was shown both by their preparations (for it is said that never before or since were there so many thousand Romans under arms), and by their extraordinary sacrifices. For though they never observe the barbarous ceremonies of foreigners, but as far as possible are humane and like the Greeks in their religion, on the outbreak of this war they were compelled to follow certain prophecies in the Sibylline books, and bury alive two Greeks, a man and a woman, and likewise two Gauls, in the place called the Cattle Market: and in accordance with these prophecies they still up to this day in the month of November perform religious mysteries, which may not be seen or spoken of by either Greeks or Gauls.

IV. At the beginning of the war the Romans were some times victorious and sometimes defeated, without coming to any decisive action, until the consulate of Flaminius and Furius, who led a great army against the Insubrians. Then the river that passes through Picenum ran blood, and it was said that three moons were seen at the city of Ariminum, and the augurs, who watch the omens at the consular elections, declared that the appointment of these consuls was wrong and of evil omen for the people. Hereupon the Senate immediately sent despatches to the camp recalling the consuls, that they might as soon as possible return and lay down their office and so undertake nothing as consuls against the enemy. Flaminius, when he received these despatches, did not open them before he had routed the barbarians in battle and overrun their country. So when he returned to Rome loaded with spoil, the people did not go out to meet him, but, because he had not at once obeyed his orders, and had treated them with insolent contempt, very nearly refused him his triumph, and after the triumph reduced him to a private station, forcing both him and his colleague to give up their office. So much regard had the Romans for religion, that they would not on occasions of the greatest good fortune overlook any neglect of the prophecies and customs of their ancestors, holding it more important for the safety of the state that their generals should reverence the gods than that they should conquer the enemy.

V. As an example of this, Tiberius Sempronius, a man second to no one in Rome for courage and virtue, named as his successors when consul Scipio Nasica and Caius Marcius, and when they were actually in possession of their provinces and armies he happened to consult a book of sacred ritual, and found in it an old custom which he did not know before. It was to this effect. When a consul has hired a house or tent outside the city to watch the flight of birds, if he be obliged before any certain omen appears, to return to the city for what cause soever, he must give up the place which he hired and take another, and make his observation over again from the beginning. This, it seems, Tiberius did not know, and it was after using the same place twice that he named these men consuls. Afterwards, having discovered his error, he laid the matter before the Senate; and that body did not despise this apparently slight irregularity, but sent despatches to the men, who at once left their provinces, returned to Rome, and resigned their office. Now this happened in later times; but in the very times of which we write two men of the best family were deprived of the priesthood: Cornelius Cethegus, because he handled the entrails improperly at a sacrifice, and Quintus Sulpicius, because when he was sacrificing, the crested hat which he wore as flamen, fell off his head. And because, when Minucius the dictator was appointing Caius Flaminius his master of the knights, the mouse which is called the coffin-mouse was heard to squeak, they turned them out of their office, and elected others. But, though so elaborately careful in trifles, they never admitted any superstitious observance, and neither altered nor added anything to their ancestral ritual.

VI. When Flaminius and his colleague had resigned their offices, Marcellus was designated consul by the interreges. On entering upon his office he nominated Cnæus Cornelius as his colleague. It was said that the Gauls were offering terms of reconciliation, and that the Senate wished for peace with them, but that Marcellus raised the spirit of the people and excited them to continue the war. But still a peace was concluded; and it seems to have been the Gæsatæ who renewed the war, by crossing the Alps and stirring up the Insubrians. Thirty thousand in number, they joined that tribe, which was many times larger, and in high spirits at once attacked Acerræ, a city beyond the river Po. From that place Britomartus with ten thousand Gæsatæ proceeded to plunder the country near the Po.

Marcellus hearing this left his colleague before Acerræ with the infantry, heavy baggage, and one-third of the cavalry, and himself, with the rest of the cavalry and about six hundred of the most active foot soldiers, marched night and day till he fell in with the ten thousand Gæsatæ at Clastidium, a Gaulish village which not long before had been subject to the Romans. There was no time for rest or refreshment; for his arrival was at once perceived by the enemy, and his force despised, as he had so little infantry with him, for the Celts thought nothing of his cavalry. Admirable horsemen and proud of their superior skill, they also had greatly the advantage of Marcellus in numbers, and at once, their king riding foremost, charged the Romans with great impetuosity and terrible threats, expecting to sweep them away. Marcellus, fearing that they might surround and outflank his small body, spread out his cavalry, thinning and widening his line, until he presented a front nearly equal to that of the enemy. He was now advancing to the charge, when his horse, scared at the terrible display of the enemy, turned short round, and forcibly carried him back. Marcellus, fearing that this might cause superstitious terror to the Romans, hastily wheeled his horse round on the bridle hand, and having again directed him against the enemy, paid his adorations to the sun, as though he had made this circle not by chance, but of set purpose; for the Romans have this custom, of turning round to worship the gods, and so he, as he was on the point of joining battle, vowed that he would consecrate the finest of the enemies' arms to Jupiter Feretrius.

VII. At this moment the king of the Gauls, seeing him, and conjecturing from his dress that he was the Roman leader, rode out far beyond the rest, and made directly for him, defiantly shouting a challenge, and brandishing his spear. He was a man distinguished from the rest of the Gauls by his tall stature and his complete armour, which glittered like the lightning with gold and silver and all kinds of gay devices with which it was incrusted. Marcellus, as he looked along the enemy's line, thought that these were the finest arms, and were those about which he had made his vow to Jupiter Feretrius. He rushed upon the Gaul, pierced his breastplate with his spear, and by the impetus of his horse bore him to the ground alive, and with a second and third thrust killed him at once. Leaping from his horse and seizing the armour of the dead man, he said, looking up to heaven, "Jupiter Feretrius, thou that seest the great deeds of generals and captains in war, I call thee to witness that I am the third Roman general that has slain the enemy's general and king, by killing this man here with my own hand: and having killed him I consecrate to thee the first and fairest of the spoils. But do thou grant us like good fortune in the rest of this war."

Hereupon the Roman cavalry charged, not against cavalry by itself, but they fought against infantry and cavalry mixed together, and won a victory of an unparalleled and wonderful kind; for never before or since that day did such a body of horsemen rout such numbers of horse and foot.

Having slain the greater part of them, and collected their arms and stores, he returned to his colleague, who was with difficulty holding his own against the Celts before the walls of the largest and most populous of Gaulish cities. It is called Mediolanum, and is regarded by the Cisalpine Gauls as their metropolis: consequently they fought vigorously in its defence, and more besieged Cornelius than were besieged by him. But when Marcellus arrived, the Gæsatæ, as soon as they heard of the defeat and death of their king, went home. Mediolanum fell, and the Celts of their own accord surrendered the other cities, and threw themselves upon the mercy of the Romans. They received moderate terms of peace.

VIII. By a decree of the Senate Marcellus alone triumphed. His procession was glorious, as few others have been, with the splendour and value of the booty exhibited, and the great stature of the captives; but the strangest and most interesting sight of all was the general himself, as he appeared carrying the suit of armour of the Gaul to offer it to the god. He had cut and trimmed the trunk of a tall young oak tree, and had tied and hung the spoils upon it, each put in its proper place. When the procession began, he himself mounted his chariot and four, and carried in state through the city, this the most glorious of all his trophies of victory. The army marched after him with their finest armour, singing as they went songs and pæans of victory in honour of the gods and their leader. Thus he proceeded till he reached the temple of Jupiter Feretrius. Here he dismounted, and dedicated his spoils, being the third, and, up to our day, the last who ever did so: first comes Romulus, with the spoils of Acron of Cæninum; second, Cornelius Cossus offered the spoils of Tolumnius the Etruscan; third, Marcellus offered these spoils of Britomartus, the king of the Gauls; after Marcellus, no man.

The god to whom they are offered is called Jupiter Feretrius, according to some, from the trophy being carried upon a feretrum, or bier, as it is called in the Greek tongue, which then was much mixed with the Latin; but according to others, it is an attribute of Jupiter the Thunderer, for the Romans call striking ferire. Others say that the name comes from striking the enemy; for even now in battle when they are pursuing the enemy they keep shouting, "Feri," that is, "Strike," to one another. The word for ordinary spoils is spolia, but for these spolia opima. Yet it is said that Numa Pompilius speaks of first, second, and third degrees of spolia opima, ordering the first to be offered to Jupiter Feretrius, the second to Mars, and the third to Quirinus; and that for the first the prize is three hundred ases, two hundred for the second, and one hundred for the third. But the most common story runs that those spoils alone are spolia opima which are taken at a pitched battle, and first of all, and by the general of the one side from the general of the other. But of these things enough.

The Roman people were so overjoyed at that victory and the end of the war that they made from the money paid to ransom captives, a golden statue, and sent it to Apollo at Delphi as a thank-offering, and gave a magnificent share of the booty to their allies, and even sent many presents to Hiero the king of Syracuse, their friend and ally.

IX. When Hannibal invaded Italy, Marcellus was sent with an army to Sicily: but when the disaster at Cannæ took place, where many thousand Romans perished, and only a few fugitives collected at Canusium, it was expected that Hannibal would at once march to attack Rome, as he had cut off the greater part of the army. Marcellus at once sent a garrison of fifteen hundred men to guard the city, and afterwards, in obedience to a senatus-consultum, went to Canusium, and taking command of the fugitives collected there, led them out of their fortified camp, to show that he would not deliver up the country to the enemy. The Romans had lost many of their most capable leaders in the wars, and Fabius Maximus, who had the greatest reputation, was blamed by them for sloth and want of enterprise because of his excessive caution in avoiding a defeat. Thinking, therefore, that he was an excellent general for defence, not for attack, they cast their eyes upon Marcellus, and in order to combine his vigour and daring with the cautious and far-seeing tactics of the other, they at one time elected them both consuls, at another made the one consul with the other serving as proconsul. Poseidonius tells us that Fabius was called the shield of the state, and Marcellus the sword. And Hannibal himself said that he feared Fabius as a schoolmaster, but regarded Marcellus as an antagonist, for the former prevented his doing any mischief, while the latter might make him suffer some.

X. At first Hannibal's soldiers, elated with their victory, roamed with careless confidence out of their camp and plundered the country; where Marcellus fell upon them, and by a series of defeats considerably weakened them. Next, he went to Naples and Nola. At Naples he encouraged the citizens, who of their own accord wished well to the Roman cause; but at Nola he found the city in a state of faction, as the senate were unable to restrain the populace, who favoured Hannibal. There was one Bandius, a man of the first nobility of the city, and renowned for bravery. This man had fought at Cannæ with conspicuous valour, and had slain many Carthaginians. When after the battle he was found in a heap of slain with his body pierced with darts, Hannibal, in admiration of his courage, not only dismissed him without ransom, but gave him presents and made him a personal friend. Bandius, out of gratitude, was one of the most eager partisans of Hannibal, and, having great influence with the people, was urging them to revolt. Marcellus thought that it would be a crime to put to death a man of such glorious antecedents, and who had taken part in one of the greatest struggles of the Romans; and, besides his natural kindliness, being able by his conversation to win over any man of noble nature, he on one occasion when greeted by Bandius inquired who he might be, though he knew very well, but merely wanted a pretext and opportunity for conversation with him. For, when he answered, "Lucius Bandius," Marcellus, as though surprised and pleased, said, "Are you indeed that Bandius, of whom all those who fought at Cannæ told us at Rome, the only man who did not desert Paulus Æmilius the consul, but who received upon his own body the greater part of the darts which were aimed at him?" Bandius admitted that he was the man, and endeavoured to speak lightly of his wounds, but Marcellus went on: "Then, as you bear about you such marks of your devotion to our cause, why did you not at once come to me? Do you think us slow to requite the valour of our friends, when it is honoured even by the enemy." Having spoken to him thus courteously, he embraced him, and presented him with a war-horse and five hundred silver drachmas.

XI. After this Bandius became the firmest partisan and ally of Marcellus, and a terrible denouncer and assailant of the opposite party. This was a numerous one; and their design was, when the Romans should march out of the town against the enemy, to attack their baggage. Marcellus, therefore, having marshalled his troops within the city, brought the baggage to the gates, and by proclamation forbade the people of Nola to approach the walls. Thus no force was visible, and he induced Hannibal to march up to the city in disorderly array, as he supposed that within it all was confusion. Then

Marcellus ordered the gate nearest him to be thrown open, and with the best equipped of his cavalry charged out of it and fell upon the enemy hand to hand. Presently the infantry poured out of another gate, running with loud shouts; and while Hannibal was dividing his forces to deal with them a third gate opened, and from it issued the remainder of the army, and from all sides attacked the Carthaginians, who were bewildered at the unexpectedness of the attack, and fought without spirit against their immediate assailants, because of the others who they saw would soon beset them.

There first did Hannibal's troops give way before the Romans, and were chased with great loss into their camp. It is said that more than five thousand perished, and that no more than five hundred Romans fell. But Livy does not consider that a great defeat took place, or that so many of the enemy fell, but he points out that Marcellus gained much glory by that battle, and that the Roman people took courage after their misfortunes, thinking that it was not against an unconquerable and invulnerable foe that they were fighting, but one who could be made to suffer as well as themselves.

XII. For this reason, as one of the consuls was dead, the people called for Marcellus, though he was absent, to become his successor; and in spite of the efforts of the government they put off the day of election until he came to Rome from the army. He was elected consul by the votes of all the tribes, but it thundered at the time, and as the priests declared this an unpropitious omen, but did not dare openly to oppose his election for fear of the people, he himself voluntarily resigned his office. But he did not avoid military service, but was created proconsul, and returning to Nola and his army he harassed those who had chosen the side of Hannibal. When the latter hastily marched to the assistance of his friends, and offered to fight a pitched battle with Marcellus, he declined; but subsequently, when the greater part of the Carthaginian army was scattered in search of plunder, and no longer expecting an attack, he fell upon it. He had distributed long lances, such as are used on ship-board, among his infantry, and instructed them to watch their opportunity and hurl these from a distance at the Carthaginians, who had no javelin-men, and whose heavy spears were only used to thrust with at close quarters. In consequence, it seems, of this, all who engaged with the Romans that day turned their backs and shamefully fled, losing five thousand killed, six hundred prisoners; while of their elephants, four were killed and two taken alive. And, what was of the greatest importance of all, on the third day after the above battle, three hundred Spanish and Numidian cavalry deserted to the Romans, a thing which never had happened to Hannibal before, as, although his army was composed of so many different nations, he had been able for a very long time to inspire it with the same spirit. These men faithfully served Marcellus and the generals who succeeded him.

XIII. Marcellus, when elected consul for the third time, sailed to Sicily; for Hannibal's successes in the war had encouraged the Carthaginians to recover that island, especially as Syracusan politics were in a disturbed state in consequence of the death of the despot Hieronymus; and on this account a Roman army under Appius had already been sent there. When Marcellus had taken the command of this army, he received a large accession of Roman soldiers, whose misfortune was as follows. Of the troops who fought with Hannibal at Cannæ, some fled, and some were taken alive, in such numbers that the Romans scarcely thought that they had left sufficient citizens to man the city walls, but this remnant was so full of pride and so great of soul, that, though Hannibal offered to release the captives for a small ransom, they would not take them, but refused by a decree of the Senate, and endured to see some of them put to death, and others sold out of Italy as slaves. The mass of those who had saved themselves by flight they sent to Sicily, with orders not to set foot on the soil of Italy until the war with Hannibal was over. So when Marcellus went to Sicily, these men came in a body into his presence, and falling on the ground before him besought him to permit them to serve as honourable soldiers, promising with cries and tears that they would prove by their actions that it was more by their bad fortune than their cowardice that the defeat at Cannæ took place. Marcellus was touched with compassion, and wrote to the Senate asking to be allowed to fill up from these men the vacancies which would occur in the ranks of his army. Much discussion followed; and at last the Senate decreed that Rome did not require the services of cowardly citizens, but, if Marcellus nevertheless wished to make use of them, they must not receive any of the crowns and other rewards which are commonly bestowed by generals as the prizes of valour. This decree vexed Marcellus, and after the war in Sicily he returned to Rome and blamed the Senate that, in spite of all that he had done for them, they would not allow him to relieve so many citizens from such a miserable position.

XIV. In Sicily, at this time, he had just cause of complaint against Hippokrates the Syracusan general, who, favouring the Carthaginian side, and wishing to establish himself as despot, put to death many Romans at Leontini. Marcellus took Leontini by storm, and did no harm to the inhabitants, but flogged and executed all the deserters whom he found. Hippokrates first sent to Syracuse a story that Marcellus was exterminating the people of Leontini, and when this report had thrown the city into confusion he fell upon it and made himself master of it. Marcellus hereupon proceeded to Syracuse with his whole army, and encamping near the city sent ambassadors to tell them what had really happened in Leontini. By this, however, he gained nothing, as the Syracusans would not listen to him (for the party of Hippokrates was in the ascendant). He now attacked the city both by sea and land, Appius commanding the land forces, while Marcellus directed a fleet of sixty quinqueremes full of armed men and missile weapons. He raised a vast engine upon a raft made by lashing eight ships together, and sailed with it to attack the wall, trusting to the numbers and excellence of his siege engines, and to his own personal prestige. But Archimedes and his machines cared nothing for this, though he did not speak of any of these engines as being constructed by serious labour, but as the mere holiday sports of a geometrician. He would not indeed have constructed them but at the earnest request of King Hiero, who entreated him to leave the abstract for the concrete, and to bring his ideas within the comprehension of the people by embodying them in tangible forms.

Eudoxus and Archytas were the first who began to treat of this renowned science of mechanics, cleverly illustrating it, and proving such problems as were hard to understand, by means of solid and actual instruments, as, for instance, both of them resorted to mechanical means to find a mean proportional, which is necessary for the solution of many other geometrical questions. This they did by the construction, from various curves and sections, of certain instruments called mesographs. Plato was much vexed at this, and inveighed against them for destroying the real excellence of geometry by making it leave the region of pure intellect and come within that of the senses, and become mixed up with bodies which require much base servile labour. So mechanics became separated from geometry, and, long regarded with contempt by philosophy, was reckoned among the military arts. However Archimedes, who was a relative and friend of Hiero, wrote that with a given power he could move any given weight whatever, and, as it were rejoicing in the strength of his demonstration, he is said to have declared that if he were given another world to stand upon, he could move this upon which we live. Hiero wondered at this, and begged him to put this theory into practice, and show him something great moved by a small force. Archimedes took a three-masted ship, a transport in the king's navy, which had just been dragged up on land with great labour and many men; in this he placed her usual complement of men and cargo, and then sitting at some distance, without any trouble, by gently pulling with his hand the end of a system of pullies, he dragged it towards him with as smooth and even a motion as if it were passing over the sea. The king wondered greatly at this, and perceiving the value of his arts, prevailed upon Archimedes to construct for him a number of machines, some for the attack and some for the defence of a city, of which he himself did not make use, as he spent most of his life in unwarlike and literary leisure, but now these engines were ready for use in Syracuse, and also, the inventor was present to direct their working.

XV. So when the Romans attacked by sea and land at once, the Syracusans were at first terrified and silent, dreading that nothing could resist such an armament. But Archimedes opened fire from his machines, throwing upon the land forces all manner of darts and great stones, with an incredible noise and violence, which no man could withstand; but those upon whom they fell were struck down in heaps, and their ranks thrown into confusion, while some of the ships were suddenly seized by iron hooks, and by a counter-balancing weight were drawn up and then plunged to the bottom. Others they caught by irons like hands or claws suspended from cranes, and first pulled them up by their bows till they stood upright upon their sterns, and then cast down into the water, or by means of windlasses and tackles worked inside the city, dashed them against the cliffs and rocks at the base of the walls, with terrible destruction to their crews. Often was seen the fearful sight of a ship lifted out of the sea into the air, swaying and balancing about, until the men were all thrown out or overwhelmed with stones from slings, when the empty vessel would either be dashed against the fortifications, or dropped into the sea by the claws being let go. The great engine which Marcellus was bringing up on the raft, called the Harp, from some resemblance to that instrument, was, while still at a distance, struck by a stone of ten talents weight, and then another and another, which fell with a terrible crash, breaking the platform on which the machine stood, loosening its bolts, and tearing asunder the hulks which supported it. Marcellus, despairing of success, drew off his ships as fast as possible, and sent orders to the land forces to retreat. In a council of war, it was determined to make another assault by night; for they argued that the straining cords which Archimedes used to propel his missiles required a long distance to work in, and would make the shot fly over them at close quarters, and be practically useless, as they required a long stroke. But he, it appears, had long before prepared engines suited for short as well as long distances, and short darts to use in them; and from many small loop-holes pierced through the wall small scorpions, as they are called, stood ready to shoot the enemy, though invisible to them.

XVI. When then they attacked, expecting that they would not be seen, they again encountered a storm of blows from stones which fell perpendicularly upon their heads and darts which were poured from all parts of the wall. They were forced to retire, and when they came within range of the larger machines missiles were showered upon them as they retreated, destroying many men and throwing the ships into great disorder, without their being able to retaliate. For most of the engines on the walls had been devised by Archimedes, and the Romans thought that they were fighting against gods and not men, as destruction fell upon them from invisible hands.

XVII. However, Marcellus escaped unhurt, and sarcastically said to his own engineers: "Are we to give in to this Briareus of a geometrician, who sits at his ease by the seashore and plays at upsetting our ships, to our lasting disgrace, and surpasses the hundred-handed giant of fable by hurling so many weapons at us at once?" For indeed all the other Syracusans were merely the limbs of Archimedes, and his mind alone directed and guided everything. All other arms were laid aside and the city trusted to his weapons solely for defence and safety. At length Marcellus, seeing that the Romans had become so scared that if only a rope or small beam were seen over the wall they would turn and fly, crying out that Archimedes was bringing some engine to bear upon them, ceased assaulting the place, and trusted to time alone to reduce it. Yet Archimedes had so great a mind and such immense philosophic speculations that although by inventing these engines he had acquired the glory of a more than human intellect, he would not condescend to leave behind him any writings upon the subject, regarding the whole business of mechanics and the useful arts as base and vulgar, but placed his whole study and delight in those speculations in which absolute beauty and excellence appear unhampered by the necessities of life, and argument is made to soar above its subject matter, since by the latter only bulk and outward appearance, but by the other accuracy of reasoning and wondrous power, can be attained: for it is impossible in the whole science of geometry to find more difficult hypotheses explained on clearer or more simple principles than in his works. Some attribute this to his natural genius, others say that his indefatigable industry made his work seem as though it had been done without labour, though it cost much. For no man by himself could find out the solution of his problems, but as he reads, he begins to think that he could have discovered it himself, by so smooth and easy a road does he lead one up to the point to be proved. One cannot therefore disbelieve the stories which are told of him: how he seemed ever bewitched by the song of some indwelling syren of his own so as to forget to eat his food, and to neglect his person, and how, when dragged forcibly to the baths and perfumers, he would draw geometrical figures with the ashes on the hearth, and when his body was anointed would trace lines on it with his finger, absolutely possessed and inspired by the joy he felt in his art. He discovered many beautiful problems, and is said to have begged his relatives and friends to place upon his tomb when he died a cylinder enclosing a sphere, and to write on it the proof of the ratio of the containing solid to the contained.

XVIII. Such was Archimedes, who at this time rendered himself, and as far as lay in him, the city, invincible.

During the blockade Marcellus took Megara, one of the most ancient of the Greek cities in Sicily, and also captured Hippokrates' camp at Acrillæ, with a destruction of more than eight thousand of his men, attacking them just as they were planting the palisades of the rampart. He overran a great part of Sicily, induced cities to revolt from Carthage, and beat all forces that opposed him. As time went on, he took prisoner one Damippus, a Spartan, as he was sailing out of the harbour of Syracuse. The Syracusans desired to ransom this man, and Marcellus, in the course of many negotiations and conferences about him, noticed that a certain tower was carelessly guarded, and that men might be introduced into it secretly, as the wall near it was easy to climb. Having, from his frequent journeys to confer with the besieged near this tower, gained a good idea of its height, he prepared scaling-ladders, and waited till the Syracusans were engaged in celebrating the feast of Artemis, and given up to drinking and amusement. Not only did he gain the tower unobserved, but was able to occupy the whole circuit of wall with his troops, and to break into the Hexapylon. When the Syracusans began to discover their position and muster for their defence, he ordered trumpets to sound on all sides, which produced great terror and tumult, as they imagined that no part of the walls remained untaken. Yet the strongest, and that too the largest and finest part of the city, was still left, called Achradina, because it is fortified on the side near the outer town, part of which is called Neapolis, and part Tyche.

XIX. These parts of the city were captured, and at daybreak Marcellus moved down through the Hexapylon, amidst the congratulations of his officers. It is said that when, from the high ground he surveyed that great and fair city, he burst into tears, thinking how sadly it would soon be changed in appearance when sacked by his soldiers. For none of his officers dared to oppose the soldiers when they demanded the privilege of plunder, and many encouraged them to burn and destroy. But Marcellus would not so much as entertain the idea of this, but, much against his will, was forced to permit them to carry off the movable property and slaves, though he forbade them to touch freemen, and gave strict orders that none of the citizens of Syracuse should be slain, dishonoured, or enslaved. Yet even after moderating their license to this extent he thought that the city was sadly ill-treated, and even in such a moment of triumph he showed great sorrow and sympathy for it, as he saw such great wealth and comfort swept away in a few hours; for the treasure was said to be not less than that which was afterwards taken in Carthage itself. The rest of the city was taken after a short time by treachery, and the soldiers insisted upon plundering it, with the exception of the royal treasury, which was confiscated to the state.

Marcellus was especially grieved at the fate of Archimedes. He was studying something by himself upon a figure which he had drawn, to which he had so utterly given up his thoughts and his sight that he did not notice the assault of the Romans and the capture of the city, and when a soldier suddenly appeared before him and ordered him to follow him into the presence of Marcellus, he refused to do so before he had finished his problem and its solution. The man hereupon in a rage drew his sword and killed him. Others say that the Roman fell upon him at once with a sword to kill him, but he, seeing him, begged him to wait for a little while, that he might not leave his theorem imperfect, and that while he was reflecting upon it, he was slain. A third story is that as he was carrying into Marcellus's presence his mathematical instruments, sundials, spheres, and quadrants, by which the eye might measure the magnitude of the sun, some soldiers met with him, and supposing that there was gold in the boxes, slew him. But all agree that Marcellus was much grieved, that he turned away from his murderer as though he were an object of abhorrence to gods and men, and that he sought out his family and treated them well.

XX. The Romans up to this time had given foreign nations great proofs of their skill in war and their courage in battle, but had not shown any evidences of kindness of heart, clemency, or any social virtue. Marcellus seems to have been the first who exhibited the Romans in a more amiable light to the Greeks. For he so dealt with his adversaries, and treated so many individuals and cities with kindness that even if any harsh treatment did befall Enna, or Megara, or Syracuse, it was thought to be more by the fault of the vanquished than of the victors. I will mention one instance out of many. There is a city in Sicily called Engyion, of no great size, but very ancient, and renowned for the appearance there of the goddesses called 'Mothers.' The foundation of the temple is ascribed to the Cretans, and they used to show certain lances and helmets inscribed, some with the name of Meriones, some of Ulixes, that is, Odysseus, which were dedicated to these goddesses. This city was eager to espouse the Carthaginian side, but was prevailed upon by one Nikias, the leading man of the city, to join the Romans, by freely speaking his mind in the public assembly and proving that his opponents did not consult the true interests of the state. These men, fearing his power and high reputation, determined to kidnap him, and deliver him up to the Carthaginians. Nikias, discovering this plot, quietly took measures for his own security, but publicly made unseemly speeches about the "Mothers," and spoke of the received tradition of their appearance with doubt and contempt, to the delight of his enemies, as he seemed to be by these actions justifying the treatment which they meant to inflict upon him. When all their preparations for seizing him were complete there was a public assembly of the citizens, and Nikias, in the midst of a speech upon state policy, suddenly fell to the ground, and after a short time, as all men were, naturally, silent with surprise, he raised his head, and turning it round he began to speak in deep and trembling tones, which he gradually made shriller and more intense, until, seeing the whole theatre, where the meeting was, silent with horror, he threw off his cloak, tore his tunic, and, half naked, rushed to the gate of the theatre, crying out that he was pursued by the "Mothers." As no one dared to touch or stop him, from fear of the gods, but all made way for him, he passed out of the city gate, not omitting any of the cries and trembling of body of a person under demoniacal possession. His wife, who was in the secret, and her husband's confederate, first brought her children and prostrated herself as a suppliant before the goddesses, and then under pretence of seeking her wandering husband managed to leave the city without opposition. Thus they safely reached Marcellus at Syracuse; and when, after enduring many affronts and insolent proceeding from the people of Engyion Marcellus took them all prisoners, and imprisoned them, meaning to put them all to death, Nikias at first stood by weeping, but at length, embracing Marcellus as a suppliant, he begged for the lives of his countrymen, beginning with his own personal enemies, until he relented, and set them all at liberty. Nor did he touch their city, but gave Nikias ample lands and rich presents. This story is told by Poseidonius the philosopher.

XXI. When the Romans recalled Marcellus, to conduct the war in their own country, he removed most of the beautiful ornaments of the city of Syracuse, to be admired at his triumphal procession, and to adorn Rome. For at that time Rome neither possessed nor knew of any works of art, nor had she any delicacy of taste in such matters. Filled with the blood-stained arms and spoils of barbarians, and crowded with trophies of war and memorials of triumphs, she was no pleasant or delightful spectacle, fit to feed the eyes of unwarlike and luxurious spectators, but, as Epameinondas called the plain of

Bœotia "the Stage of Ares," and Xenophon called Ephesus "the Workshop of War," so, in my opinion, you might call Rome at that time, in the words of Pindar, "the Domain of Ares, who revels in war." Wherefore Marcellus gained the greater credit with the vulgar, because he enriched the city with statues possessing the Hellenic grace and truth to nature, while Fabius Maximus was more esteemed by the elders. He neither touched nor removed anything of the kind from the city of Tarentum, which he took, but carried off all the money and other property, and let the statues remain, quoting the proverb: "Let us," said he, "leave the Tarentines their angry gods." They blamed Marcellus's proceedings as being invidious for Rome, because he had led not only men, but also gods as captives in his triumph, and also because the people, who before this were accustomed either to fight or to till the ground, and were ignorant of luxury and indolent pleasures, like the Herakles of Euripides,

"Unpolished, rough, but skilled in useful arts,"

were made by Marcellus into idle, babbling connoisseurs of the fine arts, and wasted the greater part of the day in talk about them. He, however, prided himself upon this even before Greeks, saying that he had taught the ignorant Romans to prize and admire the glories of Greek art.

XXII. Marcellus, whose enemies opposed his claim to a triumph, on the ground that the campaign in Sicily was not completely finished, and that he did not deserve a third triumph, so far gave way as to lead the greater triumphal procession as far as the Alban Mount, and only to enter the city in the lesser form which the Greeks call euan, and the Romans an ovation. The general conducts this, not, as in the triumph, riding in a chariot and four with a crown of laurel, and with trumpets sounding before him, but walking on foot in low shoes surrounded by flute players, and crowned with myrtle, so as to look unwarlike and joyous rather than terrible. And this is a great proof to me that in old times it was the manner and not the importance of the things achieved that settled the form of triumph. Those generals who had gained their point by battle and slaughter probably made their entry in that martial and terrible fashion, having, as is customary in lustrations of armies, crowned the men and wreathed their arms with abundance of laurel: whereas the generals who without an appeal to arms had settled matters satisfactorily by negotiation and persuasive eloquence, were given by custom this peaceful and festive entry into the city. For the flute is a peaceful instrument, and the myrtle is the favorite plant of Aphrodite, who above all the gods hates violence and war. This form of triumph is called ovation, not from the cry of "Evan," as most people think, for the other also is accompanied with shouts and songs, but the word had been twisted by the Greeks into one that has a meaning in their language, and also they are convinced that some honour is paid to Dionysus in this ceremony, which God we name Evius and Thriambos. It is curious to observe that the great Laconian lawgiver arranged the sacrifices differently to those of Rome. In Sparta those ex-generals who have accomplished their purpose by persuasion or fraud sacrifice an ox, while those who have done it by battle offer a cock. For, though warlike to excess, they thought that a victory gained by clever negotiation was greater and more befitting human beings than one gained by force and courage. Which is to be preferred, I leave to my readers' consideration.

XXIII. When Marcellus entered upon his fourth consulship, his enemies induced the Syracusans to send a deputation to Rome, to complain loudly to the Senate of the cruel and unjust treatment which they had received from him. Marcellus chanced to be performing some sacrifice in the Capitol; so when the Syracusans came to the assembled Senate, begging for a hearing that justice might be done them, the other consul stopped them, feeling that Marcellus ought not to be attacked in his absence. But Marcellus as soon as he heard of it, came to the Senate-house, seated himself as consul, on the curule chair, and despatched business; then, when this was finished, he came down and placed himself as a private person in the place where men on their trial usually stood, and called on the Syracusans to prove their charges against him. They were abashed at his majestic confidence of demeanour, and he who had been invincible in arms seemed to them yet more terrible and unapproachable in his consular purple. Nevertheless, encouraged by the enemies of Marcellus, they began their impeachment, and pleaded their cause in a piteous fashion, their chief point being that they, who were friends and allies of the Romans, had been treated in a way in which many other generals had forborne to treat hostile cities. Marcellus answered that they had done the Romans much harm, for which they had received no punishment, except such as could not be prevented in war, because victorious soldiers cannot be restrained from sacking a town which they have won, and their city, he said, was taken because they had refused his frequent offers of terms of agreement. They could not urge that they had been forced into war by their despots, for they had themselves chosen those very despots with the intention of going to war. After both parties had been heard, the Syracusans, according to custom, left the Senate-house. Marcellus came out with them, leaving his colleague to preside over the assembly, and stood outside the doors, without altering his usual demeanour, either from fear of the result or anger against the Syracusans, but serenely awaiting the verdict of the Senate.

When the question was voted upon, and he was announced successful, the Syracusans prostrated themselves before him, beseeching him with tears to put away his anger against themselves, and to show pity on the city, which was sensible to kindness, and would be grateful to him. Marcellus was touched by their appeal; he became reconciled to them, and was a constant benefactor to their city. He restored them their freedom, their laws, and what remained of their property, and the Senate confirmed his acts. In return for this, besides many other honours they passed a law that whenever Marcellus or any of his descendants should land in Sicily, the Syracusans should wear garlands of flowers and hold a festival with sacrifices to the gods.

XXIV. Next he proceeded against Hannibal; and whereas nearly all the other consuls and generals, after the disaster at Cannæ had thought of nothing but avoiding battles with him, and no one had dared to measure himself with him in the field, he adopted the opposite course, arguing that while they fancied that they were wearing out Hannibal's army they did not perceive that Italy was being consumed by it. Fabius, he urged, thought too much of safety, and by his policy of waiting, Rome, already drooping under its burdens, would at the end of the war perish as well as Hannibal. He was, he said, like those timid surgeons who shrink from using decisive remedies, and who mistake the sinking strength of the patient for the abatement of disease. His first act was to take some important Samnite towns which had revolted. Here he found great stores of corn and money, and took three thousand of Hannibal's soldiers who were there as garrison. Next, when Hannibal defeated and killed Cnæus Fulvius, the proconsul in Apulia, with a loss of eleven military tribunes and the greater part of his army, Marcellus sent despatches to Rome, bidding the citizens be of good courage, for he was already on the march, and would abate Hannibal's exultation. Livy tells us that these despatches when read did not diminish the grief of the Romans, but added to their fear, as they reflected that the risk they were about to run was so much more serious than the defeat they had sustained, as Marcellus was superior to Fulvius.

According to his despatch, he instantly marched against Hannibal into Lucania, and finding him entrenched on some strong hills near the city of Numistro, he himself encamped in the plain. On the following day he was the first to draw out his army in battle array. Hannibal descended from his position, and fought a great and well-contested battle, for it began at the third hour, and was scarcely over by dark, but without any decisive result. At daybreak he again led out his army and defied Hannibal to fight. But Hannibal retired; and Marcellus, after stripping the corpses of the enemy, and burying his own dead, pursued. His skill and good fortune were greatly admired in this campaign, as he did not fall into any of the numerous ambuscades which were prepared for him by Hannibal, and in all his skirmishes came off victorious. For this reason, as the comitia were impending, the Senate thought that it would be better to call the other consul away from Sicily than to recall Marcellus just as he was thoroughly engaged with Hannibal. When the other consul arrived, they bade him name Quintus Fulvius dictator. For a dictator is not chosen by the people or by the Senate, but one of the consuls or prætors comes forward publicly and names whom he pleases dictator. And this is the reason that the man so named is called dictator; for dicere in Latin means to name. But some think that the dictator is so called because he does not require any vote or show of hands, but on his own responsibility dictates his orders; indeed, the orders of magistrates which are called by the Greeks diatagmata, are called edicts by the Romans.

XXV. When Marcellus's colleague came to Rome from Sicily, he wished to name another person dictator, and, that he might not be forced to act against his inclination, he sailed away by night back to Sicily. Under these circumstances the people nominated Quintus Fulvius dictator, and the Senate wrote to Marcellus bidding him vote for this person. He did so, confirming the choice of the people, and was himself elected proconsul for the following year. After a conference with Fabius Maximus, at which it was arranged that the latter should make an attempt on Tarentum, while Marcellus should constantly engage Hannibal and so prevent his affording the town any assistance, he set out, and came upon Hannibal near Canusium. Hannibal frequently shifted his camp, and tried to avoid a battle, but Marcellus was not to be shaken off, and at length attacked his position, and by skirmishing provoked him to fight. Marcellus sustained his attack, and the battle was put an end to by night. Next morning his troops were again beheld under arms, so that Hannibal in great anxiety called together the Carthaginians and besought them to fight as they had never done before. "You see," said he, "that even after our great victories, we cannot rest in peace, unless we drive away this fellow." The armies met; and Marcellus seems to have lost the day by an unseasonable manœuvre. His right wing was suffering, and he ordered up one of the legions to support it; but this change produced confusion in the ranks, and gave the victory to the enemy, with a loss of two thousand seven hundred men to the Romans. Marcellus, after retiring to his fortified camp, called together his soldiers, and reproached them, saying that he saw before him the arms and bodies of many Romans, but not one true Roman. They begged forgiveness, but he answered that he could not forgive them when defeated, but would forgive them if victorious. On the morrow he said that he would renew the battle, in order that the Romans might hear of their victory before they heard of their defeat. After these words he gave orders that the troops which had given way should be supplied with rations of barley instead of corn; which had such an effect upon them, that although many were suffering from the hurts in the battle, yet, there was not one who did not suffer more from the reproaches of Marcellus than from his wounds.

XXVI. At daybreak the scarlet robe, the well known signal of battle, was displayed from the general's tent. The disgraced troops, at their own request, were placed in the first rank; the rest of the army followed under their officers. Hannibal hearing of this exclaimed: "Hercules! What can one do with a man who knows not how to bear either good or bad fortune. This is the only general who, when victorious allows his foe no rest, and when defeated takes none himself. We shall always, it seems, have to be fighting this man, who is equally excited to attack by his confidence when victor, and his shame when vanquished."

In the battle the men on each side were fighting on equal terms, when Hannibal ordered his elephants to be brought into the front rank and to attack the Roman lines. Great tumult and disturbance was produced by this, but one of the tribunes, by name Flavius, seizing a standard, stood his ground, and struck the first elephant with the spiked end of the staff, till he forced him to turn back. He then attacked the next one, and those that followed. Marcellus, seeing this, ordered his cavalry to ride as fast as they could to the scene of the confusion and complete the rout of the enemy. They charged briskly and pursued the flying Carthaginians, cutting them down up to their very camp. Great havoc was wrought by the wounded elephants among them; and in all, over eight thousand are said to have perished. Of the Roman force three thousand were killed, and almost all the survivors were wounded, which circumstance enabled Hannibal to leave his camp by night unmolested, and remove himself from the neighbourhood of Marcellus; for Marcellus could not pursue, because of the number of wounded, but marched in a leisurely manner towards Campania, and passed the summer at Sinuessa, recruiting the health of his soldiers.

XXVII. Hannibal, after he had thus torn himself free from Marcellus, sent his army to plunder Italy as recklessly as though it were disbanded; and in Rome Marcellus was ill spoken of. His enemies induced Publius Bibulus, a clever and violent partisan, to attack him. This man frequently addressed assemblies of the people and urged them to transfer the command to another general, since "Marcellus," he said, "after a little sparring with the enemy had gone to the hot baths to refresh himself as if after a gymnastic contest." Marcellus, hearing of this, left the army in charge of his legates, and went to Rome to clear his reputation from these slanders; but, in consequence of them he found that he was to undergo a trial. A day was fixed; the people assembled in the Circus Flaminius; Bibulus rose and impeached him. Marcellus spoke shortly and simply in his own defence, but the highest and noblest citizens spoke at great length in his praise, calling on the people not to show themselves by their vote worse judges of war than Hannibal, who was always as eager to avoid fighting with Marcellus, as he was to fight with other generals. After these speeches had been delivered the accuser was proved to be so far wrong in his impeachment, that Marcellus was not only honourably acquitted, but actually elected consul for the fifth time.

XXVIII. On assuming his office, he first put down an insurrectionary movement in Etruria, by visiting the various towns and using conciliatory language; after this, he wished to consecrate a temple, which he had built out of the spoils of Sicily, to Glory and Valour, but being prevented by the priests on the ground that two gods could not be included in one temple, he began to build another one, being very much vexed at the opposition he encountered, but influenced by omens: for he was disturbed at this time by many portentous occurrences, such as several temples being struck by lightning, and the gold in the temple of Jupiter being gnawed by the mice. It was also reported that an ox had spoken with a human voice, and that a child had been born with the head of an elephant—so the priests kept him in Rome to conduct the expiatory rites and atonements for these, though he was fretting and eager to take the field; for no man ever was so passionately desirous of anything as he was to measure himself with Hannibal in battle. His one dream by night, his only talk to his friends and colleagues, his sole prayer to the gods was that he might meet Hannibal in a fair field. I believe that he would most willingly have enclosed both armies within a wall or palisade, and there have fought out the quarrel. Had it not been that he was now loaded with honours, and had given proofs of his superiority in wisdom and conduct to any other general, men would have said that he showed a more boyish ambition than befitted a man of his age; for he was over sixty years old when he entered upon his fifth consulship.

XXIX. However, when he had completed the necessary sacrifices and purifications enjoined by the soothsayers, he took the field with his colleague, and harassed Hannibal much in the country between the towns of Bantia and Venusia. Hannibal declined battle, but, learning that a force was detached from the Roman army to attack the Epizephyrian Lokrians, he laid an ambuscade on the mountain near Petelia, and defeated them with a loss of two thousand five hundred men. This excited Marcellus, and he led his forces nearer to those of Hannibal. There was between the two camps a hill of some strength as a military post, overgrown with wood. Its sloping sides afforded a view of either camp, and upon them appeared the sources of several mountain streams.

The Romans were surprised at Hannibal, that, having had the first choice of so excellent a position as this, he had not occupied it, but left it to the enemy. It seems that he indeed thought it a good place to encamp in, but much better to lay an ambuscade in; and, wishing to use it rather for this purpose, he filled the woods and glens with javelin-men and spearmen, persuaded that the place itself would, from its excellent qualities, attract the Romans into it. Nor was he deceived in this expectation; for at once there was much talk in the Roman army about the necessity of occupying the hill, and men pointed out the advantages which would be gained over the enemy by encamping on it, or if necessary, by fortifying it. Now Marcellus determined to ride forward with a few horsemen and reconnoitre it, so he sent for a soothsayer and offered sacrifice. When the first victim was slain, the soothsayer showed him that the liver had no head. On sacrificing for the second time the head appeared of unusual size, while all the other organs were excellent, and this seemed to set at rest the fear which had been caused by the former. Yet the soothsayers said that they were even more disturbed and alarmed at this; for when after very bad and menacing victims unusually excellent ones appear, the sudden change is itself suspicious. But

"Not fire, not walls of iron can hinder fate,"

as Pindar says. Marcellus rode forth with his colleague Crispinus and his son, who was military tribune, in all two hundred and twenty horsemen. Of these none were Romans; they were Etruscans, with the exception of twenty men from Fregellæ, who had given constant proofs of their courage and devotion to Marcellus. On the overhanging crest of the woody hill, a man, unseen by the Romans, was watching their army. He signalled to the men in ambush what was going on, so that they permitted Marcellus to ride close to them, and then suddenly burst out upon him, and surrounding his little force on all sides, struck and threw their darts, pursued such as ran away, and fought with those who stood their ground. These were the twenty Fregellans. The Etruscans at the outset ran away panic-stricken; but these men forming together defended the consuls until Crispinus, struck by two darts, galloped away, and Marcellus was pierced through the side with a lance. Then even the few survivors of the Fregellans left him lying there, and snatching up his son, who was wounded, made their way back to the camp. The loss amounted to little over forty killed, and five lictors and eighteen horsemen taken. Crispinus, after a few days, died of his wounds. Such a misfortune as this, losing both consuls in one battle, never before befel the Romans.

XXX. Hannibal heard of the fate of all the rest with indifference, but when he was told that Marcellus had fallen he himself hastened to the place, and stood for a long time beside the corpse, admiring its strength and beauty. He made no boastful speech, and showed no joy in his countenance, as a man who had slain a troublesome and dangerous enemy, but, wondering at the strangeness of his ending, he drew the ring from the dead man's finger, and had the corpse decently attired and burned. The relics he gathered into a silver urn, upon which he placed a golden crown, and sent it to Marcellus's son. But on the way some Numidians fell in with the party who were escorting the urn, and while they tried to take it away and the others struggled to retain it, the bones were scattered on the ground. Hannibal, on hearing of this, said, "Nothing can be done against the will of heaven." He ordered the Numidians to be punished, but took no further thought about collecting or sending away the relics of Marcellus, concluding that some god had decreed the strange death and strange lack of burial which had befallen him. This is the story related by Cornelius Nepos and Valerius Maximus, but Livy and Augustus Cæsar declare that the urn was brought to his son, and that it was splendidly buried. Besides his monuments at Rome there was a gymnasium at Katana in Sicily which bore his name, and statues and votive tablets from the plunder of Syracuse were set tip in Samothrace in the temple of the gods called Kabeiri, and in Lindus (in Rhodes) in the temple of Athena.

On his statue there, according to Poseidonius, these verses are written: "This monument, O stranger, doth enshrine Marcellus, of the famous Claudian line, Who seven times was consul, and in fight His country's foes o'erthrew and put to flight."

For the writer of this epitaph counted his two proconsulates as well as his five consulates. His family remained one of the chief in Rome down to the time of Marcellus, the nephew of Augustus, who was the son of Octavia, Augustus's sister, and Caius Marcellus. He died in the office of ædile while yet a bridegroom, having just married Augustus's daughter Julia. In honour of his memory his mother Octavia established a library, and Augustus built a theatre, both of which bore his name.

# The Comparison of Pelopidas
# with Marcellus.

I. The particulars which we thought worth extracting from the histories of Pelopidas and Marcellus are related above. Their dispositions and habits were so nearly identical (for both were brave, laborious, and high-spirited) that the only point in which they differ appears to be that Marcellus put the inhabitants of several captured cities to the sword, whereas Epameinondas and Pelopidas never slew any one after they had conquered him, nor enslaved any captured city; indeed, had they been alive, it is said that the Thebans never would have so treated the town of Orchomenus. As to their exploits, that of Marcellus against the Gauls was great and wonderful, when he drove before him with his little band of horsemen so great a multitude of horse and foot together, the like of which one cannot easily find to have been done by any other general, and the killing of the chief of the enemy. The same thing was attempted by Pelopidas, but the despot was too quick for him, and he perished without succeeding in his effort. Yet with these we may compare his deeds at Leuktra and Tegyra, the most important and glorious of all his feats of arms, while we have no exploit of Marcellus which corresponds to his management of the ambuscade by which he brought back the exiled popular party to Thebes, and destroyed the despots. Indeed, of all deeds performed by secrecy and stratagem, this takes the van. Hannibal, no doubt, was a terrible enemy to Rome, as were the Lacedæmonians to Thebes; yet it is an established fact that at Tegyra and at Leuktra they gave way before Pelopidas, whereas Marcellus, according to Polybius, never once defeated Hannibal, but that general appears to have remained undefeated until the time of Scipio. But we believe, following Livy, Cæsar, Cornelius Nepos, and, among Greek historians, king Juba, that Hannibal suffered some defeats at the hands of Marcellus; yet they never produced any signal result, and we may suspect that the African sometimes only pretended to have lost the day. But what Marcellus is so justly admired for, is that after such great armies had been routed, their generals killed, and the whole military system of Rome thrown into confusion, he inspired his troops with a confidence that enabled them to hold their own against the enemy. He roused his men from their former timid and disheartened condition, making them eager to distinguish themselves in battle, and, what is more, never to yield the victory without a determined struggle. And all this, as far as any single man could, was effected by

Marcellus; for whereas his troops had been accustomed to be well satisfied if they escaped with their lives from Hannibal, he taught them to be ashamed of surviving defeat, to blush to give way ever so little, and to grieve if they were not victorious.

II. Since, then, Pelopidas never was defeated when he was in command, and Marcellus gained more victories than any Roman of his time; perhaps he who was so hard to conquer may, in consideration of his many successes, be held equal to him who never suffered a reverse. Moreover, the one took Syracuse, while the other failed before Lacedæmon. But I hold it a greater feat than taking Sicily, to have marched upon Sparta, and been the first man to cross the Eurotas, unless indeed it should be said that the credit of this exploit belongs more to Epameinondas than to Pelopidas, as also does the battle of Leuktra, whereas the glory of Marcellus's achievements is all his own. For he took Syracuse alone, and beat the Gauls without his colleague, and, with no one to assist him, but every one hanging back, he measured himself with Hannibal and changed the whole complexion of the war, by being the first to introduce a daring policy.

III. As for their deaths, I can praise neither one nor the other, but I am grieved at the unworthy manner of their end. It is strange, that Hannibal was never even wounded in a number of battles which it would weary one to recount; and I admire the conduct of Chrysantas in Xenophon's 'Cyropædia,' who, when standing with his weapon drawn, about to strike an enemy, heard the trumpet sound the recall, and leaving his man, quietly and orderly retreated. Yet Pelopidas may be excused by his excitement during a battle, and his courage, which urged him to avenge himself on the enemy, for the best thing is for the general to be victorious and to survive, and the next, for him to die "breathing forth his life in valour" as Euripides says. Thus his death becomes no accident, but a premeditated act. And besides Pelopidas's spirit, the assured victory which he saw within his grasp, could he but kill the despot, not unreasonably made him make his desperate attack; for it would have been hard for him to obtain another opportunity of distinguishing himself so gloriously. But Marcellus, without any necessity, without the excitement which sometimes in perilous circumstances overpowers men's reason, pushed heedlessly into danger, and died the death of a spy rather than a general, risking his five consulships, his three triumphs, his spoils and trophies won from kings against the worthless lives of Iberian and Numidian mercenaries. They themselves must have felt ashamed at their success, that the bravest, most powerful, and most celebrated of the Romans should have fallen among a reconnoitring party of Fregellans. Still, let not this be regarded as a reproach to these great men, but rather a complaint addressed on their own behalf to them, especially to that courage, to which they sacrificed all their other virtues, disregarding their lives, as though their loss would fall upon themselves only, and not upon their friends and native country. After his death, Pelopidas was buried by his allies, fighting for whom he died; but Marcellus was buried by the enemy at whose hands he fell. The first was an enviable end, but the other is greater, as the spectacle of an enemy honouring the valour by which he has suffered is greater than that of a friend showing gratitude to a friend. In the one case it is the man's glory alone that is respected, in the other, his usefulness and value are as much thought of as his courage.

# Life of Aristeides.

Aristeides, the son of Lysimachus, was of the tribe Antiochis, and the township of Alopekæ. There are various reports current about his property, some saying that he lived in poverty, and that on his death he left two daughters, who remained a long while unmarried because of their poverty; while this general opinion is contradicted by Demetrius of Phalerum in his book on Sokrates, where he mentions an estate at Phalerum which he knew had belonged to Aristeides, in which he was buried, and also adduces other grounds for supposing him to have been a wealthy man. First, he points out that Aristeides was Archon Eponymus, an office for which men were chosen by lot from the richest class, that of the Pentakosiomedimni, or citizens who possessed a yearly income of five hundred medimni of dry or liquid produce. Secondly, he mentions the fact that he was ostracised: now, ostracism never was used against poor men, but against those who descended from great and wealthy houses, and whose pride made them feared and disliked by their fellow citizens. Thirdly, and lastly, he writes that Aristeides placed in the temple of Dionysus tripods dedicated to the god by a victorious chorus, which even in my own time are still to be seen, and which bear the inscription: "The tribe Antiochis won the prize; Aristeides was choragus; Archestratus taught the chorus." Now this, which seems to be the strongest argument of all, is really the weakest. Epameinondas, whom all men know to have been born and to have passed his life in the greatest possible poverty, and Plato the philosopher, both exhibited excellent choruses, the former bearing the expense of a chorus of men playing on the flute, while the latter exhibited a cyclic chorus of boys. Plato's expenses were borne by Dionysius of Syracuse, and those of Epameinondas by Pelopidas and his friends. Good men do not always refuse to receive presents from their friends, but, though they would scorn to make money by them, they willingly receive them to further an honourable ambition. Panætius, moreover, proves that Demetrius is wrong in the matter of the tripods, because from the time of the Persian war to the end of the Peloponnesian war there are only two Aristeides recorded as victors, neither of whom can be identified with the son of Lysimachus, as the father of one of them was Xenophilus, and the other was a much more modern personage, as is proved by his name being written in the characters which came into use after the archonship of Eukleides, and from the name of the poet or teacher of the chorus, Archestratus, whose name we never meet with in the time of the Persian war, but who taught several choruses (that is, wrote several successful plays) during the Peloponnesian war. These remarks of Panætius must, however, be received with caution. As to ostracism, any man of unusual talent, nobility of birth, or remarkable eloquence, was liable to suffer from it, for Damon, the tutor of Perikles, was ostracised, because he was thought to be a man of superior intellect. Idomeneus tells us that Aristeides obtained the office of archon, not by lot, but by the universal voice of the people. Now, if he was archon after the battle of Platæa, as Demetrius himself admits, it is highly probable that his great reputation after such glorious successes may have obtained for him an office usually reserved for men of wealth. Indeed, Demetrius evidently tries to redeem both Aristeides and Sokrates from the reproach of poverty, as though he imagined it to be a great misfortune, for he tells us that Sokrates not only possessed a house, but also seventy minæ which were borrowed by Krito.

II. Aristeides became much attached to Kleisthenes, who established the democratic government after the expulsion of the sons of Peisistratus; but his reverence and admiration for Lykurgus the Lacedæmonian led him to prefer an aristocratic form of government, in which he always met with an opponent in Themistokles, the son of Neokles, the champion of democracy. Some say that even as children they always took opposite sides, both in play and in serious matters, and so betrayed their several dispositions: Themistokles being unscrupulous, daring, and careless by what means he obtained success, while the character of Aristeides was solid and just, incapable of deceit or artifice even in sport. Ariston of Keos tells us that their hatred of one another arose from a love affair. Stesilaus of Keos, the most beautiful youth of his time, was passionately adored by both of them with an affection which passed all bounds. Nor did they cease their rivalry when this boy's youthful bloom had passed away, but, as if this had merely been a preliminary trial, they each plunged into politics with great vigour and with utterly different views. Themistokles obtained a large following, and thus became an important power in the state, so that, when some one said to him that he would make a very good governor of Athens, provided he were just and impartial with all, he answered, "Never may I bear rule if my friends are to reap no more benefit from it than any one else."

Aristeides, on the other hand, pursued his way through political life unattended, because, in the first place, he neither wished to do wrong in order to please his friends, nor to vex them by refusing to gratify their wishes; and also because he observed that many men when they were supported by a strong party of friends were led into the commission of wrong and illegal acts.

He, therefore, conceived that a good citizen ought to trust entirely to his own rectitude, both in word and in deed.

III. In spite of this, however, when Themistokles was using every kind of political manœuvre to thwart him, he was forced to retaliate by similar measures, partly in order to defend himself, and partly to check the power of his opponent, which depended on the favour shown him by the people. He thought it better that he should occasionally do the people some slight wrong than that Themistokles should obtain unlimited power. At last, when Themistokles even proposed some useful measure, he opposed it and threw it out. On this occasion he could not refrain from saying, as he left the public assembly, that the Athenians could not be saved unless they threw both himself and Themistokles into the barathrum. Another time he brought forward a bill, which was vehemently debated upon, but was at length carried. But just before the votes of the people were given, he, perceiving from what had been said that it would prove a bad law, withdrew it. Frequently he made use of other persons to bring forward propositions, lest the public should suffer from the contest which would otherwise take place between Themistokles and himself. Indeed, his evenness of temper was the more remarkable when contrasted with the changefulness of other politicians, for he was never unduly excited by the honours which were bestowed upon him, and bore misfortune with a quiet cheerfulness, thinking it to be his duty to serve his country, not merely without being paid for it in money, but without even gaining honour for so doing. This was the reason, I suppose, that when Æschylus's verses on Amphiaraus wore being recited in the theatre;
"Not just to seem, but just he loves to be; And deep he ploughs his noble mind with thought, To reap a harvest thence of great designs,"
all men turned and looked towards Aristeides, thinking that he came nearest to this ideal virtue.

IV. He stood up vigorously for justice, not merely when it was his interest and that of his friends, but when it was in favour of his enemies and contrary to his own personal feelings to do so. It is said that once when arguing a cause against one of his enemies in a court of law, the judges refused to hear the other party speak in his own defence, after listening to the speech of Aristeides, but were about to condemn him unheard. At this Aristeides came forward and vigorously supported his antagonist's claim to be allowed his legal right of reply. Again, when acting as arbitrator between two persons, one of them said that his adversary had done much wrong to Aristeides. "My good man," said he, "do not tell me of this, but tell me whether he has wronged you or not, for I am judging your cause, not my own."

When elected to administer the revenues of the state he proved that not only his own colleagues, but those who had previously held office, had embezzled large sums, especially Themistokles,

"A clever man, but with an itching palm."

For this cause Themistokles, when Aristeides' accounts were audited, prosecuted him on a charge of malversation, and, according to Idomeneus, obtained a verdict.

However, the better class of citizens being grieved at this, not only remitted the fine, but at once elected him to the same office. He now pretended to regret his former rigour, and was much more remiss in performing his duties, which rendered him very popular with those who were in the habit of embezzling the public money, so that they were loud in his praise, and canvassed the people on his behalf, trusting that he might be re-elected archon. But when the voting was about to begin, he rose and rebuked the Athenians. "When," he said, "I did you true and honourable service, I was disgraced by you; now, when I have permitted much of the public money to be stolen, I am thought to be an excellent citizen. But I myself am more ashamed of the honour which you now pay me, than I am of my former conviction, and I am sorry for you, because among you it is esteemed more honourable to abet evil-doers than to guard the national property."

By speaking thus and exposing the peculation which was being practised, he closed the mouths of all those who were so loudly commending him as an honest man, but gained the applause of all true and honourable men.

V. When Datis was sent by Darius, nominally to punish the Athenians for the burning of Sardis, but really to enslave the whole of Greece, he landed at Marathon, and commenced laying waste the country. Of the ten generals appointed by the Athenians for the conduct of the war, Miltiades had the highest reputation, while Aristeides held the second place. He used his influence in the council of war to support the proposition of Miltiades to fight the enemy at once, and also, as each general had sole command for one day, when his day came round, he gave it to Miltiades, thus teaching his colleagues that obedience to those who know how to command is not any disgrace, but a noble and useful act. By this means he was enabled to put an end to the rivalries between the generals, and to strengthen Miltiades by concentrating in him the power which had before been passed from hand to hand. In the battle the Athenian centre was hard pressed, as the Persians resisted longest in that part of their line which was opposed to the tribes Leontis and Antiochis. Here Themistokles and Aristeides each showed conspicuous valour, fighting side by side, for the former was of the tribe Leontis, the latter of the tribe Antiochis. After the victory was won, and the Persians forced into their ships, they were observed not to sail towards the Archipelago, but to be proceeding in the direction of Athens. Fearing that they might catch the city defenceless, the Athenians determined to hurry back with nine tribes to protect it, and they accomplished their march in one day. Aristeides, with his own tribe, was left to guard the prisoners and the plunder, and well maintained his reputation. Although gold and silver was lying about in heaps, with all kinds of rich tapestry and other countless treasures, he would neither touch them himself nor allow the others to do so, though some helped themselves without his knowledge. Among these was Kallias, the torch-bearer in the Eleusinian mysteries. One of the prisoners, taking him for a king because of his long hair and fillet, fell on his knees before him, and having received his hand as a pledge for his safety pointed out to him a great store of gold concealed in a pit. Kallias now acted most cruelly and wickedly. He took the gold, and killed the poor man for fear that he should tell it to the others. It is said that ever afterwards the descendants of Kallias were jeered at by the comic poets, as being of the family of the man who found the gold in the pit.

Immediately after those events, Aristeides was chosen as Archon Eponymus, that is, the archon who gives his name to the year. Demetrius of Phalerum says that he filled this office shortly before his death, and after the battle of Platæa. But in the public records of Athens one cannot find any archon of the name of Aristeides among the many who filled the office after Xanthippides, in whose archonship Mardonius was defeated at Platæa, whereas the name of Aristeides does occur next to that of Phanippus, in whose archonship the victory at Marathon was won.

VI. Of all the virtues of Aristeides his justice was that which chiefly commended itself to the people, being that which is of most value in ordinary life. Hence it was that he, although a poor man of mean birth, yet gained for himself the truly imperial title of the Just; a title which has never been emulated by kings and despots, who delight in being called the City-taker, the Thunderbolt, or the Victorious, while some are known as the Eagle or the Hawk, because apparently they prefer strength and lawless violence to justice and goodness. Yet for all this, the gods, to whom they so presumptuously liken themselves, excel mankind chiefly in three attributes, namely in immortality, in power, and in goodness, whereof goodness is by far the most glorious and divine quality. Mere empty space, and all the elements possess immortality, while earthquakes, thunderbolts, violent winds and rushing waters have great power, but justice and equity belong to the gods alone, because of the reason and intelligence which they possess. Now most men regard the gods with admiration, with fear, and with reverence; with admiration, because they are eternal and unchangeable; with fear, because of their power and dominion, with reverence and love because of their justice. Yet men covet immortality, which no flesh can attain to; and also power, which depends mostly upon fortune; while they disregard virtue, the only godlike attribute which it is in our power to obtain; not reflecting that when a man is in a position of great power and authority he will appear like a god if he acts justly, and like a wild beast if he does not.

VII. The character of Aristeides for justice at first made him beloved by the people, but afterwards it gained him their ill-will, chiefly because Themistokles circulated reports that Aristeides had practically closed the public courts of justice by the fact of all cases being referred to him as arbitrator, and that he was virtually king of Athens, although he had not yet surrounded himself with a body-guard. By this time too the common people, elated with their victory at Marathon, and thinking themselves capable of the greatest exploits, were ill pleased at any private citizen being exalted above the rest by his character and virtues. They flocked into the city from all parts of the country and ostracised Aristeides, veiling their envy of his glory under the pretence that they feared he would make himself king. This custom of ostracism was not intended as a punishment for crime, but was called, in order to give it a plausible title, a check to excessive power. In reality, it was nothing more than a safety-valve, providing a vent for the dislike felt by the people for those whose greatness offended them. It did no irreparable injury to those who fell under its operation, but only banished them for a space of ten years. In later times mean and contemptible persons were subjected to ostracism, until at last, after the ostracism of Hyperbolus the practice was discontinued. The ostracism of Hyperbolus is said to have been brought about in the following manner. Alkibiades and Nikias, the two most powerful citizens in the state, were at the head of two rival parties. The people determined to apply the ostracism to them, and would certainly have banished one or the other of them. They, however, came to terms with one another, combined their several factions, and agreed to have Hyperbolus banished. The people, enraged at this, and thinking that they had been treated with contempt, abolished the practice of ostracism. The way in which it was conducted was as follows. Each man took an oyster-shell, wrote upon it the name of the citizen whom he wished to be banished, and then carried it to a place in the market-place which was fenced off with palings. The archons now first of all counted the whole number of shells; for if the whole number of voters were less than six thousand, the ostracism was null and void. After this, they counted the number of times each name occurred, and that man against whom most votes were recorded they sent into exile for ten years, allowing him the use of his property during that time. Now while the shells were being written upon, on the occasion of which we have been speaking, a very ignorant country fellow is said to have brought his shell to Aristeides, who was one of the bystanders, and to have asked him to write upon it the name of Aristeides. Aristeides was surprised, and asked him whether Aristeides had ever done him any harm. "No," answered the man, "nor do I know him by sight, but I am tired of always hearing him called 'The Just.'" When Aristeides heard this he made no answer, but wrote his name on the man's shell and gave it back to him. When he was leaving the city he raised his hands to heaven, and prayed exactly the opposite prayer to that of Achilles, that no crisis might befall the Athenians which would compel them to remember Aristeides.

VIII. However, three years afterwards, when Xerxes was advancing upon Attica through Thessaly and Bœotia, the Athenians annulled their decree, and permitted all exiles to return, being especially afraid of Aristeides, lest he should join the enemy and lead many of the citizens to desert with him. In this they took a very false view of his character, for even before this decree he had never ceased to encourage the Greeks to defend their liberty, and after his return, when Themistokles was in sole command of the forces of Athens, he assisted him in every way by word and deed, cheerfully raising his bitterest enemy to the highest position in the state, because the state was benefited thereby.

When Eurybiades and his party were meditating a retreat from Salamis, the Persian ships put to sea at night and hemmed them in, surrounding both the strait and the islands. No one knew that escape was impossible, but Aristeides sailed from Ægina, passed safely through the enemy's fleet by a miracle, and while it was still night proceeded straight to the tent of Themistokles. Here he called him out, and when they were alone together, he said: "We two, Themistokles, if we are wise, must cease our vain and silly rivalry with one another, and begin a more generous contest to preserve our country, you acting as general and chief, while I help and advise you. Already I perceive that you alone take a right view of the crisis, end desire to fight a battle in the narrow waters as quickly as possible. Now, while your allies have been opposing you, the enemy have been playing your game, for the sea, both in our front and rear, is full of their ships, so that the Greeks even against their will must play the man and fight; for no way of escape is left for them." To this Themistokles answered, "I would not willingly, Aristeides, be overcome by you in generosity on this occasion; and I shall endeavour, in emulation of this good beginning which you have made, to surpass it by the glory of my exploits." At the same time he explained the trick which he had played on the barbarian, and begged Aristeides to argue with Eurybiades, and point out how impossible it was for the Greeks to be saved without fighting; for he thought that the opinion of Aristeides would have more weight than his own. Consequently, when in the assembly of the generals Kleokritus the Corinthian attacked Themistokles, and said that even Aristeides did not approve of his plans, because he was present and said nothing, Aristeides answered that he would not have been silent if Themistokles had not spoken to the purpose, but that as it was he held his peace, not for any love he bore him, but because his counsel was the best.

IX. While the Greek admirals were engaged in these discussions, Aristeides, perceiving that Psyttaleia, a small island in the straits near Salamis, was full of the enemy, placed some of the boldest Athenians on board of small boats, attacked the Persians, and slew them to a man, except a few of the chiefs, who wore taken alive. Among these were the three children of Sandauke the sister of the Persian king, whom he at once sent to Themistokles, and it is said that in accordance with some oracle they were sacrificed to Dionysus Omestes, at the instance of the prophet Euphrantides. Aristeides now lined the shores of the islet with soldiers, ready to receive any vessel which might be cast upon it, in order that neither any of his friends might be lost, nor any of the enemy take refuge upon it. Indeed, the severest encounter between the two fleets and the main shock of the battle seems to have taken place at that spot; wherefore the trophy that marks the victory stands on the isle of Psyttaleia.

After the battle was won, Themistokles, wishing to feel Aristeides's opinion, said to him that they had done a good work, but that a greater one remained, which was to shut up Asia in Europe by sailing as quickly as possible to the Hellespont, and destroying the bridge of boats there. Aristeides answered that he must never propose such a plan, but must take measures to drive the Persians out of Greece as quickly as possible, for fear that so great a multitude, shut up there without the means of retreat, should turn to bay and attack them with the courage of despair. Upon this, Themistokles again sent the eunuch Arnakes, a prisoner, on a secret errand to tell the Persian king that when all the Greeks wished to sail to the Hellespont and destroy the bridge of boats, he had dissuaded them from doing so, wishing to save the king's life.

X. At this Xerxes became terrified, and at once hurried back to the Hellespont. Mardonius, with about three hundred thousand of the best troops remained behind, and was a formidable enemy, trusting in his land force, and sending defiant proclamations to the Greeks. "You," he said, "with your ships have beaten landsmen that knew not how to handle an oar; but the land of Thessaly is wide, and the plain of Bœotia is a fair place for good horsemen and heavy armed soldiers to fight upon."

To the Athenians he sent privately proposals from the Great King, who offered to rebuild their city, present them with a large sum of money, and make them lords over all Greece, if they would desist from the war. The Lacedæmonians, hearing this, were much alarmed, and sent ambassadors to beg the Athenians to send their wives and children to Sparta, and offering to support their old people, as the Athenians were in great distress for food, having lost their city and their country. However, after listening to the Lacedæmonian ambassadors, at the instance of Aristeides they returned a spirited answer, saying that they could forgive their enemies, who knew no better, for supposing that everything could be bought with money, but that they were angry with the Lacedæmonians for only regarding the present poverty and distress of the Athenians, and that forgetting how bravely they had fought, they should now offer them food to bribe them to fight for Greece. Having passed this motion Aristeides called the ambassadors back into the assembly, and bade them tell the Lacedæmonians that there was not as much gold in the world, either above or under-ground, as the Athenians would require to tempt them to betray Greece.

In answer to the herald sent from Mardonius he pointed to the sun, and said: "As long as yonder sun shall continue its course the Athenians will be enemies to the Persians, because of their ravaged lands and desecrated temples." Further, he made the priests imprecate curses on any one who had dealings with the Persians or deserted the Greek cause.

When Mardonius invaded Attica a second time, the Athenians again took refuge in Salamis. Aristeides was sent to Lacedæmon and upbraided the Spartans with their slowness and indifference, for allowing the enemy to take Athens a second time, and begged them to help what remained of Greece. The Ephors, on hearing this, pretended to pass the rest of the day in feasting and idleness, for it was the festival of the Hyacinthia; but at nightfall they chose five thousand Spartans, each attended by seven Helots, and sent them off without the knowledge of the Athenian embassy. So when Aristeides next day resumed his reproachful strain, they answered with mocking laughter, that he was talking nonsense and was asleep, for that the army was by this time at the tomb of Orestes in its march against the strangers (by strangers they meant the Persians). To this Aristeides answered that it was a sorry jest to have deceived their friends instead of their enemies. These particulars are related by Idomeneus, but in the decree of Aristeides for sending ambassadors it is not his name, but those of Kimon, Xanthippus, and Myronides that are mentioned.

XI. He was elected general with unlimited powers, and proceeded to Platæa with eight thousand Athenians. Here he was met by Pausanias, the commander-in-chief of the Greek forces, with the Spartan contingent, and the rest of the Greek troops joined them there. The Persian army was encamped along the course of the river Asopus. On account of its enormous size it was not contained in a fortified camp, but a quadrangular wall was constructed round the baggage and most valuable material. Each side of this square was ten furlongs in length.

Tisamenus of Elis, the prophet, now told Pausanias and all the Greeks that they would win the victory if they stood on the defensive and did not attack. Aristeides sent to Delphi, and received a response from the oracle, that the Athenians would conquer if they prayed to Zeus, to Hera of Kithæron, and to Pan and the nymphs Sphragitides, and if they sacrificed to the heroes Androkrates, Leukon, Peisander, Damokrates, Hypsion, Aktaion, and Polyïdus, and if they would fight in their own territory, in the plain of Demeter of Eleusis and her daughter.

This oracle greatly disturbed Aristeides. The heroes to whom he was bidden to sacrifice are the original founders of the city of Platæa, and the cave of the nymphs called Sphragitides, is on one of the peaks of Kithæron, looking towards the point where the sun sets in summer. It is said that there was formerly an oracle there, and that many of the people became possessed, and were called "nympholeptæ." But as to the plain of the Eleusinian Demeter, and the promise of victory to the Athenians if they fought in their own country, this meant no less than to recall them to Attica and forbid their taking any further part in the war. Whilst Aristeides was thus perplexed, Arimnestus, the general of the Platæans, saw a vision in his sleep. In his dreams he thought that Zeus the Preserver appeared and enquired of him what the Greeks had decided to do, and that he answered, "Lord, to-morrow we shall lead away the army to Eleusis, and fight the Persians there, according to the oracle." Upon this the god answered, that they had missed the meaning of the oracle, for the places mentioned were near Platæa, where they themselves were encamped, and if they sought they would find them. Arimnestus, after this distinct vision, awoke. He at once sent for the oldest and most learned of the citizens of Platæa, and after debating the matter with them, discovered that near Hysiæ, under Mount Kithæron, stood a very ancient temple, dedicated to the Eleusinian Demeter and her daughter. He immediately took Aristeides with him and proceeded to the spot, which was excellently placed for the array of an infantry force in the presence of an overwhelming cavalry, because the spurs of Mount Kithæron, where they run down into the plain by the temple, render the ground impassable for cavalry. Close by is the chapel of the hero Androkrates, in the midst of a thick matted grove of trees. In order, however, that the oracle might in no way be defective in its promise of victory, Arimnestus proposed, and the Platæans decreed, that the boundary marks of their territory on the side towards Attica should be removed, and the country given to the Athenians, so that they might fight in their own land for Greece, according to the oracle. This noble act of the Platæans became so famous in later times, that, many years afterwards, Alexander the Great himself, when he had conquered all Asia, caused the walls of Platæa to be rebuilt, and made proclamation at the Olympian games by a herald, "that the king bestowed this honour upon the Platæans in memory of their magnanimous conduct in giving up their territory, and venturing their lives on behalf of the Greeks in the Persian war."

XII. A controversy arose between the Athenians and the men of Tegea about their respective places in the line of battle. The Tegeans argued that if the Lacedæmonians had the right wing, they ought to be posted on the left; and they spoke at great length about the achievements of their ancestors, as entitling them to that honour. The Athenians were vexed at their pretensions, but Aristeides said: "The present time is not suitable for disputing with the Tegeans about bravery; but to you, men of Sparta, and to the rest of the Greeks, we say that a particular post neither confers courage nor takes it away, but, that in whatever part of the line you may think fit to place us, we will endeavour so to array our ranks and fight the enemy as not to impair the honour which we have gained in former battles. We did not come hither to quarrel with our allies, but to fight the enemy; not to boast about our ancestors, but to fight bravely for Greece. The coming struggle will clearly show to all the Greeks the real worth and value of each city, each general, and each single citizen." When the council of generals heard this speech, they allowed the claim of the Athenians, and gave up the left wing to them.

XIII. While the cause of Greece was thus trembling in the balance, and Athens was especially in danger, certain Athenians of noble birth, who had lost their former wealth during the war, and with it their influence in the city, being unable to bear to see others exalted at their expense, met in secret in a house in Platæa and entered into a plot to overturn the free constitution of Athens. If they could not succeed in this, they pledged themselves to ruin, the city and betray it to the Persians. While these men were plotting in the camp, and bringing many over to their side, Aristeides discovered the whole conspiracy. Afraid at such a crisis to take any decisive step, he determined, while carefully watching the conspirators, yet not at once to seize them all, not knowing how far he might have to proceed if he acted according to strict justice. From all the conspirators he arrested eight. Two of these, who would have been the first to be put on their trial, Æschines of Lampra, and Agesias of Acharna, made their escape out of the camp, and Aristeides pardoned the others, as he wished to give an opportunity to those who believed themselves unsuspected, to take courage and repent. He also hinted to them that the war afforded them a means of clearing themselves from any suspicion of disloyalty by fighting for their country like good men and true.

XIV. After this, Mardonius made trial of Grecian courage, by sending the whole of his cavalry, in which he was much the stronger, to attack them where they were, all except the Megarians, encamped at the foot of Mount Kithæron, in an easily-defended rocky country. These men, three thousand in number, were encamped nearer the plain, and suffered much from the attacks of the horsemen, who surrounded them on all sides. They sent a messenger in great haste to Pausanias, begging him to send assistance, as they could not by themselves resist the great numbers of the barbarians. Pausanias, hearing this, and seeing the camp of the Megarians overwhelmed with darts and arrows, while the defenders were huddled together in a narrow compass, knew not what to do. He did not venture to attack cavalry with the heavy-armed Lacedæmonian infantry, but offered it as an opportunity for winning praise and honour, to the generals who were with him, that they should volunteer to go to help the Megarians in their extremity. All hesitated, but Aristeides claimed the honour for the Athenians, and sent the bravest of his captains, Olympiodorus, with three hundred picked men, besides some archers. As they quickly got into array and charged at a run, Masistius, the leader of the enemy, a man of great bodily strength and beauty, seeing them, wheeled round his horse, and rode to attack them. They sustained his attack and closed with his horsemen, and a sharp struggle took place, both parties fighting as though the issue of the war depended on their exertions. The horse of Masistius was at length wounded by an arrow and threw his rider. Encumbered by his armour, Masistius was too heavy for his own men to carry him away, but also was protected by it from the stabs of the Athenians who fell upon him, for not only his head and breast, but his limbs also were protected by brass and iron. Some one, however, drove the spike at the lower end of his spear through the eye-hole of the helmet, and then the rest of the Persians abandoned the body and fled. The Greeks discovered the importance of their exploit, not from the number of the dead, for but few had fallen, but from the lamentations of the enemy. They cut off their own hair, and the manes of their horses and mules, in sign of mourning for Masistius, and filled the whole plain with weeping and wailing, having lost a man who for courage and high position, was second only to Mardonius himself.

XV. After this cavalry action, both the parties remained quiet for a long time, for the soothsayers foretold victory both to the Greeks and to the Persians if they fought in self-defence, but foretold defeat if they attacked. At length Mardonius, as he only had provisions for a few days longer, and as the Greek army kept growing stronger by the continual reinforcements which it received, determined, sorely against his will, to delay no longer, but to cross the Asopus at daybreak and fall upon the Greeks unexpectedly. In the evening he gave orders to his captains to this effect. About midnight a solitary horseman rode up straight to the Greek camp. He bade the guard send for Aristeides the Athenian, who was at once brought, when the stranger spoke as follows:

"I am Alexander of Macedon, and I have come hither at the greatest risk to myself to do you a service, for fear you should be taken by surprise. Mardonius will attack to-morrow, not because he has any new hope of success, but because he is destitute of provisions, although the soothsayers all forbid him to fight because the sacrifices and oracles are unfavourable, and the army is disheartened. Thus he is forced to put all on a venture, or else to starve if he remains quiet." When he had said this, Alexander begged Aristeides to keep the secret to himself, and communicate it to no one else. Aristeides, however, answered that it would not be right for him to conceal it from Pausanias, who was commander-in-chief. Before the battle he said that he would keep it secret from every one else, but that if Greece was victorious, all men then should know the good service so bravely rendered by Alexander. After these words the king of Macedon rode away, and Aristeides, proceeding to the tent of Pausanias, told him the whole matter; they then sent for the other generals, and ordered them to keep the troops under arms, as a battle was expected.

XVI. At this time, Herodotus tells us, Pausanias asked Aristeides to remove the Athenians from the left to the right wing, so as to be opposite to the native Persian troops, on the ground that they would be better able to contend with them, because they understood their mode of fighting, and were confident because they had beaten them once before, while he with the Spartans would take the left wing of the army, where he would be opposed to those Greeks who had taken the Persian side. Most of the Athenian generals thought this a silly and insolent proceeding of Pausanias, that he should leave all the other Greeks in their place, and march them backwards and forward like helots, only to place them opposite the bravest troops of the enemy. Aristeides, however, said that they were entirely mistaken, for a few days before they had been wrangling with the Tegeans for the honour of being posted on the left wing, and had been delighted when they obtained it; but now, when the Lacedæmonians of their own free will yielded the right wing to them, and in some sort offered them the post of honour in the whole army, they were not delighted at it, and did not consider what an advantage it was to have to fight against foreign barbarians, and not against men of their own race and nation. After these words, the Athenians cheerfully exchanged places with the Lacedæmonians, and much talk went on among them as each man reminded his comrades that the Persians who would come to attack them were no braver, nor better armed than those whom they had defeated at Marathon, but that they had the same bows and arrows, the same embroidered robes and gold ornaments on their effeminate bodies, while we, they said, have arms and bodies such as we had then, and greater confidence because of our victories. We also fight, not merely as other Greeks do, in defence of our city and territory, but for the trophies of Marathon and Salamis, lest the battle of Marathon should be thought to have been won more by Miltiades and Fortune, than by the valour of the Athenians. With such encouraging talk as this the Athenians took up their new position; but the Thebans discovered what had been done from deserters and told Mardonius. He at once, either from fear of the Athenians, or from a chivalrous wish to fight the Spartans himself, led the native Persian troops to his right wing, and ordered the renegade Greeks to take ground opposite the Athenians. When these changes were being observed, Pausanias returned to his original position on the right. Mardonius then returned to the left as before, and the day passed without an engagement. The Greeks now determined in a council of war, to remove their camp to a place farther away and better supplied with water, because they were prevented from using the springs near where they were by the enemy's great superiority in cavalry.

XVII. When night fell the generals began to lead the army to the place selected for a new camp. The soldiers were very unwilling to follow them thither and keep together in a body, but as soon as they quitted their first entrenchments, most of them made for the city of Platæa; and there was much confusion as they wandered about and pitched their tents here and there. The Lacedæmonians, much against their will, chanced to be left behind, and quite separated from the rest. One Amompharetus, a spirited and daring man, who had long been eager to fight, and chafed much at the long delays and countermarches which had taken place, now cried aloud that this change of position was no better than a cowardly flight. He refused to leave his post, and said that he and his company would stand where they were, and withstand Mardonius alone. When Pausanias came and assured him that the Greeks in council had decided upon this measure, Amompharetus heaved up a huge stone with both his hands and flinging it down at the feet of Pausanias, said, "With this pebble I give my vote for battle, and for disregarding the cowardly counsels of other Greeks." Pausanias, not knowing what to do, sent to the Athenians, who were already on the march, begging them to wait and support them, while he set off with the rest of the Spartans in the direction of Platæa, hoping thus to make Amompharetus move.

While these movements were being executed day broke, and Mardonius, who had perceived that the Greeks were leaving their camp, at once marched in order of battle to attack the Lacedæmonians, the Persians shouting and clattering their arms as though they were not going to fight, but to destroy the Greeks as they retreated, which indeed they very nearly succeeded in doing; for Pausanias, when he saw what was taking place, halted his own men, and placed them in battle array, but either because of his anger at Amompharetus, or his excitement at the suddenness of the attack, forgot to send any orders to the main body of the Greeks.

For this reason they came up not in a regular body, but straggling, and after the Lacedæmonians wore already engaged. Pausanias was busy sacrificing to the gods, and as the sacrifices were unfavourable, he ordered the Lacedæmonians to hold their shields quietly rested on the ground at their feet and await his orders, without attempting any resistance, while he sacrificed again. The enemy's cavalry was now close at hand, their arrows reached the Lacedæmonians and killed several of them. It was at this moment that Kallikrates, the tallest and handsomest man in the whole Greek army, is said to have been mortally wounded by an arrow. When dying, he said that he did not lament his death, for he left his home meaning to lay down his life for Greece, but that he was grieved that he had never exchanged blows with the enemy before he died. At this time the Lacedæmonians were offering no resistance to the assaults of the enemy, but were standing still in their ranks, shot at by the arrows of the enemy, awaiting the time when it should be the will of the gods and their general that they should fight. Some writers tell us that while Pausanias was offering sacrifice and prayer a little beyond the ranks, some Lydians suddenly fell upon him, and began to plunder the sacrificial vessels, but that Pausanias, and those with him, having no arms, drove them away with sticks and whips; in memory of which they beat young men on the altar at Sparta at the present day, and afterwards lead what is called the Lydian procession.

XVIII. Pausanias was deeply grieved at what was taking place, seeing the priests offering sacrifice after sacrifice, not one of which pleased the gods; at last he turned his eyes towards the temple of Hera and wept. Holding up his hands he besought Hera of Mount Kithæron and all the other gods of the land of Platæa that if it were not the will of the gods that the Greeks should conquer, they might at any rate do some valorous deed before they died, and let their conquerors know that they had fought with brave and experienced warriors. When Pausanias prayed thus, the sacrifices at once became favourable and the soothsayers prophesied victory. The word was given to sot themselves in order of battle, and then at once the Lacedæmonian force resembled some fierce beast turning to bay and setting up his bristles, while the barbarians saw that they had to deal with men who were prepared to fight to the death. Wherefore they set up their great wicker shields in front of them, and from this shelter shot their arrows at the Lacedæmonians. But the latter advanced without breaking their ranks, overturned the line of wicker shields, and with, terrible thrusts of their spears at the faces and breasts of the Persians, laid many of them low by their fierce and well-disciplined charge. The Persians too fought bravely, and resisted for a long while, laying hold of the spears with their bare hands and breaking most of them in that manner, fighting hand to hand, with their scimitars and axes, and tearing the Lacedæmonians' shields out of their hands by force.

Meanwhile the Athenians had for a long time stood quietly awaiting the Lacedæmonians. When, however, they heard the shouting and noise of the battle, and a messenger, it is said, reached them from Pausanias, they marched with all speed to help him. As they were hurrying over the plain to where the shouts were heard, the Greeks who had taken the Persian side attacked them. At first when Aristeides saw them, he ran out far before the rest and besought them in a loud voice in the name of the gods of Greece not to hinder the Athenians when they were going to assist those who were venturing their lives on behalf of Greece. But when he saw that they took no notice of his appeal, he no longer attempted to help the Lacedæmonians, but attacked these troops, who numbered about fifty thousand. Of these the greater part gave way at once and retreated, because they saw their barbarian allies retreating, but a fierce battle is said to have raged where the Thebans were, because the best and noblest men of that state had eagerly taken the Persian side from the beginning, while the common people followed them, not of their free will, but being accustomed to obey the nobles.

XIX. Thus was the battle divided into two parts. The Lacedæmonians were the first to rout the Persians. A Spartan, named Arimnestus, killed Mardonius by a blow on the head with a stone, as the oracle in the temple of Amphiaraus had foretold to him. For Mardonius sent a Lydian thither, and another man, a Karian, to the oracle in the cave of Trophonius. This latter was spoken to in the Karian language by the prophet, but the other slept in the sacred enclosure round the temple of Amphiaraus, and in his dreams saw a servant of the god standing beside him and bidding him begone. When he refused to go, the figure cast a great stone at his head, so that he dreamed that he died of the stroke. This is the story which is told of Mardonius. The Persian fugitives were now driven to take shelter within their wooden fortification. Shortly after these events took place, the Athenians defeated the Thebans, who lost three hundred of their noblest citizens in that battle. After this there came a messenger to them, telling them that the Persians were being besieged in their fortified camp. Hearing this, the Athenians allowed the renegade Greeks to escape, and marched at once to the assault of the camp. Here they found the Lacedæmonians, who were not pressing the enemy, because they had no experience in sieges and attacks on fortified places. The Athenians forced their way in and took the camp with an immense slaughter of the enemy. It is said that out of three hundred thousand only forty thousand under Artabazus escaped. On the side of the Greeks fell only thirteen hundred and sixty men. Of these there were fifty-two Athenians of the Aiantid tribe, which, we are told by Kleidemus, distinguished itself beyond all others on that day. For this reason, the Aiantid tribe offered the sacrifice to the nymphs Sphragitides, ordered by the oracle for the victory, at the public expense. Of the Lacedæmonians, there fell ninety-one, and of the Tegeans sixteen. It is hard, therefore, to understand Herodotus when he says that these alone came to blows with the enemy, and that no other Greeks were engaged at all; for both the number of the slain and the tombs of the fallen prove that the victory was won by all the Greeks together. If only three cities had fought, and the rest had done nothing, they never would have inscribed on the altar:

"The Greeks in battle drove the Persian forth By force of arms, and bravely Greece set free, To Zeus Protector they this altar reared, Where all might thank him for their victory."

This battle was fought on the day of the month Boedromion, according to the Athenian calendar; and on the twenty-sixth of the month Panemus according to that of the Bœotians, on which day the Hellenic meeting still takes place at Platæa, and sacrifice is offered to Zeus, the Protector of Liberty, in memory of this victory. The discrepancy of the dates is no marvel, seeing that even at the present day, when astronomy is more accurately understood, different cities still begin and end their months on different days.

XX. After the battle, as the Athenians would not assign the prize of valour to the Lacedæmonians, nor suffer them to set up a trophy, the common cause of Greece was within a little of being ruined by the quarrels of the two armies, had not Aristeides by argument and entreaty prevailed upon his colleagues, especially Leokrates and Myronides, to submit the dispute to the decision of all the Greeks. Upon this a council was held, at which Theogeiton of Megara said that the prize for valour ought to be given to another city, and not either to Athens or Sparta, if they did not wish to bring about a civil war. To this Kleokritus of Corinth made answer. All men expected that he would demand the honour for Corinth, which city had acquitted itself best, next to Athens and Sparta; but he made a very excellent and conciliatory speech, demanding that the prize should be bestowed on the Platæans, by which means neither of the claimants would be aggrieved. This proposal was agreed to by Aristeides on behalf of the Athenians, and by Pausanias on behalf of the Lacedæmonians. Having thus settled their differences, they set apart from the plunder eighty talents for the Platæans, with which they built the temple of Athena, and the shrine, and also decorated the temple with paintings, which even to this present day retain their lustre. The Lacedæmonians set up a trophy for themselves, and the Athenians another one apart. When they enquired at Delphi what sacrifice was to be offered, the oracle bade them set up an altar to Zeus the Protector of the Free, and not to sacrifice upon it until they had first put out all fires throughout the country, because it had been defiled by the presence of the barbarian, and had then fetched a new fire pure from pollution, from the hearth at Delphi, which is common to all Greece. The chiefs of the Greeks at once proceeded throughout the Platæan territory, forcing every one to extinguish his fire, even in the case of funeral piles, while Euchidas of Platæa, who promised that he would fetch fire as quickly as possible, proceeded to Delphi. There he purified his body, and having been besprinkled with holy water and crowned with laurel, took fire from the altar, set off running back to Platæa, and arrived there about sunset, having run a distance of a hundred and twenty-five miles in one day. He embraced his fellow citizens, handed the fire to them, fell down, and in a few moments died. The Platæans, to show their admiration of him, buried him in the temple of Artemis Eukleia, with this inscription on his tomb:

"Euchidas ran to Delphi and back again in one day."

As for Eukleia, most persons believe her to be Artemis, and worship her as that goddess; but some say that she was a daughter of Herakles and Myrto, the daughter of Menœtius, who was the sister of Patroklus, and who, dying a virgin, is worshipped by the Bœotians and Lokrians. An altar and image of her stands in every market-place in these countries, and those who are about to marry, sacrifice to her.

XXI. After this Aristeides proposed at a general assembly of all the Greeks, that all the cities of Greece should every year send deputies and religious representatives to the city of Platæa, and that every fifth year Eleutheria, or a festival in honour of Freedom, should be celebrated there. Also he proposed that there should be a general levy throughout Greece, for the war against the Persians, of ten thousand heavy armed troops, a thousand horse, and a hundred ships of war; and that the Platæans should be held inviolable, and consecrated to the service of the gods, to whom they offered sacrifice on behalf of all Greece. These things were ratified, and the people of Platæa undertook to make yearly sacrifices in honour of those who had fallen fighting for Greece, and whose bodies were buried there. This they perform even at the present day in the following fashion. On the sixteenth day of the month Maimakterion, which in the Bœotian calendar is called Alalkomenius, they make a procession headed by a trumpeter sounding the charge. After him follow waggons full of myrtle and garlands of flowers, a black bull, libations of wine and milk in jars, and earthenware vessels full of oil and perfume. These are carried by young men of noble birth, for no slave is allowed to take any part in the proceedings, because the men in whose honour the sacrifice is made, died fighting for liberty. Last of all comes the chief magistrate of Platæa, who, during the rest of his term of office, is not allowed to touch iron, or to wear clothes of any colour but white. On this day, however, he wears a scarlet tunic, takes an urn from the public record office in one hand, and a sword in the other, and proceeds through the middle of the city to the sepulchres. There he with his own hands draws water from the well, washes the head-stones of the graves, and anoints them with oil. After this he cuts the throat of the bull, places his bones on a funeral pile, and with prayer to Zeus, and Hermes who conducts men's souls into the nether world, he calls on the brave men who died for Greece, to come to the feast and drink the libations of blood. Next he mixes a large bowl of wine and water, pours out a cup for himself, and says, "I drink to those who died in defence of the freedom of Greece." This custom is observed even to this day by the Platæans.

XXII. After the return of the Athenians to their own city, Aristeides observed that they desired to adopt a democratic form of government. As he considered that the people had by their bravery deserved a share in the management of affairs, and likewise thought that it would be hard to turn them from their purpose as they had arms in their hands, and were confident in their strength because of the victories which they had won, he carried a decree that every citizen should have a share in the government, and that the archons should be chosen out of the whole body of Athenians.

When Themistokles told the Athenian assembly that he had in his mind a proposition most valuable to the state, which nevertheless could not be openly discussed, the people bade Aristeides alone listen to what it was and give his opinion upon it. Then Themistokles told Aristeides, that he meditated burning the entire fleet of the Greeks, as they lay drawn up on the beach, as by this means Athens would become the greatest state in Greece, and mistress of all the others. Aristeides, on hearing this, came forward to the assembly and said that the proposal of Themistokles, although most advantageous, was yet most wicked and unjust. When the people heard this, they forbade Themistokles to prosecute his design. So highly did the Athenians prize justice, and so well and faithfully did Aristeides serve them.

XXIII. Being sent as general, with Kimon as his colleague, to the war with Persia, he perceived that Pausanias and the other Spartan generals were harsh and insolent to their allies; and he himself, by treating them with kindness and consideration, aided by the gentle and kindly temper shown by Kimon in the campaign, gradually obtained supreme authority over them, not having won it by arms or fleets, but by courtesy and wise policy. The Athenians, already beloved by the Greeks, on account of the justice of Aristeides and the kindliness of Kimon, were much more endeared to them by the insolent brutality of Pausanias, who always spoke roughly and angrily to the chiefs of the various contingents of allies, and used to punish the common men by stripes, or by forcing them to stand all day with a heavy iron anchor on their shoulders. No one was permitted to obtain straw or forage for their horses, or to draw water from a well before the Spartans had helped themselves, and servants were placed with whips to drive away any who attempted to do so. Aristeides once endeavoured to complain of this to Pausanias, but he knitting his brows, rudely told him that he was not at leisure, and took no notice of his words. At this the generals and admirals of the Greek states, especially those from Chios, Samos, and Lesbos, besought Aristeides to make himself commander-in-chief, and rally round him all the allied cities, who had long desired to get rid of the Spartan supremacy and to take the side of Athens. He answered that he admitted the justice and even the necessity of their proposals, but that they must prove themselves to be in earnest by some act which would make it impossible for the great body of them to draw back. Upon this, Ouliades of Samos, and Antagoras of Chios conspired together, and off Byzantium, they ran on board of the ship of Pausanias, which was sailing before the rest. He on seeing this, rose up in a rage and threatened that in a short time he would let them know that they had not endangered his ship, but their own native cities. They in answer bade him go his way and be thankful for the victory at Platæa won under his command, for that it was which alone restrained the Greeks from dealing with him as he deserved. Finally they left him, and sailed away to join the Athenian ships. On this occasion the magnanimous conduct of the Lacedæmonians deserves high praise. When they perceived that the heads of their generals were being turned by the greatness of their power, they of their own accord withdrew from the supreme power, and no longer sent any generals to the wars, choosing rather to have moderate citizens who would abide by their laws at home, than to bear rule over the whole of Greece.

Even while the Lacedæmonians remained in command, the Greeks paid a certain contribution to pay the expenses of the war; and as they wished each city to be assessed to pay a reasonable sum, they asked the Athenians to appoint Aristeides to visit each city, learn the extent of its territory and revenues, and fix upon the amount which each was capable of contributing according to its means. Although he was in possession of such a power as this—the whole of Greece having as it were given itself up to be dealt with at his discretion—yet he laid down his office a poorer man than when he accepted it, but having completed his assessment to the satisfaction of all. As the ancients used to tell of the blessedness of the golden age, even so did the states of Greece honour the assessment made by Aristeides, calling the time when it was made, fortunate and blessed for Greece, especially when no long time afterwards it was doubled, and subsequently trebled. The money which Aristeides proposed to raise amounted to four hundred and sixty talents; to which Perikles added nearly a third part, for Thucydides tells us that at the commencement of the Peloponnesian war, the Athenians received six hundred talents a year from their allies. After the death of Perikles, the popular orators gradually raised the sum total to thirteen hundred talents. It was not so much that the money was required for the expenses of a long and costly war, as that these men had accustomed the people to largesses of money, dramatic representations, and the erection of statues and temples. Themistokles was the only man who had sneered at the great reputation which Aristeides had won by his assessment of the Greek states, saying that the praise which was lavished on him was not suitable to a man, but to a chest which kept money safe. This he said as a retort to a saying of Aristeides, who once, when Themistokles said that he thought it the most valuable quality for a general to be able to divine beforehand what the enemy would do, answered, "That, Themistokles, is very true, but it is also the part of an honourable general to keep his hands clean."

XXV. Aristeides, moreover, bound all the Greeks by an oath to keep the league against the Persians, and himself swore on behalf of Athens, throwing wedges of red hot iron into the sea after the oath was taken, and praying that the gods might so deal with those that broke their faith. But afterwards, when circumstances forced the Athenians to govern with a stronger hand, he bade the Athenians act as they pleased, for he would take upon himself any guilt of perjury which they might incur. And throughout his life Theophrastus observes that Aristeides, though scrupulously just in his dealings with his fellow-citizens, yet sometimes in dealing with other states was guided rather by advantage than by equity. For instance, when the Athenians were debating a proposal of the Samians, that the treasure of the league should be removed from Delos to Athens, a thing distinctly contrary to the articles of the alliance, Aristeides said that it was not just, but that it was expedient to do so. He himself, at the end of his life, after raising his city to be the ruler of so many people, remained in his original poverty, and took no less pride in his poverty than in the victories which he had won. This is proved by the following anecdote. Kallias, the torch-bearer in the Eleusinian mysteries, a relation of his, was being prosecuted on a capital charge by his private enemies. After speaking with great moderation upon the subject of the indictment, they used the following argument to the jury: "Gentlemen, you all know Aristeides the son of Lysimachus, whose name is renowned throughout Greece. How think you that man fares at home, when you see him appearing in public with such a worn-out cloak? May we not suppose when we see him shivering out of doors, that he has but little to eat at home, and is in want of common necessaries? Yet Kallias, the richest man in Athens, allows this man, who is his own cousin, to be in want, he and his wife and children, though he has often benefited by him and profited by his influence with you." Kallias, perceiving that the jury were especially wrought upon by this appeal and that it was likely to tell against him, called Aristeides into the court, and begged of him to bear witness to the jury that although he had often offered him money and begged him to accept it he had always refused, answering that he prided himself more upon his poverty than Kallias did upon his wealth; for one may see many persons making both a good and a bad use of riches, but it is hard to meet with a man who bears poverty with honour. Those only should be ashamed of poverty who are poor against their wills. When Aristeides bore witness to the truth of this, on behalf of Kallias, there was no one who heard him but left the court wishing rather to be poor like Aristeides than rich like Kallias. This story is preserved by Æschines, the companion of Sokrates.

Plato considers that this man alone, of all the great men of Athens, is worthy of mention by him. Themistokles, and Kimon, and Perikles, did indeed fill the city with public buildings, and money, and folly, but Aristeides in his political acts cared for nothing but virtue. One great proof of this is his kindly treatment of Themistokles. Though this man was his enemy throughout, and was the cause of his banishment by ostracism, yet when Themistokles gave him an opportunity of revenging himself in a similar manner he never remembered the injuries which he had received at his hands, but while Kimon, and Alkmæon, and many others, were endeavouring to drive him into exile and bringing all kinds of accusations against him, Aristeides alone never did or said anything against him, and did not rejoice over the spectacle of his enemy's ruin, just as he never envied his previous prosperity.

XXVI. Some writers say that Aristeides died in Pontus, to which country he had been sent on matters of state: while others say that he died of old age at Athens, respected and honoured by all his countrymen there. Kraterus of Macedonia tells us the following particulars about his end. After Themistokles went into exile the common people grew insolent and produced a numerous brood of informers, who constantly assailed the noblest and most powerful citizens through envy of their prosperity and influence. One of these men, Diophantus of Amphitrope by name, obtained a verdict against Aristeides on a charge of receiving bribes. It was stated that when he was regulating the assessment of the Ionians he received money from them to tax them more lightly. As he was unable to pay the fine of fifty minæ, which the court laid upon him, he left Athens and died somewhere in Ionia. But Kraterus offers no documentary evidence of this, neither of the sentence of his condemnation nor the decree of the people, although in general it is his habit to quote his authority for statements of this kind. And almost all others who have spoken of the harsh treatment of generals by the people mention the banishment of Themistokles, the imprisonment of Miltiades, the fine imposed on Perikles, and the suicide of Paches in court when sentence was pronounced against him, but although they speak of the banishment of Aristeides, they never allude to this trial and sentence upon him.

XXVII. Moreover, there is his tomb at Phalerum, which is said to have been constructed at the public expense, because he did not leave enough money to defray his funeral expenses. It is also related that his daughters were publicly married at the charges of the state, which provided them each with a dowry of three thousand drachmas. At the instance of Alkibiades, his son Lysimachus was also presented with a hundred silver mines, and as many acres of planted land, and in addition to this, an allowance of four drachmas a day. Kallisthenes also tells us that this Lysimachus leaving a daughter named Polykrite, she was assigned by the Athenians the same daily allowance of food as is bestowed upon the victors in the Olympian games. But Demetrius of Phalerum, Hieronymus of Rhodes, Aristoxenus the musician, and Aristotle, (if we are to believe the 'Treatise on Nobility' to be a genuine work of his) say, that Myrto, the granddaughter of Aristeides, lived in the house of Sokrates the philosopher, who was indeed married to another woman, but who took her into his house because she was a widow and destitute of the necessaries of life. These authors are sufficiently confuted by Panætius in his writings on Sokrates. Demetrius of Phalerum says, in his book about Sokrates, that he knew one Lysimachus, a very poor man, who dwelt near the Temple of Iacchus and made his living by the interpretation of dreams. Demetrius further states that he carried a bill before the Assembly by which this man's mother and sister were provided with a pension of three obols daily at the public expense. Demetrius, however, when himself a legislator, appointed that each of these women should receive a drachma instead of three obols a day. And we need not wonder at the people taking such care of the resident citizens, when we read that, hearing that the granddaughter of Aristogeiton was living in poverty at Lemnos, so poor that no one would marry her, they brought her back to Athens, gave her in marriage to a man of high birth, and bestowed upon her a farm at Potamus for a marriage portion. The city of Athens has shown many instances of this kindness and goodness of heart even down to our times, and is justly praised and admired for it.

# Life of Marcus Cato.

I. Marcus Cato is said to have been born at Tusculum, but to have been brought up and spent his time upon a farm belonging to his father in the Sabine territory, before he began to take part in war or politics. We know nothing of his ancestry, except that he himself tells us that his father, Marcus, was a good man and brave soldier, and that his grandfather, Cato, received several military rewards for his services, and that having had five horses killed under him, he received the value of them from the public treasury, as an acknowledgment of his gallantry.

It was the Roman custom to call those who had no ancestry to recommend them, but who rose by their own merits, new men. This name was applied to Cato, who said that he was indeed new to honours and posts of importance, but that, in respect of his brave and virtuous ancestry, he was a man of ancient family. His third name originally was not Cato, but Priscus, and was changed to Cato on account of his wisdom, for in Latin catus means "clever." In appearance he was rather red-haired, and grey-eyed, peculiarities which are ill-naturedly dwelt upon by the writer of the epigram—
"Red-haired, grey-eyed, and savage-tusked as well, Porcius will find no welcome e'en in hell."

Accustomed as he was to hard exercise, temperate living, and frequent campaigns, his body was always both healthy and strong; while he also practised the power of speech, thinking it a necessary instrument for a man who does not intend to live an obscure and inactive life. He consequently improved his talents in this respect by pleading causes in the neighbouring villages and towns, so that he was soon admitted to be a capable speaker, and afterwards to be a good orator. From this time all who conversed with him perceived a gravity and wisdom in his mind which qualified him to undertake the most important duties of a statesman. Not only was he so disinterested as to plead without receiving money from his clients, but he also did not think the glory which he gained in these contests to be that after which a man ought to strive, in comparison with that which is gained in battle and campaigns, in which he was so eager to distinguish himself that when quite a lad his body was covered with wounds, all in front. He himself tells us that he made his first campaign at the age of seventeen, when Hannibal was ranging through Italy uncontrolled. In battle he was prompt, stedfast, and undismayed, and was wont to address the enemy with threats and rough language, and to encourage the others to do so, as he rightly pointed out that this often cows the enemy's spirit as effectually as blows. When on the march he used to carry his own arms, and be followed by one servant who carried his provisions. It is said that he never spoke harshly to this man, no matter what food he placed before him, but that he would often help him to do his work when he was at leisure from military duty. He drank only water when campaigning, except that when suffering from parching thirst he would ask for some vinegar, and sometimes when his strength fairly failed he would drink a little wine.

II. Near his estate was a cottage which had once belonged to Manius Curius, who three times received the honour of a triumph. Cato used frequently to walk over and look at this cottage, and, as he observed the smallness of the plot of ground attached to it, and the simplicity of the dwelling itself, he would reflect upon how Curius, after having made himself the first man in Rome, after conquering the most warlike nations, and driving King Pyrrhus out of Italy, used to dig this little plot of ground with his own hands, and dwelt in this little cottage, after having thrice triumphed. It was there that the ambassadors of the Samnites found him sitting by the hearth, cooking turnips, and offered him much gold; but he sent them away, saying, "that a man who was contented with such a supper, had no need of gold, and that it was more honourable for him to conquer those who possessed gold, than to possess it himself." Cato, after leaving the cottage, full of these memories, returned to his own house and farm, and after viewing its extent and the number of slaves upon it, he increased the amount of his own daily labour, and retrenched his superfluous expenses.

When Fabius Maximus took the city of Tarentum, Cato, who was a very young lad at the time, was serving in his army. He became intimate there with one Nearchus, a philosopher of the Pythagorean school, and listened with much interest to his discourses. Hearing this man, like Plato, describe pleasure as the greatest temptation to evil, and the body as the chief hindrance to the soul, which can only free and purify itself by such a course of reasoning as removes it from and sets it above all bodily passions and feelings, he was yet more encouraged in his love of simplicity and frugality. In other respects he is said to have studied Hellenic literature late in life, and not to have read Greek books till extreme old age, when he greatly improved his style of oratory, partly by the study of Thucydides, but chiefly by that of Demosthenes. Be this as it may, his writings are full of Greek ideas and Greek anecdotes: and many of his apophthegms and maxims are literally translated from the Greek.

III. The estate adjoining that of Cato belonged to one of the most powerful and highly born patricians of Rome, Valerius Flaccus, a man who had a keen eye for rising merit, and generously fostered it until it received public recognition. This man heard accounts of Cato's life from his servants, how he would proceed to the court early in the morning, and plead the causes of all who required his services, and then on returning to his farm would work with his servants, in winter wearing a coarse coat without sleeves, in summer nothing but his tunic, and how he used to sit at meals with his servants, eating the same loaf and drinking the same wine. Many other stories of his goodness and simplicity and sententious remarks were related to Valerius, who became interested in his neighbour, and invited him to dinner. They became intimate, and Valerius, observing his quiet and ingenuous disposition, like a plant that requires careful treatment and an extensive space in which to develop itself, encouraged and urged him to take part in the political life of Rome. On going to Rome he at once gained admirers and friends by his able pleadings in the law courts, while he obtained considerable preferment by the interest of Valerius, being appointed first military tribune, and then quæstor. After this he became so distinguished a man as to be able to compete with Valerius himself for the highest offices in the state, and they were elected together, first as consuls, and afterwards as censors. Of the older Romans, Cato attached himself particularly to Fabius Maximus, a man of the greatest renown and power, although it was his disposition and mode of life which Cato especially desired to imitate. Wherefore he did not hesitate to oppose Scipio the Great, who was then a young man, but a rival and opponent of Fabius. Cato was appointed to act as his quæstor in the war in Africa, and on perceiving that Scipio was living with his usual lavish expenditure, and supplying his soldiery with extravagant pay, he sharply rebuked him, saying, "that it was not the waste of the public money that vexed him so much as the ruin of the old frugal habits of the soldiers, who were led to indulge in pleasure and luxury by receiving more pay than was necessary to supply their daily wants." When Scipio answered that he did not require an economist for his quæstor, at a time when he was preparing to wage war on a grand scale, and reminded him that he would have to give an account to the Roman people of battles won, not of money expended, Cato left the army of Scipio, which was then being assembled in Sicily. He proceeded at once to Rome, and by adding his voice to that of Fabius in the Senate, in blame of Scipio's unspeakable waste of money, and his childish and unsoldierly love of the public games and the theatre, conduct more worthy of the president of a public festival than of the commander-in-chief of an army, prevailed upon the people to send tribunes to enquire into the charges against him, and if they proved true, to bring him back to Rome. When they arrived in Sicily, however, Scipio pointed out to them that the preparations which he had made would ensure him the victory, and that although he loved pleasant society in his hours of leisure, yet that he had never allowed his pleasures to interfere with his serious duties. The tribunes were perfectly satisfied with this explanation, and Scipio sailed for Africa.

IV. Cato, however, gained considerable credit by his speeches on this occasion, and the Romans generally called him the new Demosthenes; yet his manner of life was more admired than his eloquence. Cleverness of speech was a quality which nearly all the young men of the time sought to attain, but Cato was singular in his keeping up the severe traditions of his ancestors in labouring with his own hands, eating a simple dinner, lighting no fire to cook his breakfast, wearing a plain dress, living in a mean house, and neither coveting superfluities nor courting their possessors. The Romans were at this period extending their empire so much as to lose much of their own original simplicity of living, as each new conquest brought them into contact with foreign customs and new modes of life. They therefore naturally looked with admiration upon Cato, observing that while they became enervated by pleasures and broke down under labours, he on the other hand seemed unaffected by either, and that too, not only while he was young and eager for fame: but even when he was an old grey-headed man, after he had been consul and had triumphed, he yet, like a victorious athlete, still kept himself in training, and never relaxed his severe discipline. He himself tells us that he never wore a garment worth more than a hundred drachmas, that when he was general and consul he still drank the same wine as his servants, that his dinner never cost him more than thirty ases in the market, and that he only indulged himself to this extent for the good of the state, that he might be strong and able to serve his country in the field. When he was left a piece of Babylonian tapestry he at once disposed of it; none of his rooms were whitewashed, and he never bought a slave for more than fifteen hundred drachmas, seeing that he required, not effeminate and handsome servants, but hardworking and strong men, to tend his horses and herd his cattle: and these, too, when they grew old and past work he thought it best to sell, and not feed them at his expense when they were useless. His rule was that nothing is cheap which one does not want, but that superfluities are dearly purchased even if they cost but one penny: and that it is better to buy land which can be ploughed, or where cattle can graze, than beds of flowers which require watering, and paths which have to be swept and kept in order.

V. These habits some ascribed to narrowness of mind, while others thought that he carried parsimony and avarice to excess in himself in order by his example to reform and restrain others. Be this as it may, I for my own part consider that his conduct in treating his slaves like beasts of burden, and selling them when old and worn out, is the mark of an excessively harsh disposition, which disregards the claims of our common human nature, and merely considers the question of profit and loss. Kindness, indeed, is of wider application than mere justice; for we naturally treat men alone according to justice and the laws, while kindness and gratitude, as though from a plenteous spring, often extend even to irrational animals. It is right for a good man to feed horses which have been worn out in his service, and not merely to train dogs when they are young, but to take care of them when they are old. When the Athenian people built the Parthenon, they set free the mules which had done the hardest work in drawing the stones up to the acropolis, and let them graze where they pleased unmolested. It is said that one of them came of its own accord to where the works were going on, and used to walk up to the acropolis with the beasts who were drawing up their loads, as if to encourage them and show them the way. This mule was, by a decree of the people of Athens, maintained at the public expense for the rest of its life. The racehorses of Kimon also, who won an Olympic victory, are buried close to the monument of their master. Many persons, too, have made friends and companions of dogs, as did Xanthippus in old times, whose dog swam all the way to Salamis beside his master's ship when the Athenians left their city, and which he buried on the promontory which to this day is called the Dog's Tomb. We ought not to treat living things as we do our clothes and our shoes, and throw them away after we have worn them out; but we ought to accustom ourselves to show kindness in these cases, if only in order to teach ourselves our duty towards one another. For my own part I would not even sell an ox that had laboured for me because he was old, much less would I turn an old man out of his accustomed haunts and mode of life, which is as great an affliction to him as sending him into a foreign land, merely that I might gain a few miserable coins by selling one who must be as useless to his buyer as he was to his seller.

Cato, however, as if taking a perverse pleasure in flaunting his meannesses, relates that he left behind him in Spain the horse which he rode when consul there, in order to save the state the cost of carrying him over to Italy. Whether those acts of his are to be ascribed to magnanimity or narrow-mindedness the reader must decide for himself.

VI. He was a man of wonderful temperance, in all other respects also. For example, when he was general, he only drew from the public stock three Attic bushels of wheat a month for himself and his servants, and less than three half-bushels of barley a day for his horses. When he was Governor of Sardinia, where former governors had been in the habit of charging their tents, bedding, and wearing-apparel to the province, and likewise making it pay large sums for their entertainment and that of their friends, he introduced an unheard-of system of economy. He charged nothing to the province, and visited the various cities without a carriage, walking on foot alone, attended by one single public servant carrying his robe of state and the vessel to make libations at a sacrifice. With all this he showed himself so affable and simple to those under his rule, so severe and inexorable in the administration of justice, and so vigilant and careful in seeing that his orders were duly executed, that the government of Rome never was more feared or more loved in Sardinia than when he governed that island.

VII. His conversation seems also to have had this character, for he was cheerful and harsh all at once, pleasant and yet severe as a companion, fond of jokes, but morose at the same time, just as Plato tells us that Sokrates, if judged merely from his outside, appeared to be only a silly man with a face like a satyr, who was rude to all he met, though his inner nature was earnest and full of thoughts that moved his hearers to tears and touched their hearts. For this reason I cannot understand how any persons can see a likeness between the orations of Lysias and those of Cato; however, this point must be decided by those who are more skilled than myself in the comparison of oratorical styles. I shall now relate a few of his more remarkable sayings, believing that a man's real character can be better judged of by his words than by his looks, although some people hold the contrary opinion.

VIII. Once when he wished to restrain the Romans from distributing a large quantity of corn as a largesse to the people, he began his speech: "It is difficult, my fellow-citizens, to make the stomach hear reason, because it has no ears." When desiring to blame the extravagance of the Romans, he said that a city could not be safe in which a fish sold dearer than an ox. He said, too, that the Romans were like sheep, who never form opinions of their own, but follow where the others lead them. "Just so," said he, "when you are assembled together you are led by men whose advice you would scorn to take about your own private affairs." With regard to female influence he once said, "All mankind rule their wives, we rule all mankind, and we are ruled by our wives." This remark, however, is borrowed from Themistokles. He one day, when his child was instigating its mother to lay many commands upon him, said, "Wife, remember that the Athenians rule the Greeks, I rule the Athenians, you rule me, and your child rules you; wherefore let him not abuse his power, which, though he knows it not, is greater than that of anyone else in Greece." Cato also said that the Romans fixed the price, not only of different dyes, but of different professions. "Just as the dyers," said he, "dye stuff of whatever colour they see people pleased with, so do our young men only study and apply themselves to those subjects which are praised and commended by you." He used also to beg of them, if they had become great by virtue and self-restraint, not to degenerate; and if, on the other hand, their empire had been won by licentiousness and vice, to reform themselves, since by the latter means they had become so great as not to need any further assistance from them. Those who were always seeking office, he said, were like men who could not find their way, who always wished to walk with lictors before them to show them the road. He blamed his countrymen for often electing the same men to public offices. "You will appear," said he, "either to think that the office is not worth much, or else that there are not many worthy to fill it." Alluding to one of his enemies who led a dissolute and discreditable life, he said: "That man's mother takes it as a curse rather than a blessing if any one hopes that her son will survive her." When a certain man sold his ancestral estate, which was situated by the seashore, Cato pretended to admire him, as being more powerful than the sea itself, "for this man," said he, has "drunk up the fields which the sea itself could not swallow." When King Eumenes came to Rome the Senate received him with special honours, and he was much courted and run after. Cato, however, held himself aloof and would not go near him, and when some one said "Yet he is an excellent man, and a good friend to Rome," he answered, "It may be so, but a king is by nature an animal that lives on human flesh." None of those who had borne the title of king, according to Cato, were to be compared with Epameinondas, or Perikles, or Themistokles, or with Manius Curius or Hamilcar Barcas. He used to say that his enemies hated him because he began his day's work while it was still dark, and because he neglected his own affairs to attend to those of the public. He also was wont to say that he had rather his good actions should go unrewarded than that his bad ones should be unpunished; and that he pardoned all who did wrong except himself.

IX. When the Romans sent three ambassadors to Bithynia, one of whom was crippled by the gout, another had been trepanned and had a piece taken out of his head, and the third was thought to be a simpleton, Cato remarked that the Romans had sent an embassy which had neither feet, head, nor heart. When, for the sake of Polybius the historian, Scipio entreated Cato to exert his influence on behalf of the Achæan exiles, after a long debate in the Senate, where some advised that they should be sent back to their own country, and some that they should still be detained at Rome, he got up and said, "Have we nothing better to do than to sit all day discussing whether a parcel of old Greeks shall be buried here or in Achaia?" A few days after the Senate had decreed the restoration of the exiles, Polybius proposed to make another application, that they should be restored to all the offices which they formerly held in Achaia. He asked Cato whether he thought that he should succeed in this second appeal to the Senate; to which Cato answered with a smile, that he was imitating Ulysses, when he returned again into the cave of the Cyclops to fetch the hat and girdle which he had left behind and forgotten. He said that wise men gained more advantage from fools, than fools from wise men; for the wise men avoid the errors of fools, but fools cannot imitate the example of wise men. He said that he loved young men to have red cheeks rather than pale ones, and that he did not care for a soldier who used his hands while he marched and his feet while he fought, or one who snored louder in bed than he shouted in battle. When reproaching a very fat man he said, "How can this man's body be useful to his country, when all parts between the neck and the groin are possessed by the belly?" Once when an epicure wished to become his friend, he said that he could not live with a man whose palate was more sensitive than his heart. He said also that the soul of a lover inhabits the body of his beloved. He himself tells us, that in his whole life he repented of three things only:—First, that he had trusted a woman with a secret. Secondly, that he had gone by water when he might have gone by land. Thirdly, that he had passed one day without having made his will. To an old man who was acting wrongly he said, "My good sir, old age is ugly enough without your adding the deformity of wickedness to it." When a certain tribune, who was suspected of being a poisoner, was endeavouring to carry a bad law, Cato remarked, "Young man, I do not know which is the worst for us, to drink what you mix, or to enact what you propose." Once when he was abused by a man of vicious life, he answered, "We are not contending upon equal terms; you are accustomed to hearing and using bad language, while I am both unused to hearing it and unwilling to use it."

X. When he was elected consul, together with his friend and neighbour Valerius Flaccus, the province which fell to his lot was that which the Romans call Hither Spain. While he was there engaged in establishing order, partly by persuasion, and partly by force, he was attacked by a large army of the natives, and was in danger of being disgracefully defeated by their overwhelming numbers. Consequently he applied for aid to the neighbouring tribe of the Celtiberians, who demanded as the price of their assistance the sum of two hundred talents. At this every one protested that it was unworthy of Romans to pay barbarians for their alliance, but Cato said that he saw no evil in the practice, since, if the Romans were victorious, they would pay them from the spoils of the enemy, while if they were defeated there would be no one to demand the money and no one to pay it. He won a pitched battle on this occasion, and was very successful in his whole campaign. Polybius indeed tells us that in one day at his command all the cities on this side of the river Guadalquiver pulled down their walls; and yet they were very numerous, and filled with a warlike population. Cato himself tells us that he took more cities than he spent days in Spain; nor is this a vain boast, if the number captured really, as is stated, amounted to four hundred. His soldiers enriched themselves considerably during the campaign; and at the termination of it he distributed a pound of silver to each man, saying that it was better that many Romans should return to Rome with silver in their pockets than that a few should return with gold. He himself states that he received no part of the plunder except what he ate or drank. "I do not," said he, "blame those who endeavour to enrich themselves by such means, but I had rather vie with the noblest in virtue than with the richest in wealth, or with the most covetous in covetousness." He not only kept his own hands clean, but those of his followers also. He took five servants to the war with him. One of these, Paccius by name, bought three boys at a sale of captives; but when Cato heard of it, Paccius, rather than come into his presence, hanged himself. Cato sold the boys, and paid the price into the public treasury.

XI. While he was still in Spain, Scipio the Great, who was his personal enemy, desiring to check his career of success, and to obtain the management of Spanish affairs for himself, contrived to get himself appointed to succeed Cato in his government. He at once hurried to Spain and brought Cato's rule to an end. Cato, however, at once marched to meet Scipio with an escort of five companies of infantry and five hundred horsemen. On his way he conquered the tribe of the Lacetani; and finding among them six hundred deserters from the Roman army, he put them to death. When Scipio expressed his dissatisfaction with this, Cato sarcastically answered, that Rome would be greatest if those of high birth and station, and those of plebeian origin like himself, would only contend with one another in virtue. However, as the Senate decreed that nothing that Cato had settled in the province should be altered or rearranged, Scipio found that it was he rather than Cato that was disgraced, as he had to pass his time in inglorious idleness, while Cato, after enjoying a triumph, did not retire into a life of luxury and leisure, as is done by so many men whose object is display rather than true virtue, after they have risen to the highest honours in the state by being elected consuls and enjoying the honour of a triumph. He did not impair the glorious example which he had given, by withdrawing his attention from the affairs of his country, but offered his services to his friends and fellow-countrymen, both in the courts of law and in the field, as willingly as those who have just begun their public career, and are keenly eager to be elected to some new office in which they may win fresh distinction.

XII. He went with the consul Tiberius Sempronius as legate, and assisted him in regulating the country about the Danube and Thrace; and he also served as military tribune under Manius Acilius during his campaign in Greece against Antiochus the Great, who caused more terror to the Romans than any one man since the time of Hannibal. Antiochus had originally inherited nearly the whole of Asia, that is, as much as Seleukus Nikator had possessed, and having added many warlike tribes to his empire, was so elated by his conquests as to attack the Romans, whom he regarded as the only nation remaining in the whole world which was worthy to be his antagonist. He put forward as a plausible reason for beginning the war that he intended to liberate the Greeks, who did not require his interference, as they had just been made free and independent by the Romans, who had delivered them from the tyranny of Philip and the Macedonians. Antiochus crossed over into Greece, which at once became unsettled, and a prey to hopes and fears suggested by her political leaders. Manius at once sent ambassadors to the various cities. Titus Flamininus, as has been related in his Life, restrained the greater part of them from revolutionary proceedings, and kept them to their allegiance, but Cato won over Corinth, Patræ, and Ægium. Most of his time was spent in Athens; and there is said to be still extant a speech which he made to the people there in Greek, in which he speaks with admiration of the virtue of the Athenians of old, and dwells upon his own pleasure in viewing so great and beautiful a city. This, however, is a fabrication, for we know that he conversed with the Athenians through an interpreter, though he was able to speak their language, because he wished to keep to the ways of his fathers, and administer a rebuke to those who extravagantly admired the Greeks. Thus he laughed at Postumius Albinus, who wrote a history in Greek and begged that his mistakes might be pardoned, saying that it would be right to pardon them if he wrote his history by a decree of the council of Amphiktyons. He himself says that the Athenians were surprised it the shortness and pregnant nature of his talk; for what he said in a few words, his interpreter translated by a great many: and in general he concludes that the Greeks talk from the lips, and the Romans from the heart.

XIII. When Antiochus occupied the pass of Thermopylæ with his army, and, after adding to the natural strength of the place by artificial defences, established himself there as if in an impregnable position, the Romans decided that to attack him in front was altogether impossible, but Cato, remembering how the Persians under Xerxes had turned the Greek forces by a circuitous march over the mountains, took a part of the force and set off by night. When they had gone for some distance over the mountains, the prisoner who served as their guide lost his way, and wandered about in that precipitous and pathless wilderness so as to cause great discouragement to the soldiers. Seeing this, Cato ordered every one to halt and await his orders, and himself, with one companion, one Lucius Manlius, an experienced mountaineer, laboriously and daringly plunged along through intense darkness, for there was no moon, while the trees and rocks added to their difficulties by preventing their seeing distinctly whither they were going, until they came to a path, which, as they thought, led directly down upon the camp of the enemy. Hereupon they set up marks to guide them upon some conspicuous crags of Mount Kallidromus, and returning to the army, led it to these marks, and started along the paths which they had descried. But before they had proceeded far the path ended in a precipice, at which they were both surprised and disheartened; for they could not tell, either by sight or hearing, that they were close to the enemy. It was now about daybreak, and they thought that they heard voices near at hand, and soon were able to see a Greek camp and an outpost at the foot of the precipice. Cato hereupon halted his army, and ordered the Firmiani, in whom he reposed especial confidence, to come forward alone. When they had assembled round him, he said, "I wish to take one of the enemy prisoner, and learn from him of what troops this outpost is formed, what their numbers are, how the rest of the army are placed, and what preparations they have made to resist us. You must dash upon them as quickly and boldly as lions do upon their defenceless prey." At these words of Cato's the Firmiani at once rushed down and attacked the outpost. The suddenness of their onset threw the enemy into complete confusion, and they soon caught one of them and brought him before Cato. Learning from this man that all the rest of the army was with King Antiochus himself, guarding the pass of Thermopylæ, and that only a body of six hundred picked Ætolians were watching the path over the mountains, Cato despising so small and contemptible a force, at once drew his sword, and led on his troops with shouts and trumpets sounding the charge. The Ætolians, as soon as they saw the Romans descending from the hills, fled to the main body, and filled it with confusion and terror.

XIV. Meanwhile Manius on the lower ground had attacked the fortifications in the pass with his entire force. Antiochus was struck on the mouth with a stone which knocked out several of his teeth, and the pain of his wound compelled him to wheel round his horse and retreat. His troops nowhere withstood the Romans, but, although they had endless means of escape by roads where they could scarcely be followed, yet they crowded through the narrow pass with deep marshy ground on the one hand and inaccessible rocks upon the other, and there trampled each other to death for fear of the swords of the Romans.

Cato never seems to have been sparing of his own praise, and thought that great deeds required to be told in boastful language. He gives a very pompous account of this battle, and says that all those who saw him pursuing and cutting down the enemy felt that Cato did not owe so much to the Romans, as the Romans owed to Cato. He also says that the consul Manius immediately after the victory was won, enfolded him for a long time in a close embrace, and loudly declared that neither he nor all the Roman people could ever do as much for Cato as he had that day done for them. He was sent immediately after the battle to bear the news of the victory to Rome, and reached Brundusium after a prosperous voyage.

From that place he drove in one day to Tarentum, and in four more days reached Rome with the news, on the fifth day after his landing. His arrival filled the whole city with feasting and rejoicing, and made the Roman people believe that there was no nation in the world which could resist their arms.

XV. Of Cato's warlike exploits these which we have related are the most remarkable. In his political life he seems to have thought one of his most important duties to be the impeachment and prosecution of those whom he thought to be bad citizens. He himself attacked many persons, and aided and encouraged others in doing so, a notable example being his conduct towards Scipio in the affair of Petillius. However, as Scipio was a man of noble birth and great spirit, he treated the attack made upon him with contempt, and Cato, perceiving that he could not succeed in getting him condemned to death, desisted from annoying him. But he was active in obtaining the condemnation of Scipio's brother Lucius, who was adjudged to pay a heavy fine, which was beyond his means to provide, so that he had nearly been cast into prison, but was set free by the intervention of the tribunes of the people.

It is related of him that he once met in the forum a young man who had just succeeded in obtaining the disfranchisement, by an action at law, of an enemy of his father, who was dead. Cato took him by the hand and said, "Thus ought men to honour their parents when they die, not with the blood of lambs and kids, but with the tears and condemnation of their enemies." He himself is said to have been the defendant in nearly fifty actions, the last of which was tried when he was eighty-six years of age: on which occasion he uttered that well-known saying, that it was hard for a man who had lived in one generation to be obliged to defend himself before another. And this was not the end of his litigations, for four years later, when at the age of ninety, he impeached Servius Galba. Indeed his life, like that of Nestor, seems to havo reached over three generations. He, as had been related, was a bitter political opponent of Scipio Africanus the Great, and he continued his enmity to Scipio's adopted son, called Scipio the Younger, who was really the son of Æmilius Paulus, the conqueror of Perseus and the Macedonians.

XVI. Ten years after his consulship, Cato became a candidate for the office of censor. This is the highest dignity to which a Roman can aspire, and may be regarded as the goal of political life. Its powers are very extensive, and it is especially concerned with the regulation of public morals, and the mode of life of the citizens of Rome. The Romans thought that none of a man's actions, his marriage, his family, his mode of life, his very entertainments, ought to be uncontrolled, and managed according to his own will and pleasure. They considered that a man's true character was much more clearly shown by his private life than by his public behaviour, and were wont to choose two citizens, one a patrician, and the other a plebeian, whose duty it was to watch over the morals of the people, and check any tendency to licentiousness or extravagance. These officers they called censors, and they had power to deprive a Roman knight of his horse, and to expel men of loose and disorderly life from the Senate. They also took a census of property, and kept a register of the various tribes and classes of the citizens; and they likewise exercised various other important powers. Cato's candidature was opposed by nearly all the most distinguished members of the Senate, for the patricians viewed him with especial dislike, regarding it as an insult to the nobility that men of obscure birth should attain to the highest honours in the state, while all those who were conscious of any private vices or departures from the ways of their fathers, feared the severities of one who, they knew, would be harsh and inexorable when in power.

These classes consequently combined together against Cato, and put up no less than seven candidates to contest the censorship with him, and endeavoured to soothe the people by holding out to them hopes of a lenient censor, as though that were what they required. Cato on the other hand would not relax his severity in the least, but threatened evil doers in his speeches from the rostra, and insisted that the city required a most searching reformation. He told the people that if they were wise, they would choose not the most agreeable, but the most thorough physicians to perform this operation for them, and that these would be himself and Valerius Flaccus; for with him as a colleague he imagined that he might make some progress in the work of destroying, by knife and cautery, the hydra of luxury and effeminacy. Of the other candidates he said that he saw that each one was eager to get the office and fill it badly, because he was afraid of those who could fill it well. The Roman people on this occasion showed itself so truly great and worthy to be courted by great men, as not to be alarmed at the earnest severity of Cato; but, setting aside all those plausible candidates who promised merely to consult their pleasure, elected Cato and Valerius censors. It seemed, indeed, as if Cato, inatead of being a candidate for election, was already in office and issuing his commands to the people, which were at once obeyed.

XVII. As soon as he was elected, Cato appointed his friend and colleague, Lucius Valerius Flaccus, chief of the Senate. He expelled several senators, amongst whom was Lucius Quintius, who had been consul seven years before, and, which was even a greater distinction than the consulship, was the brother of Titus Quintius Flamininus, the conqueror of Philip. He was expelled from the Senate for the following reason. Lucius had a favourite boy who never left his person, and followed him even on his campaigns. This boy had more power and received greater attention than the most trusty of his friends and relatives. Now, when Lucius was governor of a province as proconsul, this boy once, at a drinking party, was flattering him over his wine, saying that "Although there was going to be a show of gladiators at Rome, yet I did not stay to see it, but came out here to you, although I longed to see a man killed." Lucius, to please him, answered in the same tone, "If that be all, do not lie there and fret, for I will soon gratify your wish." He at once ordered a condemned criminal to be brought into the banqueting hall, and one of his servants to stand by him with an axe, and then again asked his favourite whether he wished to see a man struck dead. When the boy said that he did, he bade the servant cut off the man's head. This is the account which most writers give of the transaction, and it is that which Cicero introduces Cato as relating in his dialogue "On Old Age;" but Livy says that the man who was put to death was a Gaulish deserter, and that Lucius did not employ a servant, but slew him with his own hand, and this is the version which Cato has followed in his written account of the matter. When Cato discussed what took place at this wine party, Lucius endeavoured to deny it, but on being

challenged to state exactly what happened he refused to answer. He was most
justly condemned to lose his right as a senator; but afterwards, when some
spectacle was being witnessed in the theatre, he walked past the place
reserved for men of consular rank, and sat down in the humblest seat of all,
which so moved the people to compassion, that they forced him by their
clamour to resume his former seat, thus as far as they were able reversing the
sentence upon him and condoning his offence.

Cato expelled another senator, who was thought likely to be soon elected
consul, named Manilius, because he had kissed his wife in the daytime in the
presence of his daughter. He himself said that his own wife never embraced
him except when it thundered loudly, and added by way of joke, that he was
happy when Jupiter was pleased to thunder.

XVIII. His conduct in depriving of his horse Lucius Scipio, the brother of
Scipio Africanus, a man who had been decreed a triumph, was censured, as
being merely prompted by private spite; as he seemed merely to do it in order
to insult Scipio Africanus after his death. But what caused the greatest
dissatisfaction were his restrictions on luxury. This he could not attack
openly, because it had taken such deep root among the people, but he caused
all clothes, carriages, women's ornaments, and furniture, which exceeded
fifteen hundred drachmas in value to be rated at ten times their value and
taxed accordingly, as he thought that those who possessed the most valuable
property ought to contribute most largely to the revenues of the state. In
addition to this he imposed a tax on all citizens of three copper ases for every
thousand, in order that those who were burdened with an excessive taxation
on objects of luxury, when they saw persons of frugal and simple habits paying
so small a tax on the same income, might cease from their extravagance. This
measure gained him the hatred of those who were taxed so heavily for their
luxuries, and of those who, to avoid excessive taxation, were obliged to give
up their luxuries. Most persons are as much irritated at losing the means of
displaying their wealth as at losing their wealth itself, and it is in superfluities,
not in necessaries, that wealth can be displayed. This is what is said to have
so much surprised Ariston the Philosopher, that men should consider those
persons fortunate who possess what is superfluous, rather than those who
possess what is necessary and useful. Skopas the Thessalian also, when one
of his friends asked him for something which was not particularly useful to
him, and added, that he did not ask for anything necessary or useful,
answered, "Indeed, it is in these useless and superfluous things that my wealth
chiefly consists." For the desire of wealth is not connected with any of our

physical necessities, and is an artificial want arising from too much regard for the opinion of the vulgar.

XIX. Cato paid no attention to those who blamed his conduct, and proceeded to measures of still greater severity. He cut off the water-pipes, by which water was conveyed from the public fountains into private houses and gardens, destroyed all houses that encroached upon the public streets, lowered the price of contracts for public works, and farmed out the public revenues for the highest possible rents. All this made him still more unpopular. Titus Flamininus and his friends attacked him, and prevailed upon the Senate to annul the contracts which he had made for the building of temples and the construction of public works, on the ground that they were disadvantageous to the state. They also encouraged the boldest of the tribunes to prosecute him before the people, and to fine him two talents. He likewise received violent opposition in the matter of the basilica, or public hall, which he built at the public expense in the forum below the senate house, and which was called the Basilica Porcia.

In spite of all this, his censorship seems to have been wonderfully popular with the Roman people. When they placed his statue in the Temple of Hygieia, they did not enumerate his campaigns or triumphs in the inscription on the base, but wrote what we may translate as follows: "This statue was erected to Cato because, when Censor, finding the state of Rome corrupt and degenerate, he, by introducing wise regulations and virtuous discipline, restored it."

At one time Cato affected to despise those who took pleasure in receiving honours of this kind, and used to say that while they plumed themselves on being represented in brass or marble, they forgot that the fairest image was that of himself which every citizen bore in his heart. When any one expressed surprise at his not having a statue, when so many obscure men had obtained that honour, he answered, "I had rather that men should ask why I have no statue, than that they should ask why I have one." A good citizen, he said, ought not even to allow himself to be praised, unless the state were benefited thereby. He has glorified himself by recording that when men were detected in any fault, they would excuse themselves by saying that they must be pardoned if they did anything amiss, for they were not Catos: and that those who endeavoured clumsily to imitate his proceedings were called left-handed Catos. Also he states that the Senate looked to him in great emergencies as men in a storm look to the pilot, and that when he was not present, they frequently postponed their more important business. This indeed is confirmed by other writers: for he had great influence in Rome on account of his virtuous life, his eloquence, and his great age.

XX. He was a good father and a good husband, and was in his private life an economist of no ordinary kind, as he did not despise money-making or regard it as unworthy of his abilities. For this reason I think I ought to relate how well he managed his private affairs. He married a wife who was well born, though not rich; for he thought that though all classes might possess equally good sense, yet that a woman of noble birth would be more ashamed of doing wrong, and therefore more likely to encourage her husband to do right. He used to say that a man who beat his wife or his children laid sacrilegious hands on the holiest of things. He also said that he had rather be a good husband than a great statesman, and that what he especially admired in Sokrates the Philosopher was his patience and kindness in bearing with his ill-tempered wife and his stupid children. When his son was born, he thought that nothing except the most important business of state ought to prevent his being present while his wife washed the child and wrapped it in swaddling clothes. His wife suckled the child herself; nay, she often gave her breast to the children of her slaves, and so taught them to have a brotherly regard for her own son.

As soon as he was able to learn, Cato himself taught him his letters, although he had a clever slave named Chilon, who taught many children to read. He himself declares that he did not wish a slave to reprove his son or pull his ears because he was slow at learning. He taught the boy to read, and instructed him also in the Roman law and in bodily exercises; not confining himself to teaching him to hurl the javelin, to fight in complete armour, and to ride, but also to use his fists in boxing, to endure the extremes of heat and cold, and to swim through swiftly-flowing and eddying rivers. He tells us that he himself wrote books on history with his own hands in large letters, that the boy might start in life with a useful knowledge of what his forefathers had done, and he was as careful not to use an indecenr expression before his son as he would have been before the vestal virgins. He never bathed with him; which indeed seems to have been customary at Rome, as even fathers-in-law scrupled to bathe naked before their sons-in-law. In later times, however, the Romans learned from the Greeks the habit of bathing naked, and have taught the Greeks to do so even in the presence of women.

While Cato was engaged in this great work of forming his son's character and completing his education he found him eager to learn, and able to make great progress from his natural ability: but he appeared so weak and delicate that his father was obliged to relax the stern simplicity of his own life in his favour, and allow him some indulgences in diet. The young man, although so weakly, yet proved himself a good soldier in the wars, and distinfuished himself greatly in the battle in which Æmilius Paulus defeated King Perseus. Afterwards, upon the same day, he either had his sword struck from his hand or let it fall from weakness, and in his grief at the loss got together some of his friends and prevailed upon them again to charge the enemy. With great exertions they succeeded in clearing a space, and at length discovered his sword under a great heap of arms and corpses of friends and foes alike which were piled upon it. Paulus, the commander-in-chief, was much pleased with the youth's eagerness to regain his sword, and sent a letter to Cato in which he spoke in the highest terms of the courage and honourable feeling which he had shown. He afterwards married Tertia, the sister of Scipio, and had the gratification of pleasing his father as much as himself by thus allying himself with one of the noblest families in Rome. Thus was Cato rewarded for the care which he had bestowed upon his son's education.

XXI. He possessed a large number of slaves, and when captives were for sale he always purchased those who were young, and who, like colts or puppies, could be taught and trained to their duties. None of them ever entered any house but his own, unless sent thither by Cato or by his wife: and if they were asked what Cato was doing, they always answered that they did not know. His rule was, that a slave ought either to be doing his business or to be asleep; and he greatly preferred good sleepers, as he thought that they were more easy tempered than wakeful persons, and also that men who had slept well were better able to work than those who had lain awake. Knowing that love affairs lead slaves into mischief more than anything else, he permitted them to consort with his own female slaves at a fixed price, but forbade them to have anything to do with other women.

Cato in his earlier days, being a poor man, and always employed in service in the field, never complained of any thing that he ate, and thought it most disgraceful to quarrel with his servant for not having pleased his palate. Subsequently, however, as he became richer, he used to invite his friends and colleagues to dinner, and after the repast was wont to punish with the scourge those servants who had made mistakes or cooked the food badly. He always endeavoured to establish some quarrel amongst his slaves, so that they might plot against one another, instead of combining against himself; and when any of them appeared to have committed any crime deserving to be punished by death, the offender was formally tried, and if found guilty, was put to death in the presence of all his fellow-servants.

As Cato grew more eager to make money, he declared that farming was more an amusement than a source of income, and preferred investing his money in remunerative undertakings, such as marshes that required draining, hot springs, establishments for washing and cleaning clothes, land which would produce an income by pasturage or by the sale of wood, and the like, which afforded him a considerable revenue, and one which, as he said, not Jupiter himself could injure, meaning that he was not dependent upon the weather for his income, as farmers are. He also used to deal in marine assurance, which is thought to be a most dangerous form of investment, which he managed in the following manner. For the sake of security he made those who wished to borrow money form themselves into an association of fifty persons, representing as many ships, and held one share in the undertaking himself, which was managed by his freedman Quintio, who himself used to sail in the ships of the association and transact their mercantile business.

He used to lend money to his slaves, if they desired it. They used with the money to buy young slaves, teach them a trade at Cato's expense for a year, and then dispose of them. Many of these Cato retained in his own service, paying the price offered by the highest bidder, and deducting from it the original cost of the slave. When endeavouring to encourage his son to act in a similar manner, he used to say that it was not the part of a man, but of a lone woman, to diminish one's capital; and once, with an excessive exaggeration, he said that the most glorious and godlike man was he who on his death was found to have earned more than he inherited.

XXII. When he was an old man, Karneades the academic, and Diogenes the stoic philosopher, came as ambassadors to Rome on the part of the Athenians, to beg that they might not be forced to pay a fine of five hundred talents which had been imposed upon them in consequence of an action at law, brought against the Athenians by the people of Oropus, before the people of Sikyon as judges, having been allowed to go against them by default. Such of the Roman youths as had any taste for literature frequented the society of these men, and took great interest in hearing their discussions. They were especially delighted with Karneades, a man of great and recognised ability, who obtained large and enthusiastic audiences at his lectures, and filled the whole city with his fame. Nothing was talked of except how a single Greek with wonderful powers of eloquence and persuasion had so bewitched the youth of Rome that they forsook all other pleasures, and plunged wildly into philosophic speculations. The greater part of the citizens were well pleased with this, and looked on with great satisfaction at their sons' study of

Greek literature, and their intimacy with such celebrated men; but Cato, when the taste for philosophy first sprang up in Rome, was vexed at it, and feared that the young men might become more eager to gain distinction by fluent speaking than by warlike exploits. However, when the fame of the philosophers increased, and a distinguished man, Caius Acilius, at the general request, translated their first lectures to the Senate, Cato decided that the philosophers must at once be conducted with all due honours out of the city. He came to the Senate and made a speech, in which he blamed them for having allowed an embassy to remain so long at Rome without accomplishing its purpose, although nothing was easier than for it to gain its point. He called upon them therefore, to decide as soon as possible and come to a vote upon the matter about which this embassy was come, in order that these philosophers might return to their schools and instruct the young men of Greece, while those of Rome might, as before, give their attention to the laws and the magistrates.

XXIII. Cato acted thus, not as some writers imagine, from any private quarrel with Karneades, but because he disliked the philosophy altogether, and from a feeling of patriotism, regarded all Greek literature and methods of education with hatred and contempt. He used to say that Sokrates was a wordy and dangerous man, who endeavoured in his own way to make himself supreme in Athens, by destroying the best of the national customs and teaching the citizens to hold opinions at variance with the laws. He ridiculed Isokrates as a teacher of rhetoric, saying that his disciples stayed with him so long learning their profession, that they were only able to practice what they had learned in the court where Minos sat as judge in the next world. In his endeavours to dissuade his son from the study of Greek literature, he abused the privileges of old age so far as to utter a prophecy that the Romans would ruin their empire by too intimate an acquaintance with the arts of Greece. Time, however, has proved this to be a mere empty slander, seeing that since then Rome has risen to a wonderful height of power and glory, and yet is thoroughly familiar with Greek writings and studies. Cato not only disliked the Greek philosophers, but also looked with suspicion on the Greek physicians who then practised at Rome. He had heard some story about Hippokrates, who, when the king of Persia offered him a large sum of money if he would come to Persia, answered that he never would give his services to barbarians who were the enemies of Greece. Cato used to say that all Greek physicians had sworn an oath to act like Hippokrates, and warned his son never to have any dealings with any of them. He himself had a book full of recipes, according to which he used to physick and regulate the diet of any who fell sick in his house, being careful never to allow the patient to fast, but making him eat salad, with ducks, pigeons, and hares, which he said were light food, and suitable for sick persons, except that it often happened that those who ate of them suffered from nightmares. He used to declare that by following this regimen, he kept both himself and all his household in perfect health.

XXIV. He seems to have been justly rewarded for his quackery, for he lost both his wife and his son by sickness. He himself, however, being of an iron constitution, made a second marriage, in spite of his advanced age, being led into it by the following circumstances. After the death of his wife he arranged a marriage between his son and the daughter of Æmilius Paulus, who was the sister of Scipio. He himself meanwhile solaced himself by an intrigue with a maid-servant who visited him by stealth. However, in a small house with a daughter-in-law in it this could not be kept secret; and one day when this woman was insolently swaggering into his father's bedchamber, young Cato was observed by the old man to glance at her with bitter hatred and then turn away in disgust. As soon as Cato perceived that his conduct vexed his children, he said not a word, but went into the forum with his friends, as was his wont. Here one Salonius, who was one of his under-secretaries, met him and began to pay his respects to him, when Cato asked him in a loud voice whether he had provided a husband for his daughter. On the man's replying that he had not, and would not presume to do so without consulting him, Cato replied, "Well, I, by Jupiter, have found a very suitable person to marry her, unless his age be any objection: for he is very passable in all respects except that he is very old." As Salonius upon this bade him carry out his intention and marry the girl to whomsoever he pleased, seeing that she was his client and he was her patron, Cato without a moment's delay told him that he wished to marry the girl himself. This proposal at first, as might be expected, astonished the secretary, who had thought that a man at Cato's time of life was very unlikely to marry, and had never dreamed that his humble family would be allied with a house which could boast of consulates and triumphs; but as he saw that Cato was in earnest he gladly accepted his offer. While the preparations for the marriage were in progress, young Cato, taking his relatives with him, went and inquired of his father whether he had reproached or annoyed him in any way, that he was putting a mother-in-law over him. Cato at this question cried out aloud, "Hush, my son; I approve of all that you have done, and find no fault with you: I only desire to leave behind me more sons of my race, and more citizens to serve the state." It is said that this remark was first made by Peisistratus, the despot of Athens, when, although he had sons grown up, he married Timonassa of Argos, by whom we are told that he had two sons, Iophon and Thessalus. Cato also had a son by his second marriage, whom he named Salonius after his mother. His eldest son died during his prætorship. Cato often mentions him in his writings as having been a brave and good man, but is said to have borne his loss with philosophic resignation, and to have taken as keen an interest in politics as before. He did not, as was afterwards done by Lucius Lucullus or Metellus Pius, abandon public life when he grew old, and think that it was a burden to take part in politics; still less did he imitate Scipio Africanus, who some years before had proudly turned his back on the people who grudged him the glory he had won, and spent the rest of his life in ease and retirement. Some one is said to have told Dionysius of Syracuse that an absolute monarchy is the best thing for a man to die in, and so Cato seemed to think that political life was the best for him to grow old in, while he amused himself in his leisure moments by writing and farming.

XXV. He compiled works on various subjects, especially on history. Farming he applied himself to when very young, on account of his poverty, for he himself tells us that he had only two sources of income, farming and frugality. In later life he derived both amusement and instruction from watching the operations of agriculture, and he has written a farmer's manual, in which there is even an account of how to cook cakes and preserve fruits, so desirous was he to show a thorough knowledge of every subject. His table was never so well served as when he was in the country; for he used to invite all his friends and acquaintances from the neighbourhood, and make himself very agreeable to them, as he was a pleasant companion not only to men of his own age, but also to the young, having in the course of his long life seen and heard from others much that was interesting and curious. He regarded the table as the best means of forming friendships, and when dining used to praise the good without stint, but never would allow the names of worthless men to be mentioned, either by way of praise or blame, at his entertainments.

XXVI. The last of his political acts is said to have been the destruction of Carthage. This was actually brought to pass by Scipio the Younger, but it was chiefly owing to the counsels of Cato that the war was begun. His reason for insisting on its destruction was this. He was sent on a mission to Africa to investigate the grounds of a quarrel which existed between the Carthaginians and Masinissa, the king of the Numidians. Masinissa had always been the friend of Rome, whereas the Carthaginians, after their defeat by Scipio, had been subjected to hard conditions, having lost their sovereignty over the neighbouring tribes, and having been compelled to pay a large sum as tribute to Rome. Cato, however, found the city, not, as the Romans imagined it to be, crushed by its recent overthrow, but full of young men, overflowing with wealth, well provided with arms and munitions of war, and, as may be expected, full of warlike spirit. He concluded that it was no time for the Romans to arbitrate about the grievances of Masinissa and his Numidians, but that, unless they at once destroyed a city which bore them an undying hatred and which had recovered its strength in an incredibly short space of time, they would have as much to fear from Carthage as ever. He quickly returned home, and pointed out to the Senate that the former defeats and misfortunes suffered by the Carthaginians had not really broken their strength so much as they had dissipated their overweening self-confidence, and that in the late war they had not lost so much in strength as they had gained in experience and skill. Their present difference with the Numidians was, he urged, merely a prelude to an attack upon Rome, with which city they kept up the fiction of a peace which would soon upon a suitable opportunity be exchanged for war.

XXVII. After these words it is said that Cato threw down in the senate house some ripe figs which he had brought on purpose; and when the senators admired their size and beauty, he remarked that "the country which produced this fruit is only three days' sail distant from Rome." Another and a more violent method of forcing the Romans to attack them was his habit, when giving his opinion on any subject whatever, to append the words, "And I also am of opinion that Carthage must he destroyed." On the other hand, Publius Scipio, called Nasica, used to end all his speeches with the words, "And I further am of opinion that Carthage should be left alone." Scipio's reason for this was that he perceived that the lower classes in Rome, elated by success, were becoming difficult for the Senate to manage, and practically forced the State to adopt whatever measures they chose. He thought that to have this fear of Carthage kept constantly hanging over them would be a salutary check upon the insolence of the people, and he thought that although Carthage was too weak to conquer the Romans, yet that it was too strong to be despised by them. Cato, on the other hand, thought it a dangerous thing that, at a time when the Romans were giddy and drunk with power, they should leave in existence a city which always had been important, and which now, sobered by defeat, was biding its time and lying in wait for a favourable opportunity to avenge itself. He argued that it was better to set the Romans free from any fear of foreign states, in order that they might be able to devote themselves uninterruptedly to the task of political reform.

These are said to have been Cato's reasons for urging his countrymen to begin the third and last Punic war. He died as soon as the war was begun, leaving a prophecy that it would be finished by a young man who was then serving as military tribune, and who had given remarkable proofs of courage and generalship. Cato, on hearing of his exploits is said to have quoted Homer's line—

"He alone has solid wisdom; all the rest are shadows vain."

This opinion Scipio soon confirmed by his actions.

Cato left one son by his second wife, who, as has been said, was named Salonius, and one grandson, the child of his eldest son who was dead. Salonius died during his prætorship, but his son Marcus became consul. This man was the grandfather of Cato the Philosopher, who was one of the foremost men of his day in courage and ability.

# Comparison of Aristeides and Cato.

Now that we have related all the important events of each of these men's lives, it will be seen that the points in which they differ are very trifling when compared with those in which they agree. If, however, we are to take each of their qualities separately, as one would in comparing two speeches or two pictures, we observe that they both agree in having begun life in a humble station, and having won political distinction and power by sheer ability and force of character. It is true that Aristeides rose to power at a period when Athens was poor, and when the orators and generals whom he attacked were men whose means were little superior to his own; for the men of greatest incomes at that time were assessed as having five hundred bushels of wet or dry produce a year, while the next class, that of the knights, had three hundred, and the lowest, or those who could afford to keep a yoke of oxen, had only two hundred. Cato, on the other hand, came from an obscure village and a rustic mode of life, and boldly launched himself upon the turbid sea of Roman politics, although the days of Curius, Fabricius and Atilius were long past, and Rome was not accustomed to find her magistrates and party leaders in labouring men fresh from the plough or the workshop, but in men of noble birth and great wealth, who canvassed extensively, and bribed heavily; while the populace, insolent with the consciousness of power, were growing ripe for a revolt against the governing class.

It was a very different thing for Aristeides to have only Themistokles for an antagonist, a man of no birth or fortune (for it is said that he only possessed between three and five talents when he first embarked on politics) and for Cato to contend for the mastery with men like Scipio Africanus, Sergius Galba, and Titus Quintius Flamininus, with nothing to help him but his eloquent voice and his good cause.

II. Furthermore, Aristeides, both at Marathon and at Platæa, acted as general with nine colleagues, while Cato was elected one of the two consuls and afterwards one of the two censors, though there were many other candidates for both offices. Aristeides never conspicuously distinguished himself, as the credit of the victory at Marathon belongs to Miltiades, and that of Salamis to Themistokles, while Herodotus tells us that Pausanias obtained the most glorious success of all at Platæa, and even the second place is disputed with Aristeides by Sophanes, Ameinias, Kallimachus, and Kynægyrus, all of whom won great glory in those battles. On the other hand, Cato not only when consul gained the greatest credit, both by his wise conduct, and his personal prowess in the Spanish war, but, when at Thermopylæ he was acting as tribune under another person's command as consul, contributed mainly to winning the victory by his flank movement, by which he established himself in the rear of Antiochus while that prince was intent upon the enemy in his front. This victory, which was so manifestly due to Cato, had the important result of driving the Asiatic troops out of Greece back to their own country, and so of preparing the way for Scipio's subsequent invasion of Asia.

Neither of them were ever defeated in battle, but in political matters Aristeides was overcome by his rival Themistokles, who drove him into exile by ostracism, while Cato held his own against all the greatest and most influential men in Rome to the end of his life without once being overthrown by them. He was often impeached, and always acquitted, while he frequently succeeded in his impeachments of others, using, both as a bulwark to defend himself and as a weapon to attack others, his power of speaking in public, which indeed is a quality more to be relied upon than good fortune to protect a man from suffering wrong. Antipater, in the account which he wrote of the philosopher Aristotle after his death, observes that besides his other qualities and accomplishments this man had the power of persuasion.

III. It is generally admitted that political virtue is the highest to which a man can aspire, and of this, most think domestic virtue to be a very important part; for as a city is merely a collection of houses, the public virtue of the state must be increased if it contain many well-regulated households. Lykurgus, when he banished silver and gold from Sparta, and gave his countrymen useless iron money, did not wish to discourage good household management among them, but he removed the dangerous seductions of wealth out of their reach, in order that they all might enjoy a sufficiency of what was useful and necessary. He saw, what no other legislator appears to have seen, that the real danger to a commonwealth arises from the poor and desperate rather than from the excessively rich.

Now we have seen that Cato was as well able to manage his household as to govern the state; for he improved his fortune and became a teacher of household management and husbandry to others, by collecting much useful information on these matters. On the other hand, Aristeides made his poverty a reproach to justice, which by his example was made to seem a ruinous virtue which brought men to want, and was totally useless to those who practised it. Yet the poet Hesiod, when encouraging men to act justly and manage their household affairs well, blames idleness as the origin of injustice, and the same idea is well stated in Homer's lines:—

"Work was never my delight, Nor household cares, that breed up children bright; But ever loved I ships with banks of oars, And arrows keen, and weapons for the wars,"

where we see that the same men neglect their duties at home, and gain their living by injustice and piracy abroad. The physicians tell us that oil is most useful, outwardly used, and most harmful when taken inwardly; but it is not true of the just man that he is most useful to his friends, but useless to himself. It seems to me to be a blot on Aristeides' fame, if it be true that he could not even provide money for his daughters' dowry or for his own funeral expenses. The family of Cato for four generations, supplied Rome with prætors and consuls, for his grandchildren, and their children too, all rose to the highest offices in the state; while the hopeless poverty of Aristeides, though he was the foremost man of his time in Greece, reduced some of his family to the disreputable profession of interpreting dreams, and forced others to live on public charity, putting it quite out of their power to emulate the glorious actions of their ancestor.

IV. Some, indeed, may dispute this; for it is true that poverty is no disgrace in itself, but only when it is a proof of indolence, extravagance, or folly. The poverty of a laborious, upright, temperate statesman combines well with his other virtues, and shows true greatness of mind: for a man whose attention is given to little things, can never succeed in doing great ones; nor can a man help others if he is in need of help himself. A statesman requires, not wealth, but contentment, in order that his attention may not be diverted from public affairs by his own cravings for useless luxuries. God alone is entirely without wants, and we approach nearest to the divine ideal when we can reduce our wants to the fewest possible. Just as a healthy man requires neither excess of clothing or of food, so a man's life and that of his family, if properly regulated, can be maintained at a trifling cost. His income, however, must exactly tally with his requirements; for we cannot call that man contented who earns much, and spends little. He is a foolish man if he troubles himself to amass what he cannot enjoy; while he must be a miserable man if he is able to enjoy the use of wealth, and yet through meanness of spirit forbids himself its use.

I would willingly put this question to Cato: "If we ought to enjoy our wealth, why do you make a virtue of simplicity of living when you are a rich man? If, on the other hand, it is a noble thing, as no doubt it is, to eat common bread, to drink the same wine as our servants and farm labourers do, and not to want fine clothes or comfortable houses, then Aristeides and Epameinondus, Manius Curius and Caius Fabricius were to be applauded for their neglect of the wealth, whose use they rejected." Surely it was not necessary for a man who thought turnips made a delicious meal, and who used to boil them himself while his wife baked the bread, to write so much about how to save a penny, and how a man might most quickly make a fortune. The great advantage of simplicity and contentment is, that it prevents our wishing for superfluities, or even thinking about them. Aristeides, when cited as a witness during the trial of Kallias, is said to have observed that those who were poor against their will, ought to be ashamed of it, but that those who, like himself, were poor from their own choice, gloried in their poverty. It would be absurd to suppose that the poverty of Aristeides was not voluntary, when, without doing any criminal act, he might by stripping the body of one dead Persian, or by plundering one tent, have made himself a rich man. But enough of this.

V. As to their campaigns, those of Cato added but little to the already vast empire of Rome, while Aristeides was present at Marathon, Salamis, and Platæa, the most glorious of all Grecian victories. We cannot compare Antiochus with Xerxes, nor the destruction of the walls of the Spanish cities by Cato, with the tremendous slaughter of the barbarians by the Greeks, both on sea and land. Aristeides was present at every action of importance, although he gave up his share of glory and rewards, even as he did with gold and silver, to those who needed them more than himself. I cannot blame Cato for always glorifying himself and claiming the first place for himself, although he says in one of his books that it is absurd for a man either to praise or to blame himself; still I think that he who does not even wish for the praises of others, is a more perfect character than he who is always exalting himself. An indifference to popular applause does much to soften the bitterness of political controversy, while on the other hand a love of distinction often leads men to be ill-natured and spiteful to others, a fault which Aristeides entirely avoided, and to which Cato was peculiarly liable. Aristeides saved Athens by supporting the authority of Themistokles on several critical occasions, and even acting as his subordinate; while Cato by his opposition, nearly ruined Scipio's famous expedition to Carthage, in which he defeated the hitherto invincible Hannibal. Nor did he cease his intrigues against Scipio until by calumnious and false accusations he drove him out of Rome, and stigmatized his brother with the disgraceful charge of embezzling the public money.

VI. Self-denial, upon which Cato has bestowed such lavish praise, was practised in its purest and brightest form by Aristeides, while Cato seems to have forfeited all claim to this virtue by his unsuitable and unseasonable second marriage. It could not be to his honour, when he was of such a great age, to marry the daughter of his own servant, a man who acted as a public clerk, and to bring her into the house to act as mother-in-law to his son, who was now himself grown up and married. Whether he acted thus from natural inclination, or to spite his son for his behaviour about his mistress, the marriage and the motives which led to it are equally discreditable to him. The sarcastic explanation of it which he gave to his son is utterly untrue; for had he wished to beget other children as noble as his son, he ought to have married a well-born lady at once, and not to have been satisfied with a low intrigue until it was detected, and then to have chosen as his father-in-law, the man whom he could most easily influence, rather than some one whose alliance would bring him honour and advantage.

# Life of Philopœmen.

I. In the city of Mantinea there was a citizen named Kleander, of one of the first families, and of great influence. Nevertheless he was so unfortunate as to be forced to leave his native city, and take refuge in Megalopolis, to which he was chiefly attracted by Kraugis, the father of Philopœmen, a man eminent in every respect, and an especial private friend of Kleander. While Kraugis lived, Kleander wanted for nothing, and after his death endeavoured to repay the debt which he owed him by devoting himself to the education of his orphan son, just as Homer tells us that Achilles was nurtured by the exile Phœnix. The child, who always was of a noble and commanding spirit, grew under his care into a youth of great promise. As he came near to manhood Ekdemus and Megalophanes, two citizens of Megalopolis, took charge of his education. These men had studied in the Academy with Arkesilaus, and more than any others brought the lessons of philosophy to bear upon politics and the daily affairs of life. They freed their own country of the despot Aristodemus by secretly contriving his assassination, drove out the despot Nikokles from Sikyon, with the help of Aratus, and, at the request of the people of Kyrene, whose state was a prey to revolution, they went to that country and restored order and respect for the laws. They themselves, however, reckoned their most important work to have been the education of Philopœmen, because by bringing him up in the precepts of true philosophy they made him a benefactor to all Greece. And truly Greece loved him exceedingly, as the last great man born of her old age, after so many great and famous men of former times. A Roman speaking in his praise called him the last of the Greeks, as though he thought that Greece had never after him produced any son worthy of herself.

II. His appearance was not repulsive, as some think; for we can see the statue of him which exists at Delphi at this day. The mistake of his Megarian hostess seems to have arisen from his good-nature and simplicity. She, when she heard that the commander-in-chief of the Achæans was coming to her house, was in a great state of excitement about the preparation of dinner, her husband happening to be away. Meanwhile, Philopœmen entered, dressed in a coarse cloak, and she, supposing him to be a servant sent on in advance, ordered him to help her to get things ready. He at once threw off his cloak and began to split up firewood. While he was thus engaged his friend the master of the house came in, and seeing him, said, "What is this that you are doing, Philopœmen?" "Why," answered he in the Doric dialect, "I am suffering for my ugly face." Titus, also, when jesting upon his bodily shape, said, "Philopœmen, what fine hands and legs you have; but you have no belly," as indeed he had a very small waist. However, the jest was directed more against his power, for though he had plenty of good infantry and cavalry he was frequently in great distress for money to pay them. These are the common anecdotes which are current about Philopœmen.

III. His love of distinction was not entirely unmixed with feelings of rivalry and passion. He desired to emulate the fame of Epameinondas, but though he imitated that great man in energy, good sense, and contempt of money, yet he was unable in political struggles to maintain his calm unruffled good-nature, but was often betrayed by his fiery temper into sallies more befitting a soldier than a statesman. Indeed, from a child he had always been fond of war, and eagerly devoted himself to soldier-like exercises, such as fighting in complete armour and riding on horseback. He was thought to be a good wrestler, and was invited by his friends to contend with them in that sport, but he asked them whether the practice would not impair his efficiency as a soldier, when they answered truly that the body and the life of an athlete differs from that of a soldier in every respect, more particularly in diet and exercise. The athlete takes long sleep, frequent meals, regular exercise and intervals of rest, being likely to be put out of condition by the least change of his accustomed routine, while the life of a soldier makes him accustomed to all kinds of change and diversity of life, especially to enduring hunger and want of sleep. On learning this Philopœmen not only himself avoided wrestling and ridiculed it, but when he was in command of an army took every means in his power to bring every kind of athletic exercise into contempt, as likely to unfit the best men's bodies for the most important struggles in battle.

IV. On leaving his schoolmasters he took part in the incursion made by his fellow citizens into the Laconian territory for the purpose of plunder. In these raids it was his wont always to be first in the attack, and last in the retreat. In time of peace he would exercise his body, and make it both swift and strong, either by hunting or by tilling the ground. He possessed a fine estate about twenty furlongs from the city: to this he would walk after his morning or evening meal, and sleep there on any bed he could find, like one of the farm labourers. Then he would rise early, help the vine-dressers or cattle-herds to do their work, and, returning to town, take part in public business. The profits arising from the plunder gained in the forays he used to spend on horses, arms, and the redeeming of captives, while he endeavoured to increase his income by the skilful cultivation of his farm, considering the most just way of making money, and his strict duty to be, so to manage his fortune as to avoid the temptation of wronging others. He used to listen to conversation and to read treatises upon philosophy, yet not all, but only those which he thought would teach him to be virtuous. He also devoted much time to reading those passages of Homer which stir up and excite manly courage, His other reading consisted chiefly of Evangelus's treatise on military tactics, and of the history of Alexander the Great; but he always thought that reading, unless it led to action, was a useless waste of time. In his studies of tactics he used to disregard the diagrams in the books and consider what could be done in the field itself, observing the slopes and inequalities of the ground, the direction of brooks and water-courses, and the effect which they would have upon a body of troops advancing in line or in column. These reflections he was wont to make during his walks, and to exercise the minds of his companions by questions about them; for he devoted his whole mind to the study of military matters, regarding war as the widest arena for the display of virtue, utterly despising those who were not soldiers, as useless members of society.

V. When he was thirty years old Kleomenes, the king of the Lacedæmonians, made a night attack upon Megalopolis, forced his way through the guard on the wall and reached the market-place. Philopœmen came to the rescue, but was not able to dislodge the enemy, although he assaulted them with the greatest spirit. However, he gained time for the citizens to leave the town, while he bore the whole brunt of the attack of Kleomenes, so that at last he had great difficulty in extricating himself, as he had lost his horse and was wounded. The citizens of Megalopolis escaped to Messene, whither Kleomenes sent to offer them their town and territory again. Philopœmen, when he saw his fellow-citizens eager to embrace this offer, restrained them from accepting it by pointing out that Kleomenes did not really offer them their city back again, but meant to get the citizens as well into his power, in order to be able to hold it more securely for the future; because he could not remain there guarding naked walls and empty houses, but would be compelled to leave them and go his way. By these arguments he withheld the Megalopolitans from coming to terms, but gave Kleomenes a pretext for destroying a great part of the city, and carrying away a great booty from it.

VI. When King Antigonus some time after this joined the Achæan forces in a campaign against Kleomenes, they came upon his army advantageously posted so as to command the defiles near Sellasia. Philopœmen was among the cavalry that day with his fellow-citizens, and next to him were posted the Illyrians, numerous and warlike, who covered the flank of the allies. Their orders were to remain in reserve until they saw a red flag raised upon a pike by king Antigonus on the other wing. The generals of the allies attacked the Lacedæmonians with the Illyrian troops, but Eukleides, the brother of Kleomenes, perceiving that by this movement the foot were completely severed from the horse, sent the swiftest of his light-armed troops to outflank them and cut them off. When this was done, and the Illyrians were thrown into great disorder, Philopœmen saw that the cavalry could charge the Lacedæmonian light troops with great effect, and pointed this out to Antigonus's generals. Meeting with a scornful refusal, as his reputation was not yet sufficiently great to warrant his suggesting such a manœuvre, he collected his own fellow-countrymen and charged with them alone. At the first onset he threw the light-armed troops into confusion, and presently routed them with great slaughter. Wishing to encourage the allies and to come more quickly to blows with the retreating enemy, he dismounted, and with great difficulty, encumbered by his heavy horseman's cuirass and accoutrements, pursued over a rough piece of ground full of water-courses and precipitous rocks. While struggling over these obstacles he was struck through both thighs by a javelin with a strap attached to it, a wound which was not dangerous, though the javelin struck him with such force as to drive the iron head quite through. This wound for the time rendered him helpless, as it bound both his legs as if with a chain, while the strap made it hard to pull the javelin out again through the wound. As his friends hesitated, not knowing what to do, while the battle now at its height, excited his courage, and made him long to take part in it, he violently strained one leg forward and the other back, so as to break the javelin in the middle, after which the pieces were pulled out. Being thus set free, he drew his sword, ran through the first of the combatants and attacked the enemy, animating all his men and setting them on fire with emulation. After the victory was won Antigonus enquired of the Macedonians why the cavalry had charged without orders. They answered that they were forced to charge against their will by a young citizen of Megalopolis, who attacked on his own account. Antigonus smiled, and answered, "That young man acted like a veteran commander."

VII. Philopœmen, as may be supposed, gained great glory by this action. Antigonus was eager to obtain his services, and offered him a command and high pay, but he excused himself, knowing that his temper would not endure to be under the orders of another man. Still, as he could not be idle, he sailed for Crete to serve a campaign there, in order to gain experience of war. He spent a considerable time there, living amongst warlike, sober, and temperate men, and returned to the Achæans with so great a reputation that they at once put him in command of the knights. These horsemen, he found, were in the habit of using any chance horses they could pick up when required for a campaign, while in many cases they did not serve in person, but sent substitutes. They were entirely without discipline or bravery, while all this was passed over unnoticed by their commanders, because the knights were the most influential men among the Achæans, and were able to promote or degrade whom they pleased. Philopœmen, however, could not allow this state of things to continue. He went round to each of the cities of the Achæan League, and by personally appealing to the young men's sense of honour, by punishment where it was necessary, and by careful training, exercises, and contests among them before as many spectators as possible, in a short time produced great efficiency and military spirit. He made them quick at manœuvring in squadrons, and in wheeling round and managing their horses, which is so valuable a quality in cavalry soldiers, and taught the whole body to move with ease at the will of one man. Once during a severe battle with the Eleans and Ætolians on the banks of the river Larissa, Damophantus, the commander of the Elean horse, rode furiously to attack Philopœmen. He awaited Damophantus's onset, and with his spear thrust him from his saddle. When he fell the Eleans at once turned and fled, to the great glory of Philopœmen, who had proved himself as brave as the youngest and as skilful as the oldest soldier, equally able to fight or to command.

VIII. The Achæan League was first organised by Aratus, who formed its scattered and despicable cities into a noble and truly Greek commonwealth; then, as in running streams, when first a few small stones resist the flow of the water, soon much more is brought down by the stream and lodged against them until a firm ground is formed; so did the Achæans, by assisting some of the neighbouring cities and freeing them from despots, and by uniting and incorporating others with themselves, endeavour to combine the whole of Peloponnesus into one single state, at a time when Greece was especially weak, having lost all cohesion, each city relying solely on itself. While Aratus lived they depended much on the Macedonians, courting first Ptolemy, then Antigonus and Philip, who all were constantly interfering in the affairs of Greece. But when Philopœmen came to command they already felt themselves a match for the most powerful states, and no longer paid their court to foreign patrons. Aratus, who was no soldier, had effected most of his successes by suave diplomacy and personal friendship with foreign princes, as we have written in his Life: but Philopœmen, a brave and vigorous, and, what is more, an eminently successful commander in his first essays, greatly raised the spirit and the strength of the Achæans, by making them confident of victory under his leadership.

IX. His first task was to alter the military equipment and arms of the Achæans. They had hitherto used light shields, too narrow to protect the body, and spears much smaller than the long Macedonian pike. This light armament rendered them effective as skirmishers, but unable to hold their own in close fighting. Their order of battle, too, was loose and without cohesion, having neither the projecting pikes nor the serried shields of the Macedonian phalanx, in consequence of which they were easily thrust aside and routed. Philopœmen pointed this out to them, and persuaded them to adopt the heavy shield and pike in place of their light arms, to accoutre themselves with helmet, corslet, and greaves, and to endeavour to move in a steady unbroken mass instead of in a loose irregular skirmishing order. When he had induced them to put on complete armour he raised their spirit by telling them that they would be unconquerable, while he also effected a most wholesome change in their luxurious habits of life. It was impossible entirely to do away with their long-standing passion for fine purple robes and tapestry, rich banquets, and furniture: but he directed this love of finery to useful purposes, and soon brought them all to retrench their private expenditure, and to take a pride in the splendour of their military equipments. Their plate was sent to the crucible, and employed to gild corslets, shields, and caparisons; their public places were full of young men training chargers or exercising themselves in arms, while the women were busy fitting plumes to helmets, and ornamenting buff coats and military cloaks. The sight of all this activity roused up their courage, and made them eager for battle. In all other cases too much care for outward show and display leads to effeminacy and luxury, because the pleasure which our senses receive from these things blunt our better judgment, but in military matters this is not so, for a splendid appearance under arms increases men's courage; as Homer tells us that Achilles, when his new arms were brought to him, was at once excited by a vehement desire to make use of them. The youth, thus equipped, were incessantly exercised and practised in their new manœuvres, which they performed with zealous goodwill, being delighted with the close formation of the phalanx, which seemed as though it could never be broken. They soon began to move with ease in their heavy armour, priding themselves upon its splendour, and longing to prove its value in battle against their enemies. The Achæans at this time were at war with Machanidas the despot of Lacedæmon, who had immense resources at his disposal, and menaced the whole of Peloponnesus. As soon as news came that he had invaded Arcadia and had reached Mantinea, Philopœmen with his army marched rapidly to attack him. Both sides drew up their forces near the city of Mantinea, and both brought into the field not only nearly all their own countrymen, but also large bodies of foreign mercenary troops. Machanidas began the battle by a charge of his mercenaries, who routed the Tarentines and other light troops of the Achæans, but then instead of moving at once to attack and overwhelm their main body, hurried away in pursuit, leaving the Achæan phalanx standing untouched. Philopœmen made light of the disaster which had happened to the light troops, and, perceiving the fault which the enemy had committed in leaving their heavy infantry unprotected, so that he had an open plain over which to march against them, disregarded those Lacedæmonians who were pursuing his own auxiliaries, and bore straight down upon their main body, which he took in flank, without any cavalry to protect it, or any general to give it orders, as the men did not expect to be attacked, and imagined that the victory was already won when they saw Machanidas so eager in the pursuit. Philopœmen broke and routed them with great slaughter, four thousand men being said to have perished, and then turned to encounter Machanidas, who was returning with his mercenaries, and found his retreat cut off. A deep and wide watercourse here divided the two leaders, the one of whom endeavoured to pass it and escape, while the other tried to prevent this. They looked no longer like two generals, but the despot seemed more like some savage beast driven to bay by Philopœmen, that mighty hunter. At length the despot spurred his horse, a fiery animal, to attempt the leap. The horse gained the other bank with its fore feet, and was struggling up it, when Simias and Polyænus, the constant companions and aides-de-camp of Philopœmen, rode to attack him with levelled lances. Philopœmen, however, came up with Machanidas before them. Seeing that the despot's horse was rearing its head so as to protect its master's body, he turned his own horse a little to one side, and, seizing his lance firmly with both hands, drove it through his body and cast him from his horse. It is in this posture that Philopœmen is represented in the statue at Delphi, which was placed there by the Achæans in token of their admiration of his courage and conduct on that day.

XI. It is said that when the Greeks were assembled at the Nemean Games, Philopœmen, who had been elected commander-in-chief for the second time, and not long before had won his victory at Mantinea, being at leisure during the festival displayed his phalanx to the Greeks, with the troops drawn up in their serried array, and manœuvring with quickness and precision. Afterwards, while the musicians were contending for the prize in the theatre he entered it accompanied by his young soldiers in their military cloaks and purple uniform, all of them strong men in the prime of life, showing a modest respect for their general, combined with a martial bearing due to their many brave feats of arms. Just as they came into the theatre Pylades the musician began to recite the 'Persians' of Timotheus

"He wrought for Greece a noble work of freedom"

in a loud voice and with suitable solemnity. At this, all the spectators turned their eyes upon Philopœmen and broke into joyous applause, remembering the ancient glories of Greece, and feeling such confidence in him as almost to recover the ancient spirit of their nation.

XII. But just as horses like their accustomed rider, and if another mounts them are scared and unmanageable, so the power of the Achæans become feeble under any other general than Philopœmen. When they saw him, the whole army rejoiced, and were filled with cheerful confidence, well knowing that he was the only one of their generals before whom the enemy always fled, terrified by his name, as, indeed, appeared by their acts. For Philip king of Macedon, thinking that if Philopœmen were put out of the way, the Achæans would become subject to himself as they were before, sent men privately to Argos to assassinate him: but his plot was disclosed, and he became an object of universal hatred to the Greeks. The Bœotians too, when they were besieging Megara and were expecting shortly to take it, retreated in such hot haste that they actually left their scaling ladders planted against the walls, in consequence of a rumour, which proved a false one, that Philopœmen was coming to raise the siege and was close at hand. When Nabis, who became despot over the Lacedæmonians after Machanidas, by a sudden attack captured the town of Messene, Philopœmen was not holding any office, but was a mere private citizen. He could not prevail upon Lysippus, who was commander-in-chief of the Achæans, to go to assist the Messenians, because the latter said that the city must be lost if the enemy were inside the walls. Hereupon Philopœmen went himself to the rescue with the men of his own city, who did not delay for any formal vote to empower him to do so, but followed him because he was born to command. When Nabis heard of his approach he would not await his coming, but although he was in possession of the city he marched out by the opposite gate with all speed, thinking that he would be fortunate if he reached home safe, as indeed he did. Thus was Messene delivered.

XIII. All these exploits of Philopœmen are without doubt glorious to him; but he was much blamed for going a second time to Crete at the request of the people of Gortyna, to act as their general, leaving his own country to be attacked by Nabis, because he avoided the war at home to gather unseasonable laurels abroad. Indeed, the citizens of Megalopolis were so hard pressed at that period as to be forced to live entirely within their walls, and grow corn in the very streets, as they were quite cut off from their fields by the enemy, who was encamped before the gates. Philopœmen, by his remaining beyond seas at this time acting as general for the Cretans, gave his enemies an opportunity of charging him with dishonourably shirking the war at home. Some, however, said that since the Achæans had chosen other men generals, Philopœmen, who had no office to fill, had a right to use his leisure in acting as general to the people of Gortyna when they begged him to do so. Indeed, his nature abhorred rest, and he desired his courage and generalship to be in constant action, like everything else belonging to him. This is clearly shown by his saying about king Ptolemy. When some one praised that prince for carefully training his army and exercising himself under arms every day, Philopœmen answered, "Who can admire a king of Ptolemy's age who is still practising and not performing." However, the citizens of Megalopolis were much vexed by his conduct, which they considered to be that of a traitor, and would have banished him had they not been restrained by the whole body of the Achæans. They sent the general Aristænetus to Megalopolis, who, although he was politically opposed to Philopœmen, would not allow sentence of banishment to be passed against him. After this Philopœmen, being treated with neglect and indifference by his fellow-citizens, induced many of the outlying villages to rebel against the city, telling them to say that they were not originally made subject to it, and he himself openly took their part against his own city when the matter was referred to the general council of the Achæan league. But these things happened afterwards. At the time of which we speak he carried on war in Crete with the Gortynians, not in a simple straightforward manner, as one would expect a Peloponnesian, and especially an Arcadian would do, but he adopted the Cretan character, and by using all their subtle devices and ambushes against themselves, proved that such contrivances are but child's play when tried against a truly experienced general.

XIV. Returning to Peloponnesus with a great reputation from his Cretan successes, he found Philip beaten by Titus Quintius, and Nabis at war both with the Romans and the Achæans. He was at once elected general to attack Nabis, and in a sea fight suffered the same misfortune as Epameinondas, that is to say, he effected much less at sea than was expected of a man of his courage and reputation.

Indeed some writers tell us that Epameinondas was unwilling that his countrymen should taste the advantages of the sea, and fearing that, as Plato says, they might from steady soldiers be transformed into licentious wandering sailors, purposely returned from the coast of Asia Minor and the islands without having effected anything.

Philopœmen, imagining that his knowledge of war on land would enable him to fight equally well at sea, learned by experience how greatly practice assists men's courage, and how much their strength is increased by being trained to use it. Not only was he worsted in a sea-fight through inexperience, but having selected an old ship, which had once been a famous vessel, but now was forty years old, she leaked so much as to endanger the lives of those on board. After the action, finding that the enemy despised him, as though his ships had been entirely driven from the sea, and that they were ostentatiously besieging Gythium, he sailed straightway thither and found them quite unprepared, and with their discipline relaxed in consequence of their victory. He landed his men at night, burned the enemy's tents, and slew many of them. A few days afterwards, being surprised by Nabis in a mountainous spot, while all the Achæans gave themselves up for lost, despairing of extricating themselves from such a difficult position, Philopœmen, after a short survey of the country, proved that strategy is the greatest of military qualities. He quietly and steadily changed his front, manœuvred his army out of its disadvantageous position, attacked the enemy, and completely routed them. Perceiving that the fugitives did not make for the city, but scattered themselves all over the country, which was hilly and wooded, full of torrents and precipices, and impassable for cavalry, he made no pursuit, but encamped before dark. As he conjectured that the enemy after their rout would straggle back into the city by twos and threes under cover of the darkness, he concealed many of the Achæans, armed with daggers, in the rough ground near the city. By this stratagem Nabis's force suffered great losses, for as they did not retreat in a body, but each man as best he could, they fell into their foemen's hands at the city gate like birds into a snare.

XV. Philopœmen gained so much glory by these exploits, and was so much honoured by the Greeks wherever he appeared in public, that he roused the jealousy of Flamininus, who thought that he, a consul of Rome, was worthier of respect than a mere Arcadian, while he had moreover done much more for Greece, having by one proclamation restored those liberties of which Philip and his Macedonians had deprived it. Flamininus put an end to the war with Nabis, who was shortly afterwards assassinated by the Ætolians. As this event threw Sparta into disorder, Philopœmen seized the opportunity, marched thither with an army, and partly by persuasion, partly by force, prevailed upon the city to join the Achæan league. This wonderfully raised his fame throughout Greece, that he should have won over so famous and powerful a city, for Sparta formed a most important member of the league. He also gained the good will of the Lacedæmonian nobles, who hoped that he would protect their newly-won liberty. They sold the house and property of Nabis, and decreed that the money, amounting to a hundred and twenty talents, should be presented to him by a deputation. On this occasion Philopœmen showed himself to be a man of real virtue. At the interview none of the Spartans liked to propose to him to receive the money, but they excused themselves, and made his own especial friend Timolaus undertake to do this. Timolaus, however, when he reached Megalopolis, and living in the house of Philopœmen had an opportunity of observing the noble simplicity of his character and his lofty integrity, in the familiar intercourse of private life, dared not mention the bribe, but gave some other excuse for his visit and returned home. He was sent a second time, with the same result. On a third visit he with great hesitation broached the subject. Philopœmen listened to him without anger, and sent him back to the Spartans with the advice that they should not corrupt their friends, whose services they could obtain gratis, but keep their money to bribe those who endeavoured to countermine their city in the public assembly of the Achæan league, as, if muzzled in this way, they would cease to oppose them. It was better, he added, to restrain the freedom of speech of their enemies than that of their friends. So uncorrupt was he, and inaccessible to bribes.

XVI. When Diophanes, the commander-in-chief of the Achæans, endeavoured to punish the Lacedæmonians for a change in their policy, and they by their resistance threw the whole of Peloponnesus into confusion, Philopœmen tried to act as mediator, and to soothe the anger of Diophanes, pointing out to him that at a time when the Romans and king Antiochus with enormous forces were about to make Greece their battle ground, a general ought to direct all his thoughts to their movements, and to avoid any internal disturbance, willingly accepting any apologies from those who did wrong. But as Diophanes took no notice of him, but together with Flamininus invaded Laconia, Philopœmen, disregarding the exact letter of the law, performed a most spirited and noble action. He hurried to Sparta, and, though only a private man, shut its gates in the faces of the commander-in-chief of the Achæans and of the Roman consul, put an end to the revolutionary movement there, and prevailed upon the city to rejoin the Achæan league. Some time afterwards however, we are told by Polybius that Philopœmen, when commander-in-chief, having some quarrel with the Lacedæmonians, restored the exiles to the city, and put to death eighty, or, according to Aristokrates, three hundred and fifty Spartans. He also pulled down the walls of Sparta, and annexed a large portion of its territory to Megalopolis, while he forced all those persons who had been created citizens of Sparta under the rule of the despots to leave the city and proceed to Achæa, except three hundred. These, because they refused to obey him and leave Lacedæmon he sold for slaves, and with the money, as a wanton insult, built a public portico in Megalopolis. Moreover, in his wrath against the Lacedæmonians, he did them a most cruel wrong, for he abolished the Lycurgean system of education and forced them to educate their children like those of the Achæans, because he saw that they never would be humble-minded as long as they lived under the discipline of Lycurgus. Thus was the haughty city of Sparta brought so low by its misfortunes as to permit Philopœmen to cut, as it were, its very sinews, and render it tame and crushed. Afterwards, however, the citizens obtained permission from Rome to retire from the Achæan confederation, upon which they restored their original constitution as far as their great disasters permitted.

XVII. When the Romans were fighting king Antiochus in Greece, Philopœmen was in a private station, but, seeing Antiochus lying idly at Chalkis, wasting his time in unseasonable courtships and weddings, while his Syrian troops, in great disorder and without officers to control them, were scattered through the various Greek cities, living in riotous debauchery, he was vexed at not being elected commander in chief, and said that he envied the Romans their victory. "I," said he, "if I had been in command, would have cut off the whole of Antiochus's army in the taverns."

After the defeat of Antiochus the Romans began to tighten their hold upon Greece, and to absorb the Achæan league. Many of the popular leaders took their side, and the growing power of Rome was fated by the divine blessing before long to become absolute in Greece. Philopœmen, like a skilful pilot, struggling against a rough sea, was often compelled to yield and give way for a time, yet as he was utterly opposed to the Romans he did his best to induce the most influential men to defend the liberties of Greece. Aristænetus of Megapolis, a man of great influence with the Achæans, who urged them in the public assembly not to oppose or to thwart the Romans in anything, was listened to by Philopœmen for some time in silence, until at length he was moved to exclaim, "My good sir, why be in such a hurry to behold the end of Greece?" When Manius the Roman consul had conquered Antiochus, he begged the Achæans to permit the Lacedæmonian exiles to return. Titus

Flamininus seconded this request, but Philopœmen opposed it; not because he had any quarrel with the exiles, but because he wished their restoration to be effected by himself and the Achæans, of their own free will, not as a favour to Flamininus and the Romans. Afterwards, when commander-in-chief, he himself restored them. Thus did his high spirit make him impatient of control and authority.

XVIII. When he was in his seventieth year, and eighth term of office as commander-in-chief, he might reasonably expect to finish not only his year of office, but also the rest of his life in peace; for just as in human bodies as their strength wastes away the violence of their diseases abates, so in the Greek states as their power failed their quarrels gradually ceased. However some Nemesis overtook him, as it does a too successful athlete just at the termination of his course. It is said that when some persons in society were praising a man who was thought to be a good general, Philopœmen said, "How can you think that man worth consideration, who was taken by his enemy alive."

A few days after this Deinokrates of Messene, a personal enemy of Philopœmen, and one who was generally disliked because of his wicked and licentious life, caused Messene to revolt from the Achæan league, and was announced to be marching upon a village named Kolonis. Philopœmen was at this time lying ill with a fever in the city of Argos, but on hearing this he proceeded at once to Megalopolis, a distance of four hundred furlongs, in one day. From that city he set out straightway with a body of cavalry, composed of the noblest citizens, but mostly very young men, who were proud to serve as volunteers under Philopœmen. They rode into the Messenian territory, met Deinokrates near the hill of Evander, and put him to flight. However as the Messenian frontier patrol of five hundred men suddenly came up, the defeated body rallied again, and Philopœmen, fearing to be surrounded, and wishing to be careful of the lives of his men, retired into mountainous ground, himself protecting the rear, making frequent charges, and drawing the whole attack of the enemy upon himself. They did not dare to encounter him personally, but clamoured and wheeled about at a distance. In his eagerness to save each one of his young soldiers he ventured forward so often, to cover their retreat, that at last he found himself alone in the midst of his enemies. None of them dared to meet him, but pelted him with stones and darts from a distance, so that he was with difficulty able to guide his horse over the rocky and precipitous ground, and fatigued the animal greatly.

His age was no hindrance to him, because of his habit of constant exercise, but unluckily he was weak from his sickness, and wearied by his long journey, so as to feel faint. His horse at length stumbling threw him to the ground. He fell heavily on his head, and lay speechless for some time, so that his enemies thought that he was dead, and began to turn over his body and strip it. But when he raised his head and opened his eyes they fell upon him in a body, tied his hands behind his back, and led him away, jeering much at a man who never even dreamed that he could have been so triumphed over by Deinokrates.

XIX. The Messenians who were in the city, greatly excited at the news, assembled at the gates. When they saw Philopœmen dragged along and treated in a manner so unworthy of a man who had gained such glorious victories, most of them felt compassion for him, and were moved to tears as they reflected how uncertain a thing is human power. Thus gradually they expressed aloud their kindly feeling towards him, saying that his former benefits and the liberty which he bestowed upon them by driving out the despot Nabis, ought to be had in remembrance. There were some few, however, who in order to gain favour with Deinokrates, advised him to put Philopœmen to death by torture, pointing out that he was a dangerous enemy, and would be peculiarly exasperated against Deinokrates if he now were to regain his freedom after having been his captive and having been insulted by him. Finally they put him into what was called the Treasury, a subterranean chamber with no window or communication with the outward air, and no door even, but closed by a great stone. There they left him, putting the great stone over the entrance, and placing a guard of armed men round it.

Meanwhile the Achæan horsemen rallied from their flight, and as Philopœmen was nowhere to be seen, they thought that he must have fallen. They remained for a long while, searching for him, and reproaching themselves with having obtained dishonourable safety by abandoning to the enemy their leader, who had laid down his life for them. Afterwards they pushed forward, inquiring everywhere for him, and at length learned that he had been captured. They at once sent the news to the various cities of the Achæan league, who took the matter greatly to heart, determined to demand Philopœmen publicly from the Messenians, and prepared for a campaign on his behalf.

XX. While they were acting thus, Deinokrates feared that delay might save Philopœmen's life. Wishing therefore to be beforehand with the Achæans, as soon as night came on, and the greater part of the Messenians had retired, he opened the prison and sent into it a public slave with a draught of poison, ordering him to stand by Philopœmen until he had drunk it. Philopœmen was lying down wrapped in his cloak, not asleep, but full of trouble and distress of mind. When he saw the light and the slave with the poison standing beside him, he, with great difficulty on account of his weakness, raised himself into a sitting posture. He then took the cup into his hand, and inquired whether he knew anything about the knights, especially about one Lykortas. When the slave answered that most of them had escaped, he nodded his head, looked kindly upon him, and answered, "You tell me good news, if we are not all unfortunate." He uttered no other word, but drank the poison and laid down again. In his weak condition he was unable to offer any resistance to the operations of the drug, and died immediately.

XXI. When the Achæan cities heard of his death, they went into a general mourning for him. The men of military age assembled at Megalopolis without delay, chose Lykortas as their leader, invaded the Messenian territory, and ravaged it until the Messenians came to their senses and made terms with the Achæans. Deinokrates escaped his merited fate by suicide, as did those who had advised that Philopœmen should be put to death, while those who had advised that he should be tortured were themselves reserved for a death of torture by Lykortas. They burned his body and collected the ashes into an urn, not carelessly, but mingling a sort of triumphal pomp with his funeral procession. There one might see men crowned with garlands but weeping at the same time, and leading along his enemies in chains. The urn itself, which was scarcely to be seen for the garlands and ribbons with which it was covered, was carried by Polybius, the son of the Achæan commander-in-chief, accompanied by the noblest of the Achæans. The soldiers followed in complete armour, with caparisoned horses, not cast down, but yet too sad to feel any pride in their victory. As they passed through the towns and villages on their way the inhabitants came out as if to welcome him on his return from a successful campaign, laid their hands on his urn, and joined in the procession to Megalopolis. When here the old men, women, and children joined them, a wail of distress ran through the whole army for the unhappy city which was mourning for its hero, and which thought itself to have lost, by his death, the first place in Greece. He was buried with great honour, as we may well believe, and round his tomb the Messenian captives wore stoned to death. Many statues were made of him, and many honours voted to him by the Greek cities, which afterwards during that unfortunate time for Greece when Corinth was destroyed, a Roman proposed to destroy, accusing Philopœmen, as if he had been yet alive, of being always an enemy to the Romans. But after Polybius had answered this contemptible fellow, neither the consul Mummius nor his lieutenants would suffer him to deface and take away the honours done in memory of so famous and worthy a man, although he had frequently offered great opposition both to Flamininus and to Manius. They distinguished properly between honour and expediency, rightly thinking that men should reward those who benefit them, but that the brave should always be honoured by all brave men. Thus much have I to tell about Philopœmen.

# Life of Titus Flamininus.

Those who wish to know what Titus Quintius Flamininus, whom we have selected as a parallel to Philopœmen, was like, may see his brazen statue in Rome, which stands beside the great statue of Apollo from Carthage, opposite to the Circus, with a Greek inscription upon it. His temper is said to have been warm, both in love and in anger, though he was ever moderate and placable in inflicting punishment, while he was never weary in conferring favours, and was always eager to help those upon whom he had bestowed some benefit, preserving and protecting them as though they were the most precious of his possessions. Being ambitious and eager to distinguish himself, he wished to take the leading part in everything, and consequently preferred those who hoped to receive to those who were able to confer favours, because the former were his assistants and the latter his rivals in the struggle for honour.

He received a military training, being born at a time when Rome was engaged in most important wars, and when young men learned how to act as officers not by theory but by actual service in the field. He first served as military tribune under the consul Marcellus in the war with Hannibal. Marcellus perished in an ambuscade, but Titus was made governor of Tarentum after its recapture, and of the surrounding territory. In this government, he won as great a reputation for justice as for courage, so that when the Romans sent colonists to the two cities of Narnia and Cossa, he was appointed to lead them and act as founder of the colonies.

II. This so elated him that he at once aspired to the consulship, passing over all the usual steps of Ædile, Tribune, or Prætor, by which young men generally rose to that office. When the day of election arrived, he appeared with a strong following of devoted partisans from those two towns. When the tribunes of the people, Fulvius and Manius, came forward and protested against a young man taking the highest office in the state by storm, contrary to the laws, and being as it were uninitiated in the very elements of the constitution, the Senate referred the matter to the votes of the people, who elected him consul together with Sextus Ælius, although he was not yet thirty years old. In casting lots for provinces the war with Philip of Macedon fell to his share, greatly to the advantage of the Romans, because in that war they needed a general who would deal with the enemy not entirely by main force, but also win them over by persuasion and diplomacy. The kingdom of Macedonia was amply sufficient for Philip, if he only fought once with the

Romans; but to maintain the cost of a long war, to supply his troops, and afford him necessary resources, the co-operation of Greece was essential to him. Unless therefore Greece could be detached from his alliance, the war could not be decided by a single battle. Greece at this time had been brought but little into contact with the Romans, who then for the first time interfered in her politics. Unless, therefore, the Roman general had been a man of high character, willing to act by diplomacy rather than by war, and combining affability of address with a strict sense of justice, the Greeks would have been unwilling to throw off their allegiance to their former masters in order to place themselves under the new and untried dominion of Rome. Of these honourable traits in Titus's character many instances will be found in his acts.

III. He learned that his predecessors, Sulpicius and Publius, had both invaded Macedonia when the season was far advanced, had begun warlike operations too late, and had failed because Philip occupied the strong places in the country and harassed them by constant attacks upon their communications and foraging parties. Flamininus did not wish to follow their example, and, after wasting a year at home in the enjoyment of the consular dignity, and in taking part in the politics of Rome, to set out late in the year to begin his campaign, although by this means he might have extended his command over two years, by acting as consul in the first, and carrying on the war as proconsul during the second. He preferred to throw the weight of his power as consul into the conduct of the war, cared not to display the insignia of his office at Rome, but obtained from the Senate the appointment of his brother Lucius to the command of the fleet which was to co-operate with him, took as the nucleus of his army three thousand of the strongest of those veterans who under Scipio had beaten Hasdrubal in Spain and Hannibal in Africa, and safely crossed over with them into Epirus. Here he found Publius, with his army, watching that of Philip, which held the passes near the river Apsus, but unable to effect anything on account of the enemy being so strongly posted. After taking over the army from Publius, whom he superseded in its command, he reconnoitred the position. Its strength is as great as that of the vale of Tempe, although it wants the lovely meadows and groves of trees for which the latter is celebrated. The river Apsus runs in a deep ravine between vast and lofty mountains, like the Peneus in appearance and swiftness, and beside it, at the foot of the mountains, runs one narrow and rocky path, along which it is difficult for an army to proceed even if unmolested, and utterly impossible if it be held by an enemy.

IV. Titus was advised by some to turn Philip's flank, marching through the Dassaretid country along the Lykus, which would offer no such difficulties;

but he feared to march far from the coast lest, like his predecessors, he should become entangled in a country which could furnish no supplies, be unable to force Philip to fight, and be obliged to retreat to the sea again from want of the means of subsistence. He determined to force his way through the mountains in front, and as these were held by Philip with his main body, the phalanx, his flanks being secured by archers and light armed troops, skirmishes took place between him and the Romans daily, with considerable loss on both sides, but without any result, until some of the natives of the country informed him of a path, neglected by the enemy, by which they undertook to lead his army, and on the third day at the latest to place it upon the heights. As a guarantee of their good faith they referred the Romans to Charops, the chief of the Epirot tribes, who was friendly to the Romans, and co-operated with them secretly, being afraid of Philip. Titus trusting in this man's word sent one of the military tribunes with four thousand infantry and three hundred cavalry. They were guided by these peasants, who were strictly guarded, and marched by night, resting by day in woods and sheltered places: for the moon was full. Titus, after he had despatched this force, rested his army, only skirmishing slightly with the enemy lest they should entertain any suspicion, until the day upon which the turning party was expected to appear on the summit of the mountain range. On that morning he got his whole force under arms, light and heavy armed alike, and dividing it into three parts himself led one body in column up to the attack of the narrowest part of the pass beside the river, while the Macedonians shot at him from above and disputed every inequality of the ground, while on his right and left the other detachments likewise vigorously attacked the position. The sun rose while they were thus engaged, and a light cloud of smoke, not distinct, but like a mountain mist, rose from the captured heights. It was unnoticed by the enemy, being behind their backs, but kept the Romans, while they fought, in a state of hopeful excitement and suspense. When however it grew thicker and blacker, and rising in a cloud proved itself without doubt to be the looked-for signal, they rushed forward with a shout and drove the enemy into their innermost places of refuge, while those on the rocks above echoed their warlike clamour.

V. A headlong flight now took place, but the enemy lost only two thousand men, for the difficulties of the ground made it hard to pursue. The Romans, however, made themselves masters of their baggage, tents, and slaves, and marched through Epirus in such an orderly and well-disciplined fashion that, although the soldiers were far from their ships, had not had their monthly allowance of provisions served out to them, and were not often near a market, they nevertheless abstained from plundering a country which was abounding in riches. Indeed Titus had learned that Philip passed through Thessaly like a fugitive, driving the inhabitants of the city to fly to the mountains for refuge, burning the cities and giving all the property which could not be carried away to his soldiers as plunder.

As Philip therefore had given up the country to the Romans, Titus besought his soldiers to march through it taking as much care of it as if it were their own. This good discipline was not long in bearing fruit; for as soon as the Romans entered Thessaly the cities surrendered themselves to Titus, while the Greeks beyond Thermopylæ were excited and eager for him to come to them, and in Peloponnesus the Achæan league threw off allegiance to Philip, and agreed to wage war against him in conjunction with the Romans. The Opuntian Lokrians also sent for Titus and delivered themselves up to him, although they had been pressed by the Ætolians, who were allies of the Romans, to allow them to take charge of their city. It is said that king Pyrrhus, when from a mountain watch-tower he first saw the Roman army drawn up in regular order, said:—"These barbarians have nothing barbarous in their military discipline." And in truth all those who met Titus were compelled to echo these words. They heard from the Macedonians that the leader of a barbarian army was coming to destroy everything and to reduce everyone to slavery: and then meeting a young and pleasant looking man, who was a thorough Greek in language and address, and a man of really noble character, they were marvellously fascinated by him, and on leaving him filled their cities with his praises, saying that at length they had found a champion for the liberties of Greece. After he had proposed to Philip, as terms of peace, that he should withdraw his garrisons and leave Greece independent, which Philip refused to do, then even those who had previously been on the side of Philip admitted that the Romans had not come to fight against the Greeks, but to fight with the Greeks against the Macedonians.

VI. The whole of Greece came to terms with him without a struggle, Thebes being the first city to send a deputation to welcome him as he peacefully marched through Bœotia. It was Brachyllus who had kept the Thebans loyal to Philip, but now they desired to show their admiration and esteem for Flamininus, being, as they imagined, on terms of amity with both parties. Titus received them with great courtesy, and walked gently forwards with them, conversing with them and asking them questions, until his soldiers, who were marching some distance behind, came up with him. Then he walked into the city in the company of the Thebans, not altogether to their satisfaction, although they did not like to attempt to keep him out, as he was accompanied by a good many soldiers. Yet, as if the town were not entirely at his mercy, he made them a speech, urging them to side with the Romans, while King Attalus spoke to the same effect, encouraging the Thebans to rally to the Roman cause. Attalus, indeed, over-exerted himself in his speech, considering his great age, and in consequence of a sudden dizziness or faintness fell down in a fit. He was shortly afterwards conveyed by sea to Asia Minor, and died there. However, the Bœotians accepted the Roman alliance.

VII. Philip now sent an embassy to Rome; and Flamininus also sent thither to beg the Senate to allow him to retain his office of consul, in case they should continue the war, or if they decided otherwise, to permit him to have the honour of concluding a peace with Philip; for his ambitious spirit could not endure to be superseded by another commander. His friends succeeded in obtaining the rejection of Philip's demands, and his own continuance in office. As soon as he received this intelligence, he started, full of hope, to attack Philip in Thessaly, with an army of more than twenty-six thousand men, of which the Ætolians supplied six thousand infantry and four hundred cavalry. The army of Philip was of nearly equal numbers, and they began to march towards one another until they both drew near the city of Skotussa, where they determined to fight a decisive battle. When the two armies found themselves so near each other they felt no fear, as one might have expected, but each was confident of victory. The Romans were eager for the honour of overcoming the Macedonians, who had gained such glory under Alexander the Great; while the Macedonians, admitting the Romans to be very different soldiers to the Persians, swelled with pride at the thought that if they could conquer them, they would prove their king Philip to be even more invincible than Alexander himself. Titus also encouraged his soldiers to quit them like men, pointing out that they were about to fight in Greece, a noble theatre in which to display deeds of daring, and against worthy antagonists; while Philip, either by chance, or not noticing what he was doing in his haste, mounted upon a large sepulchre outside his camp, and from it began to make the usual speech to his men to encourage them for the coming struggle, but at length observing the evil omen was much disheartened by it, broke off in confusion, and would not fight that day.

VIII. On the following morning about dawn, as the night had been warm and damp, the whole plain was covered with fog, and a thick mist poured down from the neighbouring hills; which rendered it impossible to distinguish any object. The parties which were sent out by each army to reconnoitre fell in with one another and fought near the place called Kynoskephalæ, that is,

Dogs' Heads, which is so named because a number of small hills near together have something of this appearance. In the combat, as usually happens in such rough ground, each side alternately had the advantage, and as each gave way they were reinforced from the respective camps. Now the fog lifted, and the two commanders resolved upon a general engagement. Philip's right wing, on which the phalanx charged down-hill with all its weight, was victorious, the Romans being unable to stand before that hedge of spears, or break through that closely-locked array of shields. But on the left the Macedonians were unable to maintain their line, because of the inequalities of the ground, and Titus, seeing that his left was hopelessly routed, rode quickly to his own right, and suddenly attacked the enemy, who, because of the uneven nature of the ground, were unable to form their phalanx with its deep ranks, in which lies the peculiar strength of that order of battle, while the soldiers of which it is composed are armed in an unwieldy fashion which renders them helpless in a hand-to-hand fight. For the Macedonian phalanx is like some huge beast of invincible strength so long as it remains one body, close locked together in serried ranks; but when broken up it loses even the advantage of each individual soldier's strength, because of the fashion in which they are armed, as they can only act together, not separately. When this body was routed some of the Romans pursued the fugitives, while others charged the victorious Macedonians in flank, soon forcing them to break up their array and fly in confusion, throwing away their arms. There fell no less than eight thousand of them, and five thousand were taken prisoners. The Ætolian cavalry were blamed for letting Philip escape, because they betook themselves to plundering the camp of the Macedonians even before the Romans ceased their pursuit, so that on their return they found that nothing had been left for them.

IX. From this there arose quarrels between the Ætolians and the Romans; and afterwards they exasperated Titus by taking to themselves the credit of the victory, and being the first to spread abroad that report among the Greeks so that they received all the honours due to victors, and were mentioned first in all the poems and ballads written about the battle. Of these, that which was most in vogue was the following:—

"Unwept, unburied, on this mountain high, Stranger, Thessalians thirty thousand lie; They fell before Ætolia's sons in war. And Romans, brought by Titus from afar. Æmathia weeps their loss. Bold Philip too, Flies like a deer, and knows not what to do."

This was written by Alkæus to insult Philip, exaggerating the number of the slain; but when it came to be repeated many times and by many men, it vexed Titus more than Philip. The latter indeed parodied it in the following lines.

"Unshaped, unpolished, stands a gibbet strong, Upon this hill to hang Alkæus on."

But Titus, who felt that the eyes of Greece were upon him, was wonderfully vexed by these incidents. For this reason he conducted the operations which followed without in the least degree consulting the Ætolians. They were angry at this neglect, and when Titus began negotiations with Philip, and received an embassy from him to treat for peace, they spread it abroad throughout Greece that Titus was being bribed by Philip into making peace, when he had it in his power to utterly cut off and destroy that power which first destroyed the independence of Greece. Philip himself however put an end to this suspicion, by placing himself and all his resources in the hands of Titus and the people of Rome. So now Titus brought the war to a close. He restored Philip to his kingdom of Macedonia, but forbade him to interfere in the affairs of Greece. He also imposed upon him a fine of a thousand talents, took away all but ten of his ships of war, and sent one of his two sons, Demetrius, to Rome as a hostage for the fulfilment of these conditions. In their making terms with Philip Titus showed himself wise and provident: for Hannibal the Carthaginian, who was at that time an exile, was already at the court of King Antiochus, urging him to follow up his good fortune and increase his empire. Antiochus had already been so successful as to have gained the surname of 'the Great,' and was now aiming at universal dominion. He especially intended to attack the Romans, and unless Titus had foreseen this, and granted favourable terms of peace, Philip would have been his ally, the two most powerful kings of the age would have been arrayed against the Romans, and a struggle no less important than that of Rome against Hannibal would have begun. As it was, Titus interposed this peace between the two wars, finishing the one before he began the other; by which means he took from one of the kings his last, and from the other his first hope.

X. The ten commissioners, whom the Senate despatched to assist Titus in settling the affairs of Greece, advised him to leave it free and independent, only keeping garrisons in Corinth, Chalkis, and Demetrias, for safety against Antiochus. Upon this the Ætolians threw off all disguise, openly urged these cities to revolt, and called upon Titus to loose the chains of Greece, as Philip was wont to call these three cities. They asked the Greeks whether they were pleased at their present bonds, which were heavier, though smoother than before; and whether they still thought Titus to be their benefactor because he had removed the fetters from the feet of Greece and fastened them round her throat. Titus was much grieved at these imputations, and at length by his representations induced the Senate to desist from its design of placing garrisons in these three cities, in order that the liberty which he was about to bestow upon Greece might be unclogged by any conditions.

When the Isthmian games were being celebrated, a great number of people were assembled in the arena witnessing the gymnastic contests, as was natural now that wars had ceased throughout Greece, and the people could attend their national festivals in safety. Proclamation was now suddenly made by the sound of a trumpet that every man should keep silence; and a herald coming forward into the midst of the assembly announced that the Senate of Rome, and Titus Quintius their consul and general, having overcome King Philip and the Macedonians, did now henceforth give liberty to the Corinthians, Lokrians, Phokians, Eubœans, Achæans of Phthia, Magnetes, Thessalians, and Perrhæbians, with exemption from garrisons and tribute, and permission to govern themselves by their hereditary laws. At first all did not clearly hear the proclamation, and there was a disorderly tumult in the assembly, as men wondered at the words, asked one another their meaning, and called upon the herald to repeat them. But when silence had again been obtained, and the herald, exerting his voice to the utmost, repeated the proclamation, such a shout was raised that it was heard as far as the sea coast, and all the spectators rose from their seats, caring nothing more for the games, but rushing with one accord to greet, with transports of delight, the saviour and protector of Greece. On this occasion was observed what is often mentioned as an example of the power of human voices; some crows, which were flying over the racecourse at that moment, fell down among the people. The reason of this is that the air is broken and cut asunder by the vehemence and strength of the voices, so as not to have its natural power to support the birds, which, fell down just as if they were flying through a place where there was no air at all; unless indeed it was the violence of the cry that struck the birds like a shot, and so caused them to fall down dead. It may be also that the air is driven round in whirlpools by such shouts, as we observe happens in violent disturbances of the sea.

XI. As for Titus, unless he had escaped betimes when the assembly broke up and rushed towards him, it is thought that he could not have survived the pressure of so great a multitude. The crowd surrounded his tent, shouting and applauding until nightfall, when they dispersed: but as they went, if they met any of their kin, their friends, or fellow-citizens, they kissed and embraced them for joy, and then supped and made merry together. We may well think that they had no other talk at the table but of the great and terrible wars which Greece had fought for her liberty, and that nevertheless she never had obtained so perfect and delightful a state of freedom as that which had been won for her by other men's labours, almost without any blood of her own being spilt. It is indeed rare to find bravery and wisdom combined in any man, but it is even rarer to find a perfectly just man. Agesilaus and Lysander, Nikias and Alkibiades knew well how to wage war and win battles both by land and by sea, but they never could make their victories yield any honourable benefit to others, or true glory to themselves. Indeed with the exception of Marathon and Salamis, Platæa and Thermopylæ, and the campaigns of Kimon on the Eurymedon and in Cyprus, all the other battles of Greece have been fought against herself, to bring about her slavery, and every trophy has been a misfortune, and a monument of shame rather than glory, arising chiefly from the rivalry between the leading cities. Yet a strange nation, from which it was inconceivable that Greece should receive any benefit, with scarcely any glimmering embers, as it were, of a common origin, had nevertheless, with great risk and hard fighting, rescued Greece from her harsh tyrants and oppressors.

XII. These were the thoughts which occupied men's minds: and the events which took place were all in conformity with the proclamation. Titus had at the same time sent Lentulus to Asia Minor to free the Bargylians, and Stertinius to Thrace to remove the garrisons of Philip from the towns and islands in that quarter, while Publius Villius set sail to treat with Antiochus about the freedom of the Greeks in his dominions. Titus himself proceeded to Chalkis, and thence he took ship for Magnesia, where he removed the foreign garrisons from the cities and re-established a democratic constitution in them. After this he was elected President of the Nemean games at Argos, where he made admirable arrangements for the conduct of the festival, and made a herald repeat his proclamation to the Greeks assembled there. He now made a progress through the cities of Greece, in which he established tranquillity and good laws, encouraged them to regard each other with good will, put an end to faction, and brought back exiles, taking no less pride in acting as counsellor and mediator to the Greeks than he did in having conquered the Macedonians, so that liberty seemed to be the least of the benefits which he had bestowed on the Greeks.

It is said that when at Athens Lykurgus the orator had rescued Xenokratos the philosopher from the tax-gatherers who were taking him to prison for non-payment of the tax upon resident aliens, and had them punished for their insolent conduct towards him, Xenokrates, afterwards meeting the sons of Lykurgus, said, "My children, I am making your father an honourable return for his kindness, he has the praises of the whole people for what he did for me." Flamininus and the Romans, however, not only obtained the praise of the Greeks in return for the benefits which they had conferred upon them, but also gained the trust and confidence of all mankind by their noble acts. Not only cities, but even kings who had been wronged by other kings came to them for redress, so that in a short space of time, with the assistance, no doubt, of the divine favour, all the world became subject to them. Flamininus especially prided himself on having liberated the Greeks, and when he dedicated at Delphi silver shields and his own Roman buckler, he wrote upon them the following verses:—

"To you, the Twins, delighting in the chase, Great Zeus's sons, of Sparta's royal race, This offering gives the Roman Titus, he Who set the children of fair Hellas free."

He also dedicated a golden wreath to Apollo, with the inscription—

"To thee, Latona's child, this chaplet fair Doth Titus, leader of Rome's army, send; The crown will well beseem thy glorious hair; Do thou the donor from all ill defend."

Indeed it was in the city of Corinth that this favour has twice been bestowed upon the Greeks, for it was in Corinth that Titus made the proclamation of which we have spoken, and Nero again, in our own time, in nearly the same manner, during the Isthmian games, declared the Greeks free and independent, except that Titus proclaimed it by means of a herald, while Nero mounted upon a platform in the market place and made the announcement himself. However, this took place long afterwards.

XIII. Titus now began a war against that most hateful and lawless of despots, Nabis of Lacedæmon, but betrayed the confidence of the Greeks; for when he had the opportunity of destroying him he would not do so, but made terms with him, leaving Sparta in a shameful bondage. Either he was afraid that if the war went on for any length of time some new commander would be sent from Rome who would gain the credit of it, or else he was jealous of the honours which were paid to Philopœmen, who was by far the greatest warrior in Greece at that period, and who surpassed himself in acts of bravery and strategy during the campaign against Nabis. The homage which was paid Philopœmen in all public assemblies by the Achæans vexed Flamininus, who felt angry that a mere Arcadian, who had gained some credit as a leader in obscure border warfare, should be treated with as much respect as the Roman consul, who was acting as the protector of all the peoples of Greece. The excuse which Titus himself made for terminating the war was that he saw that the despot could not be dethroned without causing great suffering to the other Spartans. Though the Achæans passed many decrees in his honour he cared for none of them except one gift which they bestowed upon him, which was as follows. Many of the Romans who had been taken prisoners in the war with Hannibal had been sold for slaves, and were in servitude in different countries. In Greece there were twelve hundred of them, men who were in any case much to be pitied for their misfortune, but especially now, when as may be supposed, they met their sons, brothers, and relations, who were free Roman soldiers, while they themselves were slaves. Titus, though grieved at their lot, did not take them forcibly from their owners, but the Achæans paid a ransom of five minæ for each man, collected them into one body, and just as Titus was about to set sail for home, presented them to him, so that he left the scene of his glorious labours having received an honourable reward, and one which well befitted so great and patriotic a man, besides being the most glorious ornament of his triumph: for these men of their own accord, like ordinary slaves who have been emancipated, shaved their heads, put on felt skull caps, and followed in the train at his triumph.

XIV. A more splendid spectacle was afforded by the spoils of war, the Greek helmets, Macedonian shields, and long sarissæ, or pikes used by the phalanx, which were carried along in the procession. There was also no inconsiderable sum of money, for Tuditanus tells us that in this triumph there were displayed three thousand seven hundred and thirteen pounds of gold coin, forty-three thousand two hundred and seventy pounds of silver coin, and fourteen thousand five hundred and fourteen gold coins of King Philip, besides the thousand talents which he owed. These, however, the Romans, at the instance of Flamininus, forgave him, and released his son who had been kept as a hostage for their payment.

XV. When Antiochus entered Greece with a large naval and military force, many of the Greek states joined him, especially the Ætolians, who eagerly espoused his cause because of their old quarrel with Rome. They gave out as a pretext for beginning the war, that they intended to restore freedom to the Greeks, who required nothing of the sort, being free already. This, however, was merely said because it was the most plausible excuse for their conduct, for which they could not assign any creditable reason. The Romans were much alarmed at the importance of this insurrection. They sent Manius Acilius as consul and commander-in-chief to conduct the war, and dispatched Titus Flamininus on a diplomatic mission to the cities of Greece. The mere sight of him confirmed the wavering loyalty of some of these states, while his personal influence induced many which had taken the first steps towards revolt, to return to their allegiance. Some few, however, were hopelessly lost to the

Roman cause, having been previously won over by the Ætolians; yet, vexed and exasperated as he was by their conduct, he took care, after the victory had been won, that even these should not be destroyed. Antiochus, it is well known, was defeated at Thermopylæ, and at once set sail for Asia Minor, while the consul Manius besieged some of the Ætolian strongholds himself, and arranged for others to be taken by King Philip of Macedon. But when the towns in Dolopia, Magnesia, and Aperantia were being despoiled by Philip, and the consul Manius had taken Heraklea and was besieging Naupaktus, an Ætolian fortress, Flamininus, pitying the Greeks, left Peloponnesus and sailed to the consul at Naupaktus. At first he reproached him with conquering Antiochus, and then allowing Philip to reap all the advantages of his victory, and with wasting time in besieging one city out of pique, while the Macedonians were adding tribes and kingdoms to their empire. After this, as the besieged, when they saw him, called upon him by name from the walls, and stretched out their hands to him with tears and entreaties, he made no answer to them but turned away and wept. Afterwards, however, he reasoned with Manius, and persuaded him to put aside his resentment, and to grant the Ætolians a truce, and time to send an embassy to Rome to arrange reasonable terms of peace.

XVI. He was given most trouble of all by the petitions of the Chalkidians to Manius for peace. These people were especially obnoxious to the Romans because Antiochus, at the commencement of the war, had married the daughter of a citizen of Chalkis. The match was both unseasonable in point of time, and unequal in respect of age, as he was an elderly man when he fell in love with the girl, who was the daughter of one Kleoptolemus, and is said to have been of exceeding beauty. This marriage caused the Chalkidians to become eager partizans of King Antiochus, and even to offer him their city for his headquarters during the war. After his defeat he retreated at once to Chalkis, and then, taking his bride, his treasure, and his friends with him, set sail for Asia. Manius at once marched upon Chalkis in a rage, but Flaminius accompanied him, and by his entreaties at length calmed and pacified him. The people of Chalkis, after this narrow escape, dedicated the largest and most magnificent of all their public buildings to Titus, the inscriptions on which may be read even at the present day. "The people dedicate this gymnasium to Herakles and to Titus." And on the other side of the road we read "The people dedicate the Delphinium to Apollo and to Titus." Moreover even in our own times a priest of Titus is chosen by show of hands, who offers sacrifice to him. After the libations they sing a specially-written poem, too long for quotation from which we extract the following verses:—

"Sing, maidens, sing, Of Rome's good faith that keeps its oath, And gentle
Titus full of truth, Our city's saviour, Titus and Apollo sing."

XVII. He also received honours from the Greeks at large, and that which
gives reality to honours, great goodwill from all for his kindly disposition. For
though indeed he had some slight differences with Philopœmen, and again
with Diophanes when chief of the Achæan league, he was not rancorous, and
never acted under the impulse of anger, but soon laid aside his displeasure.
He was harsh to no one, but was thought by most men to be clever and witty,
and the pleasantest of companions. When the Achæans were endeavouring
to gain for themselves the island of Zakynthus, he discouraged their enterprise
by saying that if they proceeded so far from Peloponnesus they would be in
the same danger as the tortoise when he stretches his head out beyond his
shell.

When Philip first met him to discuss terms of peace, and observed that
Titus had come with a large suite, while he was alone, Titus answered, "You
by your own act have made yourself lonely, by having killed all your friends
and relations." Once at Rome Deinokrates the Messenian got drunk and
danced in women's clothes, and on the next day begged Titus to assist him in
his design of detaching Messenia from the Achæan league. Titus answered
that he would consider the matter, but that he wondered that a man engaged
in such important designs should sing and dance over his wine. When the
ambassadors of Antiochus were telling the Achæans the number of the king's
army and were enumerating the various forces of which it was composed
under various designations, Titus remarked that when dining with his host he
had been surprised at the variety of meats, and had expressed his wonder as
to how he had been able to obtain so many different kinds; but his host
informed him that it was all nothing more than pork disguised by various
sauces and cooked in various ways. "So now," continued he, "men of Achæa,
do not be alarmed at the power of Antiochus when you hear these catalogues
of spearmen and lance-bearers and foot-guards; for they are all nothing more
than Syrians disguised with different kind of arms."

XVIII. After the pacification of Greece and the end of the war with
Antiochus, Flamininus was elected censor, which is the highest office at
Rome, and is as it were the goal of political life. His colleague was Marcellus,
the son of him that was five times consul. They ejected from the Senate four
men of no reputation, and admitted into it all the candidates who were of free
birth, being forced to do so by the tribune of the people Terentius Culeo, who
by his invectives against the patricians had induced the people to pass a
decree to that effect.

The two most prominent men in Rome at this time were Scipio Africanus and Marcus Cato. Of these Titus appointed Scipio to be President of the Senate, as being the first man in the state, but he quarrelled with Cato for the following reason. Titus had a brother, Lucius Flamininus, who was very unlike himself in disposition, being licentious in his pleasures and careless of his reputation. He had a favourite whom he always took with him even when he was in command of an army or governor of a province. This boy once at a wine party said that he was so greatly attached to Lucius, that he left a show of gladiators before he had seen a man killed, to please him. Lucius, delighted at this proof of affection, said, "That is easily remedied; I will gratify your wish." He ordered a condemned criminal to be brought, sent for the executioner, and bade him strike off the man's head in the banquetting chamber. Valerius of Antium says that Lucius did this to please a female, not a male favourite. But Livy says that in Cato's own speech on the subject we are told that Lucius, to gratify his favourite, slew with his own hand a Gaulish deserter who came with his wife and children to the door, and whom he had himself invited into the banquetting chamber. It is probable that Cato added these particulars to exaggerate the horror of the story, for Cicero the Orator, who gives the story in his book 'On Old Age,' and many other writers, say that the man was not a deserter, but a criminal, and condemned to death.

XIX. In consequence of this, Cato, when censor, removed Lucius from the Senate, although he was of consular rank, and although his degradation affected his brother as well as himself. Both of them now presented themselves before the people poorly clad and in tears, and appeared to be making a very reasonable demand in begging Cato to state the grounds upon which he had cast such ignominy upon an honourable family. Cato, however, not in the least affected by this, came forward with his colleague and publicly demanded of Titus whether he was acquainted with what happened at the banquet. When Titus answered that he knew nothing of it, Cato related the circumstances, challenging Lucius to contradict him if he spoke untruly. As Lucius remained silent, the people saw that his degradation had been deserved, and Cato retired in triumph. Titus, vexed at what had befallen his brother, now joined the party of Cato's enemies, objected to all purchases, lettings, and sales by the Senate of public property which had been made by Cato, and carried his point so far as to have them all declared void. Thus he, I cannot say justly, became the violent opponent of a legally constituted official and an excellent citizen, for the sake of a man who, though his brother, was a worthless character and had only met with his deserts. Nevertheless, on one occasion, when the Roman people were witnessing some spectacle in the theatre, the Senate, as is customary, sitting in the best place in great state, they were filled with compassion on seeing Lucius Flamininus sitting on the back benches in a mean dress, and the people became so excited that they could not restrain their cries to him to resume his former seat, until at length he did so, and was welcomed by the other consulars.

XX. The ambitious character of Titus gained him much glory, while he was in the prime of life, in the wars of which we have made mention: for after his consulship he again served in the army as military tribune; but when he retired from public life, being an elderly man, he often incurred the blame of his countrymen from his desire to distinguish himself. For instance, his conduct in regard to Hannibal made him much disliked at Rome. Hannibal after his escape from Carthage, joined king Antiochus, but when Antiochus, after his defeat in Phrygia, was glad to accept terms of peace from the Romans, he again became an exile, and after many wanderings, at length settled at the court of Prusias, king of Bithynia. Every one at Rome knew that he was there, but no one wished to meddle with him because of his age and weakness, as he appeared to be deserted by fortune. However, Titus was sent to Prusias on an embassy about certain other matters, and seeing Hannibal there took offence at his being alive, and would not accede to the prayers and entreaties of Prusias on behalf of his suppliant. There was, it seems, a certain oracle which ends with this verse:—

"Libyssa's earth shall cover Hannibal."

Now Hannibal himself took this to mean Libya, and that he should be buried at Carthage; but in Bithynia there is a shingly tract by the seashore near which is a large village named Libyssa, in which Hannibal was living. As he mistrusted the weakness of Prusias and feared the Romans, he had previously to this arranged seven ways of escape leading from his own room into different subterranean passages, all of which led into the open air by concealed apertures. When then he heard that Titus insisted upon his death he endeavoured to escape by one of those passages, but finding every outlet watched by the soldiers of Prusias he determined to die by his own hand. Some say that he destroyed himself by winding his cloak round his neck, and ordered a slave to place his knee in the small of his back and pull the cloak violently until he choked; while some tell us that he imitated Themistokles and Midas, by drinking bull's blood. Livy says that he prepared some poison which he kept by him ready for such an emergency, and that as he was about to drink it he said:—"Let us set the Roman people free from their terrible anxiety, since they think it long to wait for the death of the old man whom they hate. However, Titus will not gain a glorious victory, or one worthy of his ancestors, who sent to bid Pyrrhus beware of poison, although he was their enemy and actually at war with them."

XXI. Thus is Hannibal said to have perished. When the news was brought to the Senate many thought that Titus had acted officiously and cruelly in putting Hannibal to death, when he was living unharmed and helpless, merely in order to obtain the credit of having killed him. When they reflected upon the mildness and magnanimity of Scipio Africanus they wondered yet more, for Scipio, after vanquishing the terrible and unconquered Hannibal in Libya, did not drive him into exile, or insist upon his countrymen delivering him up. He actually met him on friendly terms before the battle, and when he made a treaty with him after his victory he did not bear himself unseemly or insult his rival's misfortune. It is related that they met again in Ephesus, and that as they walked together Hannibal took the place of honour, while Africanus walked contentedly beside him. Their conversation turned upon great generals, and when Hannibal stated his opinion that the best of generals was Alexander, next to him Pyrrhus, and next himself, Scipio, with a quiet smile, asked him: "What would you have said, if I had not conquered you?" "In that case, Scipio," answered Hannibal, "I should not have reckoned myself third but first of generals." The people remembering this cried shame upon Titus, for having laid hands upon a man whom another had slain. Some few, however, praised the deed, thinking that Hannibal, as long as he lived, was a fire which might easily be fanned into a destructive conflagration. They pointed out that even when he was in the prime of life it was not his bodily strength or personal prowess that made him so terrible to the Romans, but his intellect and skill, together with his inveterate hatred of Rome, none of which had been diminished by age, but that his natural gifts remained the same, while also fortune was wont to change, and so those who had any permanent cause of enmity with another nation were ever encouraged by hopes of success to make new attacks. Indeed subsequent events seemed to prove Titus right, as Aristonikus, the son of the harp-player, in his admiration for Eumenes, filled the whole of Asia with revolt and revolution, while Mithridates, after his tremendous losses at the hands of Sulla and Fimbria, again gathered together such great forces both by land and sea to oppose Lucullus. Yet Hannibal did not fall so low as Caius Marius. The former was to the last the friend of a king, and spent his time in sailing in ships, riding on horseback, and in the study of how to keep a military force efficient; whereas the Romans, who had laughed Marius to scorn as he wandered a beggar in Africa, soon licked the dust before him while he flogged and slaughtered them in Rome. Thus no one of our present circumstances can be said to be either important or trifling, great or small, in comparison with what is to come, but we only cease to change when we cease to exist.

For this reason some say that Titus did not effect this of his own free will, but that he was sent with Lucius Scipio as a colleague on an embassy whose sole object was the death of Hannibal. Now, as after these events we know of no other acts of Titus either as a warrior or statesman, and as he died a peaceful death, it is time to begin our comparison.

# Comparison of Philopœmen and Titus.

I. It would be impossible to compare Philopœmen, or many better men than Philopœmen, with Titus, in respect of the benefits which each conferred upon the Greeks. Philopœmen and the others were all Greeks, who fought with other Greeks, while Titus was not a Greek, and yet fought on behalf of the Greeks. When Philopœmen despaired of helping his hard-pressed follow citizens and sailed to Crete, Titus was gaining a victory in the centre of Greece, in consequence of which he bestowed freedom on Philip himself, and on all the nations and cities which had been subject to him. If one carefully examines the battles fought by each commander, it will appear that Philopœmen killed more Greeks when he was general of the Achæans than Titus killed Macedonians when he was fighting for Greece. The faults of the one arose from ambition, those of the other from party spirit; the latter was easily moved to anger, the former hard to appease. Titus preserved for Philip the semblance of royal power, and treated even the Ætolians with indulgence, while Philopœmen in his anger detached the confederation of villages from his native city. Moreover, Titus was always a friend to those whom he had once befriended, while Philopœmen's kindly feelings were easily overruled by passion. Indeed he appears to have sacrificed his life to rage and bitter personal rancour, by invading Messenia before anything was ready, without showing any of the prudent caution of Titus in military matters.

II. The fame of Philopœmen's skill as a general, however, rests on a more secure basis, the number of his battles and trophies of victory. Flamininus decided his campaign against Philip by two battles, but Philopœmen fought innumerable battles, and never let it be supposed that he owed more to fortune than to skill. Moreover, Titus had at his disposal the resources of Rome, then in the zenith of her strength, while Philopœmen had the glory of performing his greatest exploits at a time when Greece was in her decadence, so that his work was all his own, while the glory of the Roman must be shared with his countrymen. The one was the leader of good soldiers, but the other by his leadership made good soldiers. That his conflicts were all against Greeks was unfortunate, but gives a strong proof of his powers; for among men who are alike in other respects, victory must be won by sheer courage. He fought the most warlike of the Greeks, the Cretans and the Lacedæmonians, the first of whom are the most deeply versed in stratagem, while the latter are most renowned for bravery, and overcame them both. In addition to this it must be remembered that Titus found his materials ready for use, as he received the arms and disciplined troops of his predecessor, while Philopœmen himself introduced a new method of armament and discipline; so that the one was obliged to discover the means of obtaining victory, while the other had only to use them. Philopœmen too did many great feats in hand to hand fight, whereas Titus did nothing, for which one of the Ætolians, Archedemus, jeered at him, saying that while he himself was running sword in hand to attack the Macedonian phalanx, Titus was standing still and raising his hands to heaven in prayer to the gods.

III. Nevertheless Titus both as a general and an ambassador always met with complete success, while Philopœmen acted as vigorously and successfully on behalf of the Achæans when in a private station as when he was their general. It was as a private citizen that he drove Nabis out of Messene and liberated the Messenians, and as a private citizen he shut the gates of Sparta against Diophanes the Achæan general and Titus himself when they were on their march against it, and so saved the Lacedæmonians from destruction. Thus, having the true spirit of a commander, he knew when to obey and when to override the laws, acting according to them when it was fitting to do so, but holding him to be the true general who upheld the spirit of the laws without being fettered by them. The kindly treatment of the Greeks by Titus was honourable to him, but the sturdy spirit of independence which Philopœmen showed towards the Romans was still more honourable, because it is much easier to grant a request to suppliants, than to irritate those who are more powerful by opposing them. Since, then, it is difficult to distinguish their respective merits by comparison, let us see whether we shall not decide best between them by assigning the palm for military and soldier-like qualities to Greek, and to the Roman that for justice and goodness of heart.

# Life of Pyrrhus.

I. Historians tell us that after the flood the first king of the Thesprotians and Molossians was Phæthon, who was one of those who came into Epirus under Pelasgus; while some say that Deukalion and Pyrrha after founding the temple at Dodona lived there in the country of the Molossians. In later times Neoptolemus, the son of Achilles, brought an army thither, obtained possession of the country, and founded a dynasty of kings, who were named after him the sons of Pyrrhus: for Pyrrhus was his own nickname as a child, and he also gave the name of Pyrrhus to one of his children by his wife Lanassa, the daughter of Kleodæus, who was the son of Hyllus. From this period Achilles has been honoured like a god in Epirus and is called Aspetus in the dialect of the country. After the earliest kings, the dynasty sunk into barbarism, and ceased to attract attention from its weakness and obscurity. Of those of later days, Tharrhypas was the first of those who made himself famous. He adopted the customs and letters of Greece, and gave just laws to his country. Tharrhypas was the father of Alketas, who was the father of Arybas, who married Troas and by her became the father of Æakides. This man married Phthia the daughter of Menon of Thessaly, who had gained great distinction in the Lamian war, and who yielded in reputation to no one except to Leosthenes himself. By Phthia Æakides had two daughters, Deidameia and Troas, and one son, Pyrrhus.

II. When the Molossians revolted, drove out their king Æakides, and invited back the children of Neoptolemus to the kingdom, the friends of Æakides were seized and put to death, but Androkleides and Angelus stole away Pyrrhus, who was still an infant and was being searched for by his enemies. They took with them some wet nurses for the child and some few other servants, but finding their flight impeded by them, they entrusted the child to Androkleion, Hippias, and Neander, strong and trusty young men, bidding them hurry on with what speed they might, and get to Megara, a fort belonging to the Macedonians, while they themselves, partly by entreaties and partly by fighting, managed to delay the pursuers till late in the evening. The enemy, after making their way through these men with some difficulty, pursued those who were carrying off Pyrrhus. The sun had now set, and the fugitives had begun to hope that they would soon be safe, when they were filled with despair by meeting with the river which runs past the fort, a wild torrent which they found it impossible to cross, as the stream was swollen with recent rains, and appeared all the more terrible because of the darkness.

They decided that they never could convey the child and his nurses across by their own exertions, but observing several of the inhabitants standing upon the further bank they besought them to assist their passage, and they showed Pyrrhus to them, crying aloud and holding out their hands to entreat for help. The men could not hear what they said because of the roaring of the water, and much time was wasted in vain clamouring until one of the fugitives, perceiving this, wrote with the tongue of a brooch upon a piece of oak bark a few words explaining who the child was, and in what danger, wrapped the piece of bark round a stone to steady its flight, and threw it across. Some say that they fastened the bark to a javelin and so hurled it across. When the men on the further bank read the letter, and perceived in what imminent peril the fugitives were, they cut down some trees, formed a raft, and so crossed over. It chanced that the first man who crossed and received Pyrrhus into his arms was named Achilles: the rest of the fugitives were ferried over by his companions.

III. Having thus escaped from their pursuers they proceeded to Glaukias, the king of the Illyrians. They found him sitting at home with his wife, and they laid the child on the ground between them. The king was full of thought, for he feared Kassander, the mortal enemy of Æakides, and he remained silent for a long time. Meanwhile Pyrrhus of his own accord crawled up to Glaukias, took hold of his cloak and then stood up at his knees, causing the king first to smile and then to feel pity for him, as he stood like a suppliant holding his knees and weeping. Some say that he did not embrace Glaukias, but that he laid hold of an altar and stood, putting his hands round it, so that Glaukias thought that he must be acting under some divine impulse. In consequence of this he at once gave Pyrrhus in charge to his wife, bidding her bring him up with her own children. Shortly after, when his enemies demanded that he should be given up, and Kassander even offered two hundred talents, Glaukias refused to betray him, and when he was twelve years of age he marched into Epirus with an army and restored him to the throne.

The appearance of Pyrrhus was more calculated to strike terror into the beholder than to impress him with an idea of the dignity which becomes a king. He had not a number of separate teeth, but one continuous bone in his upper jaw, with only slight lines showing the divisions between the teeth. He was thought to be able to cure diseases of the spleen by sacrificing a white cock, and then gently pressing with his right foot in the region of the spleen of the sufferer, who lay upon his back meanwhile. No man was so poor or despised that Pyrrhus would not touch him for this disorder if requested to do so. He also received, as a reward, the cock which was sacrificed, and was much pleased with this present. It is said that the great toe of that foot had some divine virtue, so that when the rest of his body was burned after his death, it was found unhurt and untouched by the fire. But of this hereafter.

IV. When he was about seventeen years of age, and appeared to be firmly established upon his throne, he chanced to leave the country to attend the wedding of one of the sons of Glaukias, with whom he had been brought up. The Molossians now again rose in revolt, drove out his friends, sacked the treasury, and made Neoptolemus their king. Pyrrhus having thus lost his kingdom, and being entirely destitute, fled for refuge to Demetrius, the son of Antigonus, who had married his sister Deidameia. When a young girl Deidameia had been nominally the wife of Alexander, the son of Roxana, but after the misfortunes of that family Demetrius had married her when she came of age. In the great battle of Ipsus, in which all the successors of Alexander the Great took part, Pyrrhus, while yet a youth, served with the forces of Demetrius, routed those who opposed him, and gained great distinction. He did not desert Demetrius after his defeat, but was entrusted with the care of those cities which Demetrius possessed in Greece, and kept them faithful to his cause. When he made a treaty with Ptolemy, Pyrrhus was sent to Egypt as a hostage, where he hunted and practised gymnastics with Ptolemy, showing great bodily strength and endurance. Observing that Berenike was the most powerful and intelligent of Ptolemy's wives, he paid especial court to her, and, as he knew well how to gain the favour of the powerful, though he was inclined to domineer over his inferiors, and was temperate and well-behaved, he was chosen out of many other noble youths to be the husband of Antigone, one of the daughters of Berenike, whom she bore to Philip before she married Ptolemy.

V. His influence was greatly increased by this match, and, as Antigone proved a good wife to him and furthered his designs, he prevailed upon his friends to supply him with money and troops, and send him upon an expedition to recover his throne in Epirus. When he landed, many of the people of the country were willing to accept him as their king, because of their dislike to the ferocious and arbitrary rule of Neoptolemus; but he, fearing that if he drove out his rival he would apply to some of the kings, made terms and friendship with him, and agreed to share the kingdom. As time went on, however, many encouraged him to attack Neoptolemus, and fomented suspicion between them. Pyrrhus, however, was especially exasperated by the following incidents. It was customary for the kings of Epirus to sacrifice to Zeus Areios in Passaron, a place in the Molossian country, and to take an oath to their subjects that they would govern according to the laws, while the people on their part swore to be faithful to the throne. These ceremonies were performed by both the kings, who, with their friends, afterwards conversed together, giving and receiving presents. Now Gelon, a trusty friend of Neoptolemus, after giving Pyrrhus a friendly welcome, presented to him two yoke of oxen for the plough. Myrtilus, the cupbearer, who was present, asked Pyrrhus for these oxen, and as Pyrrhus did not give them to him but to some one else, he did not conceal his annoyance, which was observed by Gelon. He at once invited Myrtilus to dinner and proposed to him that he should join the party of Neoptolemus and remove Pyrrhus by poison. Myrtilus apparently acquiesced, and accepted the offer, but told the whole intrigue to Pyrrhus, who bade him put Alexikrates, his chief cupbearer, also in communication with Gelon, on the pretence that he too wished to take part in the plot; for he wished as many persons as possible to know of the attempt which was about to be made. Thus Gelon was deceived, and in turn deceived Neoptolemus, who, imagining his plot to be on the point of success, could not restrain his delight, but let out the secret to his friends. On one occasion, when in his cups, he talked freely about this matter to his sister Kadmeia, not imagining that any one else heard him; for there was no one present except Phænarete, the wife of Samon the king's neatherd, and she lay upon a couch with her face towards the wall, apparently asleep. However she heard all that passed, unsuspected, and next day went to Antigone, the wife of Pyrrhus, and told her all that she had heard Neoptolemus say to his sister. When Pyrrhus heard this he did not act at once; but when next he offered sacrifice he invited Neoptolemus to dinner and killed him, as he knew that the strongest party in Epirus was on his side, and had often urged him to rid himself of Neoptolemus and not be satisfied with a mere share of the crown, but to engage in the great designs which his genius prompted. These considerations, together with the suspicions which he had of Neoptolemus's treachery, induced him to be beforehand with him by putting him to death.

VI. In memory of Berenike and Ptolemy he named a boy who was now born to him Ptolemy, and gave the name of Berenike to a city which he founded on the peninsula of Epirus. He now began to revolve great designs, casting his eyes especially upon the territory of his neighbours; and he was soon enabled to interfere in the affairs of Macedonia on the following grounds. The elder of the sons of Kassander put his mother, Thessalonika, to death, and drove his younger brother Alexander into exile. This prince now applied both to Demetrius and to Pyrrhus for aid. Demetrius was engaged in other matters and was slow to render him any assistance, but Pyrrhus offered his services, demanding as the price of his assistance the districts called Stymphæa and Paranæa in Macedon itself, and of the Macedonian conquests Ambrakia, Akarnania, and Amphilochia. The youth agreed to these terms, and Pyrrhus at once occupied those countries, which he secured by garrisoning their fortresses, while he began to press Antipater hard in his endeavours to gain the remainder of Macedonia for his brother. At this time king Lysimachus, an eager partisan of Antipater, was too much occupied with other matters to send him any material help, but, knowing that Pyrrhus would never disoblige or thwart Ptolemy in anything, sent a forged letter to him, in which it was stated to be Ptolemy's desire that he should withdraw his forces on the receipt of three hundred talents from Antipater. Pyrrhus, however, as soon as he opened the letter saw the deceit; for it did not begin with Ptolemy's usual greeting to him, "The father to the son wishes health" but "King Ptolemy to king Pyrrhus wishes health." He reproached Lysimachus for his conduct, but nevertheless made a peace, which they all met to ratify by a solemn oath upon a sacrifice. A bull, a boar, and a ram were brought to the altar, when suddenly the ram fell down dead. The others laughed at this, but the soothsayer Theodotus, who was conducting the sacrifice forbad Pyrrhus to swear, saying that Heaven by this portended the death of one of the three kings who were there met together. Pyrrhus therefore refused to ratify the peace.

VII. Alexander now was in a fair way to succeed, when he was joined by Demetrius, who was evidently unwelcome, and a dangerous ally. Before many days had passed the two princes, from mutual distrust, began to plot against each other. Demetrius, seizing his opportunity, assassinated the youthful Alexander, and proclaimed himself king of Macedonia. He had before this been on bad terms with Pyrrhus, who had made incursions into Thessaly, and the usual disease of princes, grasping covetousness, had made them suspicious and quarrelsome neighbours, especially since the death of Deidameia. Now, however, as they both claimed Macedonia, they were brought into direct collision, and Demetrius, after mating a campaign in Ætolia and leaving Pantauchus with a large force to guard his conquests there, himself marched against Pyrrhus. Pyrrhus, as soon as he heard of this, proceeded to meet him, but by a mistake in the road they passed by one another, so that Demetrius invaded Epirus and ravaged the country there, and Pyrrhus, falling in with Pantauchus, fought a battle with him. The struggle was a long and severe one, especially near where the generals fought, for Pantauchus, who was admitted to be the strongest and bravest of the generals of Demetrius, in the pride of his heart challenged Pyrrhus to a single combat, while Pyrrhus, who yielded to none of the kings of the age in strength and courage, and who wished to be thought a true son of Achilles by valour as well as by descent, rushed forward beyond the front ranks to meet Pantauchus. They fought with spears at first, and then, drawing their swords, contended hand to hand with equal skill and courage. Pyrrhus received one hurt, but he wounded Pantauchus in the thigh and in the throat, and overthrew him. Pyrrhus did not slay him, however, as he was rescued by his friends. The Epirots, elated at their king's victory, and filled with enthusiasm by his courage, bore everything before them, routed the phalanx of the Macedonians, and pursued the fugitives, of whom they slew many and took five thousand prisoners.

VIII. The Macedonians who had witnessed the exploits of Pyrrhus were struck with admiration, and perhaps found some solace for their defeat in the praises they bestowed on the conqueror. He was, they said, indeed a soldier, worthy to command soldiers; the only king of the age in whom there could be traced any likeness to the great Alexander. Pyrrhus revived this image by the fire and vigour of his movements in the field of battle; the rest only mimicked the hero, whose title they assumed, in their demeanour, and in the trappings and state of royalty. We can form an opinion about his knowledge and skill in military matters from the writings which he has left on these subjects. It is related, moreover, that Antigonus, when asked who was the greatest of generals, answered "Pyrrhus, if he lives to be old," speaking only of the generals of his own time. Hannibal, however, considered Pyrrhus to have been the first general that ever lived for skill and resource, placing Scipio next, and himself third, as is written in the Life of Scipio. Indeed Pyrrhus devoted the whole of his intellect to the art of war, regarding it as the only study fit for a king, and holding all other occupations to be frivolous. At a wine party he was once asked whether he thought Python or Kaphisias the better flute player, to which he answered that Polysperchon was the best general, as though that were the only subject on which a king should form or express an opinion. Yet he was mild-tempered and gentle towards his friends, full of gratitude for kindness, and eager to repay it. He grieved greatly over the death of Æropus; not so much because he was dead, for that, he said, was the common lot of mankind, but because he himself had delayed repaying him a kindness until it was too late. Debts of money, he said, can be paid to the heirs of a creditor, but men of honour are grieved at not being able to return a kindness during the lifetime of their benefactor. In Ambrakia once Pyrrhus was advised to banish a man who abused him in scurrilous terms. He answered, "I had rather he remained where he is and abused me there, than that he should wander through all the world doing so." Once some youths spoke ill of him over their wine, and being detected were asked by him whether they had used such words of him. "We did, O king," answered one of the young men, "and we should have said more evil of you if we had had more wine." At this answer Pyrrhus laughed, and acquitted them.

IX. After the death of Antigone he married several wives, for the sake of advantageous political alliances. One was the daughter of Autoleon, king of the Pæonians; another was Birkenna, daughter of Bardyllis, king of the Illyrians, while the third, Lanassa, daughter of Agathokles, despot of Syracuse, brought him as a dowry the city and island of Korkyra, which had been captured by Agathokles. By Antigone he had already one son, Ptolemy; by Lanassa he had another son, Alexander, and Helenus, the youngest of his sons, by Birkenna. They were all brought up to be good soldiers, being trained in arms by Pyrrhus himself. It is said that when one of his sons, while yet a child, asked him to which of them he would leave his kingdom, he answered "To him whose sword is the sharpest." This saying differs but little from that celebrated tragic curse upon the brothers who were to "divide their heritage with whetted steel." So savage and unsocial a quality is ambition.

X. After this battle Pyrrhus returned home, delighted at the glory which he had acquired. When the Epirotes gave him the title of the Eagle, he answered "I owe it to you that I am an eagle, for it is your arms that enable me to take so high a flight." Shortly afterwards, learning that Demetrius was dangerously ill, he suddenly invaded Macedonia, meaning merely to make a short incursion, but he very nearly obtained possession of the entire kingdom, as he overran the country without opposition and marched as far as Edessa, while many of the natives assisted him and joined his army. The danger roused Demetrius from his sick bed, and his partisans hastily collected a considerable force and marched to attack Pyrrhus. As he had only come with the intention of plundering he avoided giving battle and retreated, but on his way lost a part of his army by an attack of the Macedonians.

Demetrius, though he had thus easily driven Pyrrhus out of his kingdom, did not despise him. He had determined to go to war on a great scale to recover his father's throne, with a force of a hundred thousand men and five hundred ships of war; and he did not wish to be thwarted in this design by Pyrrhus, or to leave him as a fierce and dangerous neighbour for Macedonia. Consequently, as he had no leisure to go to war with him, he wished to come to terms with him and make peace, so that he might be at liberty to attack the other kings. These considerations led him to conclude a truce with Pyrrhus. However, the greatness of the force at Demetrius's disposal now led him to assume such an arrogant tone that the other kings were alarmed and sent letters to Pyrrhus in which they expressed their surprise that he should overlook the magnificent opportunity which Demetrius would offer him by engaging in a foreign war, and asked him whether, when he was able to drive that restless intriguer out of Macedonia, he intended not to do so, but to sit idle at home while Demetrius gained wealth and power, until at length he would have to fight for his hearth and home in Molossia, and that too when Demetrius had just deprived him of Korkyra by means of his wife. For Lanassa had quarrelled with Pyrrhus because he paid too much attention to his barbarian wives, had retired to Korkyra, and, as she still wished to be a queen, invited Demetrius to take possession of her person and of the island. He at once proceeded thither, married Lanassa, and placed a garrison in the city.

XI. Besides writing to Pyrrhus in this strain the kings themselves contrived to find work for Demetrius, who was still engaged in preparations for his campaign. Ptolemy sailed to Greece with a large force and induced many of the Greek cities to revolt from Demetrius, while Lysimachus, starting from Thrace, invaded and plundered Upper Macedonia. At the same time Pyrrhus marched upon the city of Berœa, truly conjecturing that Demetrius, in his haste to repel the invasion of Upper Macedonia, would leave the lower part of the country unprotected. That night he dreamed that he was called by Alexander the Great, and that he at once went to him, and found him reclining on a couch. The hero received him kindly, and promised him that he would aid him. When Pyrrhus mustered courage to ask, "How, O king, being yourself ill, can you assist me?" Alexander answered, "With my name," and mounting a Nisæan horse appeared to lead the way. This dream gave Pyrrhus great confidence: he quickly marched over the intervening country and took Berœa, where he fixed his headquarters, and sent out detachments to reduce other places. Demetrius, when he heard this news, and heard also the tumult of grief and indignation which it excited in his camp, feared to march any closer to Lysimachus, lest if his army came near to a king who was a Macedonian, and so distinguished a man, the troops might transfer their allegiance to him. He therefore resolved to retrace his steps, and attack Pyrrhus, as being a foreigner, and an enemy of the Macedonians. However, when he pitched his camp near Berœa, many came out from that city loudly praising Pyrrhus, as an invincible warrior and a great man, who had treated the vanquished with kindness and magnanimity. Some of these were emissaries of Pyrrhus himself, disguised as Macedonians, who said that now was the time for them to relieve themselves from the harsh tyranny of Demetrius by adopting Pyrrhus, a popular man and a true friend of the soldier, as their king. The greater part of Demetrius's troops was much excited by this means, and when the two armies met face to face, all eyes were turned in search of the hero. For a time they could not find him, for he had taken off his helmet; but when he had put it on again, and enabled them to recognise him by the lofty crest, and the goat's horns at the sides, the Macedonian soldiers quitted their ranks, and came running up to ask him, as their chief, for the pass-word. Others, seeing that his attendants wore garlands of oak-leaves, crowned themselves in like manner. Some already ventured to tell Demetrius that his best course would be to give up all as lost: and he, observing, that this advice seemed to be borne out by the temper of his army, withdrew in terror, disguised in a mean dress, and a broad-brimmed Macedonian hat. Pyrrhus, advancing without striking a blow, obtained possession of his enemy's camp, and was saluted king of the Macedonians.

XII. Lysimachus soon appeared upon the scene, pointed out that the fall of Demetrius was as much due to his own exertions as to those of Pyrrhus, and demanded a partition of Macedonia. To this Pyrrhus, not yet certain of the loyalty of his new subjects, was obliged to consent. This measure was beneficial for the moment, as it prevented their going to war; but soon it became apparent that the partition was a source of endless quarrels and recriminations. For when men are ambitious to such a degree that no seas, mountains, or wildernesses, nay not even the boundaries of Europe and Asia, will serve as barriers to their frantic desire for more territory, it is not to be expected that they will remain quiet when their frontiers touch one another, but they always are at war, from the natural jealousy of their disposition. The names of peace and war they use as mere symbols, as it suits their convenience, and they are really better men when they are openly at war than when they give the name of peace and friendship to a cessation of active wickedness. The truth of this was proved by Pyrrhus, who in order to prevent Demetrius from recovering from the great disaster which he had sustained, espoused the cause of Greece, and marched to Athens. Here he went up to the Acropolis and sacrificed to the goddess Athena. On descending he thanked the Athenians for their confidence in him, but advised them if they consulted their own interest never to admit any king within their walls. After this he made peace with Demetrius, but shortly after he was gone to Asia, Pyrrhus, at the instigation of Lysimachus, induced the Thessalians to revolt and join him, and began to besiege the fortresses on the Greek border, both because he found the Macedonians easier to manage when they were at war than when they were idle, and also because he himself was of a nature which could not endure inaction. Finally however Demetrius was irretrievably ruined in Syria, and now Lysimachus, having nothing further to fear from him, at once attacked Pyrrhus. He fell upon him suddenly near Edessa, defeated him, and reduced the troops under him to great distress for provisions. Next he began to corrupt the leading Macedonians, reproaching them with having rejected a Macedonian who had been the friend and companion of Alexander, and chosen in his stead as their master a foreigner, and one, too, of a race that had always been subject to the Macedonians. As many listened to these treacherous insinuations, Pyrrhus became alarmed, and withdrew with his Epirotes and the allied troops, thus losing Macedonia in the same way that he had gained it. So that kings have but little reason for reproaching the common people for changing sides in an emergency, for in doing so they do but imitate the kings themselves, their teachers in the art of treachery and faithlessness, who think that those men gain the greatest advantages who take least account of justice and honour.

XIII. Pyrrhus, now that he had lost Macedonia, might have spent his days peacefully ruling his own subjects in Epirus; but he could not endure repose, thinking that not to trouble others and be troubled by them was a life of unbearable ennui, and, like Achilles in the Iliad,
"he could not rest in indolence at home, He longed for battle, and the joys of war."

As he desired some new adventures he embraced the following opportunity. The Romans were at war with the Tarentines; and as that people were not sufficiently powerful to carry on the war, and yet were not allowed by the audacious folly of their mob orators to make peace, they proposed to make Pyrrhus their leader and to invite him to be their ally in the war, because he was more at leisure than any of the other kings, and also was the best general of them all. Of the older and more sensible citizens some endeavoured to oppose this fatal decision, but were overwhelmed by the clamour of the war party, while the rest, observing this, ceased to attend the public assembly. There was one citizen of good repute, named Meton, who, on the day when the final decision was to be made, when the people were all assembled, took a withered garland and a torch, like a drunkard, and reeled into the assembly with a girl playing the flute before him. At this, as one may expect in a disorderly popular meeting, some applauded, and some laughed, but no one stopped him. They next bade the girl play, and Meton come forward and dance to the music; and he made as though he would do so. When he had obtained silence he said "Men of Tarentum, you do well in encouraging those who wish to be merry and amuse themselves while they may. If you are wise you will all enjoy your freedom now, for when Pyrrhus is come to our city you will have very different things to think of, and will live very differently." By these words he made an impression on the mass of the Tarentine people, and a murmur ran through the crowd that he had spoken well. But those politicians who feared that if peace were made they should be delivered up to the Romans, reproached the people for allowing any one to insult them by such a disgraceful exhibition, and prevailed on them to turn Meton out of the assembly. Thus the vote for war was passed, and ambassadors were sent to Epirus, not from Tarentum alone, but from the other Greek cities in Italy, carrying with them presents for Pyrrhus, with instructions to tell him that they required a leader of skill and renown, and that they possessed a force of Lucanians, Messapians, Samnites and Tarentines, which amounted to twenty thousand cavalry, and three hundred and fifty thousand infantry. This not only excited Pyrrhus, but also made all the Epirotes eager to take part in the campaign.

XIV. There was one Kineas, a Thessalian, who was thought to be a man of good sense, and who, having heard Demosthenes the orator speak, was better able than any of the speakers of his age to delight his hearers with an imitation of the eloquence of that great master of rhetoric. He was now in the service of Pyrrhus, and being sent about to various cities, proved the truth of the Euripidean saw, that

"All can be done by words Which foemen wish to do with conquering swords."

Pyrrhus at any rate used to say that more cities were won for him by Kineas with words, than be himself won by force of arms. This man, observing that Pyrrhus was eagerly preparing for his Italian expedition, once when he was at leisure conversed with him in the following manner. "Pyrrhus," said he, "the Romans are said to be good soldiers, and to rule over many warlike nations. Now, if heaven grants us the victory over them, what use shall we make of it?"

"You ask what is self-evident," answered Pyrrhus. "If we can conquer the Romans, there is no city, Greek or barbarian, that can resist us, and we shall gain possession of the whole of Italy, a country whose size, richness, and power no one knows better than yourself." Kineas then, after waiting for a short time, said, "O king, when we have taken Italy, what shall we do then?" Pyrrhus, not yet seeing his drift, answered, "Close to it Sicily invites us, a noble and populous island, and one which is very easy to conquer; for, my Kineas, now that Agathokles is dead, there is nothing there but revolution and faction, and the violence of party spirit." "What you say," answered Kineas, "is very probably true. But is this conquest of Sicily to be the extreme limit of our campaign?" "Heaven," answered Pyrrhus, "alone can give us victory and success; but these conquests would merely prove to us the stepping-stones to greater things. Who could refrain from making an attempt upon Carthage and Libya when he was so close to them, countries which were all but conquered by Agathokles when he ran away from Syracuse with only a few ships? and if we were masters of these countries, none of the enemies who now give themselves such airs at our expense will dare to resist us." "Certainly not," answered Kineas; "With such a force at our disposal we clearly could recover Macedonia, and have the whole of Greece at our feet. And after we have made all these conquests, what shall we do then?" Pyrrhus laughing answered, "We will take our ease and carouse every day, and enjoy pleasant conversation with one another." Having brought Pyrrhus to say this, Kineas asked in reply, "But what prevents our carousing and taking our ease now, since we have already at hand all those things which we propose to obtain with much blood-shed, and great toils and perils, and after suffering much ourselves and causing much suffering to others?" By talking in this manner Kineas vexed Pyrrhus, because he made him reflect on the pleasant home which he was leaving, but his reasoning had no effect in turning him from his purpose.

XV. He first despatched Kineas to Tarentum with three thousand men; next he collected from Tarentum many horse-transports, decked vessels, and boats of all sorts, and embarked upon them twenty elephants, twenty-three thousand cavalry, twenty-two thousand infantry, and five hundred slingers. When all was ready he put to sea; and when half way across a storm burst upon him from the north, which was unusual at that season of the year. He himself, though his ship was carried away by the tempest, yet, by the great pains and skill of the sailors and pilots, resisted it and reached the land, with great toil to the rowers, and beyond everyone's expectation; for the rest of the fleet was overpowered by the gale and scattered. Some ships were driven off the Italian coast altogether, and forced into the Libyan and Sicilian seas, and some which could not weather the Iapygian Cape were overtaken by night, and being dashed by a violent and boisterous sea against that harbourless coast were utterly lost, except only the king's ship. She was so large and strongly built as to resist the waves as long as they broke upon her from the seaward; but when the wind changed and blew directly off the shore, the ship, which now met the waves directly with her head, was in great danger of going to pieces, while to let her drive out to sea again now that it was so rough, and the wind changed so frequently, seemed more terrible than to remain where they were. Pyrrhus rose and leapt into the water, and at once was eagerly followed by his friends and his body-guard. The darkness of night and the violent recoil of the roaring waves made it hard for them to help him, and it was not until daybreak, when the wind abated, that he reached the land, faint and helpless in body, but with his spirit invincible in misfortune. The Messapians, upon whose coast he had been thrown, now assembled from the neighbouring villages and offered their help, while some of the ships which had outlived the storm appeared, bringing a few horsemen, about two thousand foot, and two elephants.

XVI. With these Pyrrhus marched to Tarentum; Kineas, as soon as he heard of his arrival, bringing out the Tarentine army to meet him. When he reached the city he did nothing to displease the Tarentines until his fleet returned to the coast and he had assembled the greater part of his army. But then, as he saw that the populace, unless ruled by a strong hand, could neither help him nor help themselves, but intended to stay idling about their baths and entertainments at home, while he fought their battles in the field, he closed the gymnasia and public walks, in which the people were wont to waste their time in empty talk about the war. He forbade all drinking, feasting, and unseasonable revels, and forced the people to take up arms, proving himself inexorable to every one who was on the muster-roll of able-bodied citizens. This conduct made him much disliked, and many of the Tarentines left the city in disgust; for they were so unused to discipline, that they considered that not to be able to pass their lives as they chose was no better than slavery.

When news came that Lævinus, the Roman consul, was marching to attack him with a large force, and was plundering the country of Lucania as he advanced, while Pyrrhus's allies had not yet arrived, he thought it a shameful thing to allow the enemy to proceed any farther, and marched out with his army. He sent before him a herald to the Roman general, informing him that he was willing to act as arbitrator in the dispute between the Romans and the Greek cities of Italy, if they chose to terminate it peacefully. On receiving for an answer that the Romans neither wished for Pyrrhus as an arbitrator, nor feared him as an enemy, he marched forward, and encamped in the plain, between the city of Pandosia and Heraklea. Learning that the Romans were close by, and were encamping on the farther side of the river Siris he rode up to the river to view them; and when he observed their even ranks, their orderly movements, and their well-arranged camp, he was surprised, and said to the nearest of his friends: "These barbarians, Megakles, have nothing barbarous in their military discipline; but we shall soon learn what they can do." He began indeed already to feel some uncertainty as to the issue of the campaign, and determined to wait until his allies came up, and till then to observe the movements of the Romans, and prevent their crossing the river.

They however, perceiving his object, at once crossed the river, the infantry at a ford, the cavalry at many points at once, so that the Greeks feared they might be surrounded, and drew back. Pyrrhus, perceiving this, ordered his officers instantly to form the troops in order of battle and wait under arms while he himself charged with the cavalry, three thousand strong, hoping to catch the Romans in the act of crossing the river and consequently in disorder. When he saw many shields of the Roman infantry appearing over the river bank, and their horsemen all ranged in order, he closed up his own ranks and charged them first himself, a conspicuous figure in his beautiful glittering armour, and proving by his exploits that he deserved his high reputation; especially as, although he fought personally, and engaged in combat with the enemy, yet he continually watched the whole battle, and handled his troops with as much facility as though he were not in the thick of the fight, appearing always wherever his presence was required, and reinforcing those who seemed likely to give way. In this battle Leonnatus the Macedonian observing one of the Italians watching Pyrrhus and constantly following him about the field, said to him, "My king, do you see that barbarian on the black horse with white feet? He seems to be meditating some desperate deed. He is a man of spirit and courage, and he never takes his eyes off you, and takes no notice of any one else. Beware of that man." Pyrrhus answered, "Leonnatus, no man can avoid his fate; but neither that Italian nor any one else who attacks me will do so with impunity." While they were yet talking the Italian levelled his lance, and urged his horse in full career against Pyrrhus. He struck the king's horse with his spear, and at the same instant his own horse was struck a sidelong blow by Leonnatus. Both horses fell; Pyrrhus was saved by his friends, and the Italian perished fighting. He was of the nation of the Frentani, Hoplacus by name, and was the captain of a troop of horse.

XVII. This incident taught Pyrrhus to be more cautious. He observed that his cavalry were inclined to give way, and therefore sent for his phalanx, and arrayed it against the enemy. Then he gave his cloak and armour to one of his companions, Megakles, and after partially disguising himself in those of his friend, led his main body to attack the Roman army. The Romans stoutly resisted him, and an obstinate battle took place, for it is said that the combatants alternately yielded and again pressed forward no less than seven distinct times. The king's exchange of armour too, though it saved his life, yet very nearly lost him the victory: for many attacked Megakles, and the man who first struck him down, who was named Decius, snatched up his cloak and helmet, and rode with them to Lævinus, displaying them and shouting aloud that he had slain Pyrrhus. The Romans, when they saw these spoils carried in triumph along their ranks, raised a joyful cry, while the Greeks were correspondingly disheartened until Pyrrhus, learning what had taken place, rode along the line with his head bare, stretching out his hands to his soldiers and telling them that he was safe. At length he was victorious, chiefly by means of a sudden charge of his Thessalian horse on the Romans after they had been thrown into disorder by the advance of the elephants. The Roman horses were terrified at these animals, and long before they came near, ran away with their riders in panic. The slaughter was very great: Dionysius says that of the Romans there fell but little short of fifteen thousand, but Hieronymus reduces this to seven thousand, while on Pyrrhus's side there fell, according to Dionysius, thirteen thousand, but according to Hieronymus less than four thousand. These however, were the very flower of Pyrrhus's army; for he lost all his most trusty officers, and his most intimate personal friends. Still, he captured the Roman camp, which was abandoned by the enemy, induced several of their allied cities to join him, plundered a vast extent of country, and advanced within three hundred stades (less than forty English miles) of Rome itself. After the battle many of the Lucanians and Samnites came up; these allies he reproached for their dilatory movements, but was evidently well pleased at having conquered the great Roman army with no other forces but his own Epirotes and the Tarentines.

XVIII. The Romans did not remove Lævinus from his office of consul, although Caius Fabricius is reported to have said that it was not the Epirotes who had conquered the Romans, but Pyrrhus who had conquered Lævinus; meaning that he thought that the defeat was owing not to the greater force but the superior generalship of the enemy. They astonished Pyrrhus by quickly filling up their ranks with fresh levies, and talking about the war in a spirit of fearless confidence. He decided to try whether they were disposed to make terms with him, as he perceived that to capture Rome and utterly subdue the Roman people would be a work of no small difficulty, and that it would be vain to attempt it with the force at his disposal, while after his victory he could make peace on terms which would reflect great lustre on himself. Kineas was sent as ambassador to conduct this negotiation. He conversed with the leading men of Rome, and offered their wives and children presents from the king. No one, however, would accept them, but they all, men and women alike, replied that, if peace were publicly concluded with the king, they would then have no objection to regard him as a friend. And when Kineas spoke before the Senate in a winning and persuasive manner he could not make any impression upon his audience, although he announced to them that Pyrrhus would restore the prisoners he had taken without any ransom, and would assist them in subduing all Italy, while all that he asked in return was that he should be regarded as a friend, and that the people of Tarentum should not be molested. The common people, however, were evidently eager for peace, in consequence of their having been defeated in one great battle, and expecting that they would have to fight another against a larger force, because the Italian states would join Pyrrhus. At this crisis Appius Claudius, an illustrious man, but who had long since been prevented by old age and blindness from taking any active part in politics, when he heard of the proposals of Pyrrhus, and that the question of peace or war was about to be voted upon by the Senate, could no longer endure to remain at home, but caused his slaves to carry him through the Forum to the Senate House in a litter. When he reached the doors of the Senate House his sons and sons-in-law supported him and guided him into the house, while all the assembly observed a respectful silence.

XIX. Speaking from where he stood, he addressed them as follows:—"My countrymen, I used to grieve at the loss of my sight, but now I am sorry not to be deaf also, when I hear the disgraceful propositions with which you are tarnishing the glory of Rome. What has become of that boast which we were so fond of making before all mankind, that if Alexander the Great had invaded Italy, and had met us when we were young, and our fathers when they were in the prime of life, he would not have been reputed invincible, but would either have fled or perhaps even have fallen, and added to the glory of Rome? You now prove that this was mere empty vapouring, by your terror of these Chaonians and Molossians, nations who have always been a prey and a spoil to the Macedonians, and by your fear of this Pyrrhus, who used formerly to dance attendance on one of Alexander's bodyguards, and who has now wandered hither not so much in order to assist the Greeks in Italy as to escape from his enemies at home, and promises to be our friend and protector forsooth, when the army he commands did not suffice to keep for him the least portion of that Macedonia which he once acquired. Do not imagine that you will get rid of this man by making a treaty with him. Rather you will encourage other Greek princes to invade you, for they will despise you and think you an easy prey to all men, if you let Pyrrhus go home again without paying the penalty of his outrages upon you, nay, with the power to boast that he has made Rome a laughing-stock for Tarentines and Samnites."

By these words Appius roused a warlike spirit in the Romans, and they dismissed Kineas with the answer that if Pyrrhus would leave Italy they would, if he wished, discuss the question of an alliance with him, but that while he remained in arms in their country the Romans would fight him to the death, however many Lævinuses he might defeat. It is related that Kineas, during his mission to Rome, took great interest in observing the national life of the Romans, and fully appreciated the excellence of their political constitution, which he learned by conversing with many of the leading men of the state. On his return he told Pyrrhus that the Senate seemed to him like an assembly of kings, and that as to the populace, he feared that the Greeks might find in them a new Lernæan hydra; for twice as many troops had been enrolled in the consul's army as he had before, and yet there remained many more Romans capable of bearing arms.

XX. After this Caius Fabricius came to arrange terms for the exchange of prisoners; a man whom Kineas said the Romans especially valued for his virtue and bravery, but who was excessively poor. Pyrrhus, in consequence of this, entertained Fabricius privately, and made him an offer of money, not as a bribe for any act of baseness, but speaking of it as a pledge of friendship and sincerity. As Fabricius refused this, Pyrrhus waited till the next day, when, desirous of making an impression on him, as he had never seen an elephant, he had his largest elephant placed behind Fabricius during their conference, concealed by a curtain. At a given signal, the curtain was withdrawn, and the creature reached out his trunk over the head of Fabricius with a harsh and terrible cry. Fabricius, however, quietly turned round, and then said to Pyrrhus with a smile, "You could not move me by your gold yesterday, nor can you with your beast to-day." At table that day they conversed upon all subjects, but chiefly about Greece and Greek philosophy. Kineas repeated the opinion of Epikurus and his school, about the gods, and the practice of political life, and the objects at which we should aim, how they considered pleasure to be the highest good, and held aloof from taking any active part in politics, because it spoiled and destroyed perfect happiness; and about how they thought that the gods lived far removed from hopes and fears, and interest in human affairs, in a placid state of eternal fruition. While he was speaking in this strain Fabricius burst out: "Hercules!" cried he, "May Pyrrhus and the Samnites continue to waste their time on these speculations, as long as they remain at war with us!" Pyrrhus, at this, was struck by the spirit and noble disposition of Fabricius, and longed more than ever to make Rome his friend instead of his enemy. He begged him to arrange terms of peace, and after they were concluded to come and live with him as the first of his friends and officers. Fabricius is said to have quietly answered, "That, O King, will not be to your advantage; for those who now obey you, and look up to you, if they had any experience of me, would prefer me to you for their king."

Pyrrhus was not angry at this speech, but spoke to all his friends about the magnanimous conduct of Fabricius, and entrusted the prisoners to him alone, on the condition that, if the Senate refused to make peace, they should be allowed to embrace their friends, and spend the festival of the Saturnalia with them, and then be sent back to him. And they were sent back after the Saturnalia, for the Senate decreed that any of them who remained behind should be put to death.

XXI. After this, when C. Fabricius was consul, a man came into his camp bringing a letter from King Pyrrhus's physician, in which he offered to poison the king, if he could be assured of a suitable reward for his services in thus bringing the war to an end without a blow. Fabricius, disgusted at the man's treachery, brought his colleague to share his views, and in haste sent off a letter to Pyrrhus, bidding him be on his guard. The letter ran as follows: "Caius Fabricius and Quintus Æmilius, the Roman consuls, greet King Pyrrhus. You appear to be a bad judge both of your friends and of your enemies. You will perceive, by reading the enclosed letter which has been sent to us, that you are fighting against good and virtuous men, and trusting to wicked and treacherous ones. We do not give you this information out of any love we bear you, but for fear that we might be charged with having assassinated you and be thought to have brought the war to a close by treachery because we could not do so by manhood."

Pyrrhus on receiving this letter, and discovering the plot against his life, punished his physician, and, in return for the kindness of Fabricius and the Romans, delivered up their prisoners without ransom, and sent Kineas a second time to arrange terms of peace. However, the Romans refused to receive their prisoners back without ransom, being unwilling either to receive a favour from their enemy, or to be rewarded for having abstained from treachery towards him, but set free an equal number of Tarentines and Samnites, and sent them to him. As to terms of peace, they refused to entertain the question unless Pyrrhus first placed his entire armament on board the ships in which it came, and sailed back to Epirus with it.

As it was now necessary that Pyrrhus should fight another battle, he advanced with his army to the city of Asculum, and attacked the Romans. Here he was forced to fight on rough ground, near the swampy banks of a river, where his elephants and cavalry were of no service, and he was forced to attack with his phalanx. After a drawn battle, in which many fell, night parted the combatants. Next day Pyrrhus manœuvred so as to bring the Romans fairly into the plain, where his elephants could act upon the enemy's line. He occupied the rough ground on either side, placed many archers and slingers among his elephants, and advanced with his phalanx in close order and irresistible strength. The Romans, who were unable on the level ground to practise the bush-fighting and skirmishing of the previous day, were compelled to attack the phalanx in front. They endeavoured to force their way through that hedge of spears before the elephants could come up, and showed marvellous courage in hacking at the spears with their swords, exposing themselves recklessly, careless of wounds or death. After a long struggle, it is said that they first gave way at the point where Pyrrhus was urging on his soldiers in person, though the defeat was chiefly due to the weight and crushing charge of the elephants. The Romans could not find any opportunity in this sort of battle for the display of their courage, but thought it their duty to stand aside and save themselves from a useless death, just as they would have done in the case of a wave of the sea or an earthquake coming upon them. In the flight to their camp, which was not far off, Hieronymus says that six thousand Romans perished, and that in Pyrrhus's commentaries his loss is stated at three thousand five hundred and five. Dionysius, on the other hand, does not admit that there were two battles at Asculum, or that the Romans suffered a defeat, but tells us that they fought the whole of one day until sunset, and then separated, Pyrrhus being wounded in the arm by a javelin, and the Samnites having plundered his baggage. He also states the total loss on both sides to be above fifteen thousand.

The armies separated after the battle, and it is said that Pyrrhus, when congratulated on his victory by his friends, said in reply: "If we win one more such victory over the Romans, we shall be utterly ruined." For a large part of the force which he had brought with him had perished, and very nearly all his friends and officers, and there were no more to send for at home. He saw, too, that his allies were becoming lukewarm, while the Romans, on the other hand, filled up the gaps with a never-ceasing stream of fresh recruits, and did not lose confidence by their defeats, but seemed to gather fresh strength and determination to go on with the war.

XXII. While in these difficulties he conceived fresh hopes of success, and engaged in an enterprise in another quarter, which was likely to interfere with the prosecution of his original design. An embassy arrived from Sicily, offering to place the cities of Agrigentum, Syracuse, and Leontini in his hands, and begging him to aid them in driving out the Carthaginians from the island, and freeing it from despots, while at the same time messengers came from Greece with the news that Ptolemy, surnamed Keraunus, or "the thunderbolt," had perished, with all his army, in an engagement with the Gauls, and that now was his opportunity to offer himself to the Macedonians, who were in great need of a king. Pyrrhus upbraided Fortune for placing so many opportunities within his reach at the same time, and, reflecting that he could only manage one with success, for some time remained plunged in thought. At last, thinking that the Sicilian offer was likely to lead to greater things, as Africa was close to that island, he decided to accept it, and at once sent Kineas to prepare the cities for his arrival, as was his wont in such cases. He himself, meanwhile, placed a strong garrison in the city of Tarentum, much to the disgust of its citizens, who asked him either to perform what he had come thither to do, namely, to assist them in fighting against the Romans, or else to evacuate their territory, and leave their city as he found it. In answer to this demand he harshly bade them keep quiet, and wait till he was at leisure to attend to their affairs, and at once set sail for Sicily. On his arrival there he found all his hopes realised, as the cities gladly delivered themselves into his hands. At first he willingly acceded to their request, that he should wage war on their behalf, and with an army of thirty thousand foot, two thousand horse, and two hundred ships, he attacked the Carthaginians, totally defeated them, and overran the part of Sicily which was subject to them. Eryx was the strongest of their fortresses, and was strongly garrisoned. Pyrrhus, learning this, determined to assault it. When his army was ready, he came forward, in complete armour, and vowed that he would hold public games and sacrifices in honour of Herakles, if he should prove himself that day, before all the Sikeliot Greeks, to be a worthy descendant of Achilles, and to deserve to command so great a force. The trumpet then sounded the charge, the barbarians were driven from the walls by a shower of missiles, and the scaling ladders planted against them. Pyrrhus was the first man to mount the wall, and there fought singly against a host, dashing some of them over the inner, and some over the outer edge of the wall, and wielding his sword with such terrible power that he soon stood on a pile of corpses. He himself was quite unhurt, and terrified the enemy by his mere appearance, proving how truly Homer has told us that of all virtues courage alone is wont to display itself in divine transports and frenzies. After the city was taken he made a magnificent sacrifice to the gods, and held gymnastic contests of all kinds.

XXIII. He now turned his arms against the so-called Mamertines of Messina, who troubled the Greek cities much, and had even made some of them tributary to themselves. They were numerous and warlike; indeed, in Latin, their name means the "children of Mars." Pyrrhus seized and put to death any of them whom he found exacting tribute from the Greeks, and after defeating them in a pitched battle, took many of their outlying forts. The Carthaginians now were inclined to come to terms with him. They offered, if peace were concluded, to pay him tribute, and to supply a fleet for his use. To these proposals Pyrrhus, dissatisfied with obtaining so little, answered that he would only make peace and friendship with them on one condition, which was that they would evacuate Sicily altogether, and regard the African sea as their frontier towards Greece. Elated by the greatness of the force at his disposal, and the success which attended his enterprises, he now aimed at the realisation of the large hopes of conquest with which he left Greece, and meditated an attack on Libya. He had a large fleet, but required many rowers to man it, and these he proceeded to obtain from the allied cities, not by gentle means, but by harsh, arbitrary, and despotic commands. Not that he was originally of a tyrannical disposition, but his character, which at first was open, trustful, and sociable, gradually altered for the worse, as he became less dependent upon public opinion and more firmly fixed upon his throne, until at length he gained the reputation of an ungrateful and suspicious despot. The Greek cities, though with much murmuring, submitted to this arbitrary impressment, having no other alternative; but Pyrrhus soon proceeded to even harsher measures. Thoinon and Sosistratus were the leading men in Syracuse. It was they who had first invited him into Sicily, and who, when he arrived there, had placed their own city in his hands and induced most of the other Greek communities to join him. Pyrrhus now regarded these men with suspicion, and knew not whether to take them with him or leave them behind. Sosistratus, terrified at the king's evident ill-will, made his escape, upon which Pyrrhus charged Thoinon with plotting against him with the other, and put him to death. This caused a sudden revulsion of feeling from him. The Greek cities began to regard him with mortal hatred, and some of them joined the Carthaginians, whilst others invited the Mamertines to assist them. And while Pyrrhus saw nothing in Sicily but disaffection and insurrection against his power, he received despatches from the Tarentines and Samnites, informing him that they were confined to the walls of their cities, and even so could barely defend themselves against the Romans, while their lands were all being laid waste, and they urgently needed help. This intelligence prevented his withdrawal from Sicily being regarded as a flight, but in reality he had failed in his attempt to conquer that island, and was as eager to return to Italy as a shipwrecked sailor is to reach the shore. It is said that as he was sailing away he looked back at Sicily and said to his friends, "What a fair field we are leaving for the Romans and Carthaginians to fight in." This prophecy, as he expected, was soon afterwards fulfilled.

XXIV. The barbarians combined to attack him as he retreated. He fought a battle at sea with the Carthaginian fleet during his passage to Italy, in which he lost many ships, while the Mamertines, ten thousand strong, had crossed into Italy before he could reach it, and although they did not dare to fight a pitched battle, yet harassed him by attacking him when entangled in some rough ground, and threw his entire army into confusion. Two elephants and many of his rear-guard perished. Pyrrhus himself was at the head of the column of march, but at once rode to the rear and restored the fight, but was in great danger from the brave and warlike Mamertines. He received a blow upon his head from a sword, which forced him to retire a little way from the battle, and greatly elated the enemy. One of them, a powerful man, splendidly armed, ran forward far beyond the rest, and boastfully challenged him to come forward and fight, if he were alive. At this Pyrrhus was so exasperated that he broke forcibly away from the officers who tried to restrain him, and, with his face covered with blood, and a savage expression of fury on his countenance, rushed upon the barbarian, and struck him a blow on the head which showed both the strength of his arm and the admirable temper of his sword, for it clave him completely asunder, so that his body fell down in two pieces. This checked the ardour of the barbarians, who admired and feared Pyrrhus as a superior being. He was able to march unopposed for the rest of the way to Tarentum, to which city he brought a force of twenty thousand infantry and three thousand cavalry. Taking with him the best troops of the Tarentines he now marched at once to attack the Romans, who were encamped in the territory of the Samnites.

XXV. The Samnites at this period were entirely ruined and broken in spirit from the numerous defeats which they had sustained at the hands of the Romans. Some dissatisfaction also was felt with Pyrrhus for having neglected them while he was campaigning in Sicily; so that not many of that nation joined him. Pyrrhus now divided his forces, sending one portion into Lucania to harass the other consul and prevent his coming to the assistance of his colleague, while he himself led the remainder to attack Manius Curius, who was quietly encamped near the city of Beneventum, awaiting the arrival of the Lucanian forces. It is also said that his soothsayers told him, that the omens were not in favour of his moving from where he was. Pyrrhus, eager to attack him before the other consul's army joined him, made a hurried night march with his best troops and elephants, hoping to surprise the Roman camp. But during the march, which was long, and through a densely-wooded country, their torches went out, the soldiers lost their way in the darkness, and got into confusion. Day at length appeared, and showed to the Romans Pyrrhus with his army, advancing from the heights near their camp. The sight caused some disorder and excitement, but as the omens were now favourable, and the emergency required prompt action, Manius Curius led out his men, attacked the first troops of Pyrrhus's army whom he met, routed them, and dismayed the whole force, so that many were slain and several elephants captured. This success emboldened Manius to begin a general action on the more level ground, where he defeated the enemy with one wing of his army, but on the other his troops were overpowered by the charge of the elephants and driven back to their camp. Curius now called to his aid the soldiers left to guard the camp, who were standing under arms along the ramparts, and were quite fresh and unwearied. They assailed the elephants with a shower of darts, which caused them to turn and fly, trampling down their own men in their flight. The Romans thus gained the victory, and at the same time the reputation of being the first military nation in the world. For their display of valour on this occasion led to their being thought invincible, and to their at once gaining possession of the whole of Italy, and shortly afterwards of Sicily also.

XXVI. Thus did Pyrrhus fail in his Italian and Sicilian expeditions, after spending six years of constant fighting in those countries, during which he lost a great part of his force, but always, even in his defeats, preserved his reputation for invincible bravery, being thought, in warlike skill and personal strength and daring, to be by far the first prince of his age. Yet he always threw away the advantages which he gained, in following some chimerical scheme of further conquest, being unable to take proper measures for the present because of his eagerness for the future. On this account Antigonus likened him to a player who made many good throws with the dice, but who did not know how to use them. He carried back to Epirus with him eight thousand infantry and five hundred cavalry, and, having no money, began to look out for a war, by which he might support his army. Some of the Gauls now joined him, and he at once invaded Macedonia, where Antigonus, the son of Demetrius, was now king, with the intention of plundering the country. Soon, however, as he took several cities, and two thousand Macedonian soldiers deserted their colours and joined him, he began to entertain more ambitious designs, marched against Antigonus himself, and was able to surprise his army, near the issue of a defile, by a sudden attack in the rear. Notwithstanding the general confusion, however, a strong body of Gauls, who formed the rear-guard, withstood him manfully, but, after a vigorous resistance, were nearly all cut to pieces, while the elephants, whose retreat was cut off, were surrendered by their leaders. After gaining such an advantage as this, Pyrrhus, trusting to his good fortune, and without calculating the numbers opposed to him, advanced to attack the Macedonian phalanx, which was full of disorder and consternation at the defeat of the rear-guard. No attempt was made by them to strike a blow. Pyrrhus stretched out his hand and called the Macedonian officers by their names, and they at once went over to him, and were followed by all their men. Antigonus escaped to the sea-coast, where he still retained some cities in their obedience.

Pyrrhus, considering that his victory over the Gauls was the most glorious part of his recent success, hung the finest of their arms and spoils in the temple of Athene Itonis, with the following epigram.

"These spoils doth Pyrrhus the Molossian king, From the brave Gauls to thee, bright goddess, bring; He beat Antigonus, with all his men: Achilles' sons are warriors now as then."

After the battle he at once recovered the cities on the seaboard. He took Ægæ, treated the inhabitants very harshly, and left a garrison of Celtic mercenary troops in the town. These Gauls, with the insatiate greed for money for which that nation is noted, proceeded to break open the sepulchres of the Macedonian kings who were buried there, in search of plunder, and wantonly scattered their bones. Pyrrhus seemed but little disturbed at this outrage, either because his affairs gave him no leisure to think about it, or because he thought it dangerous to punish his barbarian allies: but the Macedonians were deeply grieved by it. And yet, although he was far from being firmly established in his new kingdom, he was already forming new schemes of conquest. In raillery he called Antigonus a shameless man because he had not yet laid aside the royal purple for the dress of a private man, and he eagerly accepted the invitation of Kleonymus the Spartan to go and attack Lacedæmon. This Kleonymus was by birth the rightful heir to the throne, but being thought to be a violent and tyrannical person he was hated and distrusted by the Spartans, who had chosen his nephew Areus to be their king. This was the reason of his having long borne a grudge against his countrymen, but besides this his feelings had been recently wounded by a family quarrel.

Kleonymus, now an elderly man, had married a beautiful wife of the royal blood, Chilonis, the daughter of Leotychides. She fell madly in love with Akrotatus, the son of Areus, a youth in the flower of his age, and the dishonour of Kleonymus became notorious all over Sparta. This private wrong, added to his previous exclusion from the throne, so enraged him, that he invited Pyrrhus to attack Sparta, which he did with an army of twenty-five thousand foot, two thousand horse, and twenty-four elephants, so that it was obvious that he did not mean to gain Sparta for Kleonymus, but to conquer the whole of Peloponnesus for himself, although he answered some Spartan envoys who waited on him at Megalopolis in specious language, stating that he had come with the intention of restoring to freedom the cities which were held in subjection by Antigonus, and actually going so far as to tell them that, if possible, he intended to send his younger sons to Sparta to be trained in the Laconian discipline, by which they would be able to surpass all the other kings of their age. He put off the envoys with these stories, and made them accompany his army, but on reaching the Lacedæmonian territory he at once began to plunder and lay it waste. When the envoys remonstrated with him for having invaded their country without a declaration of war, he answered—"We know well that neither do you Spartans tell any one beforehand what you mean to do." One of the envoys, by name Mandrokleides, said in his broad Laconian speech, "If you are a god, we shall not be harmed by you, for we have done no wrong; but if you are a man, you may meet with a stronger man than yourself."

XXVII. After this he marched upon Lacedæmon itself. Kleonymus urged him to make an assault immediately on the evening of his arrival, but Pyrrhus is said to have refused to do so, for fear that his soldiers might sack and destroy the city if they took it at night, while they might easily take it in the daytime. Indeed the Spartans were taken by surprise, and very few were in the city, the king Areus himself being absent in Crete on an expedition to assist the people of Gortyna. And it was this weakness and absence of defenders that really proved the salvation of the city, for Pyrrhus, not expecting any resistance, pitched his camp outside the walls, while the friends and helots of Kleonymus made ready his house and decorated it, expecting that Pyrrhus would sup there with him. At nightfall the Lacedæmonians at first proposed to send away the women to Crete, but they refused to leave the city. Archidamia even went to the senate-house with a drawn sword in her hands, and on behalf of the women of Sparta reproached the men for insulting them by supposing that they would survive the capture of their city. After this, they determined to dig a ditch along the side of the city nearest to Pyrrhus's camp, and to barricade the ends of it with waggons buried up to the axles in the ground, to resist the charge of the elephants. When this work was begun the women and girls appeared with their tunics girt up for work, and laboured at digging the ditch together with the older men. They bade those who were to fight on the morrow take rest, and they themselves alone dug one-third of the entire ditch. The width of the ditch was six cubits, its depth four cubits, and its length eight hundred feet, as we are told by Phylarchus, though Hieronymus makes its dimensions more moderate. At daybreak, when the enemy began to bestir themselves, the women armed the younger men, and handed over the ditch to them, bidding them defend it, as it would be pleasant for them to conquer in sight of their country, and glorious to die in the arms of their mothers and wives after having fought worthily of Sparta. Chilonis herself had retired to her own house, and had a halter ready about her neck, in order that if the city were taken she might not fall into the hands of Kleonymus.

XXVIII. Pyrrhus himself led a direct attack of his infantry against the Spartans, who were drawn up in deep order, and endeavoured to force his way through them, and to pass the ditch, which was difficult, because the newly dug earth afforded no secure footing to his soldiers. Meanwhile his son Ptolemy led a chosen body of two thousand Gauls and Chaonians round the end of the ditch, and endeavoured to break through the barricade of waggons. These stood so thick and so close together that they made it hard, not only for the assailants to cross them, but even for the Lacedæmonians to reach the point where they were menaced. However, as the Gauls began to pull the wheels out of the earth and to drag the waggons down towards the river, the young Akrotatus perceiving the danger, sallied out from the city at another point with three hundred men, and got round behind Ptolemy's force, from whom he was concealed by some hilly ground. Then he vigorously assailed the Gauls in the rear, and forced them to face about and defend themselves, which caused great confusion, as they were driven among the waggons and into the ditch by the Spartans until at last they were forced to retreat. This glorious exploit of Akrotatus was witnessed from the city walls by the old men and all the women. As he returned through the city to his appointed post, covered with blood and rejoicing in his victory, the Spartan women thought that he had grown taller and more handsome than before, and they envied Chilonis her lover. Some of the old men even followed him, shouting, "Go home, Akrotatus, and enjoy yourself with Chilonis: only beget brave sons for Sparta." Where Pyrrhus fought a terrible battle took place, and many valiant deeds were wrought. A Spartan named Phyllius, after greatly distinguishing himself and slaying many of the assailants, when he felt himself mortally wounded, made way for his rear rank-man to take his place, and died inside the line of shields, in order that his corpse might not fall into the hands of the enemy.

XXIX. The battle ceased at night, and during his sleep Pyrrhus dreamed a dream, that he cast thunderbolts upon Lacedæmon, set it all on fire, and rejoiced at the sight. Being awakened by his delight at this vision, he ordered his officers to hold the troops in readiness and related the dream to his friends, auguring from it that he should take the city by assault. They were all of them delighted at the vision, and certain that it portended success, except one Lysimachus, who said that he feared that, as places struck by thunderbolts may not be walked over, Heaven might mean to signify to Pyrrhus by this that he never should set foot in the city. Pyrrhus however answered that this was mere empty gossip, and that they had better take their arms in their hands and remember that

"The best of omens is King Pyrrhus's cause."

He rose, and at daybreak led his troops again to the assault. The Lacedæmonians defended themselves with a spirit and courage beyond what could be expected from their small numbers. The women mingled in the thick of the fight, supplying food, drink, and missile weapons wherever they were needed, and carrying away the wounded. The Macedonians endeavoured to fill up the ditch by flinging large quantities of wood into it, covering the arms and dead bodies which lay at the bottom. As the Lacedæmonians were resisting this attempt, they saw Pyrrhus on horseback trying to cross the line of waggons and the ditch, and force his way into the city. A shout was raised by the garrison at the spot, and the women began to scream and run wildly about. Pyrrhus had made his way through all obstacles and was about to attack the nearest of those who disputed his passage, when his horse, struck in the body by a Cretan javelin, reared in the death-agony, and threw Pyrrhus to the ground. He fell on a steep bank, and his fall caused such consternation among his followers that a timely charge of the Spartans drove them back. Upon this he gave orders to put a stop to the assault, for he imagined that the Lacedæmonians would soon offer terms of surrender, as they were nearly all wounded, and had lost many men. However, the good fortune of the city, which may have wished to test the Spartan courage to the utmost, or to prove its own power to save the city when all hope seemed lost, brought Ameinias the Phokian, one of the generals of Antigonus, with a body of mercenary troops to help the Spartans in this their darkest hour. Shortly after they had received this reinforcement, their king, Areus, arrived from Crete with two thousand men. The women now returned to their homes, not thinking it to be necessary any longer for them to take an active part in the war, while those old men too who had been forced by necessity to take up arms, were relieved by the new comers, who took their places in the line of battle against the enemy.

XXX. These reinforcements piqued Pyrrhus into making several more attempts to take the city, in which however he was repulsed and wounded. He now retired, and began to plunder the country, professing his intention to winter there. But no man can resist his destiny. There were in Argos two parties, one headed by Aristeas, and the other by Aristippus. The latter was favoured by Antigonus, which induced Aristeas to invite Pyrrhus to Argos. He was ever willing to embark on a new enterprise, because he regarded his successes merely as stepping-stones to greater things, and hoped to retrieve his failures by new and more daring exploits; so that he was rendered equally restless by victory or defeat. Accordingly he set off at once for Argos. Areus occupied the most difficult of the passes on the road with an ambuscade, and attacked the Gauls and Molossians who formed the rear-guard. Pyrrhus had been warned by his soothsayers that the livers of the victims wanted one lobe, which portended the loss of one of his relatives, but at this crisis the disorder and confusion into which his army was thrown by the ambush made him forget the omen, and order his son Ptolemy to take his guards and go to the help of the rear-guard, while he himself hurried his main body on through the defile. When Ptolemy came up a fierce battle took place. The flower of the Lacedæmonian army, led by Eualkus, engaged with the troops immediately around Ptolemy, and while they fought, a Cretan named Oryssus, a native of Aptera, running forward on the flank, struck the young man, who was fighting bravely, with a javelin, and killed him. His fall caused his troops to retreat, and they were hard pressed by the Lacedæmonians, who were so excited by their victory that they were carried by their ardour far into the plain, where their retreat was cut off by Pyrrhus's infantry. Pyrrhus himself, who had just heard of the death of his son, in an agony of grief now ordered the Molossian cavalry to charge them. He was the first to ride among the Lacedæmonians, and terribly avenged his son by cutting them down. Pyrrhus in battle was always a terrific figure, whom none dared to resist, but on this occasion he surpassed himself in courage and fury. At length he rode up to Eualkus, who avoided his charge, and aimed a blow at him with his sword which just missed Pyrrhus's bridle hand, but cut through his reins. Pyrrhus ran him through with his spear at the same moment, but fell from his horse, and, fighting henceforth on foot, slew all the chosen band commanded by Eualkus. This was a severe loss to Sparta, incurred as it was unnecessarily, after the war was really over, from the desire of their generals to distinguish themselves.

XXXI. Pyrrhus celebrated his son's obsequies with splendid games. His grief was partly satiated by the revenge which he had taken upon the enemy, and he now marched towards Argos. Hearing that Antigonus was encamped upon one of the heights near the city, he himself pitched his camp at Nauplia. On the next day he sent a herald to Antigonus with an insulting message, challenging him to come down upon the level ground and fight. Antigonus answered that he should fight only when he chose, but that if Pyrrhus was weary of his life, he could find many other ways to die. Ambassadors from Argos also came to each of them, begging them to withdraw their forces, and allow the city to remain independent and friendly to both, Antigonus accepted this offer, and handed over his son to the Argives as a hostage, while Pyrrhus agreed to retire, but, as he gave no pledge, was viewed with greater suspicion than before. A strange portent also happened to Pyrrhus, for the heads of the oxen which had been sacrificed, when lying apart from their bodies, were observed to put out their tongues and lap their own gore; and in the city the priestess of Apollo Lykius rushed about in frenzy, crying out that she saw the whole city full of slaughtered corpses, and an eagle coming to the fight and then disappearing.

XXXII. During the following night, which was very dark, Pyrrhus marched his troops up to the walls, found the gate called Diamperes opened to him by Aristeas, and was able to march his Gaulish troops into the city and seize the market-place unobserved: but the elephants could not pass through the gate until their towers were taken off their backs. The removal of these towers, in the darkness, and the replacing them when the elephants had passed through the gate, caused an amount of delay and confusion which at length roused the slumbering inhabitants; they ran together to the place called "the Shield," and the other places of strength in the city, and sent messengers to call Antigonus to their aid. He at once marched up close to the city, and remained there with a reserve, but sent his son and several of his officers with a large part of his forces to assist the Argives within their city walls. Areus the king of Sparta also arrived, with a thousand Cretans and the swiftest footed of the Spartans. All these troops now at once attacked the Gauls and threw them into great disorder. As Pyrrhus, however, marched in by the street called Kylarabis, his soldiers raised a warlike shout: and he, noticing that the shout was echoed by the Gauls in the market-place in an undecided, faint-hearted fashion, at once guessed that they were being hard pressed. He instantly pressed the horsemen with him to charge, which they did with great difficulty, as the horses kept falling into the water-courses with which the whole city is intersected. The night was spent in wild tumult and skirmishing in the narrow lanes, both parties being unable to recognize or obey their leaders, and eagerly awaiting the dawn. The first rays of light showed Pyrrhus the whole open square called "the Shield" full of enemies, while he was even more disturbed by the sight of a brazen statue in the market-place, representing a wolf and a bull about to attack one another; for he remembered an oracle which had long before foretold that he must die when he should see a wolf fighting with a bull. The Argives say that this statue commemorates the legend that

Danaus when he first landed in the country at Pyramia, near Thyrea, was marching towards Argos when he saw a wolf fighting with a bull. Danaus decided that the wolf must represent himself, because he was a stranger, and was come to attack the people of the country, like it; and he stopped and watched the fight. When the wolf gained the day, he offered prayer to Apollo Lykius, made his attempt upon the throne of Argos, and was successful, as Gelanor, who was then king, was forced into exile by a revolution. This is the account which the Argives give of these statues.

XXXIII. This sight, and the failure of his plans, disheartened Pyrrhus, and he began to think of retreating. As the gates were narrow, he sent to his son Helenus, who had been left with a large force without the city, ordering him to break down a part of the wall, and protect the fugitives, if they were pressed by the enemy. But in the hurry and confusion the messenger did not clearly explain his orders, and by some mistake the young Helenus took all the remaining elephants and the best troops, and marched through the gate with them to help his father. Pyrrhus was already beginning to retire. As long as he fought in the market-place, where there was ample room, he effected his retreat in good order, and kept off the assailants by occasional movements in advance. But when his troops began to march down the narrow street leading to the gate, they were met face to face by the reinforcement coming to their assistance. At this crisis some of the soldiers refused to obey Pyrrhus's order to retreat, while others who were willing enough to do so could not stem the tide of men marching in from the gate. At the gate itself too the largest of the elephants had fallen sideways and lay there bellowing, blocking up the way for those who were trying to pass out, while one of the elephants of the reinforcing party, called "the Conqueror," was looking for his master, who had fallen off his back mortally wounded. Charging violently back against the surging tide of fugitives, the faithful beast trampled down friends and foes alike until he found his master's body, when he seized it with his trunk and carried it upon his tusks; and then, turning round in a frenzy of grief, overturned and crushed every one whom he met. As the men were thus crowded together, no one could do anything to help himself, but the whole mass surged backwards and forwards in one solid body. The enemy who attacked them behind did them but little hurt; they suffered chiefly from one another, because when a man had once drawn his sword or couched his lance he could not put it up again, and it pierced whoever might happen to be forced against it.

XXXIV. Pyrrhus, seeing the danger with which he was menaced on every side, took off the royal diadem from his helmet, and gave it to one of his companions. He himself, trusting to the fact of his being on horseback, now charged into the mass of assailants, and was struck through his cuirass by one of them with a spear. The wound was not a dangerous or important one, and Pyrrhus at once turned to attack the man from whom he had received it. He was an Argive, not of noble birth, but the son of a poor old woman, who, like the rest, was looking on at the battle from the roof of her house. As soon as she saw Pyrrhus attacking her son, in an ecstasy of fear and rage she took up a tile and hurled it at Pyrrhus. It struck him on the helmet, bruising the spine at the back of his neck, and he fell from his horse, blinded by the stroke, at the side of the sacred enclosure of Likymnius. Few recognized him, but one Zopyrus, who was in the service of Antigonus, and two or three others, seized him just as he was beginning to recover his senses, and dragged him into an archway near at hand. When Zopyrus drew an Illyrian sword to cut off his head Pyrrhus looked so fiercely at him that he was terrified, and bungled in his work, but at length managed to sever his head from his body. By this time most men had learned what had happened, and Halkyoneus, running up, asked to see the head, that he might identify it. When he obtained this he rode off with it to his father, and finding him sitting amongst his friends, he threw it down at his feet. Antigonus when he recognized it chased his son out of his presence, striking him with his staff, and calling him accursed and barbarous, and then covered his own face with his mantle and wept, remembering how in his own family his grandfather Antigonus and his father Demetrius had experienced similar reverses of fortune. He had the body and head of Pyrrhus decently arranged on a funeral pyre and burned. Halkyoneus, meeting Helenus in poor and threadbare clothes, embraced him kindly, and led him to Antigonus, who said to him, "This meeting, my boy, is better than the other; but still you do not do right in not removing these clothes, which rather seem to disgrace us who are, as it appears, the victors." He treated Helenus with great kindness, and sent him back to his kingdom of Epirus loaded with presents, and also showed great favour towards the friends of Pyrrhus, who, together with all his army and war material, had fallen into his hands.

# Life of Caius Marius.

I. I cannot mention any third name of Caius Marius, any more than of Quintus Sertorius, who held Spain, or of Lucius Mummius, who took Corinth; for the name Achaicus was given to Mummius in commemoration of this event, just as the name Africanus was given to Scipio, and Macedonicus to Metellus. This seems to Poseidonius to be the strongest refutation of the opinion of those who suppose that the third name was the proper individual name among the Romans, such as Camillus, and Marcellus, and Cato; for he argues, if this were so, those who had only the two names would be really without a name. But Poseidonius does not perceive that by this argument he on his side makes the women to be without names: for no woman ever has the first of the three names, which first, however, Poseidonius supposes to be the name which marked individuals among the Romans; and of the other two names, he supposes the one to be common and to belong to all of one kin, such as the Pompeii and the Manlii and the Cornelii, just as the Greeks might speak of the Herakleidæ and the Pelopidæ; but the other name he supposes to be an appellation given as a distinctive name, either with reference to a man's disposition or his actions, or some character and peculiarity of his person, such as Macrinus and Torquatus and Sulla, which may be compared with the Greek Mnemon or Grypus or Kallinikus. However, in such matters as these the diversity in usage allows a variety of conjectures.

II. With respect to the personal appearance of Marius, I saw a stone statue of him at Ravenna in Gaul, which was perfectly in accordance with what is said of the roughness and harshness of his character. He was naturally of a courageous and warlike turn, and had more of the discipline of the camp than of the state, and accordingly his temper was ungovernable when he was in the possession of power. It is stated that he never studied Greek literature, and never availed himself of the Greek language for any serious purpose, for he said it was ridiculous to study a literature the teachers of which were the slaves of others; and after his second triumph, when he exhibited Greek plays on the occasion of the dedication of a certain temple, though he came to the theatre, he only sat down for a moment and then went away. Xenokrates the philosopher was considered to be rather of a morose temper, and Plato was in the habit of frequently saying to him, "My good Xenokrates, sacrifice to the Graces;" in like manner, if Marius could have been persuaded to sacrifice to the Grecian Muses and Graces, he would never have brought a most illustrious military and civil career to a most unseemly conclusion; through passion and unreasonable love of power and insatiable desire of self-aggrandizement driven to terminate his course in an old age of cruelty and ferocity. Let this, however, be judged of by the facts as they will presently appear.

III. Marius was the son of obscure parents, who gained their living by the labour of their hands, and were poor. His father's name was Marius; his mother's name was Fulcinia. It was late before he saw Rome and became acquainted with the habits of the city, up to which time he lived at Cirrhæato, a village in the territory of Arpinum, where his mode of life was rude, when contrasted with the polite and artificial fashions of a city, but temperate and in accordance with the old Roman discipline. He first served against the Celtiberians when Scipio Africanus was besieging Numantia, and he attracted the notice of his commander by his superiority in courage over all the other young soldiers, and by the readiness with which he adapted himself to the change in living which Scipio introduced among the troops, who had been corrupted by luxurious habits and extravagance. He is said also to have killed one of the enemy in single combat in the presence of the general. Accordingly Marius received from Scipio various honourable distinctions; and on one occasion, after supper, when the conversation was about generals, and one of the company, either because he really felt a difficulty or merely wished to flatter Scipio, asked him where the Roman people would find such another leader and protector when he was gone, Scipio with his hand gently touched the shoulder of Marius, who was reclining next to him, and said, "Perhaps here." So full of promise was the youth of Marius, and so discerning was the judgment of Scipio.

IV. Now it is said that Marius, mainly encouraged by these words, which he viewed as a divine intimation, entered on a political career, and obtained the tribuneship, in which he was assisted by Cæcilius Metellus, of whose house the family of Marius had long been an adherent. During his tribuneship Marius proposed a law on the mode of voting, which apparently tended to deprive the nobles of their power in the Judicia: the measure was opposed by Cotta, the consul, who persuaded the Senate to resist the proposed law, and to summon Marius to account for his conduct. The decree proposed by Cotta was drawn up, and Marius appeared before the Senate; but so far from being disconcerted, as a young man might naturally be, who without any advantages had just stepped into public life, he already assumed the tone which his subsequent exploits authorized, and threatened to carry off Cotta to prison if he did not rescind the decree. Upon Cotta turning to Metellus and asking his opinion, Metellus arose and supported the consul; but Marius, sending for the officer who was outside of the house, ordered him to carry off Metellus himself to prison. Metellus appealed to the rest of the tribunes without effect, and the Senate yielded and abandoned the decree. Marius now triumphantly came before the popular assembly and got his law ratified, having proved himself to be a man unassailable by fear, not to be diverted from his purpose by any motive of personal respect, and a formidable opponent to the Senate by his measures which were adapted to win the public favour. But he soon gave people reason to change their opinion; for he most resolutely opposed a measure for the distribution of corn among the citizens, and succeeding in his opposition, he established himself in equal credit with both parties, as a man who would do nothing to please either, if it were contrary to the public interest.

V. After the tribuneship he was a candidate for the greater ædileship. Now there are two classes of ædileships: one, which derives its name (curule) from the seats with curved feet on which the ædiles sit when they discharge their functions; the other, the inferior, is called the plebeian ædileship. When they have chosen the higher ædiles, they then take the vote again for the election of the others. Now as Marius was manifestly losing in the votes for the curule ædileship, he forthwith changed about and became a candidate for the other ædileship. But this was viewed as an audacious and arrogant attempt, and he failed in his election; but though he thus met with two repulses in one day, which never happened to any man before, he did not abate one tittle of his pretensions, for no long time after he was a candidate for a prætorship, in which he narrowly missed a failure, being the last of all who were declared to be elected, and he was prosecuted for bribery. What gave rise to most suspicion was the fact that a slave of Cassius Sabaco was seen within the septa mingled with the voters; for Sabaco was one of the most intimate friends of Marius. Accordingly Sabaco was cited before the judices; he explained the circumstance by saying that the heat had made him very thirsty, and he called for a cup of cold water, which his slave brought to him within the septa, and left it as soon as he had drunk the water. Sabaco was ejected from the Senate by the next censors, and people were of opinion that he deserved it, either because he had given false testimony or for his intemperance. Caius Herennius also was summoned as a witness against Marius, but he declared that it was contrary to established usage to give testimony against a client and that patrons (for this is the name that the Romans give to protectors) were legally excused from this duty, and that the parents of Marius, and Marius himself, originally were clients of his house.

Though the judices accepted the excuse as valid, Marius himself contradicted Herennius, and maintained that for the moment when he was declared to be elected to a magistracy, he became divested of the relation of client; which was not exactly true, for it is not every magistracy which releases a man who has obtained it, and his family, from the necessity of having a patron, but only those magistracies to which the law assigns the curule seat. However, on the first days of the trial it went hard with Marius, and the judices were strongly against him; yet on the last day, contrary to all expectation, he was acquitted, the votes being equal.

VI. During his prætorship Marius got only a moderate degree of credit. But on the expiration of his office he obtained by lot the further province of Iberia (Spain), and it is said that during his command he cleared all the robber establishments out of his government, which was still an uncivilised country in its habits and in a savage state, as the Iberians had not yet ceased to consider robbery as no dishonourable occupation. Though Marius had now embarked in a public career, he had neither wealth nor eloquence, by means of which those who then held the chief power were used to manage the people. But the resoluteness of his character, and his enduring perseverance in toil, and his plain manner of living, got him the popular favour, and he increased in estimation and influence, so as to form a matrimonial alliance with the illustrious house of the Cæsars, with Julia, whose nephew Cæsar afterwards became the greatest of the Romans and in some degree imitated his relation Marius, as I have told in the Life of Cæsar. There is evidence both of the temperance of Marius and also of his endurance, which was proved by his behaviour about a surgical operation. Both his legs, it is said, had become varicose, and as he disliked this deformity, he resolved to put himself in the surgeon's hands. Accordingly he presented to the surgeon one of his legs without allowing himself to be bound; and without making a single movement or uttering a single groan, with steady countenance and in silence he endured excessive pain during the operation. But when the surgeon was going to take the other leg, Marius refused to present it, saying that he perceived the cure was not worth the pain.

VII. When Cæcilius Metellus was appointed consul with the command of the war against Jugurtha, he took Marius with him to Libya in the capacity of legatus. Here Marius signalised himself by great exploits and brilliant success in battle, but he did not, like the rest, seek to increase the glory of Metellus and to direct all his efforts for the advantage of his general, but disdaining to be called a legatus of Metellus, and considering that fortune had offered him a most favourable opportunity and a wide theatre for action, he displayed his courage on every occasion. Though the war was accompanied with many hardships, he shrunk not from danger however great, and he thought nothing too mean to be neglected, but in prudent measures and careful foresight he surpassed all the officers of his own rank, and he vied with the soldiers in hard living and endurance, and thus gained their affections. For certainly there is nothing which reconciles a man so readily to toil as to see another voluntarily sharing it with him, for thus the compulsion seems to be taken away; and the most agreeable sight to a Roman soldier is to see his general in his presence eating common bread or sleeping on a coarse mat, or taking a hand in any trench-work and fortification. Soldiers do not so much admire a general who shares with them the honour and the spoil, as one who participates in their toils and dangers; and they love a general who will take a part in their labours more than one who indulges their licence. By such conduct as this, and by gaining the affection of the soldiers, Marius soon filled Libya and Rome with his fame and his glory, for the soldiers wrote to their friends at home and told them there would be no end to the war with the barbarian, no deliverance from it, if they did not elect Marius consul.

VIII. These proceedings evidently caused great annoyance to Metellus; but the affair of Turpillius vexed him most of all. The family of Turpillius for several generations had been connected with that of Metellus by friendly relations, and Turpillius was then serving in the army at the head of a body of engineers. It happened that he was commissioned to take charge of Vaga, which was a large city. Trusting for his security to the forbearance with which he treated the inhabitants, and his kind and friendly intercourse with them, he was thrown off his guard and fell into the hands of his enemies, who admitted Jugurtha into the city. Turpillius, however, was not injured, and the citizens obtained his release and sent him away. He was accordingly charged with treason, and Marius, who was present at the trial as an assessor, was violent against him and excited most of the rest, so that Metellus was unwillingly compelled to pronounce sentence of death against the man. Shortly after it appeared that the charge was false, and everybody except Marius sympathised with Metellus, who was grieved at what had taken place; but Marius exultingly claimed the merit of the condemnation, and was shameless enough to go about saying that he had fixed on Metellus a dæmon which would avenge the death of the man whom it was his duty to protect. This brought Metellus and Marius to open enmity; and it is reported that on one occasion when Marius was present, Metellus said in an insulting way, "You, forsooth, my good fellow, intend to leave us and make the voyage to Rome, to offer yourself for the consulship; and you won't be content to be the colleague of this son of mine." Now the son of Metellus was at that time a very young man. Marius however was still importunate to obtain leave of absence; and Metellus, after devising various pretexts for delay, at last allowed him to go, when there were only twelve days left before the consuls would be declared. Marius accomplished the long journey from the camp to Utica, on the coast, in two days and one night, and offered sacrifice before he set sail. It is said that the priest told him that the deity gave prognostications of success beyond all measure and all expectation, and accordingly Marius set sail with high hopes. In four days he crossed the sea with a favourable wind, and was most joyfully received by the people, and being introduced to the popular assembly by one of the tribunes, he began by violent abuse of Metellus, and ended with asking for the consulship and promising that he would either kill Jugurtha or take him alive.

IX. Being declared consul by a great majority, he immediately set about levying soldiers in a way contrary to law and usage, by enrolling a great number of the poorer sort and of slaves, though former generals had never admitted men of this kind into the army, but had given arms, as they would anything else that was a badge of honour, only to those who had the due qualification, inasmuch as every soldier was thus considered to pledge his property to the State. It was not this however which made Marius most odious, but his insolent and arrogant expressions, which gave offence to the nobles, for he publicly said that he considered his acquisition of the consulship a trophy gained over the effeminacy of the noble and the rich, and that what he could proudly show to the people was his own wounds, not the monuments of the dead or the likenesses of others. And he would often speak of the generals who had been defeated in Libya, mentioning by name Bestia and Albinus, men of illustrious descent indeed, but unskilled in military matters, and for want of experience unsuccessful; and he would ask his hearers whether they did not think that the ancestors of Bestia and Albinus would rather have left descendants like himself, for they also had gained an honourable fame; not by noble birth, but by their virtues and their illustrious deeds. This was not said as a mere empty boast, nor simply because he wished to make himself odious to the nobles; but the people, who were delighted to hear the Senate abused, and always measured the greatness of a man's designs by the bigness of his words, encouraged him and urged him on not to spare the nobles if he wished to please the many.

X. When Marius had crossed over to Libya, Metellus, giving way to his jealousy, and vexed to see the crown and the triumph, when he had already completed the war and it only remained to seize the person of Jugurtha, taken from him by another, a man too who had raised himself to power by ingratitude to his benefactor, would not stay to meet Marius, but privately left the country, and Rutilius, one of his legati, gave up the army to the new consul. But at last retribution for his conduct overtook Marius; for he was deprived of the glory of his victories by Sulla, just in the same way as he had deprived Metellus of his credit: and how this happened I will state briefly, since the particular circumstances are told more at length in the Life of Sulla. Bocchus, who was king of the barbarians in the interior, and the father-in-law of Jugurtha, showed no great disposition to help him in his wars, because of the faithlessness of Jugurtha, and also because he feared the increase of his power. But when Jugurtha, who was now a fugitive from place to place, made Bocchus his last resource and took refuge with him, Bocchus received his son-in-law more from a regard to decency, as he was a suppliant, than from any goodwill, and kept him in his hands; and while he openly interceded with Marius on behalf of Jugurtha, and wrote to say that he would not surrender him and assumed a high tone, he secretly entertained treacherous designs against Jugurtha, and sent for Lucius Sulla, who was the Quæstor of Marius, and had done some service to Bocchus during the campaign. Sulla confidently went to Bocchus, but the barbarian, who had changed his intentions and repented of his design, for several days wavered in his plan, hesitating whether he should deliver up Jugurtha or keep Sulla a prisoner: at last, however, he determined to carry into effect his original design, and surrendered Jugurtha into the hands of Sulla. Thus was sown the seed of that irreconcilable and violent animosity between Marius and Sulla which nearly destroyed Rome: many claimed the credit of this transaction for Sulla on account of their dislike of Marius, and Sulla himself had a seal-ring made, which he used to on which there was a representation of the surrender of Jugurtha by Bocchus. By constantly wearing this ring Sulla irritated Marius, who was an ambitious and quarrelsome man, and could endure no partner in his glory. But the enemies of Marius gave Sulla most encouragement by attributing to Metellus the credit of the first and best part of the war, and that of the latter part and the conclusion to Sulla, their object being to lower Marius in public estimation and to withdraw the people from their exclusive attachment to him.

XI. But this envy and hatred and these calumnies against Marius were dissipated and removed by the danger which threatened Italy from the west, as soon as the State saw that she needed a great commander and had to look about for a pilot whose skill should save her from such a torrent of foes; for no one would allow any of the men of noble birth or wealthy families to offer themselves at the Comitia, and Marius, in his absence from Rome, was declared consul. It happened that the Romans had just received intelligence of the capture of Jugurtha when the reports about the Cimbri and Teutones surprised them, and though the rumours as to the numbers and strength of the invaders were at first disbelieved, it afterwards appeared that they fell short of the truth. Three hundred thousand armed fighting men were advancing, bringing with them a much larger number of women and children, in quest of land to support so mighty a multitude and of cities to dwell in, after the example of the Celtæ before them, who took the best part of Italy from the Tyrrheni and kept it. As these invaders had no intercourse with other nations, and had traversed an extensive tract of country, it could not be ascertained who they were or where they issued from to descend upon Gaul and Italy like a cloud. The most probable conjecture was that they were Germanic nations belonging to those who extended as far as the northern ocean; and this opinion was founded on their great stature, their blue eyes, and on the fact that the Germans designate robbers by the name of Cimbri. Others thought that Celtica extended in a wide and extensive tract from the external sea and the subarctic regions to the rising sun and the Lake Mæotis, where it bordered on Pontic Scythia; and it was from this region, as they supposed, where the tribes are mingled, that these invaders came, and that they did not advance in one expedition nor yet uninterruptedly, but that every spring they moved forwards, fighting their way, till in the course of time they traversed the whole continent. Accordingly while the barbarians had several names according to their respective tribes, they designated the whole body by the name of Celtoscythians. But others say that the Cimmerians, with whom the ancient Greeks were first acquainted, were no large portion of the whole nation, but merely a tribe or faction that was driven out by the Scythians and passed into Asia from the Lake Mæotis, under the command of Lygdamis: they further say that the chief part of the Scythian nation and the most warlike part lived at the very verge of the continent, on the coast of the external sea, in a tract shaded, woody, and totally sunless, owing to the extent and closeness of the forests, which reach into the interior as far as the Hercynii; and with respect to the heavens, their position was in that region where the pole, having a great elevation owing to the inclination of the parallels, appears to be only a short distance from the spectator's zenith, and the days and nights are of equal length and share the year between them, which furnished Homer with the occasion for his story of Ulysses visiting the ghosts. From these parts then some supposed that these barbarians came against Italy, who were originally Cimmerii, but then not inappropriately called Cimbri. But all this is rather founded on conjecture than on sure historical evidence. As to the numbers of the invaders, they are stated by many authorities as above rather than below the amount that has been mentioned. But their courage and daring made them irresistible, and in battle they rushed forward with the rapidity and violence of fire, so that no nations could stand their attack, but all the people that came in their way became their prey and booty, and many powerful Roman armies with their commanders, which were stationed to protect Gaul north of the Alps, perished ingloriously; and indeed these armies by their unsuccessful resistance mainly contributed to direct the course of the enemy against Rome. For when they had defeated those who opposed them and got abundance of booty, they determined not to settle themselves permanently anywhere till they had destroyed Rome and ravaged Italy.

XII. Hearing this news from many quarters, the Romans called Marius to the command; and he was elected consul the second time, though it was contrary to a positive law for a man in his absence, and without a certain interval of time, to be elected again, but the people would not listen to those who made any opposition to the election. For they considered that this would not be the first time that the law had given way to convenience, and that the present was as good an occasion for such an irregularity as the election of Scipio as consul at a time when they were under no apprehension about the ruin of Rome, but merely wished to destroy Carthage. Accordingly these reasons prevailed, and Marius, after crossing the sea with his army to Rome, received the consulship, and celebrated his triumph on the calends of January, which with the Romans is the beginning of the year, and exhibited to them a sight they never expected to see, Jugurtha in chains; for no one had ever ventured to hope that the Romans could conquer their enemies while he was alive; so dexterous was Jugurtha in turning all events to the best advantage, and so much courage did he combine with great cunning. But it is said that being led in the triumph made him lose his senses. After the triumph he was thrown into prison, and while some were tearing his clothes from his body, others who were anxious to secure his golden ear-rings pulled them off and the lobe of the ear with them; in this plight being thrust down naked into a deep hole, in his frenzy, with a grinning laugh, he cried out, O Hercules, how cold your bath is! After struggling with famine for six days and to the last moment clinging to the wish to preserve his life, he paid the penalty due to his monstrous crimes. It is said that there were carried in the triumphal procession three thousand and seven pounds of gold, of silver uncoined five thousand seven hundred and seventy-five, and in coined money two hundred and eighty-seven thousand drachmæ. After the procession Marius assembled the Senate in the Capitol, and either through inadvertence or vulgar exultation at his good fortune he entered the place of meeting in his triumphal dress. But observing that the Senate took offence at this, he went out, and putting on the ordinary robe with the purple border, he returned to the assembly.

XIII. On his expedition to meet the Cimbri, Marius continually exercised his forces in various ways in running and in forced marches; he also compelled every man to carry all his baggage and to prepare his own food, in consequence of which men who were fond of toil, and promptly and silently did what they were ordered, were called Marian mules. Some, however, think that this name had a different origin; as follows:—When Scipio was blockading Numantia, he wished to inspect not only the arms and the horses, but also the mules and waggons, in order to see in what kind of order and condition the soldiers kept them. Marius accordingly produced his horse, which he had kept in excellent condition with his own hand, and also a mule, which for good appearance, docility, and strength far surpassed all the rest. The general was much pleased with the beasts of Marius and often spoke about them, which gave rise to the scoffing epithet of Marian mule, when the subject of commendation was a persevering, enduring, and labour-loving man.

XIV. Marius was favoured by a singular piece of good fortune; for there was a reflux in the course of the barbarians, and the torrent flowed towards Iberia before it turned to Italy, which gave Marius time to discipline the bodies of his men and to confirm their courage; and what was most of all, it gave the soldiers an opportunity of knowing what kind of a man their general was. For the first impression created by his sternness and by his inexorable severity in punishing, was changed into an opinion of the justice and utility of his discipline when they had been trained to avoid all cause of offence and all breach of order; and the violence of his temper, the harshness of his voice, and ferocious expression of his countenance, when the soldiers became familiarised with them, appeared no longer formidable to them, but only terrific to their enemies. But his strict justice in all matters that came before him for judgment pleased the soldiers most of all; and of this the following instance is mentioned, Caius Lusius, who was a nephew of Marius, and was an officer in the army, was in other respects a man of no bad character, but fond of beautiful youths. This Caius conceived a passion for one of the young men who served under him, by name Trebonius, and had often ineffectually attempted to seduce him. At last Caius one night sent a servant with orders to bring Trebonius; the young man came, for he could not refuse to obey the summons, and was introduced into the tent; but when Caius attempted to use violence towards him, he drew his sword and killed him. Marius was not present when this happened, but on his arrival he brought Trebonius to trial. There were many to join in supporting the accusation, and not one to speak in his favour, but Trebouius boldly came forward and told the whole story; and he produced witnesses who proved that he had often resisted the importunities of Lusius, and that though great offers had been made, he had never prostituted himself; on which Marius, admiring his conduct, ordered a crown to be brought, such as was conferred for noble deeds according to an old Roman fashion, and he took it and put it on the head of Trebonius as a fit reward for so noble an act at a time when good examples were much needed. The news of this, reaching Rome, contributed in no small degree to the consulship being conferred on Marius for the third time; the barbarians also were expected about the spring of the year, and the Romans did not wish to try the issue of a battle with them under any other commander. However, the barbarians did not come so soon as they were expected, and the period of the consulship of Marius again expired. As the Comitia were at hand, and his colleague had died, Marius came to Rome, leaving Manius Aquilius in the command of the army. There were many candidates of great merit for the consulship, but Lucius Saturninus, one of the tribunes, who had most influence with the people, was gained over by Marius; and in his harangues he advised them to elect Marius consul. Marius indeed affected to decline the honour, and begged to be excused; he said he did not wish for it; on which Saturninus called him a traitor to his country for refusing the command at so critical a time. Now though it was apparent that Saturninus was playing a part at the bidding of Marius, and in such a way that nobody was deceived, still the many seeing that the circumstances required a man of his energy and good fortune, voted for the fourth consulship of Marius, and gave him for colleague Catulus Lutatius, a man who was esteemed by the nobility and not disliked by the people.

XV. Marius, hearing that the enemy was near, quickly crossed the Alps, and established a fortified camp near the river Rhodanus (Rhône), which he supplied with abundance of stores, that he might not be compelled against his judgment to fight a battle for want of provisions. The conveyance of the necessary stores for the army, which hitherto was tedious and expensive on the side of the sea, he rendered easy and expeditious. The mouths of the Rhodanus, owing to the action of the waves, received a great quantity of mud and sand, mixed with large masses of clay, which were formed into banks by the force of the water, and the entrance of the river was thus made difficult and laborious and shallow for the vessels that brought supplies. As the army had nothing to do, Marius brought the soldiers here and commenced a great cut, into which he diverted a large part of the river, and, by making the new channel terminate at a convenient point on the coast, he gave it a deep outlet which had water enough for large vessels, and was smooth and safe against wind and wave. This cut still bears the name of Marius. The barbarians had now divided themselves into two bodies, and it fell to the lot of the Cimbri to march through the country of the Norici, over the high land against Catulus, and to force that passage: the Teutones and Ambrones were to march through the Ligurian country along the sea to meet Marius. Now on the part of the Cimbri there was some loss of time and delay; but the Teutones and Ambrones set out forthwith, and speedily traversing the space which separated them from the Romans, they made their appearance in numbers countless, hideous in aspect, and in language and the cries they uttered unlike any other people. They covered a large part of the plain, where they pitched their tents and challenged Marius to battle.

XVI. Marius cared not for all this, but he kept his soldiers within their entrenchments and severely rebuked those who made a display of their courage, calling such as through passion were eager to break out and fight, traitors to their country; he said it was not triumphs or trophies which should now be the object of their ambition, but how they should ward off so great a cloud and tempest of war, and secure the safety of Italy. This was the way in which he addressed the commanders in particular and the officers. The soldiers he used to station on the rampart in turns, and bid them look at the enemy, and thus he accustomed them to the aspect of the barbarians and their strange and savage shouts, and to make themselves acquainted with their armour and movements, so that in course of time what appeared formidable to their imagination would become familiar by being often seen. For it was the opinion of Marius that mere strangeness adds many imaginary dangers to real danger; but that through familiarity even real dangers lose their terrors. Now the daily sight of the enemy not only took away somewhat of the first alarm, but the threats of the barbarians and their intolerable arrogance roused the courage of the Roman soldiers and inflamed their passions, for the enemy plundered and devastated all the country around, and often attacked the ramparts with much insolence and temerity, so that the words and indignant expressions of the soldiers were repeated to Marius. The soldiers asked, "If Marius had discovered any cowardice in them, that he kept them from battle, like women under lock and key? Why should we not, like free men, ask him whether he is waiting for others to fight for Italy, and intends to employ us always as labourers when there may be occasion to dig canals, to clear out mud, and to divert the course of rivers? It was for this, as it seems, that he disciplined us in so many toils; and these are the exploits of his consulship, which he will exhibit to the citizens when he returns to Rome. Does he fear the fate of Carbo and Cæpio, who were defeated by the enemy? But they were far inferior to Marius in reputation and merit, and they were at the head of much inferior armies. And it is better to do something, even if we perish like them, than to sit here and see the lands of our allies plundered."

XVII. Marius, who was pleased to hear such expressions as these, pacified the soldiers by saying that he did not distrust them, but was waiting for the time and the place of victory pursuant to certain oracles. And in fact he carried about with him in a litter, with great tokens of respect, a Syrian woman named Martha, who was said to possess the gift of divination, and he sacrificed pursuant to her directions. This woman had formerly applied to the Senate, and offered to foretell future events, but her proposal was rejected. Having got access to the women, she allowed them to make trial of her skill; and especially on one occasion, when she sat at the feet of the wife of Marius, she was successful in foretelling what gladiators would win, and this led to her being sent to Marius, who was much struck with her skill. She generally accompanied the army in a litter, and assisted at the sacrifices in a double purple robe fastened with a clasp, and carrying a spear wreathed with ribands and chaplets. This exhibition made many doubt whether Marius produced the woman in public because he really believed in her, or whether he merely pretended to do so, and played a part in the matter. But the affair of the vultures, which Alexander of Myndus has related, is certainly wonderful. Two vultures were always seen hovering about the army before a victory, and accompanying it; they were known by brass rings round their necks, for the soldiers had caught the birds, and after putting on the rings had let them go. Ever after this time as the soldiers recognised the birds, they saluted them; and whenever the birds appeared on the occasion of the army moving, the soldiers rejoiced, as they were confident of success. Though there were many signs about this time, all of them were of an ordinary kind, except what was reported from Ameria and Tuder, two towns of Italy, where at night there was the appearance in the heavens of fiery spears and shields, which at first moved about in various directions, and then closed together, exhibiting the attitudes and movements of men in battle; at last part gave way, and the rest pressed on in pursuit, and all moved away to the west. It happened that about the same time Batakes, the priest of the Great Mother, came from Pessinus, and reported that the goddess from her shrine had declared to him that victory and the advantage in war would be on the side of the Romans. The Senate accepted the announcement and voted a temple to be built to the goddess in commemoration of the anticipated victory; but when Batakes presented himself to the popular assembly with the intention of making the same report there, Aulus Pompeius, one of the tribunes, stopped him, calling him an impostor, and contumeliously driving him from the Rostra; which however contributed to gain most credit for the man's assertions. For on the separation of the assembly, Aulus had no sooner returned to his house than he was seized with so violent a fever that he died within seven days; and the matter was notorious all through Rome and the subject of much talk.

XVIII. Now Marius keeping quiet, the Teutones attempted to storm his camp, but as many of them were struck by the missiles from the rampart and some lost their lives, they resolved to march forward with the expectation of safely crossing the Alps. Accordingly taking their baggage, they passed by the Roman camp. Then indeed some notion could be formed of their numbers by the length of their line and the time which they took to march by; for it is said that they continued to move past the encampment of Marius for six days without interruption. As they passed along, they asked the Romans with a laugh, if they had any message to send to their wives, for they should soon be with them. When the barbarians had marched by and advanced some distance, Marius also broke up his camp and followed close after them, always halting near the enemy, but carefully fortifying his camp and making his position strong in front, so that he could pass the night in safety. Thus advancing, the two armies came to the Aquæ Sextiæ, from which a short march would bring them into the region of the Alps. Accordingly Marius prepared for battle here, and he selected a position which was strong enough, but ill-supplied with water, with a view, as it is said, of thereby exciting his soldiers to come to an engagement. However this may be, when some of them were complaining and saying they should suffer from thirst, he pointed to a stream which ran near the barbarian camp, and said they might get drink from there, but the price was blood. Why then, they replied, don't you forthwith lead us against the enemy, while our blood is still moist? Marius calmly replied, "We must first secure our camp."

XIX. The soldiers obeyed unwillingly. In the meantime the camp servants, having no water for themselves or their beasts, went down in a body to the river, some with axes and hatchets, and others taking swords and spears, together with their pitchers, resolving to have water, even if they fought for it. At first a few only of the enemy engaged with them, for the main body of the army were eating after bathing, and some were still bathing. For a spring of warm water bursts from the ground here, and the Romans surprised some of the barbarians who were enjoying themselves and making merry in this pleasant place. The shouts brought more of the barbarians to the spot, and Marius had great difficulty in checking his men any longer, as they were afraid they should lose their slaves, and the bravest part of the enemy, who had formerly defeated the Romans under Manlius and Cæpio (these were the Ambrones, who were above thirty thousand in number), had sprung up and were running to their arms. Though full of food and excited and inflamed with wine, they did not advance in disorderly or frantic haste, nor utter confused shouts, but striking their arms to a certain measure, and advancing all in regular line, they often called out their name Ambrones, either to encourage one another or to terrify the Romans by this announcement. The Ligurians, who were the first of the Italic people to go down to battle with them, hearing their shouts, and understanding what they said, responded by calling out their old national name, which was the same, for the Ligurians also call themselves Ambrones when they refer to their origin. Thus the shouts were continual on both sides before they came to close quarters, and as the respective commanders joined in the shouts, and at first vied with one another which should call out loudest, the cries stimulated and roused the courage of the men. Now the Ambrones were separated by the stream, for they could not all cross and get into order of battle before the Ligurians, who advanced at a run, fell on the first ranks and began the battle; and the Romans coming up to support the Ligurians, and rushing on the barbarians from higher ground, broke their ranks and put them to flight. Most of the Ambrones were cut down in the stream, where they were crowded upon one another, and the river was filled with blood and dead bodies; and those who made their way across, not venturing to face about, were smitten by the Romans till they reached their camp and the waggons in their flight. There the women meeting them with swords and axes, with horrid furious yells, attempted to drive back both the fugitives and their pursuers, the fugitives as traitors and the pursuers as their enemies, mingling among the combatants, and with their bare hands tearing from the Romans their shields, laying hold of their swords, and enduring wounds and gashes till they fell, in spirit unvanquished. In this manner, it is said that the battle on the river was brought about rather from accident than any design on the part of the commander.

XX. After destroying many of the Ambrones, the Romans retreated and night came on; yet this great success was not followed, as is usual on such occasions, by pæans of victory, and drinking in the tents, and merriment over supper, and what is sweetest of all to men who have won a victory, gentle sleep, but the Romans spent that night of all others in fear and alarm. For their camp had neither palisade nor rampart, and there were still left many thousands of the enemy, and all night long they heard the lamentation of the Ambrones who had escaped and joined the rest of the barbarians, and it was not like the weeping and groaning of men, but a howl resembling that of wild beasts; and a bellowing mingled with threats and cries of sorrow proceeding from such mighty numbers, re-echoed from the surrounding mountains and the banks of the river. A frightful noise filled the whole plain, and the Romans were alarmed, and even Marius himself was disturbed, expecting a disorderly and confused battle in the night. However, the enemy made no attack either on that night or the following day, but they were occupied in arranging their forces and making preparations. In the meantime, as the position of the enemy was backed by sloping hills and deep ravines shaded with trees, Marius sent there Claudius Marcellus, with three thousand heavy-armed soldiers, with instructions to lie concealed in ambush, and to appear on the rear of the barbarians when the battle was begun. The rest of the army, who supped in good time and got a night's rest, he drew up at daybreak in front of the camp, and ordered the cavalry to advance into the plain. The Teutones, observing this, would not wait for the Romans to come down and fight with them on fair ground, but with all speed and in passion they took to their arms and advanced up the hill. Marius sent his officers to every part of the army, with orders to the soldiers to stand firm in their ranks till the enemy came within the reach of their spears, which they were to discharge, and then to draw their swords, and drive against the barbarians with their shields; for as the ground was unfavourable to the enemy, their blows would have no force, and their line no strength, owing to the unevenness of the surface, which would render their footing unstable and wavering. The advice which he gave to his soldiers he showed that he was the first to put in practice; for in all martial training Marius was inferior to none, and in courage he left all far behind him.

XXI. The Romans accordingly awaiting the enemy's attack, and coming to close quarters with them, checked their advance up the hill, and the barbarians, being hard pressed, gradually retreated to the plain, and while those in the van were rallying on the level ground, there was a shout and confusion in the rear. For Marcellus had not let the critical moment pass by, but when the shouts rose above the hills, bidding his men spring from their ambush at a rapid pace and with loud shouts he fell on the enemy's rear and began to cut them down. Those in the rear communicating the alarm to those in front of them, put the whole army into confusion, and after sustaining this double attack for no long time, they broke their ranks and fled. In the pursuit the Romans took prisoners and killed to the number of above one hundred thousand: they also took their tents, waggons, and property, all which, with the exception of what was pilfered, was given to Marius, by the unanimous voice of the soldiers. But though he received so magnificent a present, it was thought that he got nothing at all proportioned to his services, considering the magnitude of the danger. Some authorities do not agree with the statement as to the gift of the spoil, nor yet about the number of the slain. However, they say that the people of Massalia made fences round their vineyards with the bones, and that the soil, after the bodies had rotted and the winter rains had fallen, was so fertilised and saturated with the putrefied matter which sank down into it, that it produced a most unusual crop in the next season, and so confirmed the opinion of Archilochus that the land is fattened by human bodies. They say that extraordinary rains generally follow great battles, whether it is that some divine power purifies the ground, and drenches it with waters from heaven, or that the blood and putrefaction send up a moist and heavy vapour which condenses the atmosphere, which is lightly moved and readily changed to the greatest degree from the smallest cause.

XXII. After the battle, Marius caused to be collected the arms and spoils of the barbarians which were conspicuous for ornament, and unbroken, and suited to make a show in his triumphal procession: all the rest he piled up in a great heap, for the celebration of a splendid religious festival. The soldiers were already standing by in their armour, with chaplets on their heads, and Marius having put on the robe with the purple border, and fastened it up about him in the Roman fashion, had taken a burning torch, and holding it up to heaven with both his hands, was going to set fire to the heap, when some friends were seen riding quickly towards him, which caused a deep silence and general expectation. When the horsemen were near, they leaped down and greeted Marius with the news that he was elected consul for the fifth time, and they delivered him letters to this effect. This cause of great rejoicing being added to the celebration of the victory, the army transported with delight sent forth one universal shout, accompanied with the noise and clatter of their arms, and the officers crowned Marius afresh with a wreath of bay, on which he set fire to the heap, and completed the ceremony.

XXIII. But that power which permits no great good fortune to give a pleasure untempered and pure, and diversifies human life with a mixture of evil and of good—be it Fortune or Nemesis, or the necessary nature of things—in a few days brought to Marius intelligence about his companion in command, Catulus, involving Rome again in alarm and tempest, like a cloud which overcasts a clear and serene sky. For Catulus, whose commission was to oppose the Cimbri, determined to give up the defence of the passes of the Alps, for fear that he might weaken his force if he were obliged to divide it too much. Accordingly he forthwith descended into the plains of Italy, and placing the river Atiso (Adige) in his front, strongly fortified a position on each side of the river, to hinder the enemy from crossing it; and he also threw a bridge over the river, in order that he might be enabled to support those on the farther side, if the barbarians should make their way through the passes and attack the forts. The enemy had so much contempt for the Romans and such confidence, that, with the view rather of displaying their strength and courage than because it was necessary, they endured the snow-storms without any covering, and made their way through the snow and ice to the summits of the mountains, when, placing their broad shields under them, they slid down the slippery precipices over the huge rocks. When they had encamped near the river, and examined the ford, they began to dam up the stream, and tearing up the neighbouring hills, like the giants of old, they carried whole trees with their roots, fragments of rock, and mounds of earth into the river, and stopped its course; they also let heavy weights float down the stream, which drove against the piles that supported the bridge and shook it by the violence of the blows; all which so terrified the Romans, that most of them deserted the large encampment and took to flight. Then Catulus, like a good and perfect general, showed that he valued the reputation of his countrymen more than his own. Not being able to induce his soldiers to stand, and seeing that they were making off in alarm, he ordered the eagle to be moved, and running to those who were first in the retreat, he put himself at their head, wishing the disgrace to fall on himself and not on his country, and that the army should not appear to be flying, but to be following their general in his retreat. The barbarians attacked and took the fort on the farther side of the Atiso, though the Roman soldiers defended it with the utmost bravery and in a manner worthy of their country. Admiring their courage, the barbarians let them go on conditions which were sworn to upon the brazen bull, which was taken after the battle, and, it is said, was conveyed to the house of Catulus as the first spoils of the victory. The country being now undefended, the barbarians scoured it in every direction and laid it waste.

XXIV. After this Marius was called to Rome. On his arrival it was generally expected that he would celebrate his triumph, and the Senate had without any hesitation voted him one; but he refused it, either because he did not wish to deprive his soldiers and his companions in arms of the honour that was due to them, or because he wished to give the people confidence in the present emergency by intrusting to the Fortune of the State the glory of his first victory, with the confident hope that she would return it to him ennobled by a second. Having said what was suitable to the occasion, he set out to join Catulus, whom he encouraged, and at the same time he summoned his soldiers from Gaul. On the arrival of the troops, Marius crossed the Eridanus (Po), and endeavoured to keep the barbarians from that part of Italy which lay south of the river. The Cimbri declined a battle, because, as they said, they were waiting for the Teutones, and wondered they were so long in coming; but it is doubtful whether they were still really ignorant of their destruction or merely pretended not to believe it. However, they handled most cruelly those who brought the report of the defeat; and they sent to Marius to demand land for themselves and their brethren, and a sufficient number of cities for their abode. On Marius asking the ambassadors of the Cimbri whom they meant by their brethren, and being told they were the Teutones, all the Romans who were present burst out in a laugh, but Marius, with a sneer, replied, "Don't trouble yourself about your brethren: they have land, and they shall have it for ever, for we have given it to them." The ambassadors, who understood his irony, fell to abusing him, and threatened that the Cimbri would forthwith have their revenge, and the Teutones too, as soon as they should arrive. "They are here already," said Marius; "and it won't be right for you to go before you have embraced your brethren." Saying this he ordered the kings of the Teutones to be produced in their chains; for they were taken in the Alps in their flight by the Sequani.

XXV. On this being reported to the Cimbri, they forthwith advanced against Marius, who however kept quiet and remained in his camp. It is said that it was on the occasion of this engagement that Marius introduced the alteration in the spears. Before this time that part of the wooden shaft which was let into the iron was fastened with two iron nails; Marius kept one of the nails as it was, but he had the other taken out and a wooden peg, which would be easily broken, put in its place; the design being that the spear when it had struck the enemy's shield should not remain straight, for when the wooden nail broke, the iron head would bend, and the spear, owing to the twist in the metal part, would still hold to the shield, and so drag along the ground. Now Boeorix, the king of the Cimbri, with a very few men about him, riding up to the camp, challenged Marius to fix a day and place, and to come out and settle the claim to the country by a battle. Marius replied, that the

Romans never took advice of their enemies as to fighting; however, he would gratify the Cimbri in this matter, and accordingly they agreed on the third day from the present, and the battle-field was to be the plain of Vercellæ, which was suited for the Roman cavalry, and would give the Cimbri full room for their numbers. When the appointed day came, the Romans prepared for battle with the enemy. Catulus had twenty-two thousand three hundred men, and Marius thirty-two thousand, which were distributed on each flank of Catulus, who occupied the centre, as Sulla has recorded, who was in the battle. Sulla also says, that Marius expected that the line would be engaged chiefly at the extremities and on the wings, and with the view of appropriating the victory to his own soldiers, and that Catulus might have no part in the contest, and not come to close quarters with the enemy, he took advantage of the hollow front of the centre, which usually results when the line is extended, and accordingly divided and placed his forces as already stated. Some writers say that Catulus himself also made a statement to the like effect, in his apology about the battle, and accused Marius of want of good faith to him. The infantry of the Cimbri marched slowly from their fortified posts in a square, each side of which was thirty stadia: the cavalry, fifteen thousand in number, advanced in splendid style, wearing helmets which resembled in form the open mouths of frightful beasts and strange-shaped heads, surmounted by lofty crests of feathers, which made them appear taller; they had also breastplates of iron and white glittering shields. Their practice was to discharge two darts, and then closing with the enemy, to use their large heavy swords.

XXVI. On this occasion the enemy's cavalry did not advance straight against the Romans, but deviating to the right they attempted to draw the Romans little by little in that direction, with the view of attacking them when they had got them between themselves and their infantry, which was on the left. The Roman generals perceived the manoeuvre, but they could not stop their soldiers, for there was a cry from some one that the enemy was flying, and immediately the whole army rushed to the pursuit. In the meantime the barbarian infantry advanced like a huge sea in motion. Then Marius, washing his hands and raising them to heaven, vowed a hecatomb to the gods; and Catulus also in like manner raising his hands, vowed to consecrate the fortune of that day. It is said that when Marius had sacrificed and had inspected the victims, he cried out with a loud voice, "Mine is the Victory." When the attack had commenced, an incident happened to Marius which may be considered as a divine retribution, as Sulla says. An immense cloud of dust being raised, as was natural, and having covered the two armies, it happened that Marius, rushing to the pursuit with his men after him, missed the enemy, and being carried beyond their line, was for some time in the plain without knowing where he was; but it happened that the barbarians closed with Catulus, and the struggle was with him and his soldiers chiefly, among whom Sulla says that he himself fought: he adds, that the heat aided the Romans, and the sun, which shone full in the face of the Cimbri. For the barbarians were well inured to cold, having been brought up in forests, as already observed, and a cool country, but they were unnerved with the heat, which made them sweat violently and breathe hard, and put their shields before their faces, for the battle took place after the summer solstice, and, according to the Roman reckoning, three days before the new moon of the month now called Augustus, but then Sextilis. The dust also which covered their enemies helped to encourage the Romans; for they did not see their number at a distance, but running forward they engaged severally man to man with the enemy, without having been alarmed by the sight of them. And so well were the bodies of the Romans inured to toil and exertion, that not one of them was seen to sweat or pant, though the heat was excessive and they came to the shock of battle running at full speed, as Catulus is said to have reported to the honour of his soldiers.

XXVII. Now the greater part of the enemy and their best soldiers were cut to pieces in their ranks, for in order to prevent the line from being broken the soldiers of the first rank were fastened together by long chains which were passed through their belts. The fugitives were driven back to their encampments, when a most tragic scene was exhibited. The women standing on the waggons clothed in black massacred the fugitives, some their husbands, and others their brothers and fathers, and then strangling their infants they threw them under the wheels and the feet of the beasts of burden, and killed themselves. It is said that one woman hung herself from the end of the pole of a waggon with her children fastened to her feet by cords; and that the men, not finding any trees near, tied themselves to the horns of the oxen and some to their feet, and then goading the animals to make them plunge about, were dragged and trampled till they died. But though so many perished in this manner, above sixty thousand were taken prisoners, and the number of those who fell was said to be twice as many. Now all the valuable property became the booty of the soldiers of Marius, but the military spoils and standards and trumpets, it is said, were carried to the tent of Catulus; and Catulus relied chiefly on this as a proof that the victory was gained by his men. A dispute having arisen among the soldiers, as might be expected, some ambassadors from Parma who were present were chosen to act as arbitrators, and the soldiers of Catulus leading them among the dead bodies of the enemy, pointed out that the barbarians were pierced by their spears, which were recognised by the marks on them, for Catulus had taken care to have his name cut on the shafts. Notwithstanding this, the whole credit was given to Marius, both on account of the previous victory and his superior rank. And what was most of all, the people gave him the title of the third founder of Rome, considering that the danger which he had averted was not less than that of the Gallic invasion, and in their rejoicings with their wives and children at home they coupled Marius with the gods in the religious ceremonies that preceded the banquet and in their libations, and they thought that he alone ought to celebrate both triumphs. Marius, however, did not triumph alone, but Catulus shared the honour, for Marius wished to show that he was not elated by his victories: there was another reason also; he was afraid of the soldiers, who were prepared not to let Marius triumph, if Catulus were deprived of the honour.

XXVIII. Though Marius was now discharging his fifth consulship, he was more anxious to obtain a sixth than others are about the first; and he endeavoured to gain favour by courting the people and giving way to the many in order to please them, wherein he went further than was consistent with the state and dignity of the office, and further than suited his own temper, for he wished to show himself very compliant and a man of the people, when in fact his character was altogether different. Now it is said that in all civil matters and amid the noise of the popular assemblies Marius was entirely devoid of courage, which arose from his excessive love of applause; and the undaunted spirit and firmness which he showed in battle failed him before the people, where he was disconcerted by the most ordinary expressions of praise or censure. However, the following story is told of him: Marius had presented with the citizenship a thousand of the people of Camerinum, who had particularly distinguished themselves in the war; this was considered to be an illegal proceeding, and being charged with it by several persons in public, he replied that he could not hear the law for the din of arms. Still it is well known that he was discomposed and alarmed by the shouts in the popular assemblies. In military matters, it is true, he received great deference and had much influence, because his services were wanted; but in civil business he was cut off from attaining the first distinction, and accordingly there was nothing left for him but to gain the affection and favour of the many; and in order to become the first man at Rome, he sacrificed all claim to be considered the best. The consequence was, that he was at variance with all the aristocratical party, but he feared Metellus most, who had experienced his ingratitude, and, as a man of sterling worth, was the natural enemy of those who attempted to insinuate themselves into the popular favour by dishonourable means, and who had no other object than to flatter the people. Accordingly Marius formed a design to eject Metellus from the city; and for this purpose he allied himself with Glaucia and Saturninus, who were daring men, and had at their command a rabble of needy and noisy fellows, and he made them his tools in introducing his measures. He also stirred up the soldiers, and by mixing them with the people in the assemblies he overpowered Metellus with his faction. Rutilius, who is a lover of truth and an honest man, though he was a personal enemy of Marius, relates in his history, that by giving large sums of money to the tribes and buying their votes Marius kept Metellus out, and that Valerius Flaccus was rather the servant than the colleague of Marius in his sixth consulship. However, the people, never conferred the office of consul so often on any man except Corvinus Valerius; though it is said that forty-five years elapsed between the first and last consulship of Corvinus, while Marius after his first consulship enjoyed the remaining five in uninterrupted succession.

XXIX. It was in his last consulship that Marius got most odium, from his participating in many of the violent measures of Saturninus. One of them was the assassination of Nonius, whom Saturninus murdered because he was a rival candidate for the tribuneship. Saturninus, being made a tribune, introduced a measure about the land, to which was added a clause that the Senate should come forward and swear that they would abide by whatever the people should vote, and would make no opposition. In the Senate Marius made a show of opposing this clause in the proposed law, and he said that he would not take the oath, nor did he think that any man in his senses would, for if the law was not a bad one, it was an insult for the Senate to be compelled to make such concession, instead of giving their consent voluntarily. What he said, however, was not his real mind, but his object was to involve Metellus in a difficulty which he could not evade. For Marius, who considered falsehood to be a part of virtue and skill, had no intention to observe what he had promised to the Senate; but as he knew that Metellus was a man of his word, and considered truth, as Pindar calls it, the foundation of great virtue, he wished to entrap Metellus into a refusal before the Senate, and as he would consequently decline taking the oath, he designed in this way to make him odious to the people for ever: and it fell out so. Upon Metellus declaring that he would never take the oath, the Senate separated; but a few days after, Saturninus summoned the Senators to the Rostra, and urged them to take the oath. When Marius came forward there was profound silence, and all eyes were turned upon him to see what he would do. Marius, however, forgetting all his bold expressions before the Senate, said his neck was not broad enough for him to be the first to give his opinion on so weighty a matter all at once, and that he would take the oath and obey the law, if it was a law; which condition he cunningly added as a cloak to his shame. The people, delighted at Marius taking the oath, clapped their hands and applauded, but the nobility were much dejected and hated Marius for his tergiversation. However, all the senators took the oath in order, through fear of the people, till it came to the turn of Metellus, and though his friends urged and entreated him to take the oath and so to avoid the severe penalties which the law of Saturninus enacted against those who refused, he would not swerve from his purpose or take the oath, but adhering firmly to his principles and prepared to submit to any penalty rather than do a mean thing, he left the Forum, saying to those about him, that to do a wrong thing was mean, to act honourably when there was no danger was in any man's power, but that it was the characteristic of a good man to do what was right, even when it was accompanied with risk. Upon this Saturninus put it to the vote that the consuls should proclaim Metellus to be excluded from fire, water, and house; and the most worthless part of the populace was ready to put him to death. Now all the men of honourable feeling, sympathising with Metellus, crowded round him, but Metellus would not allow any commotion to be raised on his account, and he quitted the city like a wise and prudent man, saying, "Either matters will mend and the people will change their minds, when I shall be invited to return, or if things stay as they are, it is best to be out of the way." What testimonies of affection and respect Metellus received in his exile, and how he spent his time at Rhodes in philosophical studies, will be better told in his Life.

XXX. Now Marius did not perceive what incurable mischief he had done, for in return for the services of Saturninus he was obliged to wink at his audacious and violent measures, and to remain quiet while Saturninus was evidently aiming at the supreme power and the subversion of the constitution by force of arms and blood-shed. Between his fear of the disapprobation of the nobles and his wish to retain the favour of the people, Marius was reduced to an act of extreme meanness and duplicity. The first men in the State came to him by night and urged him to act against Saturninus, whom Marius, however, received by another door without their knowledge; and pretending to both parties that he was troubled with a looseness, he went backwards and forwards in the house between the nobles and Saturninus, running first to one and then to the other, and endeavouring to rouse and irritate them mutually.

However, when the Senate and the Equites began to combine and express their indignation, he drew out the soldiers into the Forum, and driving the party of Saturninus to the Capitol, he compelled them to submit for fear of dying of thirst, by cutting off the pipes that supplied them with water. The partisans of Saturninus in despair called out to Marius and surrendered on the Public Faith, as the Romans term it. Marius did all he could to save their lives, but without effect, for as soon as they came down to the Forum they were massacred. These events made him odious both to the nobles and the people, and when the time for electing censors came, contrary to all expectation he did not offer himself as a candidate, but allowed men of inferior rank to be elected, fearing he might be rejected. He, however, alleged as an excuse, though it was not true, that he did not wish to make himself many enemies by a rigid scrutiny into their lives and morals.

XXXI. A measure being proposed for recalling Metellus from exile, Marius did all he could to stop it both by word and deed, but finding his opposition useless, he at last desisted. The people received the proposed measure well, and Marius, who could not endure to see the return of Metellus, set sail for Cappadocia and Galatia, pretending that he wished to make the sacrifices he had vowed to the Great Mother, but in reality having quite a different object in view, which the people never suspected. Marius was naturally ill suited for times of peace and for taking a part in civil affairs, as he had attained his position merely by arms, and now thinking that he was gradually losing his influence and reputation by doing nothing and remaining quiet, he looked out for an opportunity of again being actively employed. He hoped to be able to stir up the kings of Asia and to rouse and stimulate Mithridates, who was supposed to be ready to go to war, in which case he expected to be appointed to take the command against him, and so to fill the city with new triumphs, and his house with Pontic spoils and the wealth of the king. Accordingly, though Mithridates paid him all attention and honour, Marius could not be bent from his purpose or induced to give way: his only answer was, "King, either try to conquer the Romans or obey their orders in silence;" an expression which startled the king, who had often heard the language of the Romans, but then for the first time heard their bold speech.

XXXII. On his return to Rome he built a house near the Forum, either, as he gave out, because he did not wish those who paid their respects to him to have the trouble of coming a great distance, or because he thought the distance was the reason why a greater number of persons did not visit his door than that of other persons. The reason, however, was not this; but as Marius was inferior to others in affability of manners and political usefulness, he was neglected, just like an instrument of war in time of peace. As for others, he cared less for their superior popularity, but he was grievously annoyed at Sulla, who had risen to power through the dislike which the nobles bore to Marius, and who made his quarrels with Marius the foundation of his political conduct. But when Bocchus, the Numidian, on receiving the title of 'Ally of the Romans,' erected in the Capitol Victories bearing trophies, and by the side of them placed gilded figures representing Jugurtha surrendered by him to Sulla, Marius was transported with passion and jealousy at Sulla thus appropriating to himself all the credit of this affair, and he was making ready forcibly to throw down the figures. Sulla prepared to oppose him, and a civil commotion was just on the point of breaking out, when it was stopped by the Social war, which suddenly burst upon the State. In this war the most warlike and populous of the Italian nations combined against Rome, and came very near to overthrowing her supremacy, for they were not only well provided with munitions of war and hardy soldiers, but they had commanders who displayed admirable courage and skill, which made them a match for the Romans.

XXXIII. This war, which was diversified by many reverses and a great variety of fortune, took from Marius as much reputation and influence as it gave to Sulla. For Marius appeared slow in his plans, and on all occasions rather over-cautious and tardy; whether it was that age had quenched his wonted vigour and fire, for he was now in his sixty-sixth year, or, as he alleged himself, his nerves were diseased and his body was incapable of supporting fatigue, and yet from a feeling of honour he endured the hardships of the campaign beyond his powers. Notwithstanding this he won a great battle, in which he slaughtered six thousand of the enemy, and he never allowed them the opportunity of getting any advantage, but when he was intrenched in his camp he submitted to be insulted by them and was never irritated by any challenge to give them battle. It is recorded that Publius Silo, who had the highest reputation and influence of any man on the side of the enemy, addressed him to this effect: "If you are a great general, Marius, come down and fight;" to which Marius replied, "Nay, do you, if you are a great general, compel me to fight against my will." And again, on another occasion when the enemy presented a favourable opportunity for attacking them, but the Romans lacked courage, and both sides retired, he summoned his soldiers together, and said, "I don't know whether to call the enemy or you greater cowards; for they could not see your back, nor you their nape." At last, however, he gave up the command, on the ground that his weakness rendered him unable to endure the fatigue of the campaign.

XXXIV. The Italians had now given in, and many persons at Rome were intriguing for the command in the Mithridatic war with the assistance of the demagogues; but, contrary to all expectation, the tribune Sulpicius, a most audacious fellow, brought forward Marius and proposed him as proconsul with power to prosecute the war against Mithridates. The people indeed were divided, some being for Marius and others in favour of Sulla; and they bade Marius go to the warm baths of Baiæ and look after his health, inasmuch as he was worn out with old age and defluxions, as he admitted himself. Marius had in the neighbourhood of Misenum a sumptuous house, furnished with luxuries and accommodation too delicately for a man who had served in so many wars and campaigns. It is said that Cornelia bought this house for seventy-five thousand; and that no long time after it was purchased by Lucius Lucullus for two millions five hundred thousand; so quickly did extravagant expenditure spring up and so great was the increase of luxury. But Marius, moved thereto by boyish emulation, throwing off his old age and his infirmities, went daily to the Campus Martius, where he took his exercises with the young men, and showed that he was still active in arms and sat firm in all the movements of horsemanship, though he was not of a compact form in his old age, but very fat and heavy. Some were pleased at his being thus occupied, and they came down to the Campus to see and admire his emulation and his exercises; but the wiser part lamented to witness his greediness after gain and distinction, and they pitied a man who, having risen from poverty to enormous wealth, and to the highest station from a low degree, knew not when to put bounds to his good fortune, and was not satisfied with being an object of admiration and quietly enjoying what he had, but as if he was in want of everything, after his triumphs and his honours was setting out to Cappadocia and the Euxine to oppose himself in his old age to Archelaus and Neoptolemus, the satraps of Mithridates. The reasons which Marius alleged against all this in justification of himself appeared ridiculous; he said that he wished to serve in the campaign in order to teach his son military discipline.

XXXV. The disease that had long been rankling in the State at last broke out, when Marius had found in the audacity of Sulpicius a most suitable instrument to effect the public ruin; for Sulpicius admired and emulated Saturninus in everything, except that he charged him with timidity and want of promptitude in his measures. But there was no lack of promptitude on the part of Sulpicius, who kept six hundred of the Equestrian class about him as a kind of body-guard and called them an Opposition Senate. He also attacked with a body of armed men the consuls while they were holding a public meeting; one of the consuls made his escape from the Forum, but Sulpicius seized his son and butchered him. Sulla, the other consul, being pursued, made his escape into the house of Marius, where nobody would have expected him to go, and thus avoided his pursuers who ran past; and it is said that he was let out in safety by Marius by another door and so got to the camp. But Sulla in his Memoirs says that he did not fly for refuge to Marius, but withdrew there to consult with him about the matters which Sulpicius was attempting to make him assent to against his will by surrounding him with bare swords and driving him on towards the house of Marius, and that finally he went from the house of Marius to the Rostra, and removed, as they required him to do, the Justitium. This being accomplished, Sulpicius, who had now gained a victory, got the command conferred on Marius by the votes of the, assembly, and Marius, who was prepared to set out, sent two tribunes to receive the army of Sulla. But Sulla encouraging his soldiers, who were thirty-five thousand men well armed, led them to Rome. The soldiers fell on the tribunes whom Marius had sent, and murdered them. Marius also put to death many of the friends of Sulla in Rome, and proclaimed freedom to the slaves if they would join him; but it is said that only three slaves accepted the offer. He made but a feeble resistance to Sulla on his entering the city, and was soon compelled to fly. On quitting Rome he was separated from his partisans, owing to its being dark, and he fled to Solonium, one of his farms. He sent his son Marius to get provisions from the estates of his father-in-law Mucius, which were not far off, and himself went to Ostia, where Numerius, one of his friends, had provided a vessel for him, and without waiting for his son he set sail with his stepson Granius. The young man arrived at the estates of Mucius, but he was surprised by the approach of day while he was getting something together and packing it up, and thus did not altogether escape the vigilance of his enemies, for some cavalry came to the spot, suspecting that Marius might be there. The overseer of the farm, seeing them approach, hid Marius in a waggon loaded with beans, and yoking the oxen to it, he met the horsemen on his road to the city with the waggon. Marius was thus conveyed to the house of his wife, where he got what he wanted, and by night made his way to the sea, and embarking in a vessel bound for Libya, arrived there in safety.

XXXVI. The elder Marius was carried along the coast of Italy by a favourable wind, but as he was afraid of one Geminius, a powerful man in Terracina, and an enemy of his, he ordered the sailors to keep clear of that place. The sailors were willing to do as he wished, but the wind veering round and blowing from the sea with a great swell, they were afraid that the vessel could not stand the beating of the waves, and as Marius also was much troubled with sickness, they made for land, and with great difficulty got to the coast near Circeii. As the storm increased and they wanted provisions, they landed from the vessel and wandered about without any definite object, but as happens in cases of great difficulty, seeking merely to escape from the present evil as worst of all, and putting their hopes on the chances of fortune; for the land was their enemy, and the sea also, and they feared to fall in with men, and feared also not to fall in with men, because they were in want of provisions. After some time they met with a few herdsmen, who had nothing to give them in their need, but they recognised Marius and advised him to get out of the way as quickly as he could, for a number of horsemen had just been seen there riding about in quest of him. Thus surrounded by every difficulty and his attendants fainting for want of food, he turned from the road, and plunging into a deep forest, passed the night in great suffering. The next day, compelled by hunger and wishing to make use of his remaining strength before he was completely exhausted, he went along the shore, encouraging his followers, and entreating them not to abandon the last hope, for which he reserved himself on the faith of an old prediction. For when he was quite a youth and living in the country, he caught in his garment an eagle's nest as it was falling down, with seven young ones in it; which his parents wondering at, consulted the soothsayers, who told them that their son would become the most illustrious of men, and that it was the will of fate that he should receive the supreme command and magistracy seven times. Some affirm that this really happened to Marius; but others say that those who were with Marius at this time and in the rest of his flight heard the story from him, and believing it, recorded an event which is altogether fabulous. For an eagle has not more than two young ones at a time, and they say that Musæus was mistaken when he wrote of the eagle thus:—

Lays three, two hatches, and one tends with care.

But that Marius frequently during his flight, and when he was in the extremest difficulties, said that he should survive to enjoy a seventh consulship, is universally admitted.

XXXVII. They were now about twenty stadia from Minturnæ, an Italian city, when they saw at a distance a troop of horse riding towards them, and as it chanced two merchant vessels sailing along the coast. Running down to the sea as fast as they could and as their strength would allow, and throwing themselves into the water, they swam to the vessels. Granius having got into one of the vessels, passed over to the island of Ænaria, which is off that coast. But Marius, who was heavy and unwieldy, was with difficulty held above the water by two slaves and placed in the other vessel, the horsemen being now close to them and calling from the shore to the sailors either to bring the vessel to land or to throw Marius overboard, and to set sail wherever they pleased. But as Marius entreated them with tears in his eyes, those who had the command of the vessel, after changing their minds as to what they should do as often as was possible in so short a time, at last told the horsemen that they would not surrender Marius. The horsemen rode off in anger, and the sailors again changing their minds, came to land, and casting anchor at the mouth of the Liris, which spreads out like a lake, they advised Marius to disembark and take some food on land and to rest himself from his fatigues till a wind should rise: they added, that it was the usual time for the sea-breeze to decline, and for a fresh breeze to spring up from the marshes. Marius did as they advised, and the sailors carried him out of the vessel and laid him on the grass, little expecting what was to follow. The sailors immediately embarking again and raising the anchor, sailed off as fast as they could, not thinking it honourable to surrender Marius or safe to protect him. In this situation, deserted by everybody, he lay for some time silent on the shore, and at last recovering himself with difficulty, he walked on with much pain on account of there being no path. After passing through deep swamps and ditches full of water and mud, he came to the hut of an old man who worked in the marshes, and falling down at his feet, he entreated him to save and help a man, who, if he escaped from the present dangers, would reward him beyond all his hopes. The man, who either knew Marius of old or saw something in the expression of his countenance which indicated superior rank, said that his hut was sufficient to shelter him if that was all he wanted, but if he was wandering about to avoid his enemies, he could conceal him in a place which was more retired. Upon Marius entreating him to do so, the old man took him to the marsh, and bidding him lie down in a hole near the river he covered Marius with reeds and other light things of the kind, which were well adapted to hide him without pressing too heavily.

XXXVIII. After a short time a sound and noise from the hut reached the ears of Marius. Geminius of Terracina had sent a number of men in pursuit of him, some of whom, had chanced to come there, and were terrifying the old man and rating him for having harboured and concealed an enemy of the Romans. Marius, rising from his hiding-place and stripping off his clothes, threw himself into the thick and muddy water of the marsh; and this was the cause of his not escaping the search of his pursuers, who dragged him out covered with mud, and leading him naked to Minturnæ, gave him up to the magistrates. Now instructions had been already sent to every city, requiring the authorities to search for Marius, and to put him to death when he was taken. However, the magistrates thought it best to deliberate on the matter first, and in the meantime they lodged Marius in the house of a woman named Fannia, who was supposed not to be kindly disposed towards him on account of an old grudge. Fannia had a husband whose name was Tinnius, and on separating from him she claimed her portion, which was considerable. The husband charged her with adultery, and Marius, who was then in his sixth consulship, presided as judge. But on the trial it appeared that Fannia had been a loose woman, and that her husband, though he knew it, took her to wife, and lived with her a long time; accordingly, Marius being disgusted with both of them, decreed that the man should return the woman's portion, but he imposed on the woman, as a mark of infamy, a penalty of four copper coins. Fannia, however, did not on this occasion exhibit the feeling of a woman who had been wronged, but when she saw Marius, far from showing any resentment for the past, she did all that she could for him under the circumstances, and encouraged him. Marius thanked her, and said that he had good hopes, for a favourable omen had occurred to him, which was something of this sort:—When they were leading him along, and he was near the house of Fannia, the doors being opened, an ass ran out to drink from a spring which was flowing hard by: the ass, looking at Marius in the face with a bold and cheerful air, at first stood opposite him, and then making a loud braying, sprang past him frisking with joy. From this, Marius drew a conclusion, as he said that the deity indicated that his safety would come through the sea rather than through the land, for the ass did not betake himself to dry food, but turned from him to the water. Having said this to Fannia, he went to rest alone, bidding her close the door of the apartment.

XXXIX. The magistrates and council of Minturnæ, after deliberating, resolved that there ought to be no delay, and that they should put Marius to death. As none of the citizens would undertake to do it, a Gallic or Cimbrian horse-soldier, for the story is told both ways, took a sword and entered the apartment. Now that part of the room in which Marius happened to be lying was not very well lighted, but was in shade, and it is said that the eyes of Marius appeared to the soldier to dart a strong flame, and a loud voice issued from the gloom, "Man, do you dare to kill Caius Marius?" The barbarian immediately took to flight, and throwing the sword down, rushed through the door, calling out, "I cannot kill Caius Marius." This caused a general consternation, which was succeeded by compassion and change of opinion, and self-reproach for having come to so illegal and ungrateful a resolution concerning a man who had saved Italy, and whom it would be a disgrace not to assist. "Let him go, then," it was said, "where he pleases, as an exile, and suffer in some other place whatever fate has reserved for him. And let us pray that the gods visit us not with their anger for ejecting Marius from our city in poverty and rags." Moved by such considerations, all in a body entered the room where Marius was, and getting round him, began to conduct him to the sea. Though every man was eager to furnish something or other, and all were busying themselves, there was a loss of time. The grove of Marica, as it is called, obstructed the passage to the sea, for it was an object of great veneration, and it was a strict rule to carry nothing out of it that had ever been carried in; and now, if they went all round it, there would of necessity be delay: but this difficulty was settled by one of the older men at last calling out, that no road was inaccessible or impassable by which Marius was saved; and he was the first to take some of the things that they were conveying to the ship and to pass through the place.

XL. Everything was soon got ready through these zealous exertions, and a ship was supplied for Marius by one Belæus, who afterwards caused a painting to be made representing these events, and dedicated it in the temple. Marius embarking, was carried along by the wind, and by chance was taken to the island Ænaria, where he found Granius and the rest of his friends, and set sail with them for Libya. As their water failed, they were compelled to touch at Erycina in Sicily. Now the Roman quæstor, who happened to be about these parts on the look-out, was very nearly taking Marius when he landed; and he killed about sixteen of the men who were sent to get water. Marius, hastily embarking and crossing the sea to the island of Meninx, there learnt for the first time that his son had escaped with Cethegus, and that they were going to Iampsas (Hiempsal), king of the Numidians, to ask aid of him. This news encouraged him a little, and he was emboldened to move from the island to the neighbourhood of Carthage. At this time the governor of Libya was Sextilius, a Roman, who had neither received injury nor favour from Marius, and it was expected that he would help him, at least as far as feelings of compassion move a man. But no sooner had Marius landed with a few of his party, than an officer met him, and standing right in front of him said, "The Governor Sextilius forbids you, Marius, to set foot on Libya, and he says that if you do, he will support the decree of the Senate by treating you as an enemy." On hearing this, grief and indignation deprived Marius of utterance, and he was a long time silent, looking fixedly at the officer. Upon the officer asking Marius what he had to say, what reply he had for the governor, he answered with a deep groan, "Tell him you have seen Caius Marius a fugitive sitting on the ruins of Carthage": a reply in which he not unaptly compared the fate of that city and his own changed fortunes. In the meantime, Iampsas, the king of the Numidians, being unresolved which way to act, treated young Marius and his companions with respect, but still detained them on some new pretext whenever they wished to leave; and it was evident that he had no fair object in view in thus deferring their departure. However, an incident happened of no uncommon kind, which brought about their deliverance. The younger Marius was handsome, and one of the king's concubines was grieved to see him in a condition unbefitting his station; and this feeling of compassion was a beginning and motive towards love. At first, however, Marius rejected the woman's proposals, but seeing that there were no other means of escape, and that her conduct proceeded from more serious motives than mere passion, he accepted her proffered favours, and with her aid stole away with his friends and made his escape to his father. After embracing one another, they went along the shore, where they saw some scorpions fighting, which Marius considered to be a bad omen. Accordingly they forthwith embarked in a fishing boat, and passed over to the island Cercina, which was no great distance from the mainland; and it happened that they had only just set sail, when some horsemen despatched by the king were seen riding to the spot where they embarked. Marius thus escaped a danger equal to any that ever threatened him.

XLI. News reached Rome that Sulla was encountering the generals of Mithridates in Bœotia, while the consuls were quarrelling and taking up arms. A battle was fought, in which Octavius got the victory and ejected Cinna, who was attempting to govern by violent means, and he put in Cinna's place as consul Cornelius Merula; but Cinna collected troops in Italy and made war against Octavius. On hearing this, Marius determined to set sail immediately, which he did with some Moorish cavalry that he took from Africa, and some few Italians who had fled there, but the number of both together did not exceed a thousand. Coming to shore at Telamo in Tyrrhenia, and landing there, Marius proclaimed freedom to the slaves; and as the freemen who were employed in agriculture there, and in pasturing cattle, flocked to the sea, attracted by his fame, Marius persuaded the most vigorous of them to join him, and in a few days he had collected a considerable force and manned forty ships. Knowing that Octavius was an honourable man and wished to direct the administration in the justest way, but that Cinna was disliked by Sulla and opposed to the existing constitution, he determined to join him with his force. Accordingly he sent to Cinna and proffered to obey him as consul in everything. Cinna accepted the proposal, and naming Marius proconsul, sent him fasces and the other insigna of the office. Marius, however, observing that such things were not suited to his fortunes, clad in a mean dress, with his hair uncut from the day that he had been an exile, and now above seventy years of age, advanced with slow steps, wishing to make himself an object of compassion; but there was mingled with his abject mien more than his usual terrific expression of countenance, and through his downcast looks he showed that his passion, so far from being humbled, was infuriated by his reverses of fortune.

XLII. As soon as he had embraced Cinna and greeted the soldiers, Marius commenced active operations and gave a great turn to affairs. First of all, by attacking the corn-vessels with his ships and plundering the merchants, he made himself master of the supplies. He next sailed to the maritime cities, which he took; and, finally, Ostia being treacherously surrendered to him, he made plunder of the property that he found there and put to death many of the people, and by blocking up the river he completely cut off his enemies from all supplies by sea. He now moved on with his army towards Rome and occupied the Janiculus. Octavius damaged his own cause, not so much from want of skill as through his scrupulous observance of the law, to which he unwisely sacrificed the public interests; for though many persons advised him to invite the slaves to join him by promising their freedom, he refused to make them members of the State from which he was endeavouring to exclude Marius in obedience to the law. On the arrival at Rome of Metellus, the son of Metellus who had commanded in Libya, and had been banished from the city through the intrigues of Marius, the soldiers deserted Octavius and came to Metellus, entreating him to take the command and save the city; they said, if they had an experienced and active commander, they would fight well and get the victory. But Metellus expressed great dissatisfaction at their conduct, and bade them go to the consul, upon which they passed over to the enemy. Metellus also in despair left the city. But Octavius was persuaded by Chaldæans and certain diviners and interpreters of the Sibylline books to stay in Rome by the assurance that all would turn out well. Octavius, who in all other matters had as solid a judgment as any Roman, and most carefully maintained the consular dignity free from all undue influence according to the usage of his country and the laws, as if they were unchangeable rules, nevertheless showed great weakness in keeping company with impostors and diviners, rather than with men versed in political and military matters. Now Octavius was dragged down from the Rostra before Marius entered the city, by some persons who where sent forward, and murdered; and it is said that a Chaldæan writing was found in his bosom after he was killed. It seemed to be a very inexplicable circumstance, that of two illustrious commanders, Marius owed his success to not disregarding divination, and Octavius thereby lost his life.

XLIII. Matters being in this state, the Senate met and sent a deputation to Cinna and Marius to invite them into the city and to entreat them to spare the citizens. Cinna, as consul, sitting on his chair of office, gave audience to the commissioners and returned a kind answer: Marius stood by the consul's chair without speaking a word, but indicating by the unchanging heaviness of his brow and his gloomy look that he intended to fill Rome with slaughter. After the audience was over, they marched to the city. Cinna entered accompanied by his guards, but Marius halting at the gates angrily affected to have some scruples about entering. He said he was an exile and was excluded from his country by a law, and if anybody wanted to have him in the city, they must go to the vote again and undo the vote by which he was banished, just as if he were a man who respected the laws and were returning from exile to a free state. Accordingly he summoned the people to the Forum, but before three or four of the tribes had voted, throwing off the mask and setting aside all the talk about being legally recalled, he entered with some guards selected from the slaves who had flocked to him, and who were called Bardiæi. These fellows killed many persons by his express orders and many on the mere signal of his nod; and at last meeting with Ancharius, a senator who had filled the office of prætor, they struck him down with their daggers in the presence of Marius, when they saw that Marius did not salute him. After this whenever he did not salute a man or return his salute, this was a signal for them to massacre him forthwith in the streets, in consequence of which even the friends of Marius were filled with consternation and horror when they approached him. The slaughter was now great, and Cinna's appetite was dulled and he was satisfied with blood; but Marius daily went on with his passion at the highest pitch and thirsting for vengeance, through the whole list of those whom suspected in any degree. And every road and every city was filled with the pursuers, hunting out those who attempted to escape and conceal themselves, and the ties of hospitality and friendship were proved to be no security in misfortune, for they were very few who did not betray those who sought refuge with them. This rendered the conduct of the slaves of Cornutus the more worthy of praise and admiration, for they concealed their master at home, and hanging up by the neck the dead body of some obscure person, and putting a gold ring on his finger, they showed him to the guards of Marius, and then wrapping up the body as if it were their master's, they interred it. The device went unsuspected, and Cornutus being thus secreted by his slaves, made his escape to Gaul.

XLIV. The orator Marcus Antonius found a faithful friend, but still he did not escape. This man, though poor, and of the lower class, received in his house one of the most illustrious of the Romans, and wishing to entertain him as well as he could, he sent a slave to one of the neighbouring wine-shops to get some wine. As the slave was more curious than usual in tasting it, and told the man to give him some better wine, the merchant asked what could be the reason that he did not buy the new wine, as usual, and the ordinary wine, but wanted some of good quality and high price. The slave replied in his simplicity, as he was speaking to an old acquaintance, that his master was entertaining Marcus Antonius, who was concealed at his house. The wine-dealer, a faithless and unprincipled wretch, as soon as the slave left him, hurried off to Marius, who was at supper, and having gained admission, told him that he would betray Marcus Antonius to him. On hearing this, Marius is said to have uttered a loud shout and to have clapped his hands with delight; and he was near getting up and going to the place himself, but his friends stopped him, and he despatched Annius with some soldiers, with orders to bring him the head of Antonius immediately. On reaching the house, Annius waited at the door, and the soldiers mounting the stairs entered the room, but on seeing Antonius, every man began to urge some of his companions and push him forward to do the deed instead of himself. And so powerful were the charm and persuasion of his eloquence, when Antonius began to speak and pray for his life, that not a man of them could venture to lay hands on him or look him in the face, but they all bent their heads down and shed tears. As this caused some delay, Annius went upstairs, where he saw Antonius speaking and the soldiers awed and completely softened by his eloquence; on which he abused them, and running up to Antonius, cut off his head with his own hand. The friends of Catulus Lutatius, who had been joint consul with Marius and with him had triumphed over the Cimbri, interceded for him with Marius, and begged for his life; but the only answer they got was, "He must die!" and accordingly Catulus shut himself up in a room, and lighting a quantity of charcoal, suffocated himself. Headless trunks thrown into the streets and trampled underfoot excited no feeling of compassion, but only a universal shudder and alarm. But the people were most provoked by the licence of the Bardiæi, who murdered fathers of families in their houses, defiled their children, and violated their wives; and they went on plundering and committing violence, till Cinna and Sertorius combining, attacked them when they were asleep in the camp, and transfixed them with spears.

XLV. In the meantime, as if the wind was beginning to turn, reports reached Rome from all quarters that Sulla had finished the war with

Mithridates, and recovered the provinces, and was sailing against the city with a large force. This intelligence caused a brief cessation and pause to unspeakable calamities, for Marius and his faction were in expectation of the immediate arrival of their enemies. Now being elected consul for the seventh time, on the very Calends of January, which is the beginning of the year, Marius caused one Sextus Lucinus to be thrown down the Tarpeian rock, which appeared to be a presage of the great misfortunes that were again to befal the partisans of Marius and the State. But Marius was now worn out with labour, and, as it were, drowned with cares, and cowed in his spirit; and the experience of past dangers and toil made him tremble at the thoughts of a new war, and fresh struggles and alarms, and he could not sustain himself when he reflected that now he would have to hazard a contest, not with Octavius or Merula at the head of a tumultuous crowd and seditious rabble, but that Sulla was advancing—Sulla, who had once driven him from Rome, and had now confined Mithridates within the limits of his kingdom of Pontus. With his mind crushed by such reflections, and placing before his eyes his long wanderings and escapes and dangers in his flight by sea and by land, he fell into a state of deep despair, and was troubled with nightly alarms and terrific dreams in which he thought he heard a voice continually calling out, "Dreadful is the lion's lair Though he is no longer there."

As he greatly dreaded wakeful nights, he gave himself up to drinking and intoxication at unseasonable hours and to a degree unsuited to his age, in order to procure sleep, as if he could thus elude his cares. At last when a man arrived with news from the sea, fresh terrors seized him, partly from fear of the future and partly from feeling the burden and the weariness of the present state of affairs; and while he was in this condition, a slight disturbance sufficed to bring on a kind of pleurisy, as the philosopher Poseidonius relates, who also says that he had an interview and talked with him on the subject of his embassy, while Marius was sick. But one Caius Piso, an historian, says that Marius, while walking about with some friends after supper, fell to talking of the incidents of his life, beginning with his boyhood, and after enumerating his many vicissitudes of fortune, he said that no man of sense ought to trust fortune after such reverses; upon which he took leave of his friends, and keeping his bed for seven successive days, thus died. Some say that his ambitious character was most completely disclosed during his illness by his falling into the extravagant delusion that he was conducting the war against Mithridates, and he would then put his body into all kinds of attitudes and movements, as he used to do in battle, and accompany them with loud shouts and frequent cheers. So strong and unconquerable a desire to be engaged in that war had his ambitious and jealous character instilled into him; and therefore, though he had lived to be seventy years of age, and was the first Roman who had been seven times consul and had made himself a family, and wealth enough for several kings, he still bewailed his fortune, and complained of dying before he had attained the fulness and completion of his desires.

XLVI. Now Plato, being at the point of death, felicitated himself on his dæmon and his fortune, first that he was born a human being, then that he was a Greek, and neither a barbarian nor an irrational animal; and besides all this, that his birth had fallen on the time when Socrates lived. And indeed it is said that Antipater of Tarsus, in like manner, just before his death, when recapitulating the happiness that he had enjoyed, did not forget his prosperous voyage from Rome to Athens, inasmuch as he considered every gift of favourable fortune as a thing to be thankful for, and preserved it to the last in his memory, which is to man the best storehouse of good things. But those who have no memory and no sense, let the things that happen ooze away imperceptibly in the course of time; and consequently, as they hold nothing and keep nothing, being always empty of all goodness, but full of expectation, they look to the future and throw away the present. And yet fortune may hinder the future, but the present cannot be taken from a man; nevertheless, such men reject that which fortune now gives, as something foreign, and dream of that which is uncertain: and it is natural that they should; for before reason and education have enabled them to put a foundation and basement under external goods, they get and they heap them together, and are never able to fill the insatiate appetite of their soul. Now Marius died, having held for seventeen days his seventh consulship. And immediately there were great rejoicings in Rome, and good hope that there was a release from a cruel tyranny; but in a few days men found that they had exchanged an old master for a young one who was in the fulness of his vigour; such cruelty and severity did the son of Marius exhibit in putting to death the noblest and best citizens. He gained the reputation of a man of courage, and one who loved danger in his wars against his enemies, and was named a son of Mars: but his acts speedily showed his real character, and he received instead the name of a son of Venus. Finally, being shut up in Præneste by Sulla, and having in vain tried all ways of saving his life, he killed himself when he saw that the city was captured and all escape was hopeless.

# Life of Lysander

I. The treasury of the Akanthians at Delphi has upon it the following inscription: "The spoils which Brasidas and the Akanthians took from the Athenians." For this reason many suppose that the stone statue which stands inside the treasure-chamber, just by the door, is that of Brasidas; but it is really a copy of a statue of Lysander, wearing his hair and beard long, in the ancient fashion. For it is not true, as some say, that when the Argives after their great defeat shaved their hair in sign of mourning, the Spartans on the other hand, in pride at their victory let their hair grow long; nor was it because the Bacchiadæ, when they fled from Corinth to Sparta had their hair cut short, and looked mean and despicable that made the Spartans, themselves eager to let their hair grow long; but the fashion was enjoined by Lykurgus. It is recorded that he said of this mode of wearing the hair, that it made handsome men look handsomer, and made ugly men look more ferocious.

II. Aristokleitus, the father of Lysander, is said to have been a descendant of Herakles, though not a member of the royal family. Lysander was brought up in poverty, and, like other Spartans, proved himself obedient to discipline and of a manly spirit, despising all pleasures except that which results from the honour paid to those who are successful in some great action. This was the only enjoyment permitted to young men in Sparta; for they wish their children, from their very birth, to dread reproach and to be eager for praise, and he who is not stirred by these passions is regarded with contempt as a pluggish fellow without ambition.

Lysander retained throughout life the emulous desire for fame which had been instilled into him by his early training; but, though never wanting in ambition, yet he fell short of the Spartan ideal, in his habit of paying court to the great, and easily enduring the insolence of the powerful, whenever his own interests were concerned. Aristotle, when he observes that the temperaments of great men are prone to melancholy, instances Sokrates, Plato, and Herakles, and observes also that Lysander, when advanced in life, became inclined to melancholy. What is especially to be noted in his character is, that while he himself lived in honourable poverty, and never received a bribe from any one, that he nevertheless brought wealth and the desire for wealth into his native country, and took away from it its old boast of being superior to money; for after the war with Athens he filled the city with gold and silver, although he did not keep a drachma of it for himself.

When the despot Dionysius sent him some rich Sicilian dresses for his daughters, he refused them, saying that he feared they would make the girls look uglier than before. However, being shortly afterwards sent as ambassador to this same despot, when he again offered him two dresses, bidding him take whichever he chose for his daughter, he took them both away with him, saying that she would be better able to choose for herself.

III. Towards the end of the Peloponnesian war, the Athenians, after their great disaster in Sicily, seemed likely to lose the command of the sea, and even to be compelled to sue for peace from sheer exhaustion. But Alkibiades, after his return from exile, effected a great change in the position of Athens, and raised the Athenian navy to such a pitch that it was able to meet that of the Lacedæmonians on equal terms. At this the Lacedæmonians again began to fear for the result of the war. They determined to prosecute it with greater earnestness than before, and as they required a skilful general, as well as a large force, they gave Lysander the command of their fleet.

When he came to Ephesus, he found the city friendly to him, and willing enough to support the Lacedæmonian cause; but it was in a weak and ill-managed condition, and in danger of falling into the Persian manners and losing its Greek nationality, because it was close to Lydia, and the Persian generals generally made it their headquarters. But Lysander formed a camp there, ordered all transports to be directed to sail thither, and established a dockyard for the construction of ships of war. By this means he filled the harbour with trading vessels, and the market with merchandise, and brought money and business into every house and workshop; so that, thanks to him, the city then first began to entertain hopes of arriving at that pitch of greatness and splendour which it has since attained.

IV. When he heard that Cyrus, the son of the king of Persia, had arrived at Sardis, he went thither to confer with him, and to complain of the conduct of Tissaphernes, who, although he received orders to assist the Lacedæmonians, and to drive the Athenians from the sea, yet by means of the influence of Alkibiades appeared to be very much wanting in zeal for the Lacedæmonian cause, and to be ruining their fleet by his parsimony. Cyrus gladly listened to anything to the discredit of Tissaphernes, who was a worthless man and also a personal enemy of his own. After this Lysander gained considerable influence with the young prince, and induced him to carry on the war with greater spirit. When Lysander was about to leave the court, Cyrus invited him to a banquet, and begged him not to refuse his courtesies, but to demand whatever boon he pleased, as he would be refused nothing. Lysander replied, "Since, Cyrus, you are so very kind to me, I ask you to add an obolus to the pay of the sailors, so that they may receive four obols a day instead of three." Cyrus, pleased with his warlike spirit, presented him with ten thousand darics, with which money he paid the extra obolus to the sailors, and so improved the equipment of his fleet, that in a short time he all but emptied the enemy's ships; for their sailors deserted in crowds to the best paymaster, and those who remained behind were so disheartened and mutinous, that they gave their officers continual trouble. Yet even after he had thus weakened his enemy's forces Lysander dared not venture on a battle, knowing Alkibiades to be a brilliant general, and that his fleet was still the more numerous, while his many victories by sea and land made him feared at this period as invincible.

V. When, however, Alkibiades sailed from Samos to Phokæa he left his pilot Antiochus in command of the fleet. This man, wishing in a foolhardy spirit to insult Lysander, sailed into the harbour of Ephesus with two triremes, and arrogantly passed along the beach where the Lacedæmonian fleet lay drawn up, with loud laughter and noise. Lysander, enraged at this, at first only launched a few triremes to pursue him, but when he saw the Athenians coming to his assistance he manned his whole fleet, and brought on a general action. Lysander was victorious, took fifteen triremes, and erected a trophy. Upon this the Athenian people were greatly incensed against Alkibiades, and removed him from his command; and he, being insulted and ill-treated by the soldiery at Samos, withdrew from the Athenian camp to the Chersonesus. This battle, though not in itself remarkable, yet became so because of the misfortunes which it brought upon Alkibiades.

Lysander now invited to Ephesus all the bravest and most distinguished Greeks from the cities on the Ionic coast, and thus laid the foundation of all those oligarchies and revolutionary governments which were afterwards established there, by encouraging them to form political clubs, and devote themselves energetically to carrying on the war, because in the event of success they would not only conquer the Athenians, but also would be able to put down all democratic government, and establish themselves as absolute rulers in their respective cities. He proved the truth of his professions to these people by his acts, as he promoted those whom he personally knew, and those with whom he was connected by the ties of hospitality, to important posts and commands, aiding and abetting their most unscrupulous and unjust acts, so that all men began to look up to him and to be eager to win his favour, imagining that if he remained in power, their most extravagant wishes would be gratified. For this reason they were dissatisfied with Kallikratidas, when he took command of the fleet as Lysander's successor, and even after he had proved himself to be as brave and honest as a man could be, they still disliked his truthful, straightforward, Dorian manners. Yet they could not but admire his virtue, as men admire some antique heroic statue, although they regretted Lysander's ready zeal for the interest of his friends so much that some of them actually wept when he sailed away.

VI. Lysander made this class of persons yet more irritated against Kallikratidas by sending back to Sardis the balance of the money which he had received from Cyrus for the fleet, bidding the sailors ask Kallikratidas for pay, and see how he would manage to maintain the men. And when he finally left Ephesus, he endeavoured to force Kallikratidas to admit that he had handed over to him a fleet which was mistress of the seas. Kallikratidas, however, wishing to expose his vainglorious boasts, answered: "If so, sail from hence, passing Samos on your left, and hand over the fleet to me at Miletus; for we need not fear the Athenians at Samos, if our fleet is mistress of the seas." To this Lysander answered that it was not he, but Kallikratidas who was in command, and at once sailed away to Peloponnesus, leaving Kallikratidas in great perplexity; for he had brought no money with him from his own country, and he could not endure to wring money out of the distressed Greek cities on the coast. There remained only one course open to him: to go to the satraps of the king of Persia, and ask them for money, as Lysander had done. Kallikratidas was the worst man in the world for such a task, being high-spirited and generous, and thinking it less dishonourable for Greeks to be defeated by other Greeks than for them to court and flatter barbarians who had nothing to recommend them but their riches. Forced by want of money, however, he made a journey into Lydia, and at once went to the house of Cyrus, where he ordered the servants to say that the admiral Kallikratidas was come, and wished to confer with him. They answered, "Stranger, Cyrus is not at leisure; he is drinking." To this Kallikratidas with the greatest coolness replied: "Very well; I will wait until he has finished his draught." At this answer the Persians took him for a boor, and laughed at him, so that he went away; and, after presenting himself a second time and being again denied admittance, returned to Ephesus in a rage, invoking curses upon those who had first been corrupted by the barbarians, and who had taught them to behave so insolently because of their riches, and vowing in the presence of his friends that as soon as he reached Sparta, he would do all in his power to make peace between the Greek states, in order that they might be feared by the barbarians, and might no longer be obliged to beg the Persians to help them to destroy one another.

VII. But Kallikratidas, whose ideas were so noble and worthy of a Spartan, being as brave, honourable, and just a man as ever lived, perished shortly afterwards in the sea-fight at Arginusæ. Upon this, as the Lacedæmonian cause was going to ruin, the allied cities sent an embassy to Sparta, begging for Lysander to be again given the chief command, and promising that they would carry on the war with much greater vigour if he were their leader. Cyrus also sent letters to the same effect. Now as the Spartan law forbids the same man being twice appointed admiral, the Lacedæmonians, wishing to please their allies, gave the chief command nominally to one Arakus, but sent Lysander with him, with the title of secretary, but really with full power and authority. He was very welcome to the chief men in the various cities, who imagined that by his means they would be able to obtain much greater power, and to put down democracy throughout Asia; but those who loved plain and honourable dealing in a general thought that Lysander, when compared with Kallikratidas, appeared to be a crafty, deceitful man, conducting the war chiefly by subtilty and stratagem, using honourable means when it was his interest to do so, at other times acting simply on the rules of expediency, and not holding truth to be in itself superior to falsehood, but measuring the value of the one and the other by the profit which was to be obtained from them. He indeed laughed at those who said that the race of Herakles ought not to make wars by stratagem, saying, "Where the lion's skin will not protect us, we must sew the fox's skin to it."

VIII. All this is borne out by what he is said to have done at Miletus. Here his friends and connections, to whom he had promised that he would put down the democratic constitution and drive their enemies out of the city, changed their minds, and made up their quarrel with their political opponents. At this reconciliation Lysander publicly expressed great satisfaction and even seemed anxious to promote a good understanding, but in private he railed at them and urged them to attack the popular party. But as soon as he heard of an outbreak having taken place, he at once marched into the city, addressed the insurgents roughly, and sent them away in custody, harshly treated, as if he meant to inflict some signal punishment upon them, while he bade those of the popular faction take courage, and not to expect any ill-treatment while he was present. By this artifice he prevailed upon the chief men of the democratic party not to leave the city, but to remain and perish in it; as indeed they did, for every one who trusted to his word was put to death. Moreover, Androkleides relates a story which shows Lysander's extreme laxity with regard to oaths. He is said to have remarked, that "We cheat boys with dice, and men with oaths!" In this he imitated

Polykrates, the despot of Samos—an unworthy model for a Spartan general. Nor was it like a Spartan to treat the gods as badly as he treated his enemies, or even worse—for the man who overreaches his enemy by breaking his oath admits that he fears his enemy, but despises his god.

IX. Cyrus now sent for Lysander to Sardis, and gave him a supply of money, with promise of more. Nay, he was so zealous to show his attachment to Lysander that he declared, if his father would not furnish him with funds, that he would expend all his own property, and if other resources failed, that he would break up the gold and silver throne on which he was sitting. Finally, when he went away to Media to see his father, he empowered Lysander to receive the tribute from the subject cities, and placed the whole of his government in his hands. He embraced Lysander, begged him not to fight the Athenians by sea until he returned from court, promised that he would return with many ships from Phœnicia and Cilicia, and so departed.

Lysander was not able to fight the Athenians on equal terms, but yet he could not remain quiet with so large a number of ships. He accordingly put out to sea, induced several of the islands to revolt from Athens, and overran Ægina and Salamis. At length he landed in Attica, where he met Agis, who came down from Dekeleia to see him, and showed the land army what his naval force was, boasting that he could sail whither he pleased, and was master of the seas. However, when he discovered that the Athenians were in pursuit he fled precipitately back to Asia Minor. Finding the Hellespont unguarded, he attacked the city of Lampsakus by sea, while Thorax, who had arrived at the same place with the land forces, attacked it on that side. He took the city by storm, and, gave it up to his soldiers to plunder. Meanwhile, the Athenian fleet of a hundred and eighty triremes had just touched at Elaius in the Chersonese, but, hearing that Lampsakus was lost, proceeded to Sestos. Having taken in provisions at that place, they sailed to the "Goat's Rivers," opposite to Lampsakus, where the enemy's fleet still lay. One of the Athenian generals on this occasion was that Philokles who once induced the people to pass a decree that all prisoners of war should have their right thumbs cut off, so that they might not be able to hold a spear, but yet might work at the oar.

X. Hereupon both parties rested, expecting a sea-fight on the morrow. Lysander, however, had other intentions, but notwithstanding ordered the sailors to man their ships at daybreak, as if he intended to fight, and to remain quietly at their posts waiting for orders; and the land force was similarly drawn up by the sea-side. When the sun rose, the Athenian fleet rowed straight up to the Lacedæmonians, and offered battle, but Lysander, although his ships were fully manned, and had their prows pointing towards the enemy, would not let them engage, but sent small boats to the first line of his ships with orders not to move, but remain quietly in their places without any noise or attempt to attack. Though the Athenians retired towards evening, he would not let his men land before two or three triremes which he had sent to reconnoitre, returned with the intelligence that the enemy had disembarked. The same manœuvres took place on the next day, and also on the third and fourth days, so that the Athenians began to be very bold, and to despise their enemy, who seemed not to dare to attack them. At this time Alkibiades, who was living in his own forts in the Chersonese, rode over to the Athenian camp and blamed the generals for having in the first place encamped in a bad position, on an exposed sea-beach without any harbour, and pointed out their mistake in having to fetch all their provisions from Sestos, which was so far off, whereas they ought to have proceeded to the harbour and city of Sestos, where they would also be farther away from a watchful enemy, commanded by one general only, and so well disciplined as to be able to carry out his orders with great rapidity. These representations of Alkibiades were not listened to by the Athenian generals, one of whom, Tydeus, insolently replied that it was they, not he, who were in command.

XI. As besides this Alkibiades had some suspicions of treachery among them, he rode away. On the fifth day however, when the Athenians, after their customary offer of battle, had returned as usual, in a careless and negligent manner, Lysander sent out some ships to reconnoitre, with orders to row back again with all speed as soon as they saw the Athenians disembark, and when they reached the middle of the straits to hoist a brazen shield over their bows as a signal for advance. He himself sailed from ship to ship, addressing the steersmen and captains of each, urging them to be in their place with their full complement both of rowers and fighting-men on deck, and at the signal to row strongly and cheerfully against the enemy.

When the shield was raised, and the signal given by trumpet from the flag-ship, the fleet put to sea, while the land force marched rapidly along the shore towards the promontory. The straits here are only fifteen furlongs wide, a distance which was soon passed by the zeal of the Lacedæmonian rowers. Konon was the first of the Athenian generals who perceived the fleet approaching. He at once called out to the men to embark, and in his agony of distress at the disaster, ordered, implored, and forced them into their ships. But all his zeal was useless, scattered as the crews were; for as soon as they disembarked they at once, not expecting any attack, began some to purchase food in the market, some to stroll about, while some went to sleep in their tents, and some began to cook, without the least mistrust of that which befel them, through the ignorance and inexperience of their leaders. As by this time the enemy were close upon them, with loud cries and noise of oars, Konon with eight ships made his way safely through the enemy, and escaped to the court of Evagoras, king of Cyprus. As to the rest of the ships, the Peloponnesians took some of them empty, and sank the others as the sailors endeavoured to get on board of them. Of these men, many perished near their ships, as they ran to them in disorderly crowds, without arms, while others who fled away on land were killed by the enemy, who landed and went in pursuit of them. Besides these, three thousand men, including the generals, were taken prisoners. Lysander also captured the entire fleet, with the exception of the sacred trireme called the Paralus, and the eight ships which escaped with Konon. After plundering the camp, and taking all the captured ships in tow, he sailed back to Lampsakus with triumphal music of flutes and pæans of victory, having won a great victory with little labour, and in a short time brought to a close the longest and most uncertain war ever known in his times. There had been innumerable battles, and frequent changes of fortune, in which more generals had perished than in all the previous wars in Greece, and yet all was brought to a close by the wisdom and conduct of one man: which thing caused some to attribute this victory to the interposition of the gods.

XII. Some affirmed, that when Lysander's ship sailed out of the harbour of Lampsakus to attack the enemy, they saw the Dioskuri, like two stars, shining over the rudders. Some also say that the fall of the great stone was an omen of this disaster: for the common belief is that a vast stone fell down from Heaven into the Goat's Rivers, which stone is even now to be seen, and is worshipped by the people of the Chersonese. We are told that Anaxagoras foretold that in case of any slip or disturbance of the bodies which are fixed in the heavens, they would all fall down. The stars also, he said, are not in their original position, but being heavy bodies formed of stone, they shine by the resistance and friction of the atmosphere, while they are driven along by the violence of the circular motion by which they were originally prevented from falling, when cold and heavy bodies were separated from the general universe. There is a more credible theory on this subject, that shooting-stars are not a rush of ærial fire which is put out as soon as it is kindled, nor yet a blaze caused by a quantity of air being suddenly allowed to rush upwards, but that they are heavenly bodies, which from some failure in their rotatory power, fall from their orbit and descend, not often into inhabited portions of the earth, but for the most part into the sea, whereby they escape notice. This theory of Anaxagoras is confirmed by Daimachus in his treatise on Piety, where he states that for seventy-five days before the stone fell a fiery body of great size like a burning cloud, was observed in the heavens. It did not remain at rest, but moved in various directions by short jerks, so that by its violent swaying about many fiery particles were broken off, and flashed like shooting-stars. When, however, it sank to the earth, the inhabitants, after their first feeling of terror and astonishment were passed, collected together, and found no traces of fire, but merely a stone lying on the ground, which although a large one, bore no comparison to that fiery mass. It is evident that this tale of Daimachus can only find credit with indulgent readers: but if it be true, it signally confutes those who argue that the stone was wrenched by the force of a whirlwind from some high cliff, carried up high into the air, and then let fall whenever the violence of the tempest abated. Unless, indeed, that which was seen for so many days was really fire, which, when quenched, produced such a violent rushing and motion in the air as tore the stone from its place. A more exact enquiry into these matters, however, belongs to another subject.

XIII. Now Lysander, after the three thousand Athenians whom he had taken prisoners had been condemned to death by the council, called for Philokles their general, and asked him what punishment he thought that he deserved for having advised his fellow-countrymen to treat Greeks in such a cruel manner. Philokles, not in the least cast down by his misfortunes, bade him not to raise questions which no one could decide, but, since he was victor, to do what he would himself have suffered if vanquished. He then bathed, put on a splendid dress, and led his countrymen to execution, according to the account given by Theophrastus. After this Lysander sailed to the various cities in the neighbourhood, and compelled all the Athenians whom he met to betake themselves to Athens, giving out that he would spare no one, but put to death all whom he found without the city. His object in acting thus was to produce famine in Athens as speedily as possible, that the city might not give him the trouble of a long siege. He now destroyed the democratic and popular constitutions in all the Greek cities which had been subject to Athens, placing a Lacedæmonian in each as harmost or governor, with a council of ten archons under him, composed of men selected from the political clubs which he had established. He proceeded leisurely along, effecting these changes alike in the cities which had been hostile to him and in those which had fought on his side, as though he were preparing for himself a Greece in which he would take the first place. He did not choose his archons by their birth, or their wealth, but favoured his own friends and political adherents, to whom he gave irresponsible power; while by being present at several executions, and driving the opponents of his friends into exile, he gave the Greeks a very unpleasant idea of what they were to expect from the empire of Lacedæmon. The comic poet Theopompus therefore appears to talk at random when he compares the Lacedæmonians to tavern-keepers, because they at first poured out for the Greeks a most sweet draught of liberty and afterwards made it bitter; whereas in truth the taste of their rule was bitter from the beginning, as Lysander would not allow the people to have any voice in the government, and placed all the power in each city in the hands of the most daring and ambitious men of the oligarchical party.

XIV. After spending a short time in arranging these matters and having sent messengers to Laconia to announce that he was coming thither with a fleet of two hundred ships, he joined the Spartan kings, Agis and Pausanias, in Attica, and expected that the city of Athens would soon fall into his hands. Finding, however, that the Athenians made an obstinate defence, he crossed over to Asia again with the fleet. Here he overthrew the existing constitutions and established governments of ten in all the cities alike, putting many citizens to death, and driving many into exile. He drove out all the inhabitants from the island of Samos in a body, and handed over the cities in that island to those who had previously been banished. He also took Sestos from the Athenians, and would not allow the people of Sestos to live there, but gave the city and territory over to those who had acted as steersmen and masters on board of his ships. This indeed was the first of his acts which was cancelled by the Lacedæmonians, who restored Sestos to its inhabitants. Yet his proceedings were viewed with satisfaction by the Greeks, when he restored the Æginetans, who had for a long time been banished from their island, and also refounded Melos and Skione, the Athenians being driven away and forced to give up the cities.

By this time he learned that the people of Athens were nearly starved out, and consequently sailed to Peiræus and received the submission of the city, which was obliged to accept whatever terms of capitulation he chose to offer. I have indeed heard Lacedæmonians say that Lysander wrote to the Ephors, saying "Athens is taken;" and that they wrote to Lysander in answer, "To have taken it is enough." But this tale is merely invented for effect. The real decree of the Ephors ran as follows:—"This is the decision of the Lacedæmonian government. Throw down the walls of Peiræus and the Long Walls. Withdraw from all other cities and occupy your own land, and then you may have peace, if you wish for it, allowing likewise your exiles to return.

With regard to the number of the ships, whatever be judged necessary by those on the spot, that do."

The Athenians accepted these terms, by the advice of Theramenes the son of Hagnon: and on this occasion it is said that when he was asked by Kleomenes, one of the younger orators, how he dared to act and speak against what Themistokles had done, by giving up to the Lacedæmonians those walls which Themistokles had built in spite of them, he answered, "My boy, I am doing nothing contrary to Themistokles; for these same walls he built up to save his countrymen, and we will throw them down to save them. Indeed, if walls made a city prosperous, then ought Sparta, which has none, to be the most miserable of all."

XV. Now Lysander, after taking all the fleet of the Athenians except twelve ships, and having taken possession of their walls, began to take measures for the subversion of their political constitution, on the sixteenth day of the month Munychion, the same day on which they had defeated the Persians in the sea-fight at Salamis. As they were greatly grieved at this, and were loth to obey him, he sent word to the people that the city had broken the terms of its capitulation, because their walls were standing although the time within which they ought to have been destroyed had elapsed. He therefore would make an entirely new decision about their fate, because they had broken the treaty. Some writers say that he actually consulted the allies about the advisability of selling the whole population for slaves, in which debate the Theban Erianthus proposed to destroy the city and make the site of it a sheep walk. Afterwards, however, when the generals were drinking together a Phokian sang the first song in the Elektra of Euripides, which begins with the words—

"Elektra, Agamemnon's child, I reach thy habitation wild."

At this their hearts were touched, and it appeared to them to be a shameful deed to destroy so famous a city, and one which had produced such great men. After this, as the Athenians agreed to everything that Lysander proposed, he sent for a number of flute-players out of the city, collected all those in his camp, and destroyed the walls and burned the ships to the sound of music, while the allies crowned themselves with flowers and danced around, as though on that day their freedom began. Lysander now at once subverted the constitution, establishing thirty archons in the city, and ten in Peiræus, placing also a garrison in the Acropolis under the command of Kallibius, who acted as harmost, or governor. This man once was about to strike Autolykus the athlete, in whose house Xenophon has laid the scene of his "Symposium," with his staff, when Autolykus tripped him and threw him down. Lysander did not sympathise with his fall, but even reproached him, saying that he did not know how to govern free men. However, the Thirty, to please Kallibius, shortly afterwards put Autolykus to death.

XVI. After these transactions Lysander set sail for Thrace, but sent home to Sparta all the money for which he had no immediate occasion, and all the presents and crowns which he had received, in charge of Gylippus, who had held a command in Sicily during the war there. His wealth was very great, as many naturally had bestowed rich presents on one who had such great power as to be in some sort dictator of Greece. Gylippus is said to have cut open the seam at the bottom of each bag of money, taken a great deal of it out, and then to have sewn it up again, not knowing that there was a written note in each bag stating the amount which it contained. When he reached Sparta he hid the money which he had stolen under the tiles of his roof, and handed the bags over to the Ephors with the seals unbroken. When the bags were opened and the money counted, the amount was found not to agree with the written notes, and the Ephors were much perplexed at this until a servant of Gylippus explained the cause of it in a riddle, telling them that under his tiles roosted many owls. For, it seems, most of the money current at that period bore the Athenian device of the owl, in consequence of the extent of the Athenian empire.

Gylippus, having sullied the glory of his great achievements by this mean and sordid action, left Sparta in disgrace. Yet the wisest Spartans, fearing the power of the money for this very reason, that it was the chief men in the state who would be tempted by it, reproached Lysander for bringing it, and implored the Ephors to convey solemnly all the gold and silver coin away out of the country, as being so much "imported ruin." On this the Ephors invited discussion upon the subject. Theopompus tells us that it was Skiraphidas, but Ephorus says that it was Phlogidas who advised the Spartans not to receive the gold and silver coinage into their country, but to continue to use that which their fathers had used. This was iron money, which had first been dipped in vinegar when red hot, so that it could not be worked, as its being quenched in this manner rendered it brittle and useless, while it was also heavy, difficult to transport from place to place, and a great quantity of it represented but a small value. It appears probable that all money was originally of this kind, and that men used instead of coin small spits of iron or copper. For this reason we still call small coins obols, and we call six obols a drachma, meaning that this is the number of them which can be grasped by the hand.

XVII. The motion for sending away the money was opposed by Lysander's friends, who were eager to keep it in the state; so that it was at last decided that for public purposes this money might be used, but that if any private person were found in possession of it, he should be put to death: as if Lykurgus had been afraid of money itself, and not of the covetousness produced by it, which they did not repress by forbidding private men to own money so much as they encouraged it by permitting the state to own it, conferring thereby a certain dignity upon it over and above its real value. It was not possible for men who saw that the state valued silver and gold to despise it as useless, or to think that what was thus prized by the whole body of the citizens could be of no concern to individuals. On the contrary, it is plain that national customs much sooner impress themselves on the lives and manners of individuals, than do the faults and vices of individuals affect the national character. When the whole becomes corrupt the parts necessarily become corrupt with it; but the corruption of some of the parts does not necessarily extend to the whole, being checked and overpowered by those parts which remain healthy. Thus the Spartans made the law and the fear of death guard the houses of their citizens so that money could not enter them, but they did not guard their minds against the seductions of money, nay, even encouraged them to admire it, by proclaiming that it was a great and important matter that the commonwealth should be rich. However, I have discussed the conduct of the Lacedæmonians in this respect in another book.

XVIII. From the proceeds of the plunder which he had taken Lysander set up a brazen statue of himself and of each of the admirals at Delphi, and also offered up golden stars to the Dioskuri, which stars disappeared just before the battle of Leuktra. Besides this, in the treasury of Brasidas and the Akanthians there used to be a trireme made of gold and ivory, two cubits long, which was sent to him by Cyrus as a present on the occasion of his victory. Anaxandrides of Delphi also tells us that Lysander deposited there a talent of silver, fifty-two minæ, and eleven of the coins called staters, which does not agree with the accounts given by other writers of his poverty.

At this time Lysander was more powerful than any Greek had ever been before, and displayed an amount of pride and arrogance beyond even what his power warranted. He was the first Greek, we are told by Douris in his history, to whom cities erected altars and offered sacrifice as though he were a god, and he was the first in whose honour pæans were sung, one of which is recorded as having begun as follows:
"The praise of our fair Græcia's king That comes from Sparta, let us sing, Io pæan."

Nay, the Samians decreed that their festival, called Hερæa in honour of Hera, should be called Lysandreia. He always kept the poet Chœrilus in his train, that he might celebrate his actions in verse, and when Antilochus wrote some stanzas in his praise he was so pleased that he filled his hat with silver and gave it to him. Antimachus of Kolophon and one Nikeratus of Heraklea each wrote a poem on his deeds, and competed before him for a prize, at the Lysandreia. He gave the crown of victory to Nikeratus, which so enraged Antimachus that he suppressed his poem. Plato, who was a young man at that time, and admired the poetry of Antimachus, consoled him for his defeat by pointing out to him that the illiterate are as much to be pitied for their ignorance as the blind are for their loss of sight. When, however, the harper Aristonous, who had six times won the victory at the Pythian games, to show his regard to Lysander, told him that if he won the prize again he intended to have his name proclaimed by the herald as Lysander's servant, Lysander said, "Does he mean to proclaim himself my slave?"

XIX. This ambition of Lysander was only a burden to the great, and to those of equal rank with himself. But as none dared to thwart him, his pride and insolence of temper became intolerable. He proceeded to extravagant lengths both when he rewarded and when he punished, bestowing absolute government over important cities upon his friends, while he was satisfied with nothing short of the death of an enemy, and regarded banishment as too mild a sentence. Indeed, when subsequently to this he feared lest the chiefs of the popular party at Miletus might escape, and also wished to tempt those who had concealed themselves to leave their hiding-place, he swore that he would not harm them; and when they, trusting to his word, came forward and gave themselves up, he delivered them over to the aristocratical party to be put to death, to the number of not less than eight hundred men. In all the other cities, too, an indiscriminate massacre of the popular party took place, as Lysander not only put to death his own personal enemies, but also those persons against whom any of his friends in each city might happen to have a grudge. Wherefore Æteokles the Lacedæmonian was thought to have spoken well, when he said that "Greece could not have borne two Lysanders." We are told by Theophrastus that Archestratus made the same remark about Alkibiades: although in his case it was insolence, luxury and self-will which gave so much offence, whereas Lysander's harsh, merciless disposition was what made his power so hateful and terrible.

At first the Lacedæmonians paid no attention to complaints brought against him; but when Pharnabazus, who had been wronged by Lysander's depredations on his country, sent an embassy to Sparta to demand justice, the

Ephors were much enraged. They put to death Thorax, one of his friends, whom they found in possession of silver coin, and they sent a skytale to him bidding him appear before them. I will now explain what a skytale was. When the Ephors sent out any one as general or admiral of their forces, they used to prepare two round sticks of wood of exactly the same length and thickness, corresponding with one another at the ends. One of these they kept themselves, and the other they gave to the person sent out. These sticks they call skytales. Now when they desire to transmit some secret of importance to him, they wrap a long narrow strip of paper like a strap round the skytale which is in their possession, leaving no intervals, but completely covering the stick along its whole length with the paper. When this has been done they write upon the paper while it is upon the stick, and after writing they unwind the paper and send it to the general without the stick. When he receives it, it is entirely illegible, as the letters have no connection, but he winds it round the stick in his possession so that the folds correspond to one another, and then the whole message can be read. The paper is called skytale as well as the stick, as a thing measured is called by the name of the measure.

XX. Lysander, when this skytale reached him at the Hellespont, was much troubled, and as he especially feared the accusations of Pharnabazus, he hastened to confer with him, with a view to settling their dispute. When they met, Lysander begged him to write a second letter to the Spartan government, stating that he had not received any wrong, and that he had no charge to bring against him. It was, however, a case of "diamond cut diamond," as the proverb has it, for Pharnabazus, while he ostensibly promised to do everything that Lysander wished, and to send publicly a letter dictated by him, had by him another privately-written despatch, and when the seals were about to be affixed, as the two letters looked exactly alike, he substituted the privately-written one for that which Lysander had seen. When then Lysander reached Lacedæmon, and proceeded, as it customary, to the senate-house, he handed over to the Ephors this letter of Pharnabazus, with the conviction that thereby he was quashing the most important of all the charges against himself; for Pharnabazus was much loved by the Lacedæmonians, because he had taken their part in the war more zealously than any other Persian satrap. When, however, the Ephors showed him the letter, and he perceived that "Others besides Odysseus can contrive," he retired in great confusion, and a few days afterwards, on meeting with the Ephors, informed them that he must go and pay a sacrifice to Ammon; which he had vowed before winning his victories. Some historians tell us that this was true, and that when he was besieging Aphytæ, a city in Thrace, the god Ammon appeared to him in a dream; in consequence of which he raised the siege, imagining this to be the will of the god, ordered the inhabitants to sacrifice to Ammon, and himself made preparations for proceeding at once to Libya to propitiate the god. Most persons, however, imagined that this was a mere pretence, but that really he feared the Ephors, and was unable to endure the harsh discipline of life at Sparta, and therefore wished to travel abroad, just as a horse longs for liberty when he has been brought back out of wide pastures to his stable and his accustomed work. As to the cause which Ephorus gives for these travels of his, I will mention that presently.

XXI. After having with great difficulty obtained permission from the Ephors, he set sail. Now as soon as he left the country, the two kings, perceiving that by means of his device of governing the cities of Greece by aristocratic clubs devoted to his interest he was virtually master of the whole country, determined to restore the popular party to power and to turn out Lysander's friends. When however this movement was set on foot, and when first of all the Athenians starting from Phyle attacked the Thirty and overpowered them, Lysander returned in haste, and prevailed upon the Lacedæmonians to assist the cause of oligarchy and put down these popular risings. They decided that the first government which they would aid should be that of the Thirty, at Athens; and they proposed to send them a hundred talents for the expenses of the war, and Lysander himself as their general. But the two kings, envying his power, and fearing that he would take Athens a second time, determined that one of themselves should proceed thither in his stead. Pausanias accordingly went to Athens, nominally to assist the Thirty against the people, but really to put an end to the war, for fear that Lysander by means of his friends might a second time become master of Athens. This he easily effected; and by reconciling all classes of Athenians to one another and putting an end to the revolution, he made it impossible for Lysander to win fresh laurels. But when shortly afterwards the Athenians again revolted he was much blamed for having allowed the popular party to gather strength and break out of bounds, after it had once been securely bridled by an oligarchy, while Lysander on the contrary gained the credit of having, in every city, arranged matters not with a view to theatrical effect, but to the solid advantage of Sparta.

XXII. He was bold in his speech, and overbearing to those who opposed him. When the Argives had a dispute with the Lacedæmonians about their frontier, and seemed to have justice on their side, Lysander drew his sword, saying, "He that is master of this is in possession of the best argument about frontier lines." When some Megarian in a public meeting used considerable

freedom of speech towards him, he answered, "My friend, your words require a city to back them." He asked the Bœotians, who wished to remain neutral, whether he should pass through their country with spears held upright or levelled. On the occasion of the revolt of Corinth, when he brought up the Lacedæmonians to assault their walls, he observed that they seemed unwilling to attack. At this moment a hare was seen to leap across the ditch, upon which he said, "Are you not ashamed to fear such enemies as these, who are so lazy as to allow hares to sleep upon their walls?" When king Agis died, leaving a brother, Agesilaus, and a son Leotychides who was supposed to be his, Lysander, who was attached to Agesilaus, prevailed upon him to lay claim to the crown as being a genuine descendant of Herakles. For Leotychides laboured under the imputation of being the son of Alkibiades, who carried on an intrigue with Timæa the wife of Agis, when he was living in Sparta as an exile. It is said that Agis, after making a calculation about the time of his wife's pregnancy treated Leotychides with neglect and openly denied that he was his father. When however he was brought to Heræa during his last illness, and was at the point of death, he was induced by the entreaties of the youth and his friends to declare in the presence of many witnesses that Leotychides was his legitimate son, and died begging them to testify this fact to the Lacedæmonians. They did indeed so testify in favour of Leotychides; and although Agesilaus was a man of great distinction, and had the powerful assistance of Lysander, yet his claims to the crown were seriously damaged by one Diopeithes, a man deep read in oracular lore, who quoted the following prophecy in reference to the lameness of Agesilaus:
"Proud Sparta, resting on two equal feet, Beware lest lameness on thy kings alight; Lest wars unnumbered toss thee to and fro, And thou thyself be ruined in the fight."

But when many were persuaded by this oracle and looked to Leotychides as the true heir, Lysander said that they did not rightly understand it; for what it meant was, he argued, not that the god forbade a lame man to reign, but that the kingdom would be lame of one foot if base-born men should share the crown with those who were of the true race of Herakles. By this argument and his own great personal influence he prevailed, and Agesilaus became king of Sparta.

XXIII. Lysander now at once began to urge him to make a campaign in Asia, holding out to him hopes of conquering the Persians and making himself the greatest man in the world. He also wrote to his friends in Asia, bidding them ask the Lacedæmonians to send them Agesilaus to act as their commander in chief in the war with the Persians. They obeyed, and sent an embassy to demand him: which was as great an honour to Agesilaus as his being made king, and which, like the other, he owed to Lysander alone. However, ambitious natures, though in other respects fit for great commands, often fail in important enterprises through jealousy of their rivals; for they make those men their opponents who would otherwise have been their assistants in obtaining success. On this occasion Agesilaus took Lysander with him, as the chief of his board of thirty counsellors, and treated him as his greatest friend; but when they reached Asia, the people there would not pay their court to Agesilaus, whom they did not know, while all Lysander's friends flocked round him to renew their former intimacy, and all those who feared him assiduously courted his favour. Thus, as in a play we often see that a messenger or servant engrosses all the interest of the spectators and really acts the leading part, while he who wears the crown and bears the sceptre is hardly heard to speak, so now it was the counsellor who obtained all the honours due to a commander in chief, while the king had merely the title without any influence whatever. It was necessary, no doubt, that this excessive power of Lysander should be curtailed, and he himself forced to take the second place: but yet to disgrace and ruin a friend and one from whom he had received great benefits, would have been unworthy of Agesilaus. Consequently at first he did not entrust him with the conduct of matters of importance, and did not give him any separate command. In the next place, he invariably disobliged, and refused the applications, of any persons on whose behalf he understood Lysander to be interested, and thus gradually undermined his power. When however after many failures Lysander perceived that his interest on his friends' behalf was a drawback rather than an advantage to them, he ceased from urging their claims, and moreover begged them not to pay their court to him, but to attach themselves to the king, and to those who were able to promote and reward their followers. Most of them on hearing this no longer troubled him on matters of business, but continued on the most friendly terms with him, and angered Agesilaus more than ever by the manner in which they flocked round him in public places and walks, showing thereby their dislike to the king. Agesilaus now bestowed the government of cities and the conduct of important expeditions upon various obscure soldiers, but appointed Lysander his carver, and then in an insulting manner told the Ionians to go and pay their court to his carver. At this Lysander determined to have an interview with him, and there took place a short and truly Laconian dialogue between them. Lysander said, "You know well, Agesilaus, how to humble your friends." "Yes," answered he, "if they desire to be greater than I am: but those who increase my power have a right to share it."

"Perhaps," said Lysander, "you have spoken better than I have acted; however, if it be only on account of the multitude whose eyes are upon us, I beg you to appoint me to some post in which I may be of more use to you, and cause you less annoyance than at present."

XXIV. Upon this he was sent on a special mission to the Hellespont, where although he was at enmity with Agesilaus, he did not neglect his duty, but, finding that the Persian Spithridates, a man of noble birth and commanding a considerable force, was on bad terms with Pharnabazus, he induced him to revolt, and brought him back with him to Agesilaus. After this Lysander was given no further share in the conduct of the war, and after some time sailed back to Sparta in disgrace, full of rage against Agesilaus, and hating the whole Spartan constitution more than ever. He now determined without any further delay to put in practice the revolutionary plans which he had so long meditated. These were as follows:—When the descendants of Herakles, after associating with the Dorians, returned to Peloponnesus, their race grew and flourished at Sparta. Yet it was not every family of the descendants of Herakles, but only the children of Eurypon and Agis who had a right to the throne, while the others gained no advantage from their noble birth, as all honours in the state were given according to merit. Now Lysander, being a descendant of Herakles, after he had gained great glory by his achievements and obtained many friends and immense influence, could not endure that the state should reap such great advantages from his success, and yet continue to be ruled by men of no better family than himself. He meditated, therefore, the abolition of the exclusive right to the throne possessed by these two families, and throwing it open to all the descendants of Herakles, or even, according to some historians, to all Spartans alike, in order that the crown might not belong to the descendants of Herakles, but to those who were judged to be like Herakles in glory, which had raised Herakles himself to a place among the gods themselves. If the throne were disposed of in this manner he imagined that no Spartan would be chosen king before himself.

XXV. First then he proposed to endeavour to win over his countrymen to his views by his own powers of persuasion, and with this object studied an oration written for him by Kleon of Halikarnassus. Soon, however, he perceived that so new and important a scheme of reform would require more violent means to carry it into effect, and, just as in plays supernatural machinery is resorted to where ordinary human means would fail to produce the wished-for termination, even so did Lysander invent oracular responses and prophecies and bring them to bear on the minds of his countrymen, feeling that he would gain but little by pronouncing Kleon's oration, unless the Spartans had previously, by superstition and religious terrors, been brought into a state of feeling suitable for its reception. Ephorus relates in his history that Lysander endeavoured by means of one Pherekles to bribe the priestess at Delphi, and afterwards those of Dodona; and that, as this attempt failed, he himself went to the oracle of Ammon and had an interview with the priests there, to whom he offered a large sum of money. They also indignantly refused to aid his schemes, and sent an embassy to Sparta to charge him with having attempted to corrupt them. He was tried and acquitted, upon which the Libyans, as they were leaving the country, said:—"We at any rate, O Spartans, will give more righteous judgments when you come to dwell amongst us"—for there is an ancient oracle which says that the Lacedæmonians shall some day settle in Libya. Now as to the whole framework of Lysander's plot, which was of no ordinary kind, and did not take its rise from accidental circumstances, but consisted, like a mathematical demonstration, of many complicated intrigues all tending to one fixed point, I will give a short abstract of it extracted from the works of Ephorus, who was both an historian and a philosopher.

XXVI. There was a woman in Pontus who gave out that she was pregnant by Apollo. As might be expected, many disbelieved in her pretensions, but many more believed in them, so that when a male child was born of her, it was cared for and educated at the charge of many eminent persons. The child, for some reason or other, was given the name of Silenus. Lysander, starting with these materials, constructed the rest of the story out of his own imagination. He was assisted in his scheme by many persons of the highest respectability, who unsuspiciously propagated the fable about the birth of the child: and who also procured another mysterious story from Delphi, which they carefully spread abroad at Sparta, to the effect that some oracles of vast antiquity are guarded by the priests at Delphi, in writings which it is not lawful to read; nor may any one examine them or look upon them, until in the fulness of time one born of Apollo shall come, and after clearly proving his birth to the guardians of these writings, shall take the tablets which contain them. This having been previously arranged, Silenus's part was to go and demand the oracles as Apollo's child, while those of the priests who were in the plot were to make inquiries and examine carefully into his birth, and at length were to appear convinced of the truth of the story, and show the writings to him, as being really the child of Apollo. He was to read aloud in the presence of many persons all the oracles contained in the tablets, especially one which said that it would be better for the Spartans to choose their kings from the best of the citizens. Silenus was nearly grown up, and the time to make the attempt had almost arrived, when the whole plot was ruined by the cowardice of one of the principal conspirators, whose heart failed him when the moment for action arrived. None of these particulars, however, were discovered till after Lysander's death.

XXVII. Before Agesilaus returned from Asia Lysander perished in a Bœotian war in which he had become involved, or rather had involved Greece; for various accounts are given of it, some laying the blame upon him, some upon the Thebans, and some upon both. It was urged against the Thebans that they overturned the altar at Aulis and scattered the sacrifice, and also that Androkleides and Amphitheus, having been bribed by Persia to induce all the Greek states to attack the Lacedæmonians, had invaded the Phokian territory and laid it waste. On the other hand Lysander is said to have been angry that the Thebans alone should claim their right to a tenth part of the plunder obtained in the war, though the other allies made no such demand, and that they should have expressed indignation at Lysander's sending such large sums of money to Sparta. He was especially wroth with them for having afforded the Athenians the means of freeing themselves from the domination of the Thirty, which he had himself established, and which the Lacedæmonians had endeavoured to support by decreeing that all exiled Athenians of the popular party might be brought back to Athens from whatever place they might be found in, and that those who protected them against being forcibly brought back should be treated as outlaws. In answer to this the Thebans passed a decree worthy of themselves, and deserving of comparison with the great acts of Herakles and Dionysus, the benefactors of mankind. Its provisions were, that every city and every house in Bœotia should be open to those Athenians who required shelter, that whoever did not assist an Athenian exile against any one who tried to force him away should be fined a talent, and that if any marched under arms through Bœotia to attack the despots at Athens, no Theban should either see or hear them. Not only did they make this kindly and truly Hellenic decree, but they also acted up to the spirit of it; for when Thrasybulus and his party seized Phyle, they started from Thebes, supplied with arms and necessaries by the Thebans, who also assisted them to keep their enterprise secret and to begin it successfully. These were the charges brought against the Thebans by Lysander.

XXVIII. His naturally harsh temper was now soured by age, and he urged on the Ephors into declaring war against the Thebans, and appointing him their general to carry it on. Subsequently, however, they sent the king, Pausanias, with an army, to co-operate with him. Pausanias marched in a circuitous course over Mount Kithæron, meaning to invade Bœotia on that side, while Lysander with a large force came to meet him through Phokis. He took the city of Orchomenus, which voluntarily came over to his side, and he took Lebadeia by storm and plundered it. He now sent a letter to Pausanias bidding him march through the territory of Platæa and join him at Haliartus, promising that at daybreak he would be before the walls of Haliartus. The messenger who carried this letter fell into the hands of the enemy, and the letter was taken to Thebes. Hereupon the Thebans entrusted their city to the care of the Athenians, who had come to their aid, and themselves started early in the evening, reached Haliartus a little before Lysander, and threw a body of troops into the town. Lysander, on discovering this, at first determined to halt his army on a hill in the neighbourhood and await the arrival of Pausanias: but as the day went on he could remain quiet no longer, but got his men under arms, harangued the allied troops, and led them in a close column down the road directly towards the city. Upon this those of the Thebans who had remained outside the walls, leaving the city on their left hand, marched to attack the extreme rear of the Lacedæmonians, near the fountain which is called Kissousa, in which there is a legend that Dionysus was washed by his nurses after his birth; for the water is wine-coloured and clear, and very sweet-tasted. Round the fountain is a grove of the Cretan Storax-trees, which the people of Haliartus point to as a proof of Rhadamanthus having lived there. They also show his tomb, which they call Alea. The sepulchre of Alkmena too is close by: for the story goes that she married Rhadamanthus here after the death of Amphitryon. Meanwhile the Thebans in the city, together with the citizens of Haliartus themselves, remained quiet until Lysander and the first ranks of the enemy came close to the walls, and then suddenly opening the gates they charged and slew him together with his soothsayer and some few more: for most of them fled quickly back to the main body. However as the Thebans did not desist but pressed on, the whole mass took to flight, and escaped to the neighbouring hills with a loss of about one thousand men. Three hundred of the Thebans also fell in an attack which they made on the enemy in rough and difficult ground. These men had been accused of favouring the Lacedæmonians, and it was to wipe out this unjust imputation before the eyes of their fellow citizens that they showed themselves so reckless of their lives.

XXIX. When Pausanias heard of this disaster, he was marching from Platæa towards Thespiæ. He at once put his troops in array and proceeded to Haliartus. Here likewise arrived Thrasybulus from Thebes, with an Athenian force. On his arrival, Pausanias proposed to apply for permission to carry

away the dead. This proposal greatly shocked the older Spartans, who could not refrain from going to the king and imploring him not to receive back Lysander's corpse by a truce which was in itself a confession of defeat, but to let them fight for his body and either bury it as victors, or else to share their general's fate as became them. However, in spite of these representations, Pausanias, perceiving that it would be no easy task to overcome the Thebans, flushed as they were with the victory of the day before, and that, as Lysander's body lay close under the walls of the town, it would be almost impossible, even if they were victorious, to recover it otherwise than by treaty, sent a herald, obtained the necessary truce, and led away his forces. As soon as the Spartans crossed the Bœotian frontier they buried the body of Lysander in the territory of the friendly and allied city of Panope, in Phokis, where at the present day his monument stands by the side of the road from Chæronea to Delphi. It is said that while the army was encamped there one of the Phokians, while describing the battle to another who had not been present, said that the enemy fell upon them just after Lysander had crossed the Hoplites. A Spartan who was present was surprised at this word, and enquired of Lysander's friend, what he meant by the Hoplites, for he did not understand it. "It was where," answered he, "the enemy overthrew our front ranks; for they call the stream which runs past the city the Hoplites." On hearing these words the Spartan burst into tears, and exclaimed, "How impossible is it for a man to escape his fate:"—for it seems Lysander had received an oracular warning in these words:
"I warn thee, shun Hoplites roaring track. And th' earth-born snake that stings behind thy back."

Some say that the Hoplites does not run by Haliartus, but that it is the name of a torrent which joins the river Philarus near Koronea, which used to be called the Hoplias, and is now called Isomantus. The man who killed Lysander was a citizen of Haliartus named Neochorus, who bore a snake as the device upon his shield, which it is supposed was alluded to by the oracle.

We are also told that during the Peloponnesian war the Thebans received an oracle from Apollo Ismenius, referring immediately to the battle of Delium, and also to this battle at Haliartus, which took place thirty years afterwards. It ran as follows:
"Beware the boundary, when you hunt The wolf with spears; And shun the Orchalian hill, the fox's haunt, For endless years."

The boundary alludes to the country near Delium, which is on the borders of Attica and Bœotia, and the Orchalian hill, which is now called Fox-hill, lies in the territory of Haliartus, on the side nearest Mount Helikon.

XXX. The death of Lysander, as related above, grieved the Spartans so much that they impeached their king on a capital charge, and he, fearing the result of the trial, fled to Tegea, where he spent the remainder of his life in the sanctuary of Athena as a suppliant of the goddess. Moreover the poverty of Lysandor, which was discovered after his death, made his virtue more splendid, for although he had handled great sums of money, and possessed immense power; though his favour had been courted by wealthy cities, and even by the great king of Persia himself, yet Theopompus tells us that he did not in the least degree improve his family estate: an account which we may the more readily believe, as it is told us by a historian who is more prone to censure than to admiration. In later times we learn from the historian Ephorus that some dispute arose between the allied cities which rendered it necessary to examine Lysander's papers, and that Agesilaus went to his house for this purpose. Here he found the scroll upon which was written the speech about altering the constitution; advising the Spartans to abolish the hereditary right to the throne enjoyed by the old royal families of Eurypon and Agis, and to throw it open to the best of the citizens without restriction. Agesilaus was eager to publish this speech abroad, and show his fellow-countrymen what sort of a man Lysander had really been; but Lakratides, a wise man, who was at that time chief of the board of Ephors, restrained him, pointing out that it would be wrong to disturb Lysander in his grave, and that it would be better that so clever and insidious a composition should be buried with him. Among other honours which were paid to Lysander after death, the Spartans fined the suitors of his daughters, because when after his death his poverty was discovered, they refused to marry them, thus showing that they had paid their court to him when they believed him to be rich, and neglected him when his poverty proved him to have been just and honourable. It appears that in Sparta there were actions at law against men who did not marry, or who married too late in life or unbecomingly: under which last head came those who tried to marry into rich families, instead of marrying persons of good birth and their own friends. This is what we have found to tell about the life of Lysander.

# Life of Sulla.

I. Lucius Cornelius Sulla, by birth, belonged to the Patricians, whom we may consider as corresponding to the Eupatridæ. Among his ancestors is enumerated Rufinus, who became consul; but is less noted for attaining this honour than for the infamy which befell him. He was detected in possessing above ten pounds' weight of silver plate, which amount the law did not permit, and he was ejected from the Senate. His immediate descendants continued in a mean condition, and Sulla himself was brought up with no great paternal property. When he was a young man he lived in lodgings, for which he paid some moderate sum, which he was afterwards reproached with, when he was prospering beyond his deserts, as some thought. It was after the Libyan expedition, when he was assuming airs of importance and a haughty tone, that a man of high rank and character said to him, How can you be an honest man who are now so rich, and yet your father left you nothing? For though the Romans no longer remained true to their former integrity and purity of morals, but had declined from the old standard, and let in luxury and expense among them, they still considered it equally a matter of reproach for a man to have wasted the property that he once had, and not to remain as poor as his ancestors. Subsequently when Sulla was in the possession of power and was putting many to death, a man of the class of Libertini, who was suspected of concealing a proscribed person, and for this offence was going to be thrown down the Tarpeian rock, reproached Sulla with the fact that they had lived together for some time in one house; that he had paid two thousand sestertii for his lodgings, which were in the upper part of the house, and Sulla three thousand for the lower rooms; and, consequently, that between their fortunes there was only the difference of a thousand sestertii, which is equivalent to two hundred and fifty Attic drachmæ. This is what is recorded of Sulla's early condition.

II. As for his person, we may judge of it by his statues, except his eyes and complexion. His eyes were an uncommonly pure and piercing blue, which the colour of his face rendered still more terrific, being spotted with rough red blotches, interspersed with the white; from which circumstance, it is said, he got his name Sulla, which had reference to his complexion; and one of the Athenian satirists in derision made the following verse in allusion to it: "Sulla is a mulberry besprinkled with meal."

It is not out of place to avail ourselves of such traits of a man who is said to have had so strong a natural love of buffoonery, that when he was still young and of no repute, he spent his time and indulged himself among mimi and jesters; and when he was at the head of the state, he daily got together from the scena and the theatre the lewdest persons, with whom he would drink and enter into a contest of coarse witticisms, in which he had no regard to his age, and, besides degrading the dignity of his office, he neglected many matters that required attention. It was not Sulla's habit when he was at table to trouble himself about anything serious, but though he was energetic and rather morose at other times, he underwent a complete change as soon as he went into company and was seated at an entertainment, for he was then exceedingly complaisant to singers of mimi and dancers, and easy of access and affable. This habit of relaxation seems to have produced in him the vice of being exceedingly addicted to women and that passion for enjoyment which stuck to him to his old age. In his youth he was for a long time attached to one Metrobius, an actor. The following incident also happened to him:—He formed an attachment to a woman named Nicopolis, who was of mean condition, but rich, and from long familiarity and the favour which he found on account of his youth, he came to be considered as a lover, and when the woman died she left him her heir. He also succeeded to the inheritance of his step-mother, who loved him as her own son; and in this way he acquired a moderate fortune.

III. On being appointed Quæstor to Marius in his first consulship, he sailed with him to Libya, to prosecute the war against Jugurtha. In this campaign he showed himself a man of merit, and by availing himself of a favourable opportunity he made a friend of Bocchus, king of the Numidians. Some ambassadors of Bocchus who had escaped from Numidian robbers were hospitably received by Sulla, and sent back with presents and a safe conduct. Now Bocchus happened for some time to have disliked his son-in-law Jugurtha, whom he was also afraid of; and as Jugurtha had been defeated by the Romans and had fled to Bocchus, he formed a design to make him his prisoner and deliver him to his enemies; but as he wished Sulla to be the agent rather than himself, he invited Sulla to come and see him. Sulla communicated the message to Marius, and, taking a few soldiers with him, ventured on the hazardous enterprise of putting himself in the hands of a barbarian who never kept his faith even with his friends, and this for the purpose of having another man betrayed to him. Bocchus, having got both of them in his power, was under the necessity of being treacherous to one of them, and after great fluctuations in his resolution, he finally carried into effect his original perfidious design, and surrendered Jugurtha to Sulla. Marius enjoyed the triumph for the capture of Jugurtha, but the honour of the success was given to Sulla through dislike of Marius, which caused Marius some uneasiness; for Sulla was naturally of an arrogant disposition, and as this was the first occasion, on which he had been raised from a mean condition and obscurity to be of some note among his fellow-citizens, and had tasted the sweets of distinction, he carried his pride so far as to have a seal-ring cut, on which the occurrence was represented, and he wore it constantly. The subject represented was Bocchus surrendering and Sulla receiving the surrender of Jugurtha.

IV. Though Marius was annoyed at this, yet as he still thought Sulla beneath his jealousy, he employed him in his campaigns—in his second consulship in the capacity of legate, and in his third consulship as tribune; and by his instrumentality Marius effected many important objects. In his capacity of legate Sulla took Copillius, king of the Tectosages; and when he was a tribune he persuaded the powerful and populous nation of the Marsi to become friends and allies to Rome. But now perceiving that Marius was jealous of him, and was no longer willing to give him the opportunity of distinguishing himself, but opposed his further rise, Sulla attached himself to Catulus, the colleague of Marius, who was an honest man, but inactive as a soldier. Sulla being entrusted by Catulus with all matters of the greatest moment, thus attained both influence and reputation. In his military operations he reduced a large part of the Alpine barbarians; and on one occasion, when there was a scarcity of provisions in the camp, he undertook to supply the want, which he did so effectually that the soldiers of Catulus had not only abundance for themselves, but were enabled to relieve the army of Marius. This, as Sulla himself says, greatly annoyed Marius. Now this enmity, so slight and childish in its foundation and origin, was continued through civil war and the inveterate animosity of faction, till it resulted in the establishment of a tyranny and the complete overthrow of the constitution; which shows that Euripides was a wise man and well acquainted with the diseases incident to states, when he warned against ambition, as the most dangerous and the worst of dæmons to those who are governed by her.

V. Sulla now thought that his military reputation entitled him to aspire to a political career, and accordingly as soon as the campaign was ended he began to seek the favour of the people, and became a candidate for the prætorship; but he was disappointed in his expectations. He attributed his failure to the populace, for he says that they knew he was a friend of Bocchus, and if he filled the office of ædile before that of prætor, they expected to have brilliant hunting exhibitions and fights of Libyan wild beasts, and that therefore they elected others to the prætorship, with the view of forcing him to serve as ædile. But that Sulla does not state the real cause of his failure appears evident from what followed. In the next year he obtained the prætorship, having gained the votes of the people, partly by solicitation and partly by bribery. It was in allusion to this, and during his prætorship when he was threatening Cæsar to use his own authority against him, that Cæsar replied with a laugh, You are right in considering your authority as your own, for you bought it. After the expiration of his prætorship he was sent to Cappadocia, for the purpose, as it was given out, of restoring Ariobarzanes to his power, but in reality to check Mithridates, who was very active and was acquiring new territory and dominion as extensive as what he already had. Sulla took with him no large force of his own, but meeting with zealous co-operation on the part of the allies, he slaughtered a great number of the Cappadocians, and on another occasion a still greater number of Armenians who had come to the relief of the Cappadocians, drove out Gordius, and declared Ariobarzanes king. While he was staying near the Euphrates, the Parthian general Orobazus, a commander of King Arsaces, had an interview with him, which was the first occasion on which the two nations met; and this also may be considered as one of the very fortunate events in Sulla's successful career, that he was the first Roman to whom the Parthians addressed themselves in their request for an alliance and friendship with Rome. Sulla is said to have had three chairs placed, one for Ariobarzanes, another for Orobazus, and a third for himself, on which he took his seat between the two, while the business was transacted. The king of the Parthians is said to have put Orobazus to death for submitting to this indignity; as to Sulla, some commended him for his haughty treatment of the barbarians, while others blamed him for his arrogance and ill-timed pride. It is said there was a man among the attendants of Orobazus, a Chaldæan, who examined the countenance of Sulla and observed the movements of his mind and body, not as an idle spectator, but studying his character according to the principles of his art, and he declared that of necessity that man must become the first of men, and he wondered that he could endure not to be the first already. On his return to Rome Censorinus instituted proceedings against Sulla on the charge of having received large sums of money, contrary to express law, from a king who was a friend and ally of the Romans. Censorinus did not bring the matter to a trial, but gave up the prosecution.

VI. His quarrel with Marius was kindled anew by fresh matter supplied by the ostentation of King Bocchus, who, with the view of flattering the Roman people and pleasing Sulla, dedicated in the Capitol some figures bearing trophies, and by the side of them placed a gilded figure of Jugurtha being surrendered by himself to Sulla. Marius was highly incensed and attempted to take the figures down, while others were ready to support Sulla, and the city was all but in a flame through the two factions, when the Social War which had long smouldered burst forth in a blaze upon Rome and stopped the civil discord. In this most serious war, which was attended with many variations of fortune, and brought on the Romans the greatest misery and the most formidable dangers, Marius by his inability to accomplish anything of importance showed that military excellence requires bodily vigour and strength: but Sulla by his great exploits obtained among his own citizens the reputation of a great commander, among his friends the reputation of the very greatest, and among his enemies too the reputation of the most fortunate of generals. Sulla did not behave like Timotheus the son of Konon, whose success was attributed by his enemies to fortune, and they had paintings made in which he was represented asleep while Fortune was throwing a net over the cities, all which he took in a very boorish way, and got into a passion with his enemies, as if they were thus attempting to deprive him of the honour due to his exploits; and on one occasion, returning from a successful expedition, he said to the people, "Well, Fortune has had no share in this campaign, at least, Athenians." Now, as the story goes, Fortune showed her spite to Timotheus in return for his arrogance, and he never did anything great afterwards, but failing in all his undertakings and becoming odious to the people, he was at last banished from the city. But Sulla by gladly accepting such felicitations on his prosperity and such admiration, and even contributing to strengthen these notions and to invest them with somewhat of a sacred character, made all his exploits depend on Fortune; whether it was that he did this for the sake of display, or because he really had such opinions of the deity. Indeed he has recorded in his memoirs, that the actions which he resolved upon without deliberation, and on the spur of the moment, turned out more successfully than those which appeared to have been best considered. And again, from the passage in which he says that he was made more for fortune than for war, he appears to attribute more to fortune than to his merit, and to consider himself completely as the creature of the dæmon; nay, he cites as a proof of good fortune due to the favour of the gods his harmony with Metellus, a man of the same rank with himself, and his father-in-law, for he expected that Metellus would cause him a good deal of trouble, whereas he was a most accommodating colleague. Further, in his memoirs which he dedicated to Lucullus, he advises him to think nothing so safe as what the dæmon enjoins during the night. When he was leaving the city with his troops for the Social War, as he tells us in his memoirs, a great chasm opened in the earth near

Laverna, from which a quantity of fire burst forth, and a bright flame rose like a column to the skies. The diviners said that a brave man, of an appearance different from and superior to ordinary men, would obtain the command and relieve the city from its present troubles, Sulla says this man was himself, for the golden colour of his hair was a peculiarity in his personal appearance, and that he had no diffidence about bearing testimony to his own merits after so many illustrious exploits. So much as to his religious opinions. As to the other parts of his character, he was irregular and inconsistent: he would take away much, and give more; he would confer honours without any good reason, and do a grievous wrong with just as little reason; he courted those whose assistance he wanted, and behaved with arrogance to those who wanted his aid; so that one could not tell whether he had naturally more haughtiness or subserviency. For as to his inconsistency in punishing, sometimes inflicting death for the slightest matters, and at others quietly bearing the greatest wrongs, his ready reconciliations with his deadly enemies, and his prosecution of slight and trifling offences with death and confiscation of property—all this may be explained on the supposition that he was naturally of a violent and vindictive temper, but sometimes moderated his passion upon calculations of interest. During this Social War his soldiers killed with sticks and stones a man of Prætorian rank, who was his legatus, Albinus by name, an outrage which Sulla overlooked, and made no inquiry about: he went so far as to say, with apparent seriousness, that the soldiers would bestir themselves the more in the war and make amends for their fault by their courage. As to any blame that was imputed to him, he cared not for it; but having already formed the design of overthrowing the power of Marius and of getting himself appointed to the command against Mithridates, as the Social War was now considered at an end, he endeavoured to ingratiate himself with his army. On coming to Rome he was elected consul with Quintus Pompeius for his colleague, being now fifty years of age, and he formed a distinguished matrimonial alliance with Cæcilia, the daughter of Metellus, the chief Pontifex. This gave occasion to the populace to assail him with satirical songs; and many of the highest class were displeased at the marriage, as if they did not think him worthy of such a wife, whom they had judged to be worthy of the consulship, as Titus Livius remarks. Cæcilia was not the only wife that Sulla had. When he was a very young man he married Ilia, who bore him a daughter; his second wife was Ælia; and his third wife was Clœlia, whom he divorced on the ground of barrenness, yet in a manner honourable to the lady, with an ample testimony to her virtues and with presents. But as he married Metella a few days after, it was believed that his alleged ground of divorce was merely a pretext.

However, he always paid great respect to Metella, which induced the Romans, when they wished to recall from exile the partisans of Marius, and Sulla refused his assent, to apply to Metella to intercede for them. After the capture of Athens also, it was supposed that he treated the citizens with more severity, because they had cast aspersions upon Metella from their walls. But of this hereafter.

VII. Sulla looked on the consulship as only a small matter compared with what he expected to attain: the great object of his desires was the command in the war against Mithridates. But he had a rival in Marius, who was moved by an insane love of distinction and by ambition, passions which never grow old in a man, for though he was now unwieldy and had done no service in the late campaigns by reason of his age, he still longed for the command in a distant war beyond the seas. While Sulla was with the army completing some matters that still remained to be finished, Marius kept at home and hatched that most pestilent faction which did more mischief to Rome than all her wars; and indeed the deity showed by signs what was coming. Fire spontaneously blazed from the wooden shafts which supported the military standards, and was quenched with difficulty; and three crows brought their young into the public road, and after devouring them, carried the fragments back to their nest. The mice in a temple gnawed the gold which was kept there, and the keeper of the temple caught one of the mice, a female, in a trap, which produced in the trap five young ones, and devoured three of them. But what was chief of all, from a cloudless and clear sky there came the sound of a trumpet, so shrill and mournful, that by reason of the greatness thereof men were beside themselves and crouched for fear. The Tuscan seers interpreted this to portend the commencement of a new period, and a general change. They say that there are in all eight periods, which differ in mode of life and habits altogether from one another, and to each period is assigned by the deity a certain number of years determined by the revolution of a great year. When a period is completed, the commencement of another is indicated by some wondrous sign on the earth or from the heavens, so as to make it immediately evident to those who attend to such matters and have studied them, that men are now adopting other habits and modes of life, and are less or more an object of care to the gods than the men of former periods. They say, in the change from one period to another there are great alterations, and that the art of the seer at one time is held in high repute, and is successful in its predictions, when the deity gives clear and manifest signs, but that in the course of another period the art falls into a low condition, being for the most part conjectural, and attempting to know the future by equivocal and misty signs. Now this is what the Tuscan wise men said, who are supposed to know more of such things than anybody else. While the senate was communicating on these omens with the seers, in the temple of Bellona, a sparrow flew in before the whole body with a grasshopper in his mouth, part of which he dropped, and the rest he carried off with him out of the place. From this the interpreters of omens apprehended faction and divisions between the landholders on the one side and the city folk and the merchant class on the other, for the latter were loud and noisy like a grasshopper, but the owners of land kept quiet on their estates.

VIII. Now Marius contrived to gain over the tribune Sulpicius, a man without rival in any kind of villainy, and so one need not inquire whom he surpassed in wickedness, but only wherein he surpassed himself. For in him were combined cruelty, audacity, and rapaciousness, without any consideration of shame or of any crime, inasmuch as he sold the Roman citizenship to libertini and resident aliens, and publicly received the money at a table in the Forum. He maintained three thousand men armed with daggers, and also a number of young men of the equestrian class always about him, and ready for anything, whom he called the Opposition Senate. He caused a law to be passed that no Senator should contract debt to the amount of more than two thousand drachmæ, and yet at his death he left behind him a debt of three millions. This man being let loose upon the people by Marius, and putting everything into a state of confusion by violence and force of arms, framed various pernicious laws, and among them that which gave to Marius the command in the Mithridatic war. The consuls accordingly declared a cessation of all public business; but while they were holding a meeting of the people near the temple of Castor and Pollux, Sulpicius with his rabble attacked them, and among many others massacred the youthful son of Pompeius in the Forum; Pompeius only escaped by hiding himself. Sulla was pursued into the house of Marius, from which he was compelled to come out and repeal the edict for the cessation of public business; and it was for this reason that Sulpicius, though he deprived Pompeius of his office, did not take the consulship from Sulla, but, merely transferred the command of the Mithridatic war to Marius, and sent some tribunes forthwith to Nola to take the army and lead it to Marius.

IX. But Sulla made his escape to the camp before the tribunes arrived, and the soldiers hearing of what had passed, stoned them to death; upon which the partisans of Marius murdered the friends of Sulla who were in the city, and seized their property. This caused many persons to betake themselves to flight, some going to the city from the camp, and others from the camp to the city. The Senate was not its own master, but was compelled to obey the orders of Marius and Sulpicius; and on hearing that Sulla was marching upon Rome, they sent to him two of the prætors, Brutus and Servilius, to forbid him to advance any further. The prætors, who assumed a bold tone before Sulla, narrowly escaped being murdered; as it was, the soldiers broke their fasces, stripped them of their senatorial dress, and sent them back with every insult. It caused dejection in the city to see the prætors return without their insignia of office, and to hear them report that the commotion could not be checked, and was past all remedy. Now the partisans of Marius were making their preparations, while Sulla with his colleague and six complete legions was moving from Nola; he saw that the army was ready to march right to the city, but he had some hesitation himself, and feared the risk. However upon Sulla making a sacrifice, the seer Postumius, after inspecting the signs, stretched out his hands to Sulla and urged him to put him in chains and keep him a prisoner till the battle took place, declaring that if everything did not speedily turn out well, he was ready to be put to death. It is said also that Sulla in his sleep had a vision of the goddess, whose worship the Romans had learned from the Cappadocians, whatever her name may be, Selene, Athena, or Enyo. Sulla dreamed that the goddess stood by him and put a thunderbolt into his hand, and as she named each of his enemies bade him dart the bolt at them, which he did, and his enemies were struck to the ground and destroyed. Being encouraged by the dream, which he communicated to his colleague, at daybreak Sulla led his forces against Rome. When he was near Picinæ he was met by a deputation which entreated him not to march forthwith against the city, for all justice would be done pursuant to a resolution of the Senate. Sulla consented to encamp there, and ordered the officers to measure out the ground for the encampment, according to the usual practice, and the deputation went away trusting to his promise. But as soon as they were gone, Sulla sent Lucius Bacillus and Caius Mummius, who seized the gate and that part of the walls which surrounds the Esquiline hill, and Sulla set out to join them with all speed. Bacillus and his soldiers broke into the city and attempted to gain possession of it, but the people in large numbers, being unarmed, mounted the house-tops, and by pelting the soldiers with tiles and stones stopped their further progress, and drove them back to the wall. In the mean time Sulla had come up, and seeing how matters stood, he called out that the houses must be fired, and taking a flaming torch, he was the first to advance: he also ordered the bowmen to shoot firebrands, and to aim at the roofs; in which he acted without any rational consideration, giving way to passion, and surrendering the direction of his enterprize to revenge, for he saw before him only his enemies, and without thought or pity for his friends and kinsmen, would force his way into Rome with the help of flames, which know no distinction between the guilty and the innocent. While this was going on, Marius, who had been driven as far as the temple of Earth, invited the slaves to join him by offering them their freedom, but being overpowered by his enemies who pressed on him, he left the city.

X. Sulla assembled the Senate, who condemned to death Marius and a few others, among whom was the tribune Sulpicius. Sulpicius was put to death, being betrayed by a slave, to whom Sulla gave his freedom, and then ordered him to be thrown down the Tarpeian rock: he set a price on the head of Marius, which was neither a generous nor a politic measure, as Marius had shortly before let Sulla off safe when Sulla put himself into his power by going to the house of Marius. Now if Marius had not let Sulla go, but had given him up to Sulpicius to be put to death, he might have secured the supreme power; but he spared Sulla; and yet a few days after, when Sulla had the same opportunity, Marius did not obtain from him a like return. The conduct of Sulla offended the Senate, though they durst not show it; but the dislike of the people and their dissatisfaction were made apparent to him by their acts. They contemptuously rejected Nonius, the son of Sulla's sister, and Servius, who were candidates for offices, and elected those whose elevation they thought would be most disagreeable to Sulla. But Sulla pretended to be pleased at this, and to view it as a proof that the people, by doing what they liked, were really indebted to him for their liberty; and for the purpose of diminishing his general unpopularity he managed the election of Lucius Cinna, who was of the opposite faction, to the consulship, having first bound him by solemn imprecations and oaths to favour his measures. Cinna ascended the Capitol with a stone in his hand and took the oath; then pronouncing an imprecation on himself, that, if he did not keep faithful to Sulla, he might be cast out of the city as the stone from his hand, he hurled it to the ground in the presence of a large number of persons. But as soon as Cinna had received the consulship, he attempted to disturb the present settlement of affairs, and prepared to institute a process against Sulla, and induced Virginius, one of the tribunes, to be the accuser; but Sulla, without caring for him or the court, set out with his army against Mithridates.

XI. It is said that about the time when Sulla was conducting his armament from Italy, many omens occurred to Mithridates, who was staying in Pergamum, and that a Victory, bearing a crown, which the people of Pergamum were letting down upon him by some machinery from above, was broken in pieces just as it was touching his head, and the crown falling upon the theatre, came to the ground and was destroyed, which made the spectators shudder and greatly dispirited Mithridates, though his affairs were then going on favourably beyond all expectation. For he had taken Asia from the Romans, and Bithynia and Cappadocia from their kings, and had fixed himself at Pergamum, where he was distributing wealth and provinces and kingdoms among his friends; one of his sons also held without any opposition the ancient dominions in Pontus, and the Bosporus as far as the uninhabited regions beyond the Mæotis; Ariarathes occupied Thrace and Macedonia with a large army; and his generals with their forces were subduing other places. Archelaus, the greatest of his generals, was master of all the sea with his navy, and was subjugating the Cyclades and all the other islands east of Malea, and had already taken Eubœa, while with his army, advancing from Athens as his starting-point, he was gaining over all the nations of Greece as far north as Thessaly, and had only sustained a slight check near Chæroneia. For there he was met by Bruttius Sura, a legatus of Sentius, prætor of Macedonia, and a man of signal courage and prudence. Archelaus was sweeping through Bœotia like a torrent, when he was vigorously opposed by Sura, who, after fighting three battles near Chæroneia, repulsed him and drove him back to the coast. On receiving orders from Lucius Lucullus to make room for Sulla, who was coming, and to allow him to carry on the war, for which he had received his commission, Sura immediately left Bœotia and went back to Sentius, though he had succeeded beyond his expectations, and Greece was well disposed to change sides on account of his great merit. However, these exploits of Bruttius were very brilliant.

XII. Now all the rest of the Grecian cities immediately sent deputations to Sulla and invited him to enter; but against Athens, which was compelled by the tyrant Aristion to be on the king's side, he directed all his energies; he also hemmed in and blockaded the Peiræus, employing every variety of engine and every mode of attack. If he had waited a short time, he might have taken the Upper City without danger, for through want of provisions it was reduced by famine to extreme necessity; but anxious to return to Rome, and fearing a new revolution there, at great risk fighting many battles and at great cost he urged on the war, wherein, besides the rest of the expenditure, the labour about the military engines required ten thousand pair of mules to be daily employed on this service. As wood began to fail, owing to many of the works being destroyed by their own weight, and burnt by the incessant fires thrown by the enemy, Sulla laid his hands on the several groves and levelled the trees in the Academia, which was the best wooded of the suburbs, and those in the Lycæum. And as he wanted money also for the war, he violated the sacred depositaries of Greece, sending for the finest and most costly of the offerings dedicated in Epidaurus and Olympia. He wrote also to the Amphiktyons to Delphi, saying that it would be better for the treasures of the god to be brought to him, for he would either have them in safer keeping, or, if he used them, he would replace them; and he sent one of his friends, Kaphis, a Phokian, to receive all the things after they were first weighed. Kaphis went to Delphi, but he was afraid to touch the sacred things, and in the presence of the Amphiktyons he deeply lamented the task that was imposed on him. Upon some of them saying that they heard the lute in the shrine send forth a sound, Kaphis either believing what they said or wishing to inspire Sulla with some religious fear, sent him this information. But Sulla replied in a scoffing tone, he wondered Kaphis did not understand that such music was a sign of pleasure and not of anger, and he bade him take courage and seize the property, as the deity was quite willing, and in fact offered it. Now all the things were secretly sent off unobserved by most of the Greeks; but the silver jar, one of the royal presents which still remained, could not be carried away by the beasts of burden owing to its weight and size, and the Amphiktyons were accordingly obliged to cut it in pieces; and this led them to reflect that Titus Flamininus, and Manius Acilius, and also Æmilius Paulus—Acilius, who drove Antiochus out of Greece; and the two others, who totally defeated the kings of Macedonia—not only refrained from touching the Greek temples, but even gave them presents and showed them great honour and respect. These generals, however, were legally appointed to command troops consisting of well-disciplined soldiers, who had been taught to obey their leaders without a murmur: and the commanders themselves were men of kingly souls, and moderate in their living and satisfied with a small fixed expenditure, and they thought it baser to attempt to win the soldiers' favour than to fear their enemies. But the generals at this time, as they acquired their rank by violence and not by merit, and had more occasion to employ arms against one another than against the enemies of Rome, were compelled to act the demagogue while they were in command; and by purchasing the services of the soldiers by the money which they expended to gratify them, they made the Roman state a thing for bargain and sale, and themselves the slaves of the vilest wretches in order that they might domineer over honest men. This is what drove Marius into exile, and then brought him back to oppose Sulla; this made Cinna the murderer of Octavius, and Fimbria the murderer of Flaccus. And Sulla mainly laid the foundation of all this by his profusion and expenditure upon his own soldiers, the object of which was to corrupt and gain over to his side the soldiers of other commanders; so that his attempts to seduce the troops of others and the extravagance by which his own soldiers were corrupted, made money always necessary to him; and most particularly during the siege of Athens.

XIII. Now Sulla was seized with a violent and irresistible desire to take Athens, whether it was that he was ambitious to contend against a city which retained only the shadow of its former glory, or that he was moved by passion to revenge the scoffs and jeers with which the tyrant Aristion irritated him and his wife Metella, by continually taunting them from the wall and insulting them. This Aristion was a compound of lewdness and cruelty, who combined in himself all the worst of the vices and passions of Mithridates, and now had brought as it were a mortal disease in its last extremities upon a city which had come safe out of so many wars and escaped from so many tyrannies and civil commotions. For now when a medimnus of wheat was selling for a thousand drachmæ in the Upper City, and men were obliged to eat the parthenium that grew about the Acropolis, and shoes and oil-flasks, he was drinking all day long and amusing himself with revels and pyrrhic dances, and making jokes at the enemy: he let the sacred light of the goddess go out for want of oil; when the hierophant sent to ask for the twelfth part of a medimnus of wheat, he sent her as much pepper; and when the members of the Senate and the priests entreated him to have pity on the city and come to terms with Sulla, he dispersed them by ordering the archers to fire on them. At last being persuaded with great difficulty, he sent two or three of his boon companions to treat of peace; but instead of making any reasonable proposals, the men began to make a pompous harangue about Theseus and Eumolpus, and the Persian wars, on which Sulla said, "Be gone, my good fellows, with your fine talk. I was not sent to Athens by the Romans to learn a lesson, but to compel rebels to submit."

XIV. In the mean time, as the story goes, some soldiers in the Keramicus overheard certain old men talking to one another, and abusing the tyrant for not guarding the approach to the wall about the Heptachalkum, which was the only part, they said, where it was practicable and easy for the enemy to get over; and the soldiers reported to Sulla what they heard. Sulla did not neglect the intelligence, but he went to the spot by night, and seeing that it was practicable, he set about the thing forthwith. He says in his Memoirs that the first man who mounted the wall was Marcus Teius, who, finding a soldier in his way, struck him a violent blow on the helmet, which broke his sword; still Marcus did not retreat, but kept his ground. The city then was taken from this quarter, as the old Athenians said it might be. Sulla having destroyed and levelled that part of the wall which lies between the Peiræic and the Sacred

Gate, about midnight entered the city, striking terror with the sound of trumpets and horns, and the shouts and cries of the soldiers, who had his full licence to plunder and kill, and made their way through the streets with naked swords. The slain were not counted, but the number is even now measured by the space over which the blood flowed. For besides those who were slaughtered in the other parts of the city, the blood of those who fell about the Agora covered all the Keramicus within Dipylum: many say that it even flowed through the gates and deluged the suburbs. But though the number of those who perished by the sword was so great, as many killed themselves for sorrow and regret at the overthrow of their native city. For all the most honest citizens were driven to despair, expecting in Sulla neither humanity nor moderation. But, however, when Meidias and Kalliphon, who were exiles, fell down at his knees with entreaties, and the Senators who were in his army urged him to save the city, being now sated with vengeance and passing some encomiums upon the ancient Athenians, he said he would pardon the many for the sake of the few, and the living for the sake of the dead. Sulla states in his Memoirs, that he took Athens on the Calends of March, which day nearly coincides with the new moon of Anthesterion, in which month it happens that the Athenians perform many ceremonies in commemoration of the great damage and loss occasioned by the heavy rain, for they suppose that the deluge happened pretty nearly about that time. When the city was taken the tyrant retreated to the Acropolis, where he was besieged by Curio, who was commissioned for this purpose: after he had held out for some time, Aristion was compelled to surrender for want of water; his surrender was immediately followed by a token from the deity, for on the very day and hour on which Curio took the tyrant from the Acropolis, the clouds gathered in the clear sky, and a violent shower descended which filled the Acropolis with water. Sulla soon took the Peiræus also, and burnt the greater part of it, including the arsenal of Philo, which was a wonderful work.

XV. In the mean time Taxiles, the general of Mithridates, coming down from Thrace and Macedonia with one hundred thousand foot, ten thousand horse, and ninety scythe-bearing four-horse chariots, summoned Archelaus, who was still lying with his ships near Munychia, and was neither inclined to give up the sea nor ready to engage with the Romans: his plan was to protract the war and to cut off the supplies of the enemy. But Sulla was as quick as Archelaus, and moved into Bœotia from a niggardly region, which even in time of peace could not have maintained his troops. Most people thought that he had made a false calculation in leaving Attica, which is a rough country and ill adapted for the movements of cavalry, to throw himself into the champaign and open tracts of Bœotia, when he knew that the strength of the barbarians lay in their chariots and cavalry. But in his flight from famine and scarcity, as I have already observed, he was compelled to seek the hazard of a battle. Besides, he was alarmed for Hortensius, a skilful general and a man ambitious of distinction, who was conducting a force from Thessaly to Sulla, and had to pass through the straits where the enemy was waiting for him. For all these reasons Sulla moved into Bœotia. But Kaphis, who was from my town, evading the barbarians by taking a different route from what they expected, led Hortensius over Parnassus, close by Tithora, which was not at that time so large a city as it is now, but only a fort on a steep rock scarped all round, to which place in time of old the Phokians who fled from Xerxes escaped with their property and were there in safety. Hortensius having encamped there during the day repelled the attacks of the enemy, and at night descending to Patronis, through a difficult path joined Sulla, who met him with his forces.

XVI. Having united their forces, Sulla and Hortensius occupied an elevation rising out of the midst of the plains of Elateia, which was fertile and extensive, and had water at its base: it is called Philobœotus, and its natural qualities and position are most highly commended by Sulla. When they were encamped, the weakness of the Roman force was apparent to the enemy; for the cavalry did not exceed fifteen hundred, and the infantry was below fifteen thousand. Accordingly the rest of the generals, against the wish of Archelaus, drew out their forces in order of battle, and filled the plain with horses, chariots, shields, and bucklers; and the heavens could not contain the shouts and cries of so many nations putting themselves in battle array. At the same time the pomp and costly splendour of the troops were not without effect nor their use in causing alarm; but the glittering of the arms, which were curiously ornamented with gold and silver, and the colour of the Median and Scythian dresses mingled with the brightness of the brass and steel, produced a firelike and formidable appearance as the masses moved like waves and changed their places, so that the Romans hid themselves behind their ramparts, and Sulla, being unable by any words to remove their fear, and not choosing to urge men to a battle who were disposed to run away, kept quiet and had to endure the insulting boasts and ridicule of the barbarians. But this turned out most favourable to the Romans; for the enemy despising them, neglected to preserve discipline, and indeed, owing to the number of commanders, the army was not generally inclined to obey orders; a few kept to their post within their ramparts, but the greater part, tempted by the hope of booty and plunder, were dispersed many days' journey from the camp. It is said that they destroyed the city of Panopeus, and plundered Lebadeia, and robbed the oracular shrine without any order from a general. Sulla, who could not endure to see the cities destroyed before his eyes and was greatly irritated, no longer allowed his soldiers to be inactive, but leading them to the Kephisus, he compelled them to divert the stream from its course and to dig ditches, allowing no man any cessation and punishing most severely all who gave in, his object being to tire his soldiers with labour and to induce them to seek danger as a release from it. And it happened as he wished. For on the third day of this labour, as Sulla was passing by, they entreated him with loud shouts to lead them against the enemy. He replied, that they said this not because they wished to fight, but because they disliked labour; but if they really were disposed to fight, he bade them move forthwith with their arms to yonder place, pointing out to them what was formerly the Acropolis of the Parapotamii, but the city was then destroyed and there remained only a rocky precipitous hill, separated from Mount Hedylium by the space occupied by the river Assus, which falling into the Kephisus at the base of the Hedylium and thus becoming a more rapid stream, makes the Acropolis a safe place for encampment. Sulla also wished to seize the height, as he saw the Chalkaspides of the enemy pressing on towards it, and as his soldiers exerted themselves vigorously, he succeeded in occupying the place. Archelaus, being repelled from this point, advanced towards Chæroneia, upon which the men of Chæroneia who were in Sulla's army entreating him not to let their city fall into the hands of the enemy, he sent Gabinius a tribune, with one legion, and permitted the men of Chæroneia to go also, who, though they had the best intention, could not reach the place before Gabinius: so brave a man he was, and more active in bringing aid than even those who prayed for it. Juba says it was not Gabinius who was sent, but Ericius. However this may be, our city had a narrow escape.

XVII. From Lebadeia and the oracle of Trophonius favourable omens and predictions of victory were sent to the Romans, about which the people of the country have a good deal to say. But Sulla, in the tenth book of his Memoirs, writes, that Quintus Titius, a man of some note among those who had mercantile affairs in Greece, came to him immediately after the victory in Chæroneia, to report that Trophonius foretold a second battle and victory there in a short time. After Titius, a soldier in his army, named Salvenius, brought an answer from the god, as to what would be the result of affairs in Italy. Both reported the same as to the vision of the god: they said, that in beauty and stature he was like the Olympian Jupiter. After crossing the Assus and advancing to the foot of Hedylium, Sulla encamped near Archelaus, who had thrown up a strong intrenchment between Mounts Akontium and Hedylium, at a place called the Assia. The spot on which he encamped is called Archelaus from his name up to the present day. After the interval of one day Sulla left Murena with one legion and two cohorts, to annoy the enemy if he should attempt to form in order of battle; he himself sacrificed on the banks of the Kephisus, and the victims being favourable, he advanced towards Chæroneia with the object of again effecting a junction with the forces there, and examining the place called Thurium, which was occupied by the enemy. This is a rough summit and a conical-shaped hill, named Orthopagus; and under it is the stream of the Morius and a temple of the Thurian Apollo. The deity has this name from Thuro, the mother of Chæron, who is said to have been the founder of Chæroneia. Some say that the cow which was given by the Pythian Apollo as a guide to Kadmus appeared there, and that the place was so called from her; for the Phœnicians call the cow Thor. As Sulla was approaching Chæroneia, the tribune who was stationed in the city led out the soldiers under arms, and met him with a chaplet of bay. No sooner had Sulla received the chaplet, and after saluting the soldiers, encouraged them to the approaching battle, than two Chæroneians (Homoloichus and Anaxidamos) presented themselves to him and undertook to drive the enemy from Thurium if he would give them a few soldiers. They said there was a path unknown to the barbarians, leading from the place called Petrachus by the Museum to the highest point of Thurium, and that by taking this direction they could, without difficulty, fall on the enemy and either roll stones down upon them from above or drive them into the plain. As Gabinius bore testimony to the courage and fidelity of the men, Sulla bade them make the attempt; and in the mean time he formed his line and distributed his cavalry on each flank, himself taking the right and giving Murena the command on the left. The legati Galba and Hortensius, with some reserved cohorts in the rear, occupied the neighbouring heights, to prevent the army from being attacked on the flank, for it was observed that the enemy were placing a strong body of cavalry and light infantry on their wings, with the view of adapting that part of their battle to ready and easy manœuvres, their design being to extend their line and to surround the Romans.

XVIII. In the mean time the Chæroneians, whom Sulla had placed under the command of Ericius, went round Thurium without being perceived, and all at once showed themselves to the enemy, who immediately falling into great confusion, took to flight and sustained considerable loss, but chiefly from themselves; for as they did not stand their ground, but ran down the hill, they got entangled among their own spears and shoved one another down the rocks, while the Chæroneians pressing upon them from above, wounded them in the parts which were unprotected; and there fell of the enemy to the number of three thousand. Part of those who got safe to the foot of the hill, being met by Murena, whose troops were already in order of battle, had their retreat cut off and were destroyed: the rest forced their way to the army of Archelaus, and, falling upon the line in disorder, caused a general alarm and confusion, and some loss of time to the generals; and this did them no small harm, for Sulla promptly led his forces against the enemy while they were still in disorder, and by quickly traversing the interval between the two lines, deprived the scythe-bearing chariots of all opportunity of being effective. The efficacy of the chariots depends mainly on the space they traverse, by which they acquire velocity and momentum; but when the space is small their attack is ineffectual and feeble, just like missiles that have not been propelled with due force. Now this happened to the barbarians. The first chariots were driven on without any vigour, and came feebly against the ranks of the Romans, who easily pushed them aside, and, clapping their hands and laughing, called for more, as the people do in the horse-races of the Circus. Upon this the infantry joined battle; the barbarians pushed forward their long spears and endeavoured by locking their shields to maintain their ranks in line: the Romans hurled their javelins, and then drawing their swords, endeavoured to beat aside the spears, that they might forthwith close with the enemy; for they were irritated at seeing drawn up in front of the enemy fifteen thousand slaves, whom the king's generals had invited from the cities by a proclamation of freedom, and enrolled among the hoplitæ. A Roman centurion is said to have remarked, that slaves had only freedom of speech at the Saturnalia, so far as he knew. Now, owing to the depth of the ranks of these slaves and their close order, it was some time before they could be made to give way before the heavy-armed Roman soldiers, and they also fought with more courage than one expects from a slave; but the missiles from the slings and the light javelins which were showered upon them unsparingly by the Romans in the rear, at last made them turn and put them into complete confusion.

XIX. While Archelaus was extending his right wing, in order to surround the Romans, Hortensius made his cohorts advance at a run, with the intention of taking the enemy in the flank; but as Archelaus suddenly wheeled round with his two thousand horsemen, Hortensius was overpowered by numbers and retreated towards the mountain region, being gradually separated from the main body of the army and in danger of being completely hemmed in by the barbarians. Sulla, who was on the right wing, which was not yet engaged in the action, hearing of the danger of Hortensius, hastened to relieve him. Archelaus conjecturing from the dust raised by Sulla's troops how the matter was, left Hortensius, and wheeling round moved towards the position which Sulla had quitted (the right), expecting to find the soldiers there without their general, and to defeat them. At the same time Taxiles led the Chalkaspides against Murena; and now the shouts being raised from both armies and re-echoed by the mountains, Sulla halted and hesitated to which quarter he should move. Having determined to maintain his own original position, he sent Hortensius with four cohorts to support Murena, and ordering the fifth to follow him, he hurried to the right wing, which unaided was bravely resisting Archelaus; but as soon as Sulla appeared, the Romans completely broke the line of Archelaus, and pursued the barbarians in disorderly flight to the river and Mount Akontium. However, Sulla did not leave Murena alone in his dangerous position, but hastened to help him. Seeing, however, that the Romans were victorious here also, he joined in the pursuit. Now many of the barbarians were cut down in the plain, but the greatest number were destroyed in the attempt to regain their entrenchments, and only ten thousand out of so large a host made their escape to Chalkis. Sulla says in his Memoirs, that he missed only fourteen of his own soldiers, and that ten of them showed themselves in the evening; in commemoration of which he inscribed on the trophies, Mars and Victory, and Venus, to signify that he had gained the victory no less through good fortune than skill and courage. One of these trophies, which commemorates the victory in the plain, stands where the soldiers of Archelaus first gave ground in the flight to the Molus: the other is placed on the summit of Thurium, to commemorate the surprise of the barbarians, with a Greek inscription in honour of the courage of Homoloichus and Anaxidamus. Sulla celebrated the festival for the victory in Thebes at the fountain of Oedipus, where he erected a stage. The judges were Greeks invited from the other cities of Greece; for Sulla could not be reconciled to the Thebans; and he took from them half of their lands, which he dedicated to the Pythian Apollo and Olympian Jupiter; and from the revenue of these lands he ordered the sums of money which he had taken from them to be repaid to the deities.

XX. After the battle Sulla received intelligence that Flaccus, who belonged to the opposite faction, was chosen consul, and was crossing the Ionian sea with a force which was said to be designed against Mithridates, but was in fact directed against himself; and accordingly he advanced towards Thessalia to meet Flaccus. He had advanced to the neighbourhood of Meliteia, when

reports from all sides reached him that the country in his rear was ravaged by
another army of Mithridates as numerous as that which he had dispersed.
Dorylaus had landed at Chalkis with a large navy, on board of which he
brought eighty thousand men of the best trained and disciplined troops of
Mithridates, and he immediately advanced into Bœotia and occupied the
country, being eager to draw Sulla to an engagement, and paying no regard
to Archelaus, who dissuaded him from fighting: he even said publicly that so
many thousands could never have been destroyed if there had not been
treachery. However, Sulla, who quickly returned to Bœotia, showed Dorylaus
that Archelaus was a prudent man and had formed a very just estimate of the
courage of the Romans; for after a slight skirmish with Sulla near
Tilphossium, Dorylaus was himself the first among those who were not for
deciding the matter by a battle, but thought it best to prolong the war till the
Romans should be exhausted by want of supplies. However, Archelaus was
somewhat encouraged by the position of their encampment near
Orchomenus, which was very favourable for battle to an army which had the
superiority in cavalry; for of all the plains in Bœotia noted for their beauty
and extent, this, which commences at the city of Orchomenus, is the only one
which spreads without interruption and without any trees, and it reaches to
the marshes in which the river Melas is lost. The Melas rises close to
Orchomenus, and is the only river of Greece that is a copious and navigable
stream at its source; it also increases like the Nile about the summer solstice,
and the same plants grow on its banks; but they produce no fruit and do not
attain any large size. Its course however is short, for the larger part of the
water is soon lost in obscure marshes overgrown with shrubs: a small part
joins the Kephisus somewhere about the point where the lake is said to
produce the reed that is adapted for making musical pipes.

XXI. The two armies being encamped near one another, Archelaus kept
quiet, but Sulla began to dig trenches on both sides with the view, if possible,
of cutting off the enemy from the hard ground and those parts which were
favourable to cavalry and driving them into the marshes. However, the
barbarians would not endure this, and as soon as their generals allowed them
to attack the Romans, they rushed forward with so much vigour and force,
that not only were the men dispersed who were working at the trenches, but
the greater part of the Roman troops that were drawn up for their protection
were involved in the fight. Upon this Sulla leapt down from his horse, and
snatching up a standard, made his way through the fugitives towards the
enemy, crying out, "For my part, Romans, it is fit I should die here; as for you,
when you are asked where you deserted your Imperator, remember to say it

was in Orchomenus." These words made the soldiers rally, and two cohorts came to their support from the right wing, which Sulla led against the enemy and put them to flight. He then led his soldiers back a short distance, and after allowing them to take some food, he began again to work at the trenches which were designed to enclose the enemy's camp. The barbarians made another attack in better order than before; in which Diogenes, the son of the wife of Archelaus, fell fighting bravely on the right wing; and the bowmen being hard pressed by the Romans and having no means of retreat, took their arrows altogether in their hands, and using them like swords, struck at the Romans, but, at last they were driven back to their camp, where they spent a wretched night owing to their wounds and great losses. As soon as day dawned Sulla again led his soldiers up to the enemy's encampment and again commenced working at the ditches. The enemy came out in a great force, but Sulla put them to flight, and as no one stood his ground after they were thrown into disorder, Sulla stormed the camp. The swamps and the lake were filled with the blood and bodies of those who fell, and even to the present day many barbarian bows, helmets, and pieces of iron cuirasses and swords are found buried in the marshes, though it is near two hundred years since the battle. Such, according to the historians, was the battle about Chæroneia and near Orchomenus.

XXII. Cinna and Carbo were now conducting themselves towards the chief men at Rome in an illegal and violent manner, and many flying from their tyranny resorted to the camp of Sulla as a harbour of refuge, so that in a short time a kind of Senate was formed about him. Metella also, who had with difficulty escaped with her children, came and reported that his house and farms were burnt by his enemies, and she entreated him to go to the assistance of his friends at Rome. Sulla was perplexed what to do: he could not endure the thoughts of neglecting his country in her present oppressed condition, nor did he see how he could leave so great an undertaking as the Mithridatic war imperfect. In the meantime there came to him a merchant of Delos, named Archelaus, who secretly brought from Archelaus, the king's general, hopes of peace and certain proposals. Sulla was so well pleased that he was eager for an interview with Archelaus, and they met at Delium on the sea-coast, where the temple of Apollo is. Archelaus, who began the conference, urged Sulla to give up Asia and the Pontus, and to sail to Rome to prosecute the war against his enemies, and he offered him money, ships, and troops on behalf of the king. Sulla in reply advised Archelaus not to trouble himself any further about Mithridates, but to assume the kingly title himself and to become an ally of Rome, and to give up the ships of

Mithridates. As Archelaus professed his detestation of such treachery, Sulla said, "You then, Archelaus, who are a Cappadocian, and the slave of a barbarian king, or, if you please, his friend—you refuse to do a base deed for so splendid a reward, and yet venture to talk about treachery to me who am a Roman general, and am Sulla, as if you were not that Archelaus who fled from Chæroneia with a few men out of your one hundred and twenty thousand, and were hid for two days in the marshes of Orchomenus, and left Bœotia with all the roads made impassable by the heaps of dead?" Upon this Archelaus changed his tone, and humbling himself, entreated Sulla to give up the war and to come to terms with Mithridates. Sulla accepted the proposal, and peace was made on the following terms:—Mithridates was to give up Asia and Paphlagonia, and to surrender Bithynia to Nikomedes, and Cappadocia to Ariobarzanes, to pay down to the Romans two thousand talents, and to give them seventy ships fitted with brass and completely equipped; Sulla was to confirm Mithridates in the rest of his possessions and to recognise him as an ally of the Romans.

XXIII. These terms being settled, Sulla retraced his steps and marched through Thessaly and Macedonia to the Hellespont in company with Archelaus, whom he treated with great respect. Archelaus fell dangerously ill at Larissa, on which Sulla stopped his march and paid as much attention to him as if he had been one of his own officers and fellow-generals. This gave rise to some suspicion that the battle of Chæroneia was not fairly fought, which was strengthened by the fact that Sulla restored all the friends of Mithridates whom he had taken prisoners, except Aristion the tyrant, who was an enemy of Archelaus, and whom he caused to be poisoned: but the most convincing proof of all was Sulla's giving the Cappadocian ten thousand plethra of land in Eubœa, and the title of friend and ally of the Romans. However, Sulla makes his apology about these matters in his Memoirs. Ambassadors from Mithridates now arrived, and were ready to accede to all the terms agreed on, except that the king would not consent to give up Paphlagonia, and as to the ships he dissented altogether; on which Sulla in a passion exclaimed, "What say ye? Mithridates claims to keep Paphlagonia, and refuses to abide by the agreement about the ships; I thought he would have been thankful if I left him his right hand, which has destroyed so many Romans. However, he will soon speak another language when I have crossed over to Asia. At present let him stay in Pergamum and there direct the conduct of a campaign which he has not seen." The ambassadors were so much alarmed that they said nothing, but Archelaus implored Sulla and tried to soften his anger, clinging to his hands with tears in his eyes. At last he prevailed on Sulla to let him go to Mithridates, and he promised to effect a peace on Sulla's own terms, or to kill himself. Sulla accordingly sent Archelaus to Mithridates, and in the mean time he invaded Mædike, and having ravaged the greater part of it, returned to Macedonia and found Archelaus at Philippi, who reported that all was favourable, but that Mithridates much wished to have an interview with him. Mithridates was minly induced to this by the circumstance that Fimbria, after murdering the consul Flaccus, who belonged to the opposite faction, and defeating the generals of Mithridates, was advancing against the king himself. It was fear of Fimbria that made Mithridates more inclined to make a friend of Sulla.

XXIV. Accordingly they met at Dardanus in the Troad: Mithridates had there two hundred rowing-ships, twenty thousand heavy-armed soldiers, six thousand horsemen, and many of his scythe-bearing chariots: Sulla had four cohorts and two hundred horsemen. Mithridates advanced to meet Sulla and held out his hand, on which Sulla asked him if he would put an end to the war on the terms agreed to by Archelaus. As the king made no reply, Sulla said, "Well, those who sue must speak first; conquerors may remain silent." Mithridates began an apology, in which he partly imputed the origin of the war to the deities, and partly threw the blame on the Romans; but Sulla cut him short by saying, that he had long ago been told, and now he knew by his own experience, that Mithridates was a most skilful speaker, inasmuch as he had no difficulty in finding words to justify acts which were so base and so contrary to all right. Sulla went on to recapitulate all that Mithridates had done, reproaching him in bitter terms, and he then asked him again, if he would abide by the agreement of Archelaus. Mithridates said that he would; on which Sulla embraced him, threw his arms round him and kissed him; he then brought forward the kings Ariobarzanes and Nikomedes, and reconciled Mithridates to them. After surrendering to Sulla seventy ships and five hundred bowmen, Mithridates sailed off to the Pontus. Sulla perceived that his soldiers were dissatisfied at the settlement of the war: they thought it a shame that the greatest enemy of the Romans, who had contrived the massacre of one hundred and fifty thousand Romans in Asia in one day, should be seen sailing off with the wealth and the spoils of Asia, which he had been plundering and levying contributions on for four years; Sulla apologised to the soldiers by saying that he should not be able to oppose both Fimbria and Mithridates, if they were united against him.

XXV. From Dardanus Sulla marched against Fimbria, who was encamped near Thyateira, and halting there, began to throw up his intrenchments. Fimbria's men coming out of their camp in their jackets embraced the soldiers of Sulla, and began to assist them zealously in their works. Fimbria seeing that his soldiers had deserted him, and fearing Sulla's unforgiving temper, committed suicide in the camp. Sulla now levied a contribution on Asia to the amount of twenty thousand talents: and he reduced individuals to beggary by the violence and exactions which he permitted to the soldiers who were quartered in their houses. He issued an order that the master of a house should daily supply the soldier who was quartered on him with four tetradrachmæ, and with dinner for himself and as many of his friends as he chose to invite; a centurion was to receive fifty drachmæ daily, and to be supplied with two garments, one to wear in the house and the other when he went abroad.

XXVI. Sulla set sail from Ephesus with all his ships, and on the third day anchored in the Peiræus. After being initiated into the Eleusinian mysteries, he appropriated to himself the library of Apellikon of Teos, which contained most of the writings of Aristotle and Theophrastus. The works of these two philosophers were not then well known to people in general. It is said that when the library was brought to Rome, Tyrannio the grammarian arranged most of the books, and that Andronikus of Rhodes having procured copies from Tyrannio, published them, and made the tables which are now in use. It appears that the older Peripatetics were indeed well-instructed men, and devoted to letters, but they did not possess many of the writings of Aristotle and Theophrastus, nor yet correct copies, owing to the circumstances that the books came into the hands of the heirs of Neleus of Skepsis, to whom Theophrastus bequeathed them, and that they were ignorant persons, who never troubled themselves about such matters. While Sulla was staying at Athens, he was seized with a numbness in his feet, accompanied with a feeling of heaviness, which Strabo calls "a stammering of gout." Accordingly he crossed the sea to Ædepsus; where he used the warm springs, at the same time indulging in relaxation and spending all his time in the company of actors. As he was walking about on the seashore, some fishermen presented him with some very fine fish; Sulla was much pleased with the present, but on hearing that the men belonged to Halæae, he said, What, is there an Halæan still alive? For it happened, that while pursuing his enemies after the victory at Orchomenus, he destroyed at once three Bœotian cities, Anthedon, Larymna, and Halæae. The men were struck speechless with fear, but Sulla with a smile bade them go away in good heart, for the intercessors they had brought were no mean ones, and not to be despised. Upon this the Halæans say they took courage and again occupied their city.

XXVII. Sulla went through Thessaly and Macedonia to the sea-coast, where he made preparations to cross from Dyrrachium to Brundisium with twelve hundred ships. Near to Dyrrachium is Apollonia, and near to Apollonia is the Nymphæum, a sacred spot, where perpetual streams of fire rise in various places out of a green grassy valley. It is said that a sleeping satyr was caught there, such a one as sculptors and painters represent, and was brought to Sulla and questioned by many interpreters as to who he was; but he spoke with difficulty, and what he did utter was unintelligible, and something like a compound of the neighing of a horse and the bleating of a goat; upon which Sulla, who was startled at the monster, ordered him to be removed. Sulla was now about to take his soldiers over the sea, but he feared that when they landed in Italy they would disperse to their several cities; however, the soldiers voluntarily took an oath to abide by him, and not to do any damage in Italy from set design; seeing also that he required much money, they all contributed something from what they had, each according to his means. However, Sulla would not receive the contribution, but after commending their zeal and encouraging them he proceeded to cross the sea, as he expresses it in his Memoirs, to oppose fifteen hostile commanders at the head of four hundred and fifty cohorts. The deity gave him sure prognostics of success; for upon his sacrificing immediately on landing in Italy near Tarentum, the liver of the animal was found to have on it the figure of a crown of bay with two ribands attached to it. A short time also before he crossed the sea, two large he-goats were seen in Campania near Mount Hephæus, in the daytime, fighting, and in all respects acting like men engaged in a contest. But it was only a vision, and it gradually rose up from the ground and dispersed in the air in various directions like dark phantoms, and finally disappeared. No long time after, in this very spot, when the younger Marius and the consul Norbanus came upon him at the head of a large force, Sulla, without having time to form his battle or to dispose his companies, but merely availing himself of the spirit that animated all his men, and their impetuous courage, put to flight his opponents, and shut Norbanus up in Capua with the loss of seven thousand of his soldiers. It was this success, as some say, which prevented his soldiers from dispersing to their several cities, and encouraged them to stay with Sulla and to despise their opponents, though many times more numerous than themselves. At Silvium, as Sulla says, a slave of one Pontius, moved by a divine impulse, met him and declared that he brought from Bellona assurance of superiority in war and victory, but that if he did not make haste the Capitol would be burnt; and this is said to have happened on the very day which the man foretold, being the day before the Nones of

Quintilis, which we now call July. Further, Marcus Lucullus, one of Sulla's commanders, was opposed at Fidentia with sixteen cohorts to fifty of the enemy, and though he had confidence in the spirit of his men, he was discouraged because a greater part of them were unarmed. While he was considering and hesitating what to do, a gentle breeze blowing from the adjoining plain, which was covered with grass, carried many of the flowers to the army of Lucullus, and spontaneously strewed them about, so that they rested and fell on the men's shields and helmets, which seemed to their opponents to be crowned with chaplets. Thus encouraged, the soldiers of Lucullus engaged, and gained a victory, with the loss to the opposite party of eighteen thousand men and their camp. This Lucullus was the brother of the Lucullus who afterwards defeated Mithridates and Tigranes.

XXVIII. Sulla, perceiving that he was still surrounded by many hostile camps and large forces, treacherously invited Scipio one of the consuls, to come to terms. Scipio accepted the proposal, which was followed by many meetings and conferences, but Sulla continually threw impediments and pretexts in the way of a final agreement, and in the mean time he corrupted Scipio's soldiers by means of his own men, who were as practised in all kinds of deceit and fraud as their commander. Going within the intrenchments of Scipio and mingling with his soldiers, they gained over some by giving them, money, others by promises, and the rest by flattery and persuasion. At last Sulla with twenty cohorts approached the camp of Scipio, and his soldiers saluted those of Scipio, who returned the salute and came over to them. Scipio, thus deserted, was taken prisoner in his tent, but set at liberty; and Sulla with the twenty cohorts, like so many tame birds, having entrapped forty of the enemy, led them all back to his camp. On this occasion, it is said, Carbo observed that he had to contend in Sulla both with a lion and a fox, but the fox gave him most trouble. After this, in the neighbourhood of Signia, Marius at the head of eighty-four cohorts challenged Sulla to battle; and Sulla was very ready for the contest on that day, for he happened to have had a vision in his sleep of this sort:—He dreamed that the elder Marius, who had long been dead, was advising his son to beware of the following day, as it would bring him heavy misfortune. This was the reason that Sulla was eager to fight, and he sent for Dolabella, who was encamped at some distance. But as the enemy occupied the roads and cut off the communications, the soldiers of Sulla were wearied with fighting and working at the roads at the same time; and it happened that much rain also fell, and added to the fatigue of their labour. Upon this, the centurions coming up to Sulla, begged him to defer the battle, and pointed out to him that the soldiers were exhausted by fatigue and were lying on the ground with their shields under them. Sulla consented unwillingly, and gave orders for the army to halt there; but while they were beginning to throw up their rampart and dig their trenches, Marius advanced against them confidently at the head of his troops, expecting to disperse them in their state of disorder and confusion. Now the dæmon made good the words that Sulla heard in his dream; for his soldiers, transported with indignation and stopping their work, fixed their spears in the ground close to the trenches, and drawing their swords with a loud shout, were forthwith at close quarters with the enemy. The soldiers of Marius did not stand their ground long, and there was a great slaughter of them in their flight. Marius, who fled to Præneste, found the gates closed, but a rope being let down from the walls, he fastened himself to it, and was drawn up into the city. Some historians say, and Fenestella among them, that Marius saw nothing of the battle, but that being exhausted by want of sleep and fatigue he lay down on the ground in the shade, and as soon as the signal was given for battle, fell asleep, and that he was roused with difficulty when the flight began. Sulla says that he lost only twenty-three men in this battle, and that he killed of the enemy twenty thousand, and took eight thousand alive. He was equally successful everywhere else through his generals Pompeius, Crassus, Metellus, Servilius; for without sustaining any but the most trifling loss, they destroyed the great armies of their opponents, and at last Carbo, who was the main support of the opposite party, stole away from his troops by night and sailed to Libya.

XXIX. In the last struggle, however, like a fresh combatant attacking an exhausted athlete, Telesinus the Samnite was very near tripping up Sulla and laying him prostrate at the gates of Rome. Telesinus was hastening with Lamponius the Lucanian and a strong force to Præneste, in order to rescue Marius, who was besieged; but finding that Sulla in his front and Pompeius in his rear were coming against him, and that he could neither advance nor retreat, like a brave and experienced man he broke up his encampment by night and marched with all his force against Rome. And indeed he was very near surprising the city, which was unguarded; however, halting about ten stadia from the Colline gate, he passed the night there, full of confidence and elated with hope, as he had got the advantage over so many great generals. At daybreak the most distinguished young men came out on horseback to oppose him, but many of them fell, and among them Claudius Appius, a man of noble rank and good character. This naturally caused confusion in the city, and there were women shrieking and people hurrying in all directions, in expectation that the city was going to be stormed, when Balbus appeared first, coming at full speed from Sulla with seven hundred horsemen. Balbus just halted long enough to allow his men to dry the sweat from their horses: then bridling them again, they advanced quickly and engaged with the enemy. In the mean time Sulla also appeared, and ordering the advanced ranks to take some refreshment, he began to put them in order of battle. Dolabella and Torquatus earnestly entreated him to pause, and not to put all to the hazard with his exhausted soldiers; they said, the contest was not with Carbo and Marius, but with Samnites and Lucanians, the most deadly and warlike enemies of Rome: but Sulla, without paying any regard to them, ordered the trumpets to sound the charge, though it was now about the tenth hour. The battle began, and was fiercer than any that was fought in this campaign. The right wing, where Crassus commanded, was completely successful; but the left was hard pressed, and in a dangerous plight, when Sulla came to its support mounted on a very spirited and fleet white horse, by which he was easily distinguished from the rest, and two of the enemy's soldiers, fixing their javelins, prepared to aim at him, Sulla did not see them, but his groom whipped the horse, which just carried his rider so far out of the reach of the spears that they passed close to the horse's tail, and stuck in the ground. It is said that Sulla always carried about with him in his bosom, in battle, a small golden figure of Apollo, which he got from Delphi, and that he then kissed it, and said, "O Pythian Apollo, after raising the fortunate Sulla Cornelius in so many contests to glory and renown, wilt thou throw him prostrate here, at the gates of his native city, and so bring him to perish most ignobly with his fellow-citizens?" After this address to the god it is said that Sulla entreated some, and threatened and laid hold of others; but at last, the left wing being completely broken, he was mingled with the fugitives and made his escape to the camp with the loss of many of his friends and men of note. Not a few of the citizens also, who had come to see the fight, were killed and trampled down, so that it was thought all was over with the city, and the blockade of Marius was all but raised, for many of the fugitives made their way to Præneste, and urged Ofella Lucretius, who had been appointed to conduct the siege, to break up his quarters with speed, as Sulla was killed, and Rome in the possession of the enemy.

XXX. It was now far on in the night when men came to Sulla's camp from Crassus to get something to eat for him and his soldiers, for after putting the enemy to flight they had pursued them to Antemnæ, and there encamped. Upon this intelligence, and that most of the enemy were killed, Sulla came to Antemnæ at daybreak. Here three thousand soldiers sent to him to propose to surrender, and Sulla promised them their lives if they would punish the rest of his enemies before they joined him. Trusting to his promise, these men attacked their comrades, and a great number on both sides were cut to pieces. However, Sulla got together the soldiers who had offered to surrender and those who had survived the massacre, to the number of six thousand, in the Circus, and at the same time he summoned the Senate to the temple of Bellona. As soon as he began to speak, the men who were appointed to do the work began to cut down the six thousand men. A cry naturally arose from so many men being butchered in a narrow space, and the Senators were startled; but Sulla preserving the same unmoved expression of countenance, bade them attend to what he was saying, and not trouble themselves about what was going on outside; it was only some villains who were being punished by his orders. This made even the dullest Roman see that there was merely an exchange of tyrants, not a total change. Now Marius was always cruel, and he grew more so, and the possession of power did not change his disposition. But Sulla at first used his fortune with moderation and like a citizen of a free state, and he got the reputation of being a leader who, though attached to the aristocratical party, still regarded the interests of the people; besides this, he was from his youth fond of mirth, and so soft to pity as to be easily moved to tears. It was not without reason, then, that his subsequent conduct fixed on the possession of great power the imputation that it does not let men's tempers abide by their original habits, but makes them violent, vain, and inhuman. Now whether fortune really produces an alteration and change in a man's natural disposition, or whether, when he gets to power, his bad qualities hitherto concealed are merely unveiled, is a matter that belongs to another subject than the present.

XXXI. Sulla now began to make blood flow, and he filled the city with deaths without number or limit; many persons were murdered on grounds of private enmity, who had never had anything to do with Sulla, but he consented to their death to please his adherents. At last a young man, Caius Metellus, had the boldness to ask Sulla in the Senate-house, when there would be an end to these miseries, and how far he would proceed before they could hope to see them stop. "We are not deprecating," he said, "your vengeance against those whom you have determined to put out of the way, but we entreat you to relieve from uncertainty those whom you have determined to spare." Sulla replied, that he had not yet determined whom he would spare. "Tell us then," said Metellus, "whom you intend to punish." Sulla said that he would. Some say that it was not Metellus, but Afidius, one of Sulla's flatterers, who made use of the last expression. Sulla immediately proscribed eighty persons without communicating with any magistrate. As

this caused a general murmur, he let one day pass, and then proscribed two
hundred and twenty more, and again on the third day as many. In an
harangue to the people, he said, with reference to these measures, that he had
proscribed all he could think of, and as to those who now escaped his
memory, he would proscribe them at some future time. It was part of the
proscription that every man who received and protected a proscribed person
should be put to death for his humanity; and there was no exception for
brothers, children, or parents. The reward for killing a proscribed person was
two talents, whether it was a slave who killed his master or a son who killed
his father. But what was considered most unjust of all, he affixed infamy on
the sons and grandsons of the proscribed and confiscated their property. The
proscriptions were not confined to Rome; they extended to every city of Italy:
neither temple nor hospitable hearth nor father's house was free from murder,
but husbands were butchered in the arms of their wives, and children in the
embrace of their mothers. The number of those who were massacred through
revenge and hatred was nothing compared with those who were murdered for
their property. It occurred even to the assassins to observe that the ruin of
such a one was due to his large house, another man owed his death to his
orchard, and another again to his warm baths. Quintus Aurelius, a man who
never meddled with public affairs, and though he was no further concerned
about all these calamities except so far as he sympathised with the sufferings
of others, happened to come to the Forum and there he read the names of the
proscribed. Finding his own name among them, he exclaimed, Alas! wretch
that I am; 'tis my farm at Alba that is my persecutor. He had not gone far
before he was murdered by some one who was in search of him.

XXXII. In the mean time Marius killed himself to avoid being taken. Sulla
now went to Præneste, and he began by examining the case of each individual
before he punished him; but having no time for this inquiry, he had all the
people brought to one spot, to the number of twelve thousand, and ordered
them to be massacred, with the exception of one man, an old friend of his,
whom he offered to pardon. But the man nobly declared he would never owe
his safety to the destroyer of his country, and mingling with the rest of the
citizens he was cut down together with them. The affair of Lucius Catilina
was perhaps the most monstrous of all. Lucius had murdered his brother
before the termination of the war, and he asked Sulla to proscribe him among
the rest as if he were still alive; which was done. To show his gratitude,
Catilina killed one Marcus Marius, who belonged to the opposite faction, and
after bringing his head to Sulla, who was then sitting in the Forum, he went

to the temple of Apollo, which was close by, and washed his hands in the sacred font.

XXXIII. Besides the massacres, there were other things to cause dissatisfaction. Sulla had himself proclaimed Dictator, and thus revived this office after an interval of one hundred and twenty years. An act of indemnity was also passed for all that he had done; for the future it was enacted that he should have power of life and death, and should confiscate property, distribute lands, found colonies, destroy them, take away kingdoms and give them to whom he pleased. The sales of confiscated property were conducted by him from his tribunal in such an arrogant and tyrannical manner, that his mode of dealing with the produce of the sales was more intolerable than the seizure of the property: he gave away to handsome women, players on the lyre, mimi and worthless libertini, the lands of whole nations and the revenues of cities; to some men he gave wives, who were compelled to marry against their will. Wishing to form an alliance with Pompeius Magnus, he made him put away his wife; and he took Æmilia, who was the daughter of Scaurus and of his own wife Metella, from her husband Manius Glabrio. though she was then with child, and married her to Pompeius. Æmilia died in the house of Pompeius in childbirth. Lucretius Ofella, who had taken Præneste, became a candidate for the consulship, and canvassed for it. Sulla at first attempted to stop him; but on Lucretius entering the Forum supported by a large party, Sulla sent one of his centurions to kill Lucretius, himself the while sitting on his tribunal in the temple of Castor and Pollux, and looking down upon the murder. The bystanders seized the centurion and brought him before the tribunal; but Sulla bidding them stop their noise, declared that he had ordered the centurion to kill Lucretius, and they must let him go.

XXXIV. The triumph of Sulla was magnificent for the splendour and rarity of the regal spoils; but the exiles formed a greater ornament to it and a noble spectacle. The most illustrious and wealthy of the citizens followed in the procession with chaplets on their heads, calling Sulla their saviour and father, inasmuch as through him they were restored to their country, their children, and their wives. When the triumph was over, Sulla before the assembled people gave an account of all the events of his life, mentioning with equal particularity his good fortune and his great deeds, and in conclusion he bade them salute him by the name of Eutyches, for this is the nearest word to express the Latin Felix: and when he wrote to Greeks or had any business to transact with them, he called himself Epaphroditus. In our country also, on the trophies of Sulla, there is the inscription: Lucius Cornelius Sulla Epaphroditus. As Metella bore him twins, Sulla named the male Faustus, and the female Fausta: for the Romans apply the name Faustus to what is fortunate and gladsome. Sulla indeed trusted so far to his good fortune rather than to his acts, that, though he had put many persons to death, and had made so many innovations and changes in the state, he laid down the dictatorship, and allowed the people to have the full control of the consular elections, without going near them, and all the while walking about in the Forum, and exposing himself to any one who might choose to call him to account, just like a private person. Contrary to Sulla's wish, a bold man, and an enemy of his, was likely to be elected consul, Marcus Lepidus, not for his own merits, but because the people wished to please Pompeius, who was earnest in his support and canvassed for him. Sulla seeing Pompeius going home well pleased with his victory, called him to him and said: "What a fine piece of policy is this of yours, young man, for Lepidus to be proclaimed consul before Catulus, the most violent in preference to the most honourable of men! It is, however, time for you not to be asleep, as you have strengthened your rival against yourself." Sulla said this in a kind of prophetic tone, for Lepidus soon broke out in great excesses, and was at war with Pompeius.

XXXV. Sulla made an offering of the tenth part of his substance to Hercules, and feasted the people magnificently: so much greater indeed was the preparation than what was required, that a great quantity of provisions was daily thrown into the river, and wine was drunk forty years old, and even older. In the midst of the entertainment, which lasted several days, Metella died. As the priests would not allow Sulla to go to her, or his house to be polluted by a dead body, Sulla sent Metella a writing of divorce, and ordered her, while still alive, to be removed from his house to another. So far he observed the custom strictly through superstition; but the law which limited the cost of funerals, though he had proposed it himself, he violated by sparing no expense. He also violated his own laws for diminishing the cost of entertainments, endeavouring to forget his grief in extravagant drinking and feasting, and in the company of buffoons. A few months after his wife's death there was a show of gladiators. As there was yet no distinction of places, but men and women sat promiscuously in the theatre, it chanced that a woman seated herself near Sulla who was very handsome and of good family; she was a daughter of Messala, and sister of the orator Hortensius: her name was Valeria, and she had lately separated from her husband. This woman, going behind Sulla, placed her hand upon him, and pulling a thread out of his dress, returned to her place. As Sulla looked on her with some surprise, she said, No mischief, Imperator; I also wish to have a bit of your good fortune. Sulla was not displeased at her words, and it was soon plain that he had conceived a passion for the woman; for he privately sent to ask her name, and made himself acquainted with her family and her mode of life. After this there were interchanges of glances, and frequent side-looks, and giving and returning of smiles, and, finally, treaties and arrangements about marriage, all which on her part perhaps deserved no censure; but as to Sulla, however chaste and reputable the woman might be that he married, it was no reputable or decent matter that induced him to it, for he was caught like a young man by mere looks and wanton airs, the nature of which is to excite the most depraved and impure feelings.

XXXVI. Though Sulla married Valeria he still associated with actresses and female lute-players and dancers, spending his time with them on beds, and drinking from an early hour of the day. These were the names of the persons who at this time enjoyed most of his favour:—Roscius the comedian, Sorix the chief mimus, and Metrobius who played women's parts in men's dress, and to whom, though Metrobius was now growing old, Sulla all along continued strongly attached, and never attempted to conceal it. By this mode of life he aggravated his disease, which was slight in its origin, and for some time he was not aware that all his viscera were full of diseased matter. The flesh, being corrupted by the disease, was changed into vermin, and though many persons were engaged day and night in taking the vermin away, what was got rid of was nothing compared with what came, for all his clothes, and the bath and the water, and his food, were filled with the matter that flowed from him, and with the vermin; such was the violence of the disorder. Though he went into the water several times a day and drenched his body and cleansed it from filth, it was of no avail, for the disease went on too quickly, and the quantity of vermin defied all attempts to clear it away. Among those in very remote times who are said to have died of the lousy disease was Akastus the son of Pelias; and in more recent times, Alkman the lyric poet, Pherekydes the theologian, Kallisthenes of Olynthus, while he was in prison, and Mucius the lawyer. And if one may mention those who have got a name, not for any good that they did, but in other ways, Eunus the runaway slave, who began the Servile war in Sicily, is said to have died of this disease, after he was captured and carried to Rome.

XXXVII. Sulla foresaw his end, and even in a manner wrote about it, for he finished the twenty-second book of his Memoirs only two days before his death. He there says, that the Chaldæans foretold him that it was his fate to die, after a happy life, at the very height of his prosperity; he says also that his son, who had died a short time before Metella, appeared to him in a dream, in a mean dress, and standing by him, entreated his father to rest from his troubles and to go with him to join his mother Metella, and live with her in ease and quiet. Yet he did not give up attending to public matters. Ten days before his death he restored tranquillity among the people of Dicæarchia, who were in a state of civil commotion, and he drew up for them a constitution; and only one day before his death, hearing that the chief magistrate Granius was a public defaulter and refused to pay the debt, waiting for Sulla's death, Sulla sent for the man to his chamber, and surrounding him with his slaves ordered him to be strangled; but with his shouting and efforts he burst an imposthume and vomited a quantity of blood. Upon this his strength failed him and he got through the night with difficulty. He left two infant children by Metella; Valeria, after his death, brought forth a daughter, whom they called Postuma, for this is the name that the Romans give to children who are born after their father's death.

XXXVIII. Now many flocked to Lepidus and combined with him to prevent the body of Sulla from receiving the usual interment. But Pompeius, though he had ground of complaint against Sulla, for he was the only friend whom Sulla had passed over in his will, turning some from their purpose by his influence and entreaties, and others by threats, had the body conveyed to Rome, and secured it a safe and honourable interment. It is said that the women contributed so great a quantity of aromatics for Sulla's funeral, that without including what was conveyed in two hundred and ten litters, there was enough to make a large figure of Sulla, and also to make a lictor out of costly frankincense and cinnamon. The day was cloudy in the morning, and as rain was expected they did not bring the body out till the ninth hour. However, a strong wind came down on the funeral pile and raised a great flame, and they had just time to collect the ashes as the pile was sinking and the fire going out, when a heavy rain poured down and lasted till night; so Sulla's good fortune seemed to follow him to his funeral, and to stay with him to the last. His monument is in the Campus Martius. The inscription, which they say he wrote and left behind him, says in substance, that none of his friends ever did him a kindness, and none of his enemies ever did him a wrong, without being fully repaid.

# Comparison of Lysander and Sulla

Now that we have completed the second of these men's lives, let us proceed to compare them with one another. Both rose to greatness by their own exertions, though it was the peculiar glory of Lysander that all his commands were bestowed upon him by his countrymen of their own free will and by their deliberate choice, and that he never opposed their wishes or acted in opposition to the laws of his country. Now,—

"In revolutions, villains rise to fame,"

and at Rome, at the period of which we are treating, the people were utterly corrupt and degraded, and frequently changed their masters. We need not wonder at Sulla's becoming supreme in Rome when such men as Glaucia and Saturninus drove the Metelli into exile, when the sons of consuls were butchered in the senate-house, when silver and gold purchased soldiers and arms, and laws were enacted by men who silenced their opponents by fire and the sword. I cannot blame a man who rises to power at such a time as this, but I cannot regard it as any proof of his being the best man in the state, if the state itself be in such a condition of disorder. Now Lysander was sent out to undertake the most important commands at a time when Sparta was well and orderly governed, and proved himself the greatest of all the foremost men of his age, the best man of the best regulated state. For this reason Lysander, though he often laid down his office, was always re-elected by his countrymen, for the renown of his abilities naturally pointed him out as the fittest man to command: whereas Sulla, after being once elected to lead an army, remained the chief man in Rome for ten years, calling himself sometimes consul and sometimes dictator, but always remaining a mere military despot.

II. We have related an attempt of Lysander to subvert the constitution of Sparta; but he proceeded by a much more moderate and law-abiding means than Sulla, for he meant to gain his point by persuasion, not by armed force; and besides this he did not intend to destroy the constitution utterly, but merely to reform the succession to the throne. And it does not seem contrary to justice, that he who is best among his peers should govern a city, which ruled in Greece by virtue, not by nobility of blood.

A huntsman tries to obtain a good hound, and a horseman a good horse, but does not trouble himself with their offspring, for the offspring of his horse might turn out to be a mule. Just so in politics, the important point is, what sort of man a ruler is, not from what family he is descended. Even the Spartans in some cases dethroned their kings, because they were not king-like but worthless men. If then vice be disgraceful even in the nobly born, it follows that virtue does not depend upon birth, but is honoured for itself.

The crimes of Lysander were committed for, those of Sulla against, his friends. Indeed, what Lysander did wrong was done chiefly on behalf of his friends, as, in order to establish them securely in their various despotic governments, he caused many of their political opponents to be put to death. Sulla, on the other hand, reduced the army of Pompeius and the fleet which he himself had given to Dolabella to command, merely to gratify his private spite. When Lucretius Ofella sued for the consulship as the reward of many great exploits, he ordered him to be put to death before his face, and thus made all men fear and hate him by his barbarous treatment of his most intimate friends.

III. Their several esteem for pleasure and for riches prove still more clearly that Lysander was born to command men; Sulla to tyrannize over them. The former, although he rose to such an unparalleled height of power never was betrayed by it into any acts of insolent caprice, and there never was a man to whom the well-known proverb

"Lions at home, but foxes in the field,"

was less applicable, Sulla, on the other hand, did not allow his poverty when young or his years when old to hinder him in the pursuit of pleasure, but he enacted laws to regulate the marriages and morals of his countrymen, and indulged his own amorous propensities in spite of them, as we read in Sallust's history. In consequence of his vices, Rome was so drained of money that he was driven to the expedient of allowing the allied cities to purchase their independence by payment, and that, too, although he was daily proscribing the richest men and selling their property by public auction. Yet he wasted money without limit upon his courtiers. What bounds can we imagine he would set to his generosity when in his cups, seeing that once, when a great estate was being sold by public auction, he ordered the auctioneer to knock it down to a friend of his own for a mere nominal sum, and when some one else made a higher bid, and the auctioneer called out the additional sum offered, Sulla flew into a passion and exclaimed: "My friends, I am very hardly used if I may not dispose of my own plunder as I please." Now Lysander sent home to his countrymen even what he had himself received as presents together with the rest of the spoils. Yet I do not approve of him for so doing: for he did as much harm to Sparta by bestowing that money upon it as Sulla did harm to Rome by the money which he took from it: but I mention it as proving how little he cared for money. Each acted strangely towards his fellow-countrymen. Sulla regulated and improved the morals of Rome, although he himself was wasteful and licentious. Lysander filled his countrymen with the passions from which he himself was free. Thus the former was worse than the laws which he himself enacted, while the latter rendered his countrymen worse than himself, as he taught the Spartans to covet what he had learned to despise. So much for their political conduct.

IV. In warlike exploits, in brilliancy of generalship, in the number of victories he won, and the greatness of the dangers which he encountered, Sulla is immeasurably the greater. Lysander did indeed twice conquer in a sea-fight, and I will even allow him the credit of having taken Athens; no difficult matter, no doubt, but one which, brought him great glory because of its being so famous a city. In Bœotia and before Haliartus he was perhaps unlucky, yet his conduct in not waiting for the arrival of the great force under Pausanias, which was at Platæa, close by, seems like bad generalship. He would not stay till the main body arrived, but rashly assaulted the city, and fell by an unknown hand in an insignificant skirmish. He did not meet his death facing overwhelming odds, like Kleombrotus at Leuktra, nor yet in the act of rallying his broken forces, or of consummating his victory, as did Cyrus and Epameinondas. All these died as became generals and kings; but Lysander ingloriously flung away his life like any common light infantry soldier, and proved the wisdom of the ancient Spartans, who always avoided the attack of fortified places, where the bravest may fall by the hand of the most worthless man, or even by that of a woman or a child, as Achilles is said to have been slain by Paris at the gates of Troy. Turning now to Sulla, it is not easy to enumerate all the pitched battles he won, the thousands of enemies that he overthrew. He twice took Rome itself by storm, and at Athens he took Peiræus, not by famine like Lysander, but after a gigantic struggle, at the end of which he drove Archelaus into the sea.

It is important also to consider who were the generals to whom they were opposed. It must have been mere child's-play to Lysander to defeat Antiochus, the pilot of Alkibiades, and to outwit Philokles, the Athenian mob-orator,

"A knave, whose tongue was sharper than his sword,"

for they were both of them men whom Mithridates would not have thought a match for one of his grooms, or Marius for one of his lictors. Not to mention the rest of the potentates, consuls, prætors and tribunes with whom Sulla had to contend, what Roman was more to be dreaded than Marius? What king more powerful than Mithridates? Who was there in Italy more warlike than Lamponius and Pontius Telesinus? Yet Sulla drove Marius into exile, crushed the power of Mithridates, and put Lamponius and Pontius to death.

V. What, however, to my mind incontestably proves Sulla to have been the greater man of the two, is that, whereas Lysander was always loyally assisted by his countrymen in all his enterprises, Sulla, during his campaign in Bœotia, was a mere exile. His enemies were all-powerful at Rome. They had driven his wife to seek safety in flight, had pulled down his house, and murdered his friends. Yet he fought in his country's cause against overwhelming numbers, and gained the victory. Afterwards, when Mithridates offered to join him and furnish him with the means of overcoming his private enemies, he showed no sign of weakness, and would not even speak to him or give him his hand until he heard him solemnly renounce all claim to Asia Minor, engage to deliver up his fleet, and to restore Bithynia and Cappadocia to their native sovereigns. Never did Sulla act in a more noble and high-minded manner. He preferred his country's good to his own private advantage, and, like a well-bred hound, never relaxed his hold till his enemy gave in, and then began to turn his attention to redressing his own private wrongs.

Perhaps their treatment of Athens gives us some insight into their respective characters. Although that city sided with Mithridates and fought to maintain his empire, yet when Sulla had taken it he made it free and independent. Lysander, on the other hand, felt no pity for Athens when she fell from her glorious position as the leading state in Greece, but put an end to her free constitution and established the cruel and lawless government of the Thirty.

We may now conclude our review of their respective lives by observing that while Sulla performed greater achievements, Lysander committed fewer crimes: and that while we assign the palm for moderation and self-denial to the latter, that for courage and generalship be bestowed upon the former.

# Life of Kimon.

Peripoltas, the soothsayer, after he had brought back King Opheltas and the people under him to Bœotia, left a family which remained in high repute for many generations, and chiefly settled in Chæronea, which was the first city which they conquered when they drove out the barbarians. As the men of this race were all brave and warlike, they were almost reduced to extinction in the wars with the Persians, and in later times with the Gauls during their invasion of Greece, so that there remained but one male of the family, a youth of the name of Damon, who was surnamed Peripoltas, and who far surpassed all the youth of his time in beauty and spirit, although he was uneducated and harsh-tempered. The commander of a detachment of Roman soldiers who were quartered during the winter in Chæronea conceived a criminal passion for Damon, who was then a mere lad, and as he could not effect his purpose by fair means it was evident that he would not hesitate to use force, as our city was then much decayed, and was despised, being so small and poor. Damon, alarmed and irritated at the man's behaviour, formed a conspiracy with a few young men of his own age, not many, for secrecy's sake, but consisting of sixteen in all. These men smeared their faces with soot, excited themselves by strong drink, and assaulted the Roman officer just at daybreak, while he was offering sacrifice in the market-place. They killed him and several of his attendants, and then made their escape out of the city. During the confusion which followed, the senate of the city of Chæronea assembled and condemned the conspirators to death—a decree which was intended to excuse the city to the Romans for what had happened. But that evening, when the chief magistrates, as is their custom, were dining together, Damon and his party broke into the senate-house, murdered them all, and again escaped out of the city. It chanced that at this time Lucius Lucullus was passing near Chæronea with an armed force. He halted his troops, and, after investigating the circumstances, declared that the city was not to blame, but had been the injured party. As for Damon, who was living by brigandage and plunder of the country, and who threatened to attack the city itself, the citizens sent an embassy to him, and passed a decree guaranteeing his safety if he would return. When he returned they appointed him president of the gymnasium, and afterwards, while he was being anointed in the public baths, they murdered him there.

Our ancestors tell us that as ghosts used to appear in that place, and groans were heard there, the doors of the bath-room were built up; and even at the present day those who live near the spot imagine that shadowy forms are to be seen, and confused cries heard. Those of his family who survive (for there are some descendants of Damon) live chiefly in Phokis, near the city of Steiris. They call themselves Asbolomeni, which in the Æolian dialect means "sooty-faced," in memory of Damon having smeared his face with soot when he committed his crimes.

II. Now the city of Orchomenus, which is next to that of Chæronea, was at variance with it, and hired a Roman informer, who indicted the city for the murder of those persons killed by Damon, just as if it were a man. The trial was appointed to take place before the prætor of Macedonia, for at that time the Romans did not appoint prætors of Greece. When in court the representatives of Chæronea appealed to Lucullus to testify to their innocence, and he, when applied to by the prætor, wrote a letter telling the entire truth of the story, which obtained an acquittal for the people of Chæronea. Thus narrowly did the city escape utter destruction. The citizens showed their gratitude to Lucullus by erecting a marble statue to him in the market-place, beside that of Dionysus; and although I live at a much later period, yet I think it my duty to show my gratitude to him also, as I too have benefited by his intercession. I intend therefore to describe his achievements in my Parallel Lives, and thus raise a much more glorious monument to his memory by describing his real disposition and character, than any statue can be, which merely records his face and form. It will be sufficient for me if I show that his memory is held in grateful remembrance, for he himself would be the first to refuse to be rewarded for the true testimony which he bore to us by a fictitious narrative of his exploits. We think it right that portrait painters when engaged in painting a handsome face should neither omit nor exaggerate its defects; for the former method would destroy the likeness and the latter the beauty of the picture. In like manner, as it is hard, or rather impossible, to find a man whose life is entirely free from blame, it becomes our duty to relate their noble actions with minute exactitude, regarding them as illustrative of true character, whilst, whenever either a man's personal feelings or political exigencies may have led him to commit mistakes and crimes, we must regard his conduct more as a temporary lapse from virtue than as disclosing any innate wickedness of disposition, and we must not dwell with needless emphasis on his failings, if only to save our common human nature from the reproach of being unable to produce a man of unalloyed goodness and virtue.

III. It appears to me that the life of Lucullus furnishes a good parallel to that of Kimon. Both were soldiers, and distinguished themselves against the barbarians; both were moderate politicians and afforded their countrymen a brief period of repose from the violence of party strife, and both of them won famous victories. No Greek before Kimon, and no Roman before Lucullus, waged war at such a distance from home, if we except the legends of Herakles and Dionysus, and the vague accounts which we have received by tradition of the travels and exploits of Perseus in Ethiopia, Media, and Armenia, and of the expedition of Jason to recover the Golden Fleece.

Another point in which they agree is the incomplete nature of the success which they obtained, for they both inflicted severe losses on their enemies, but neither completely crushed them. Moreover we find in each of them the same generous hospitality, and the same luxurious splendour of living. Their other points of resemblance the reader may easily discover for himself by a comparison of their respective lives.

IV. Kimon was the son of Miltiades by his wife Hegesipyle, a lady of Thracian descent, being the daughter of King Olorus, as we learn from the poems addressed to Kimon himself by Archelaus and Melanthius. Thucydides the historian also was connected with Kimon's family, as the name of Olorus had descended to his father, who also inherited gold mines in Thrace from his ancestors there. Thucydides is said to have died at Skapte Hyle, a small town in Thrace, near the gold mines. His remains were conveyed to Athens and deposited in the cemetery belonging to the family of Kimon, where his tomb is now to be seen, next to that of Elpinike, Kimon's sister. However, Thucydides belonged to the township of Halimus, and the family of Miltiades to that of Lakia.

Miltiades was condemned by the Athenians to pay a fine of fifty talents, and being unable to do so, died in prison, leaving Kimon and his sister Elpinike, who were then quite young children. Kimon passed the earlier part of his life in obscurity, and was not regarded favourably by the Athenians, who thought that he was disorderly and given to wine, and altogether resembled his grandfather Kimon, who was called Koalemus because of his stupidity.

Stesimbrotus of Thasos, who was a contemporary of Kimon, tells us that he never was taught music or any of the other usual accomplishments of a Greek gentleman, and that he had none of the smartness and readiness of speech so common at Athens, but that he was of a noble, truthful nature, and more like a Dorian of the Peloponnesus than an Athenian,

"Rough, unpretending, but a friend in need,"

as Euripides says of Herakles, which line we may well apply to Kimon according to the account of him given by Stesimbrotus. While he was still young he was accused of incest with his sister. Indeed Elpinike is not recorded as having been a respectable woman in other respects, as she carried on an intrigue with Polygnotus the painter; and therefore it is said that when he painted the colonnade which was then called the Peisianakteum, which is now called the Painted Porch, he introduced the portrait of Elpinike as Laodike, one of the Trojan ladies. Polygnotus was a man of noble birth, and he did not execute his paintings for money, but gratis, from his wish to do honour to his city. This we learn from the historians and from the poet Melanthius, who wrote—

"With deeds of heroes old, He made our city gay, In market-place and porch, Himself the cost did pay."

Some historians tell us that Elpinike was openly married to Kimon and lived as his wife, because she was too poor to obtain a husband worthy of her noble birth, but that at length Kallias, one of the richest men in Athens, fell in love with her, and offered to pay off the fine which had been imposed upon her father, by which means he won her consent, and Kimon gave her away to Kallias as his wife. Kimon indeed seems to have been of an amorous temperament, for Asterie, a lady of Salamis, and one Mnestra are mentioned by the poet Melanthius, in some playful verses he wrote upon Kimon, as being beloved by him; and we know that he was passionately fond of Isodike, the daughter of Euryptolemus the son of Megakles, who was his lawful wife, and that he was terribly afflicted by her death, to judge by the elegiac poem which was written to console him, of which Panætius the philosopher very reasonably conjectures Archelaus to have been the author.

V. All the rest that we know of Kimon is to his honour. He was as brave as Miltiades, as clever as Themistokles, and more straightforward than either. Nor was he inferior to either of them in military skill, while he far surpassed them in political sagacity, even when he was quite a young man, and without any experience of war. For instance, when Themistokles, at the time of the Persian invasion, urged the Athenians to abandon their city and territory, and resist the enemy at Salamis, on board of their fleet, while the greater part of the citizens were struck with astonishment at so daring a proposal, Kimon was seen with a cheerful countenance walking through the Kerameikus with his friends, carrying in his hand his horse's bridle, which he was going to offer up to the goddess Athena in the Acropolis, in token that at that crisis the city did not need horsemen so much as sailors. He hung up the bridle as a votive offering in the temple, and, taking down one of the shields which hung there, walked with it down towards the sea, thereby causing many of his countrymen to take courage and recover their spirits. He was not an ill-looking man, as

Ion the poet says, but tall, and with a thick curly head of hair. As he proved himself a brave man in action he quickly became popular and renowned in Athens, and many flocked round him, urging him to emulate the glories won by his father at Marathon. The people gladly welcomed him on his first entrance into political life, for they were weary of Themistokles, and were well pleased to bestow the highest honours in the state upon one whose simple and unaffected goodness of heart had made him a universal favourite. He was greatly indebted for his success to the support given him by Aristeides, who early perceived his good qualities, and endeavoured to set him up as an opponent to the rash projects and crooked policy of Themistokles.

VI. When, after the repulse of the Persian invasion, Kimon was sent as general of the Athenian forces to operate against the enemy in Asia, acting under the orders of Pausanias, as the Athenians had not then acquired their supremacy at sea, the troops whom he commanded were distinguished by the splendour of their dress and arms, and the exactness of their discipline. Pausanias at this time was carrying on a treasonable correspondence with the king of Persia, and treated the allied Greek troops with harshness and wanton insolence, the offspring of unlimited power. Kimon, on the other hand, punished offenders leniently, treated all alike with kindness and condescension, and became in all but name the chief of the Greek forces in Asia, a position which he gained, not by force of arms, but by amiability of character. Most of the allies transferred their allegiance to Kimon and Aristeides, through disgust at the cruelty and arrogance of Pausanias. There is a tradition that Pausanias when at Byzantium became enamoured of Kleonike, the daughter of one of the leading citizens there. He demanded that she should be brought to his chamber, and her wretched parents dared not disobey the tyrant's order. From feelings of modesty Kleonike entreated the attendants at the door of his bedchamber to extinguish all the lights, and she then silently in the darkness approached the bed where Pausanias lay asleep. But she stumbled and overset the lamp. He, awakened by the noise, snatched up his dagger, and imagining that some enemy was coming to assassinate him, stabbed the girl with it, wounding her mortally. It is said that after this her spirit would never let Pausanias rest, but nightly appeared to him, angrily reciting the verse—

"Go, meet thy doom; pride leadeth men to sin."

The conduct of Pausanias in this matter so enraged the allied Greeks that, under Kimon's command, they besieged him in Byzantium, which they took by assault. He, however, escaped, and, it is said, fled for refuge to the oracle of the dead at Heraklea, where he called up the soul of Kleonike and besought her to pardon him. She appeared, and told him that if he went to Sparta he would soon be relieved of all his troubles, an enigmatical sentence alluding, it is supposed, to his approaching death there.

VII. Kimon, who was now commander-in-chief, sailed to Thrace, as he heard that the Persians, led by certain nobles nearly related to Xerxes himself, had captured the city of Eion on the river Strymon, and were making war upon the neighbouring Greek cities. His first act on landing was to defeat the Persians, and shut them up in the city. He next drove away the Thracian tribes beyond the Strymon, who supplied the garrison with provisions, and by carefully watching the country round he reduced the city to such straits that Boutes, the Persian general, perceiving that escape was impossible, set it on fire, and himself with his friends and property perished in the flames. When Kimon took the city he found nothing in it of any value, as everything had been destroyed in the fire together with the Persian garrison; but as the country was beautiful and fertile, he made it an Athenian colony. Three stone statues of Hermes at Athens were now set up by a decree of the people, on the first of which is written:—

"Brave men were they, who, by the Strymon fair, First taught the haughty Persians to despair;"

and on the second—

"Their mighty chiefs to thank and praise, The Athenians do these columns raise; That generations yet to come, May fight as well for hearth and home;"

and on the third—

"Mnestheus from Athens led our hosts of yore, With Agamemnon, to the Trojan shore; Than whom no chief knew better to array, The mail-clad Greeks, when mustering for the fray: Thus Homer sung; and Athens now, as then, Doth bear away the palm for ruling men."

VIII. These verses, although Kimon's name is nowhere mentioned in them, appeared to the men of that time excessively adulatory. Neither Themistokles nor Miltiades had ever been so honoured. When Miltiades demanded the honour of an olive crown, Sophanes of Dekeleia rose up in the public assembly and said,—"Miltiades, when you have fought and conquered the barbarians alone, you may ask to be honoured alone, but not before"—a harsh speech, but one which perfectly expressed the feeling of the people.

Why, then, were the Athenians so charmed with Kimon's exploit? The reason probably was because their other commanders had merely defended them from attack, while under him they had been able themselves to attack the enemy, and had moreover won territory near Eion, and founded the colony of Amphipolis. Kimon also led a colony to Skyros, which island was taken by Kimon on the following pretext.

The original inhabitants were Dolopes, who were bad farmers, and lived chiefly by piracy. Emboldened by success they even began to plunder the strangers who came into their ports, and at last robbed and imprisoned some Thessalian merchants whose ships were anchored at Ktesium. The merchants escaped from prison, and laid a complaint against the people of Skyros before the Amphiktyonic council. The people refused to pay the fine imposed by the council, and said that it ought to be paid by those alone who had shared the plunder. These men, in terror for their ill-gotten gains, at once opened a correspondence with Kimon, and offered to betray the island into his hands if he would appear before it with an Athenian fleet. Thus Kimon was enabled to make himself master of Skyros, where he expelled the Dolopes and put an end to their piracies; after which, as he learned that in ancient times the hero Theseus, the son of Ægeus, after he had been driven out of Athens, took refuge at Skyros, and was murdered there by Lykomedes, who feared him, he endeavoured to discover where he was buried. Indeed there was an oracle which commanded the Athenians to bring back the bones of Theseus to their city and pay them fitting honours, but they knew not where they lay, as the people of Skyros did not admit that they possessed them, and refused to allow the Athenians to search for them. Great interest was now manifested in the search, and after his sepulchre had with great difficulty been discovered, Kimon placed the remains of the hero on board of his own ship and brought them back to Athens, from which they had been absent four hundred years. This act made him very popular with the people of Athens, one mark of which is to be found in his decision in the case of the rival tragic poets. When Sophokles produced his first play, being then very young, Aphepsion, the archon, seeing that party feeling ran high among the spectators, would not cast lots to decide who were to be the judges, but when Kimon with the other nine generals, his colleagues, entered to make the usual libation to the god, he refused to allow them to depart, but put them on their oath, and forced them to sit as judges, they being ten in number, one from each of the ten tribes. The excitement of the contest was much increased by the high position of the judges. The prize was adjudged to Sophokles, and it is said that Æschylus was so grieved and enraged at his failure that he shortly afterwards left Athens and retired to Sicily, where he died, and was buried near the city of Gela.

IX. Ion tells us that when quite a boy he came from Chios to Athens, and met Kimon at supper in the house of Laomedon. After supper he was asked to sing, and he sang well. The guests all praised him, and said that he was a cleverer man than Themistokles; for Themistokles was wont to say that he did not know how to sing or to play the harp, but that he knew how to make a state rich and great. Afterwards the conversation turned upon Kimon's exploits, and each mentioned what he thought the most important. Hereupon Kimon himself described what he considered to be the cleverest thing he had ever done. After the capture of Sestos and Byzantium by the Athenians and their allies, there were a great number of Persians taken prisoners, whom the allies desired Kimon to divide amongst them. He placed the prisoners on one side, and all their clothes and jewellery on the other, and offered the allies their choice between the two. They complained that he had made an unequal division, but he bade them take whichever they pleased, assuring them that the Athenians would willingly take whichever part they rejected. By the advice of Herophytus of Samos, who urged them to take the property of the Persians, rather than the Persians themselves, the allies took the clothes and jewels. At this Kimon was thought to have made a most ridiculous division of the spoil, as the allies went swaggering about with gold bracelets, armlets, and necklaces, dressed in Median robes of rich purple, while the Athenians possessed only the naked bodies of men who were very unfit for labour. Shortly afterwards, however, the friends and relations of the captives came down to the Athenian camp from Phrygia and Lydia, and ransomed each of them for great sums of money, so that Kimon was able to give his fleet four months' pay, and also to remit a large sum to Athens, out of the money paid for their ransom.

X. The money which Kimon had honourably gained in the war he spent yet more honourably upon his countrymen. He took down the fences round his fields, that both strangers and needy Athenians might help themselves to his crops and fruit. He provided daily a plain but plentiful table, at which any poor Athenian was welcome to dine, so that he might live at his ease, and be able to devote all his attention to public matters. Aristotle tells us that it was not for all the Athenians, but only for the Lakiadæ, or members of his own township, that he kept this public table. He used to be attended by young men dressed in rich cloaks, who, if he met any elderly citizen poorly clothed, would exchange cloaks with the old man; and this was thought to be a very noble act. The same young men carried pockets full of small change and would silently put money into the hands of the better class of poor in the market-place. All this is alluded to by Kratinus, the comic poet, in the following passage from his play of the Archilochi:

"I too, Metrobius, hoped to end My days with him, my noblest friend, Kimon, of all the Greeks the best, And, richly feasting, sink to rest. But now he's gone, and I remain unblest."

Moreover, Gorgias of Leontini says that Kimon acquired wealth in order to use it, and used it so as to gain honour: while Kritias, who was one of the Thirty, in his poems wishes to be

"Rich as the Skopads, and as Kimon great, And like Agesilaus fortunate."

Indeed, Lichas the Spartan became renowned throughout Greece for nothing except having entertained all the strangers who were present at the festival of the Gymnopædia: while the profuse hospitality of Kimon, both to strangers and his own countrymen, far surpassed even the old Athenian traditions of the heroes of olden days; for though the city justly boasts that they taught the rest of the Greeks to sow corn, to discover springs of water, and to kindle fire, yet Kimon, by keeping open house for all his countrymen, and allowing them to share his crops in the country, and permitting his friends to partake of all the fruits of the earth with him in their season, seemed really to have brought back the golden age. If any scurrilous tongues hinted that it was merely to gain popularity and to curry favour with the people that he did these things, their slanders were silenced at once by Kimon's personal tastes and habits, which were entirely aristocratic and Spartan. He joined Aristeides in opposing Themistokles when the latter courted the mob to an unseemly extent, opposed Ephialtes when, to please the populace, he dissolved the senate of the Areopagus, and, at a time when all other men except Aristeides and Ephialtes were gorged with the plunder of the public treasury, kept his own hands clean, and always maintained the reputation of an incorruptible and impartial statesman. It is related that one Rhœsakes, a Persian, who had revolted from the king, came to Athens with a large sum of money, and being much pestered by the mercenary politicians there, took refuge in the house of Kimon, where he placed two bowls beside the door-posts, one of which he filled with gold, and the other with silver darics. Kimon smiled at this, and inquired whether he wished him to be his friend, or his hired agent; and when the Persian answered that he wished him to be a friend, he said, "Then take this money away; for if I am your friend I shall be able to ask you for it when I want it."

XI. When the allies of Athens, though they continued to pay their contribution towards the war against Persia, refused to furnish men and ships for it, and would not go on military expeditions any longer, because they were tired of war and wished to cultivate their fields and live in peace, now that the Persians no longer threatened them, the other Athenian generals endeavoured to force them into performing their duties, and by taking legal proceedings against the defaulters and imposing fines upon them, made the Athenian empire very much disliked. Kimon, on the other hand, never forced any one to serve, but took an equivalent in money from those who were unwilling to serve in person, and took their ships without crews, permitting them to stay at home and enjoy repose, and by their luxury and folly convert themselves into farmers and merchants, losing all their ancient warlike spirit and skill, while by exercising many of the Athenians in turn in campaigns and military expeditions, he rendered them the masters of the allies by means of the very money which they themselves supplied. The allies very naturally began to fear and to look up to men who were always at sea, and accustomed to the use of arms, living as soldiers on the profits of their own unwarlike leisure, and thus by degrees, instead of independent allies, they sank into the position of tributaries and subjects.

XII. Moreover, no one contributed so powerfully as Kimon to the humbling of the king of Persia; for Kimon would not relax his pursuit of him when he retreated from Greece, but hung on the rear of the barbarian army and would not allow them any breathing-time for rallying their forces. He sacked several cities and laid waste their territory, and induced many others to join the Greeks, so that he drove the Persians entirely out of Asia Minor, from Ionia to Pamphylia. Learning that the Persian leaders with a large army and fleet were lying in wait for him in Pamphylia, and wishing to rid the seas of them as far as the Chelidoniæ, or Swallow Islands, he set sail from Knidus and the Triopian Cape with a fleet of two hundred triremes, whose crews had been excellently trained to speed and swiftness of manœuvring by Themistokles, while he had himself improved their build by giving them a greater width and extent of upper deck, so that they might afford standing-room for a greater number of fighting men. On reaching the city of Phaselis, as the inhabitants, although of Greek origin, refused him admittance, and preferred to remain faithful to Persia, he ravaged their territory and assaulted the fortifications. However, the Chians who were serving in Kimon's army, as their city had always been on friendly terms with the people of Phaselis, contrived to pacify his anger, and by shooting arrows into the town with letters wrapped round them, conveyed intelligence of this to the inhabitants. Finally, they agreed to pay the sum of ten talents, and to join the campaign against the Persians. We are told by the historian Ephorus that the Persian fleet was commanded by Tithraustes, and the land army by Pherendates. Kallisthenes, however, says that the supreme command was entrusted to Ariomandes, the son of Gobryas, who kept the fleet idle near the river Eurymedon, not wishing to risk an engagement with the Greeks, but waiting for the arrival of a reinforcement of eighty Phœnician ships from Cyprus. Kimon, wishing to anticipate this accession of strength, put to sea, determined to force the enemy to fight. The Persian fleet at first, to avoid an engagement, retired into the river Eurymedon, but as the Athenians advanced they came out again and ranged themselves in order of battle. Their fleet, according to the historian Phanodemus, consisted of six hundred ships, but, according to Ephorus, of three hundred and fifty. Yet this great armament offered no effective resistance, but turned and fled almost as soon as the Athenians attacked. Such as were able ran their ships ashore and took refuge with the land army, which was drawn up in battle array close by, while the rest were destroyed, crews and all, by the Athenians. The number of the Persian ships is proved to have been very great, by the fact that, although many escaped, and many were sunk, yet the Athenians captured two hundred prizes.

XIII. The land forces now moved down to the beach, and it appeared to Kimon that it would be a hazardous undertaking to effect a landing, and to lead his tired men to attack fresh troops, who also had an immense superiority over them in numbers. Yet as he saw that the Greeks were excited by their victory, and were eager to join battle with the Persian army, he disembarked his heavy-armed troops, who, warm as they were from the sea-fight, raised a loud shout, and charged the enemy at a run. The Persian array met them front to front, and an obstinate battle took place, in which many distinguished Athenians fell. At length the Persians were defeated with great slaughter, and the Athenians gained an immense booty from the plunder of the tents and the bodies of the slain.

Kimon, having thus, like a well-trained athlete at the games, carried off two victories in one day, surpassing that of Salamis by sea, and that of Platæa by land, proceeded to improve his success by attacking the Phœnician ships also. Hearing that they were at Hydrum, he sailed thither in haste, before any news had reached the Phœnicians about the defeat of their main body, so that they were in anxious suspense, and on the approach of the Athenians were seized with a sudden panic. All their ships were destroyed, and nearly all their crews perished with them. This blow so humbled the pride of the king of Persia, that he afterwards signed that famous treaty in which he engaged not to approach nearer to the Greek seas than a horseman could ride in one day, and not to allow a single one of his ships of war to appear between the Kyanean and Chelidonian Islands. Yet the historian Kallisthenes tells us that the Persians never made a treaty to this effect, but that they acted thus in consequence of the terror which Kimon had inspired by his victory; and that they removed so far from Greece, that Perikles with fifty ships, and Ephialtes with only thirty, sailed far beyond the Chelidonian Islands and never met with any Persian vessels. However, in the collection of Athenian decrees made by Kraterus, there is a copy of the articles of this treaty, which he mentions as though it really existed. It is said that on this occasion the Athenians erected an altar to Peace, and paid great honours to Kallias, who negotiated the treaty. So much money was raised by the sale of the captives and spoils taken in the war, that besides what was reserved for other occasions, the Athenians were able to build the wall on the south side of the Acropolis from the treasure gained in this campaign. We are also told that at this time the foundations of the Long Walls were laid. These walls, which were also called the Legs, were finished afterwards, but the foundations, which had to be carried over marshy places, were securely laid, the marsh being filled up with chalk and large stones, entirely at Kimon's expense. He also was the first to adorn the city with those shady public walks which shortly afterwards became so popular with the Athenians, for he planted rows of plane-trees in the market-place, and transformed the Academy from a dry and barren wilderness into a well-watered grove, full of tastefully-kept paths and pleasant walks under the shade of fine trees.

XIV. As some of the Persians, despising Kimon, who had set out from Athens with a very small fleet, refused to leave the Chersonese, and invited the Thracian tribes of the interior to assist them in maintaining their position, he attacked them with four ships only, took thirteen of the enemy's, drove out the Persians, defeated the Thracians, and reconquered the Chersonese for Athens. After this he defeated in a sea-fight the people of Thasos, who had revolted from Athens, captured thirty-three of their ships, took their city by storm, and annexed to Athens the district of the mainland containing the gold mines, which had belonged to the Thasians. From Thasos he might easily have invaded Macedonia and inflicted great damage upon that country, but he refrained from doing so. In consequence of this he was accused of having been bribed by Alexander, the king of Macedonia, and his enemies at home impeached him on that charge. In his speech in his own defence he reminded the court that he was the proxenus, or resident agent at Athens, not of the rich Ionians or Thessalians, as some other Athenians were, with a view to their own profit and influence, but of the Lacedæmonians, a people whoso frugal habits he had always been eager and proud to imitate; so that he himself cared nothing for wealth, but loved to enrich the state with money taken from its enemies. During this trial, Stesimbrotus informs us that Elpinike, Kimon's sister, came to plead her brother's cause with Perikles, the bitterest of his opponents, and that Perikles answered with a smile, "Elpinike, you are too old to meddle in affairs of this sort." But for all that, in the trial he treated Kimon far more gently than any of his other accusers, and spoke only once, for form's sake.

XV. Thus was Kimon acquitted; and during the remainder of his stay in Athens he continued to oppose the encroachments of the people, who were endeavouring to make themselves the source of all political power. When, however, he started again on foreign service, the populace finally succeeded in overthrowing the old Athenian constitution, and under the guidance of Ephialtes greatly curtailed the jurisdiction of the Senate of the Areopagus, and turned Athens into a pure democracy. At this time also Perikles was rising to power as a liberal politician. Kimon, on his return, was disgusted at the degradation of the ancient Senate of the Areopagus, and began to intrigue with a view of restoring the aristocratic constitution of Kleisthenes. This called down upon him a storm of abuse from the popular party, who brought up again the old scandals about his sister, and charged him with partiality for the Lacedæmonians. These imputations are alluded to in the hackneyed lines of Eupolis:
"Not a villain beyond measure, Only fond of drink and pleasure; Oft he slept in Sparta's town, And left his sister here alone."

If, however, he really was a careless drunkard, and yet took so many cities and won so many battles, it is clear that if he had been sober and diligent he would have surpassed the most glorious achievements of any Greek, either before or since.

XVI. He was always fond of the Lacedæmonians, and named one of his twin sons Lacedæmonius, and the other Eleius. These children were borne to him by his wife Kleitoria, according to the historian Stesimbrotus; and consequently Perikles frequently reproached them with the low birth of their mother. But Diodorus the geographer says that these two and the third, Thessalus, were all the children of Kimon by Isodike, the daughter of Euryptolemus the son of Megakles. Much of Kimon's political influence was due to the fact that the Lacedæmonians were bitterly hostile to Themistokles, and wished to make him, young as he was, into a powerful leader of the opposite party at Athens. The Athenians at first viewed his Spartan partialities without dissatisfaction, especially as they gained considerable advantages by them; for during the early days of their empire when they first began to extend and consolidate their power, they were enabled to do so without rousing the jealousy of Sparta, in consequence of the popularity of Kimon with the Lacedæmonians. Most international questions were settled by his means, as he dealt generously with the subject states, and was viewed with especial favour by the Lacedæmonians.

Afterwards, when the Athenians became more powerful, they viewed with dislike Kimon's excessive love for Sparta. He was never weary of singing the praises of Lacedæmon to the Athenians, and especially, we are told by Stesimbrotus, when he wished to reproach them, or to encourage them to do bettor, he used to say, "That is not how the Lacedæmonians do it." This habit caused many Athenians to regard him with jealousy and dislike: but the most important ground of accusation against him was the following. In the fourth year of the reign of king Archidamus, the son of Zeuxidamus, at Sparta, the Lacedæmonian territory was visited by the greatest earthquake ever known there. The earth opened in many places, some of the crags of Taygetus fell down, and the whole city was destroyed, with the exception of five houses. It is related that while the boys and young men were practising gymnastics in the palæstra, a hare ran into the building, and that the boys, naked and anointed as they were, immediately ran out in pursuit of it, while the gymnasium shortly afterwards fell upon the young men who remained and killed them all. Their tomb is at this day called Seismatia, that is, the tomb of those who perished in the earthquake.

Archidamus, perceiving the great dangers with which this disaster menaced the state, and observing that the citizens thought of nothing but saving their most valuable property from the wreck, ordered the trumpet to sound, as though the enemy were about to attack, and made every Spartan get under arms and rally round him as quickly as possible. This measure saved Sparta; for the helots had gathered together from the country round about, and were upon the point of falling upon the survivors. Finding them armed and drawn up in order, they retreated to the neighbouring cities, and openly made war against the Spartans, having won over no small number of the Periœki to their side, while the Messenians also joined them in attacking their own old enemies. At this crisis the Spartans sent Perikleides as an ambassador to Athens to demand assistance. This is the man whom Aristophanes ridiculed in his play as sitting by the altars as a suppliant, with a pale face and a scarlet cloak, begging for an army.

We are told by Kritias that Ephialtes vigorously opposed his mission, and besought the Athenians not to assist in restoring a state which was the rival of Athens, but to let the pride of Sparta be crushed and trampled in the dust. Kimon, on the other hand, postponing the interests of his own country to those of the Lacedæmonians, persuaded the people of Athens to march a numerous body of men to assist them. The historian Ion has preserved the argument which had most effect upon the Athenians, and says that Kimon besought them not to endure to see Greece lame of one foot and Athens pulling without her yoke-fellow.

XVII. When Kimon with his relieving force marched to help the Lacedæmonians, he passed through the territory of Corinth. Lachartus objected to this, saying that he had marched in before he had asked leave of the Corinthians, and reminded him that when men knock at a door, they do not enter before the master of the house invites them to come in. Kimon answered, "Lachartus, you Corinthians do not knock at the doors of the cities of Megara or of Kleonæ, but break down the door and force your way in by the right of the stronger, just as we are doing now." By this timely show of spirit he silenced the Corinthians, and passed through the territory of Corinth with his army.

The Lacedæmonians invited the aid of the Athenians a second time, to assist in the reduction of the fortress of Ithomé, which was held by the Messenians and revolted helots; but when they arrived the Lacedæmonians feared so brilliant and courageous a force, and sent them back, accusing them of revolutionary ideas, although they did not treat any other of their allies in this manner. The Athenians retired, in great anger at the treatment they had received, and no longer restrained their hatred of all who favoured the Lacedæmonians. On some trifling pretext they ostracised Kimon, condemning him to exile for ten years, which is the appointed time for those suffering from ostracism. During this time the Lacedæmonians, after setting Delphi free from the Phokians, encamped at Tanagra, and fought a battle there with the Athenians, who came out to meet them. On this occasion Kimon appeared, fully armed, and took his place in the ranks among his fellow-tribesmen. However, the senate of the five hundred hearing of this, became alarmed, and, as his enemies declared that his only object was to create confusion during the battle and so to betray his countrymen to the Lacedæmonians, they sent orders to the generals, forbidding them to receive him. Upon this he went away, after having begged Euthippus the Anaphlystian and those of his friends who were especially suspected of Laconian leanings, to fight bravely, and by their deeds to efface this suspicion from the minds of their fellow-citizens. They took Kimon's armour, and set it up in their ranks; and then, fighting in one body round it with desperate courage, they all fell, one hundred in number, causing great grief to the Athenians for their loss, and for the unmerited accusation which had been brought against them. This event caused a revulsion of popular feeling in favour of Kimon, when the Athenians remembered how much they owed him, and reflected upon the straits to which they were now reduced, as they had been defeated in a great battle at Tanagra, and expected that during the summer Attica would be invaded by the Lacedæmonians. They now recalled Kimon from exile; and Perikles himself brought forward the decree for his restoration. So moderate were the party-leaders of that time, and willing to subordinate their own differences to the common welfare of their country.

XVIII. On his return Kimon at once put an end to the war, and reconciled the two states. After the peace had been concluded, however, he saw that the Athenians were unable to remain quiet, but were eager to increase their empire by foreign conquest. In order, therefore, to prevent their quarrelling with any other Greek state, or cruising with a large fleet among the islands and the Peloponnesian coast, and so becoming entangled in some petty war, he manned a fleet of two hundred triremes with the intention of sailing a second time to Cyprus and Egypt, wishing both to train the Athenians to fight against barbarians, and also to gain legitimate advantages for Athens by the plunder of her natural enemies. When all was ready, and the men were about to embark, Kimon dreamed that he saw an angry dog barking at him, and that in the midst of its barking it spoke with a human voice, saying,
"Go, for thou shalt ever be Loved both by my whelps and me."

This vision was very hard to interpret. Astyphilus of Poseidonia, a soothsayer and an intimate friend of Kimon's, told him that it portended his death, on the following grounds. The dog is the enemy of the man at whom he barks: now a man is never so much loved by his enemies as when he is dead; and the mixture of the voice, being partly that of a dog and partly that of a man, signifies the Persians, as their army was composed partly of Greeks and partly of barbarians. After this dream Kimon sacrificed to Dionysus. The prophet cut up the victim, and the blood as it congealed was carried by numbers of ants towards Kimon, so that his great toe was covered with it before he noticed them. At the moment when Kimon observed this, the priest came up to him to tell him that the liver of the victim was defective. However, he could not avoid going on the expedition, and sailed forthwith. He despatched sixty of his ships to Egypt, but kept the rest with him. He conquered the Phœnician fleet in a sea-fight, recovered the cities of Cilicia, and began to meditate an attack upon those of Egypt, as his object was nothing less than the utter destruction of the Persian empire, especially when he learned that Themistokles had risen to great eminence among the Persians, and had undertaken to command their army in a campaign against Greece. It is said that one of the chief reasons which caused Themistokles to despair of success was his conviction that he could not surpass the courage and good fortune of Kimon. He therefore committed suicide, while Kimon, who was now revolving immense schemes of conquest as he lay at Cyprus with his fleet, sent an embassy to the shrine of Ammon to ask something secret. What it was no one ever knew, for the god made no response, but as soon as the messengers arrived bade them return, as Kimon was already with him. On hearing this, they retraced their steps to the sea, and when they reached the headquarters of the Greek force, which was then in Egypt, they heard that Kimon was dead. On counting back the days to that on which they received the response, they perceived that the god had alluded to Kimon's death when he said that he was with him, meaning that he was among the gods.

XIX. According to most authorities Kimon died of sickness during a siege; but some writers say that he died of a wound which he received in a battle with the Persians. When dying he ordered his friends to conceal his death, but at once to embark the army and sail home. This was effected, and we are told by Phanodemus that no one, either of the enemy or of the Athenian allies conceived any suspicion that Kimon had ceased to command the forces until after he had been dead for thirty days. After his death no great success was won by any Greek general over the Persians, but they were all incited by their popular orators and the war-party to fight with one another, which led to the great Peloponnesian war. This afforded a long breathing-time to the Persians, and wrought terrible havoc with the resources of Greece. Many years afterwards Agesilaus invaded Asia, and carried on war for a short time against the Persian commanders who were nearest the coast. Yet he also effected nothing of any importance, and being recalled to Greece by the internal troubles of that country, left Persia drawing tribute from all the Greek cities and friendly districts of the sea-coast, although in the time of Kimon no Persian tax-gatherer or Persian horseman was ever seen within a distance of four hundred stades (fifty miles) from the sea.

His remains were brought back to Attica, as is proved by the monument which to this day is known as the "Tomb of Kimon." The people of Kitium, also, however, pay respect to a tomb, said to be that of Kimon, according to the tale of the orator Nausikrates, who informs us that once during a season of pestilence and scarcity the people of Kitium were ordered by an oracle not to neglect Kimon, but to pay him honour and respect him as a superior being. Such a man as this was the Greek general.

# Life of Lucullus.

I. The grandfather of Lucullus was a man of consular rank, and his uncle on the mother's side was Metellus, surnamed Numidicus. His father was convicted of peculation, and his mother, Cæcilia, had a bad name as a woman of loose habits. Lucullus, while he was still a youth, before he was a candidate for a magistracy and engaged in public life, made it his first business to bring to trial his father's accuser, Servilius the augur, as a public offender; and the matter appeared to the Romans to be creditable to Lucullus, and they used to speak of that trial as a memorable thing. It was, indeed, the popular notion, that to prefer an accusation was a reputable measure, even when there was no foundation for it, and they were glad to see the young men fastening on offenders, like well-bred whelps laying hold of wild beasts. However, there was much party spirit about that trial, and some persons were even wounded and killed; but Servilius was acquitted. Lucullus had been trained to speak both Latin and Greek competently, so that Sulla, when he was writing his memoirs, dedicated them to Lucullus as a person who would put them together and arrange his history better than himself; for the style of the oratory of Lucullus was not merely suited to business and prompt, like that of the other orators which disturbed the Forum—

"As a struck tunny throws about the sea,"

but when it is out of the Forum is

"Dry, and for want of true discipline half dead"—

but he cultivated the appropriate and so-called liberal sciences, with a view to self-improvement, from his early youth. When he was more advanced in years he let his mind, as it were, after so many troubles, find tranquillity and repose in philosophy, rousing to activity the contemplative portion of his nature, and seasonably terminating and cutting short his ambitious aspirations after his difference with Pompeius. Now, as to his love of learning, this also is reported, in addition to what has been mentioned: when he was a young man, in a conversation with Hortensius, the orator, and Sisenna, the historian, which began in jest, but ended in a serious proposition, he agreed that if they would propose a poem and a history, Greek and Roman, he would treat the subject of the Marsic war in whichsoever of these two languages the lot should decide; and it seems that the lot resulted in a Greek history, for there is still extant a Greek history of the Marsic war by Lucullus. Of his affection to his brother Marcus there were many proofs, but the Romans speak most of the first; being older than his brother, he did not choose to hold a magistracy by himself, but he waited till his brother was of the proper age, and so far gained the public favour that his brother in his absence was elected ædile jointly with him.

II. Though he was a young man during the Marsic war, he gave many proofs of courage and prudence; but it was rather on account of the solidity of his character and the mildness of his temper that Sulla attached Lucullus to himself, and from the beginning he constantly employed him in affairs of the greatest importance; one of which was the matter relating to the coinage. It was Lucullus who superintended the coining of most of the money in the Peloponnesus during the Mithridatic war, and it was named Lucullean after him, and continued for a long time to have a ready circulation, in consequence of the demands of the war. Afterwards, Sulla, who was in possession of the country about Athens, but was shut out from supplies by sea by the enemy, who had the command of it, sent Lucullus to Egypt and Libya to get ships there. It was now the depth of winter, but still he set sail with three Greek piratical ships, and the same number of Rhodian biremes, exposing himself to a wide sea and to hostile vessels, which, owing to their having the superiority, were cruising about in great numbers and in all directions. However, he landed at Crete, and made the people friendly to his cause; and, finding the Cyrenæans in a state of confusion, owing to continual tyrannies and wars, he tranquillised and settled the state, by reminding the citizens of a certain expression of Plato, which the philosopher had addressed to them in a prophetic spirit. They asked him, as it appears, to draw up laws for them, and to settle their democracy after the model of a well-ordered polity; but he replied that it was difficult to legislate for the Cyrenæans while they were so prosperous. Nothing, indeed, is more difficult to govern than a man who considers himself prosperous; and, on the other hand, there is nothing more obedient to command than a man when he is humbled by fortune. And it was this that made the Cyrenæans tractable to Lucullus in his legislation for them. Sailing from Cyrene to Egypt, he lost most of his vessels by an attack of pirates; but he escaped himself, and entered Alexandria in splendid style; for the whole fleet came out to meet him, as it was used to do when a king entered the port, equipped magnificently. The young king, Ptolemæus, showed him other surprising marks of attention, and gave him a lodging and table in the palace, though no foreign general had ever before been lodged there. He also offered him an allowance for his expenditure, not such as he used to offer to others, but four times as much; Lucullus, however, would not receive anything more than his necessities required, nor yet any present, though the king sent presents to the value of eighty talents. It is said that Lucullus did not go up to Memphis, nor make inquiry about any other of the wondrous and far-famed things in Egypt; he said that such things befitted an idle spectator, and one who had only to enjoy himself: not a man like himself, who had left the Imperator encamped under the bare sky, and close to the enemy's battlements.

Plutarch begins his Treatise which is intitled To an Uninstructed Prince with the same story about Plato and the Cyrenæans (Moralia, ed. Wyttenbach, vol. iv.).]

III. Ptolemæus declined the alliance, being afraid of the war; but he gave Lucullus ships to convoy him as far as Cyprus, and when he was setting sail he embraced him and paid him great attention, and presented him with an emerald set in gold, of great price. Lucullus at first begged to be excused from taking the present; but when the king showed him that the engraving contained his royal likeness, Lucullus was afraid to refuse the present, lest, if he should be supposed to sail away at complete enmity with the king, he might be plotted against on the sea. In his voyage along the coast Lucullus got together a number of vessels from the maritime towns except such as participated in piratical iniquities, and passed over to Cyprus, where, hearing that his enemies were lying in wait for him with their ships at the headlands, he drew up all his vessels, and wrote to the cities about winter quarters and supplies, as if he intended to stay there till the fine season. As soon as a favourable opportunity offered for his voyage, he launched his ships and got out to sea, and by sailing during the day with his sails down and low, and putting them up at night, he got safe to Rhodes. The Rhodians supplied him with some more ships, and he persuaded the people of Kos and Knidus to quit the king's side, and join him in an attack on the Samians. He drove the king's party also out of Chios, and he gave the people of Kolophon freedom by seizing Epigonus, their tyrant. It happened about this time that Mithridates had left Pergamum, and was shut up in Pitane. While Fimbria was keeping the king blockaded there on the land side and pressing the siege, Mithridates, looking to the sea, got together and summoned to him ships from every quarter, having given up all design of engaging and fighting with Fimbria, who was a bold man and had defeated him. Fimbria observing this, and being deficient in naval force, sent to Lucullus, and prayed him to come with his fleet and help him to take the most detested and the most hostile of kings, in order that Mithridates, the great prize, which had been followed through many contests and labours, might not escape the Romans, now that he had given them a chance of seizing him, and was caught within the nets. He said, if Mithridates was taken, no one would have more of the glory than he who stopped his flight and laid hold of him when he was trying to steal away; that if Mithridates were shut out from the land by him, and excluded from the sea by Lucullus, there would be a victory for both of them, and that as to the vaunted exploits of Sulla at Orchomenus and Chæronea, the Romans would think nothing of them in comparison with this. There was nothing unreasonable in all that Fimbria said; and it was plain to every man that if Lucullus, who was at no great distance, had then accepted the proposal of Fimbria, and led his ships there and blockaded the port with his fleet, the war would have been at an end, and all would have been delivered from innumerable calamities. But whether it was that Lucullus regarded his duty to Sulla above all private and public interests, or that he detested Fimbria, who was an abandoned man, and had lately murdered his own friend and general, merely from ambition to command, or whether it was through chance, as the Deity would have it, that he spared Mithridates, and reserved him for his own antagonist—he would not listen to Fimbria, but allowed Mithridates to escape by sea, and to mock the force of Fimbria. Lucullus himself, in the first place, defeated off Lektum in the Troad, the king's ships, which showed themselves there, and again observing that Neoptolemus was stationed at Tenedos with a larger force, he sailed against him ahead of all the rest, in a Rhodian galley of five banks which was commanded by Demagoras, a man well affected to the Romans, and exceedingly skilful in naval battles. Neoptolemus came against him at a great rate, and ordered the helmsman to steer the ship right against the vessel of Lucullus; but Demagoras, fearing the weight of the king's vessel and the rough brass that she was fitted with, did not venture to engage head to head, but he quickly turned his ship round and ordered them to row her stern foremost, and the vessel being thus depressed at the stern received the blow, which was rendered harmless by falling on those parts of the ship which were in the water. In the meantime his friends coming to his aid, Lucullus commanded them to turn his ship's head to the enemy; and, after performing many praiseworthy feats, he put the enemy to flight, and pursued Neoptolemus.

IV. After this, Lucullus joined Sulla in the Chersonesus, as he was going to cross the Hellespont, and he made the passage safe for him, and assisted his army in getting over. When the treaty was made, and Mithridates had sailed off to the Euxine, and Sulla had imposed a contribution of twenty thousand talents on Asia, and Lucullus had been appointed to collect the money, and to strike coin, it appeared some small consolation to the cities of Asia for the harshness of Sulla that Lucullus not only behaved with honesty and justice, but conducted himself mildly in the discharge of so oppressive and disagreeable a duty. Though the Mitylenæans had openly revolted, Lucullus wished them to come to their senses, and to submit to some reasonable penalty for their ill-conduct in the matter of Marius; but perceiving that they were under the influence of some evil dæmon, he sailed against them, and defeated them in a battle, and, after shutting them up in their walls, and establishing a blockade, he sailed out in open day to Elæa, but he returned by stealth, and laying an ambuscade near the city, kept quiet. The Mitylenæans approached in disorder, and with confidence in the expectation of plundering a deserted camp; but Lucullus falling on them took a great number alive, and killed five hundred of them who made resistance. He also took six thousand slaves, and the rest of the booty was past count. But in the miseries which Sulla and Marius were at that time bringing on the people of Italy, without limit and of every kind, he had no share, being detained by his business in Asia by some happy fortune. Nevertheless, he had not less favour with Sulla than the rest of his friends; for, as I have said Sulla dedicated his memoirs to Lucullus, as a token of his affection, and finally he appointed him the guardian of his son, and passed by Pompeius. And this was probably the origin of the difference and the jealousy between Lucullus and Pompeius; for they were both young, and burning for distinction.

V. Shortly after Sulla's death, Lucullus was consul with Marcus Cotta, about the hundred and seventy-sixth Olympiad. Many persons were again attempting to stir up the Mithridatic war, and Marcus said that the war was not ended, but only stopped for a time. It was for this reason that Lucullus was annoyed at the lot giving him for his province Gaul within (south of) the Alps, which offered no opportunity for great exploits. But the reputation of Pompeius, who was now in Iberia, stung him most, as it was expected that Pompeius, in preference to any one else, would be forthwith chosen to the command of the war against Mithridates, if it should happen that the Iberian war should be brought to a close. Accordingly, when Pompeius asked for money, and wrote to say that if they did not send it he would leave Iberia and Sertorius, and lead his troops hack to Italy, Lucullus did all he could to get money sent, and to prevent Pompeius returning from Iberia on any pretence whatever while he was consul; for he considered that the whole State would be at the disposal of Pompeius if he were at Rome with so large an army. Cethegus, also, who had then the power in his hands by always speaking and acting with a view to popularity, was at enmity with Lucullus, who detested his habits of life, which were nothing but a course of unnatural lusts, insolence, and violence. With Cethegus then Lucullus was at open war. There was, indeed another demagogue, Lucius Quintius, who had set himself against

Sulla's measures, and attempted to disturb the present settlement of affairs; but Lucullus, by much persuasion in private and reproof in public, drew him from his designs, and quieted his ambition, in as politic and wholesome a way as a man could do, by taking in hand so great a disease at its commencement.

VI. In the meantime news arrived of the death of Octavius, the Governor of Cilicia. Now there were many eager competitors for the province, who courted Cethegus as the person who was best able to help them to it. As to Cilicia itself, Lucullus made no great account of that province; but, inasmuch as he thought, if he should get Cilicia, which bordered on Cappadocia, no one else would be sent to conduct the war against Mithridates, he left no means untried to prevent the province falling into other hands; and, at last, contrary to his natural disposition, he submitted from necessity to do an act which was not creditable, or commendable, though it was useful towards the end he had in view. There was a woman named Præcia, who was famed through Rome for her beauty and gallantry, and though in other respects she was no better than a common prostitute, yet, as she availed herself of her influence with those who visited her and talked to her, for the purpose of forwarding the interests and political views of her friends, she added to her other attractions the reputation of being a woman who was much attached to her friends, and very active in accomplishing anything, and she obtained great influence. Cethegus, who was then at the height of his popularity, and directed the administration, was captivated by Præcia, and began to cohabit with her, and thus the whole power of the State fell into her hands; for no public measure was transacted if Cethegus was not for it, and if Præcia did not recommend it to Cethegus. Now Lucullus gained over Præcia by presents and flattery; and, indeed, it was in itself a great boon to a proud woman, fond of public display, to be seen using her influence on behalf of Lucullus; and thus he soon had Cethegus speaking in his favour, and trying to get Cilicia for him. When Lucullus had once gained the province of Cilicia, it was no longer necessary for him to call in the aid of Præcia or Cethegus, but all alike readily put into his hands the conduct of the Mithridatic war, believing that it could not be managed better by any other person; for Pompeius was still fighting against Sertorius, and Metellus had withdrawn from service by reason of his age, and these were the only persons who could be considered as rivals to Lucullus in any dispute about the command in the war. However, Cotta, the colleague of Lucullus, after making earnest application to the Senate, was sent with some ships to watch the Propontis, and to defend Bithynia.

VII. Lucullus, with one legion which he had raised at home, crossed over into Asia, where he took the command of the rest of the forces, all of whom had long been spoiled by luxurious habits and living at free quarters; and the soldiers of Fimbria were said to have become difficult to manage, from being accustomed to obey no commander. They were the men who joined Fimbria in putting to death Flaccus, who was a consul and their general, and who gave up Fimbria himself to Sulla—self-willed and lawless men, but brave and full of endurance, and experienced soldiers. However, in a short time, Lucullus took down the insolence of these soldiers, and changed the character of the rest, who then, for the first time, as it seems, knew what it was to have a genuine commander and leader; for under other generals, they were used to be courted, and spirited on to military service in such wise as was agreeable to them. As to the enemy, matters were thus: Mithridates, like most of the sophists, full of boasting at first, and rising up against the Romans arrogantly, with an army unsubstantial in fact, but in appearance brilliant and pompous, had failed in his undertaking, and exposed himself to ridicule: but now, when he was going to commence the war a second time, taught by experience he concentrated his powers in a real and effectual preparation. Rejecting those motley numbers and many-tongued threats of the barbarians, and arms ornamented with gold and precious stones, which he considered to be the spoils of the victors, and to give no strength to those who possess them, he set about having Roman swords made, and heavy shields manufactured; and he got together horses which were well trained, instead of horses which were well caparisoned; and one hundred and twenty thousand foot-soldiers who were disciplined to the Roman order of battle, and sixteen thousand horse-soldiers, without reckoning the scythe-bearing four-horse chariots, and these were a hundred; besides, his ships were not filled with tents embroidered with gold, nor with baths for concubines, nor apartments for the women luxuriously furnished; but fitting them out fully with arms, missiles, and stores, he invaded Bithynia, where he was again gladly received by the cities, and not by these cities only, for a return of their former calamities had visited all Asia, which was suffering past endurance from the Roman money-lenders and farmers of the taxes. These men, who, like so many harpies, were plundering the people of their substance, Lucullus afterwards drove out; but, for the time, he endeavoured by reproof to make them more moderate in their conduct, and he stopped the insurrection of the towns, when, so to speak, not a single man in them was quiet.

VIII. While Lucullus was busied about these matters, Cotta, thinking it a good opportunity for himself, was preparing to fight with Mithridates; and, though many persons brought him intelligence that Lucullus was encamped in Phrygia on his advanced march, Cotta, thinking that he had the triumph all but in his hands, hastened to engage, that Lucullus might have no share in it. But he was defeated by land and by sea at the same time; and he lost sixty vessels with all the men in them, and four thousand foot-soldiers, and he was shut up in Chalkedon and besieged there, and obliged to look for help at the hands of Lucullus. Now there were some who urged Lucullus not to care for Cotta, but to advance forward, as he would be able to seize the kingdom of Mithridates, which was unprotected; and this was the language of the soldiers especially, who were indignant that Cotta, not satisfied with ruining himself and those with him by his imprudent measures, should be a hindrance to their getting a victory without a contest when it was in their power; but Lucullus said in reply to all this in an harangue, that he would rather save one Roman from the enemy than get all that the enemy had. And when Archelaus, who had commanded for Mithridates in Bœotia, and afterwards had left him, and was now in the Roman army, maintained that if Lucullus would only show himself in Pontus, he might make himself master of everything at once, Lucullus replied that he was not a greater coward than huntsmen, which he should be if he passed by the wild beasts and went to their empty dens. Saying this he advanced against Mithridates, with thirty thousand foot-soldiers and two thousand five hundred cavalry. On arriving in sight of the enemy, he was startled at their numbers, and wished to avoid a battle and to protract the time. Marius, however, whom Sertorius had sent from Iberia to Mithridates in command of a force, came out to meet Lucullus, and challenged him to the contest, on which Lucullus put his army in order of battle; and they were just on the point of commencing the engagement, when, without any evident change, but all at once, the sky opened, and there appeared a huge flame-like body, which came down between the two armies, in form most like a cask, and in colour resembling molten silver, so that both armies were alarmed at the sight and separated. This, it is said, took place in Phrygia, at a place called Otryæ. Lucullus, considering that it was not possible for any human resources or wealth to maintain for any length of time, and in the presence of an enemy, so many thousands as Mithridates had, ordered one of the prisoners to be brought to him, and asked him first how many messmates he had, and then how much provision he had left in his tent. When the man had given his answer, he ordered him to be removed, and he put the same question to a second, and to a third. Then comparing the amount of provisions that the enemy had with the number of those who were to be fed, he concluded that the enemy's provisions would fail them in three or four days. He now stuck still more closely to his plan of protracting the time, and he employed himself in getting into his camp a great store of provision, that he might have abundance himself, and so wait till the enemy was reduced to want.

IX. In the meantime Mithridates resolved to attack the Kyzikeni, who had received a blow in the battle at Chalkedon, for they had lost three thousand men and ten ships. Accordingly, wishing to give Lucullus the slip, he put himself in motion immediately after supper, taking advantage of a dark and rainy night; and he succeeded in planting his force at daybreak right opposite to the city, at the base of the mountain tract of the Adrasteia. Lucullus, who perceived his movements and followed him, was well satisfied that he had not come up with the enemy while his own troops were out of battle order; and he posted his army near the village named Thrakia, in a position excellently adapted to command the roads and the places from which and through which the soldiers of Mithridates must bring their supplies. Now, as he had in his own mind a clear comprehension of the issue, he did not conceal it from his men; but as soon as he had chosen his ground, and the men had finished the entrenchments, he summoned them together, and confidently told them that he would, in a few days, give them a victory which would cost no blood. Mithridates had hemmed in the Kyzikeni with ten camps on the land side, and towards the sea with his ships, by blocking up the narrow channel which separates the city from the mainland, and thus he was besieging them on both sides. Though the citizens were disposed to resist the enemy boldly, and had determined to sustain all hardships for the sake of the Romans, they were troubled at not knowing where Lucullus was, and at having heard nothing of him. Yet the army of Lucullus was visible and in sight of the city; but the citizens were deceived by the soldiers of Mithridates, who pointed to the Romans in their entrenchments on the higher ground, and said, "Do you see them? That is the army of the Armenians and Medes, which Tigranes has sent to support Mithridates."

The Kyzikeni were alarmed to see such a host of enemies around them, and they had no hopes that they could be released, even if Lucullus should come. However, Demonax, who was sent to them by Archelaus, was the first to inform them of Lucullus being there. While they were distrusting his intelligence, and thinking that he had merely invented this story to comfort them in their difficulties, there came a youth, who had been captured by the enemy and made his escape. On their asking him where he supposed Lucullus to be, he laughed outright, for he thought they were making sport of him; but, seeing that they were in earnest, he pointed with his hand to the Roman camp, and the citizens again took courage. Now the lake Daskylitis is navigable for boats of a considerable size, and Lucullus, drawing up the largest of them, and conveying it on a waggon to the sea-coast, put into it as many soldiers as it would hold. The soldiers crossed over by night unobserved, and got into the city.

X. It appears that the deity, also, admiring the bravery of the Kyzikeni, encouraged them by other manifest signs, and especially by this: the festival called Persephassia was at hand, and as they had not a black cow to sacrifice, they made one of dough, and placed it at the altar. The cow which was intended to be the victim, and was fattening for the goddess, was pasturing, like the other animals of the Kyzikeni, on the opposite mainland; but on that day, leaving the rest of the herd by itself, it swam over the channel to the city and presented itself to be sacrificed. The goddess also appeared in a dream to Aristagoras, the town-clerk, and said: "For my part, I am come, and I bring the Libyan fifer against the Pontic trumpeter. Bid the citizens, then, be of good cheer." The Kyzikeni were wondering at these words, when at daybreak the sea began to be disturbed by an unsteady, changing wind that descended upon it, and the engines of the king, which were placed near the walls—admirable contrivances of Nikonides the Thessalian—by their creaking and rattling showed what was going to happen: then a south-west wind, bursting forth with incredible fury, broke to pieces the other engines in a very short time, and shook and threw down the wooden tower, which was a hundred cubits high. It is told that Athena appeared to many of the people in Ilium in their sleep, streaming with copious sweat, showing part of her peplus rent, and saying that she had just returned from helping the Kyzikeni. And the people of Ilium used to show a stele which contained certain decrees and an inscription about these matters.

XI. Mithridates, so long as he was deceived by his generals and kept in ignorance of the famine in his army, was annoyed at the Kyzikeni holding out against the blockade. But his ambition and his haughtiness quickly oozed away when he had discovered the straits in which his army was held, and that they were eating one another; for Lucullus was not carrying on the war in a theatrical way, nor with mere show; but, as the proverb says, was kicking against the belly, and contriving every means how he should cut off the food. Accordingly, while Lucullus was engaged in besieging a certain garrisoned post, Mithridates, seizing the opportunity, sent off into Bithynia nearly all his cavalry, with the beasts of burden, and all his superfluous infantry. Lucullus hearing of this, returned to his camp during the night, and early in the following morning, it being winter time, getting ready ten cohorts and the cavalry, he followed the troops of Mithridates, though it was snowing, and his soldiers suffered so much that many of them gave in by reason of the cold, and were left behind: however, with the rest he came up with the enemy at the river Rhyndakus, and gave them such a defeat that the women came from the town of Apollonia and carried off the baggage and stripped the dead. Many fell in the battle, as might be supposed, but there were taken six thousand horses, with a countless number of baggage-beasts, and fifteen thousand men, all whom he led back past the camp of the enemy. I wonder at Sallustius saying that this was the first time that the Romans saw the camel; for he must have supposed that the soldiers of Scipio, who some time before had defeated Antiochus, and those who had also fought with Archelaus at Orchomenus and Chæronea, were unacquainted with the camel. Now Mithridates had determined to fly as soon as he could; but, with the view of contriving something which should draw Lucullus in the other direction, and detain him in his rear, he sent his admiral, Aristonikus, to the Grecian sea, and Aristonikus was just on the point of setting sail when he was betrayed to Lucullus, who got him into his power, together with ten thousand pieces of gold which he was carrying to bribe a part of the Roman army with. Upon this Mithridates fled to the sea, and his generals led the land forces off. But Lucullus falling upon them at the river Granikus, took many prisoners, and slew twenty thousand of them. It is said that near three hundred thousand persons were destroyed out of the whole number of camp-followers and fighting-men.

XII. Upon entering Kyzikus, Lucullus took his pleasure, and enjoyed a friendly reception suitably to the occasion; he next visited the Hellespont, and got his navy equipped. Arriving at the Troad, he placed his tent within the sacred precincts of Aphrodite, and as he was sleeping there he thought that he saw the goddess in the night standing by him, saying:
"Why slumber, lion of the mighty heart? The fawns are near at hand."

Waking from sleep, Lucullus called his friends and told them his dream, while it was still night; and there came persons from Ilium, who reported that thirteen of the king's quinqueremes had been seen near the Achæan harbour, moving in the direction of Lemnos. Immediately setting sail, Lucullus captured these vessels and killed their commander, Isidorus, and he then advanced against the other captains. Now, as they happened to be at anchor, they drew all their vessels together up to the land, and, fighting from the decks, dealt blows on the men of Lucullus; for the ground rendered it impossible to sail round to the enemy's rear, and, as the ships of Lucullus were afloat, they could make no attack on those of the enemy, which were planted close to the land and securely situated. However, with some difficulty, Lucullus landed the bravest of his soldiers in a part of the island which was accessible, who, falling on the rear of the enemy, killed some and compelled the rest to cut their cables and make their escape from the land, and so to drive their vessels foul of one another, and to be exposed to the blows of the vessels of Lucullus. Many of the enemy perished; but among the captives there was Marius, he who was sent from Sertorius. Marius had only one eye, and the soldiers had received orders from Lucullus, as they were setting out on the expedition, to kill no one-eyed man; for Lucullus designed to make Marius die a shameful and dishonourable death.

XIII. As soon as he had accomplished this, Lucullus hastened in pursuit of Mithridates; for he expected still to find him about Bithynia, and watched by Voconius, whom he had sent with ships to Nikomedia to follow up the pursuit. But Voconius lingered in Samothrakia, where he was getting initiated into mysteries and celebrating festivals. Mithridates, who had set sail with his armament, and was in a hurry to reach Pontus before Lucullus returned, was overtaken by a violent storm, by which some of his ships were shattered and others were sunk; and all the coast for many days was filled with the wrecks that were cast up by the waves. The merchant-vessel in which Mithridates was embarked could not easily be brought to land by those who had the management of it, by reason of its magnitude, in the agitated state of the water, and the great swell, and it was already too heavy to hold out against the sea, and was water-logged; accordingly the king got out of the vessel into a piratical ship, and, intrusting his person to pirates, contrary to expectation and after great hazard he arrived at Heraklea in Pontus. Now it happened that the proud boast of Lucullus to the Senate brought on him no divine retribution. The Senate was voting a sum of three thousand talents to equip a navy for the war, but Lucullus stopped the measure by sending a letter, couched in vaunting terms, in which he said, that without cost and so much preparation, he would with the ships of the allies drive Mithridates from the sea. And he did this with the aid of the deity; for it is said that it was owing to the anger of Artemis Priapine that the storm fell on the Pontic soldiers, who had plundered her temple and carried off the wooden statue.

XIV. Though many advised Lucullus to suspend the war, he paid no heed to them: but, passing through Bithynia and Galatia, he invaded the country of the king. At first he wanted provisions, so that thirty thousand Galatians followed him, each carrying on his shoulders a medimnus of wheat; but as he advanced and reduced all into his power, he got into such abundance of everything that an ox was sold in the camp for a drachma, and a slave for four drachmæ; and, as to the rest of the booty, it was valued so little that some left it behind, and others destroyed it; for there were no means of disposing of anything to anybody when all had abundance. The Roman army had advanced with their cavalry and carried their incursions as far as Themiskyra and the plains on the Thermodon, without doing more than wasting and ravaging the country, when the men began to blame Lucullus for peaceably gaining over all the cities, and they complained that he had not taken a single city by storm, nor given them an opportunity of enriching themselves by plunder. "Nay, even now," they said, "we are quitting Amisus, a prosperous and wealthy city, which it would be no great matter to take, if any one would press the siege, and the general is leading us to fight with Mithridates in the wilds of the Tibareni and Chaldæans." Now, if Lucullus had supposed that these notions would have led the soldiers to such madness as they afterwards showed he would not have overlooked or neglected these matters, nor have apologised instead to those men who were blaming his tardiness for thus lingering in the neighbourhood of insignificant villages for a long time, and allowing Mithridates to increase his strength. "This is the very thing," he said, "that I wish, and I am sitting here with the design of allowing the man again to become powerful, and to get together a sufficient force to meet us, that he may stay, and not fly from us when we advance. Do you not see that a huge and boundless wilderness is in his rear, and the Caucasus is near, and many mountains which are full of deep valleys, sufficient to hide ten thousand kings who decline a battle, and to protect them? and it is only a few days' march from Kabeira into Armenia, and above the plains of Armenia Tigranes the King of Kings has his residence, with a force which enables him to cut the Parthian off from Asia, and he removes the inhabitants of the Greek cities up into Media, and he is master of Syria and Palestine, and the kings, the descendants of Seleucus, he puts to death, and carries off their daughters and wives captives. Tigranes is the kinsman and son-in-law of Mithridates. Indeed, he will not quietly submit to receive Mithridates as a suppliant; but he will war against us, and, if we strive to eject Mithridates from his kingdom we shall run the risk of drawing upon us Tigranes, who has long been seeking for a pretext against us, and he could not have a more specious pretext than to be compelled to aid a man who is his kinsman and a king. Why, then, should we bring this about, and show Mithridates, who does not know it, with whose aid he ought to carry on the war against us? and why should we drive him against his wish, and ingloriously, into the arms of Tigranes, instead of giving him time to collect a force out of his own resources and to recover his courage, and so fight with the Kolchi, and Tibareni, and Cappadocians, whom we have often defeated, rather than fight with the Medes and Armenians?"

XV. Upon such considerations as these, Lucullus protracted the time before Amisus without pushing the siege; and, when the winter was over, leaving Murena to blockade the city, he advanced against Mithridates, who was posted at Kabeira, and intending to oppose the Romans, as he had got together a force of forty thousand infantry and four thousand horse on whom he relied most. Crossing the river Lykus into the plain, Mithridates offered the Romans battle. A contest between the cavalry ensued, in which the Romans fled, and Pomponius, a man of some note, being wounded, was taken prisoner, and brought to Mithridates while he was suffering from his wounds. The king asked him if he would become his friend if his life were spared, to which Pomponius replied, "Yes, if you come to terms with the Romans; if not, I shall be your enemy." Mithridates admired the answer, and did him no harm. Now, Lucullus was afraid to keep the plain country, as the enemy were masters of it with their cavalry, and he was unwilling to advance into the hilly region, which was of great extent and wooded and difficult of access; but it happened that some Greeks were taken prisoners, who had fled into a cave, and the eldest of them, Artemidorus, promised Lucullus to be his guide, and to put him in a position which would be secure for his army, and also contained a fort that commanded Kabeira. Lucullus, trusting the man, set out at nightfall after lighting numerous fires, and getting through the defiles in safety; he gained possession of the position; and, when the day dawned, he was seen above the enemy, posting his soldiers in a place which gave him the opportunity of making an attack if he chose to fight, and secured him against any assault if he chose to remain quiet. At present neither general had any intention of hazarding a battle; but it is said, that while some of the king's men were pursuing a deer, the Romans met them and attempted to cut off their retreat, and this led to a skirmish, in which fresh men kept continually coming up on both sides. At last the king's men had the better, and the Romans, who from the ramparts saw their comrades falling, were in a rage, and crowded about Lucullus, praying him to lead them on, and calling for the signal for battle. But Lucullus, wishing them to learn the value of the presence and sight of a prudent general in a struggle with an enemy and in the midst of danger, told them to keep quiet; and, going down into the plain and meeting the first of the fugitives, he ordered them to stand, and to turn round and face the enemy with him. The men obeyed, and the rest also facing about and forming in order of battle, easily put the enemy to flight, and pursued them to their camp. Lucullus, after retiring to his position, imposed on the fugitives the usual mark of disgrace, by ordering them to dig a trench of twelve feet in their loose jackets, while the rest of the soldiers were standing by and looking on.

XVI. Now there was in the army of Mithridates a prince of the Dandarii, named Olthakus (the Dandarii are one of the tribes of barbarians that live about the Mæotis), a man distinguished in all military matters where strength and daring are required, and also in ability equal to the best, and moreover a man who knew how to ingratiate himself with persons, and of insinuating address. Olthakus, who was always engaged in a kind of rivalry for distinction with one of the princes of the kindred tribes, and was jealous of him, undertook a great exploit for Mithridates, which was to kill Lucullus. The king approved of his design, and purposely showed him some indignities, at which, pretending to be in a rage, Olthakus rode off to Lucullus, who gladly received him, for there was a great report of him in the Roman army; and Lucullus, after some acquaintance with him, was soon pleased with his acuteness and his zeal, and at last admitted him to his table and made him a member of his council. Now when the Dandarian thought he had a fit opportunity, he ordered the slaves to take his horse without the ramparts, and, as it was noontide and the soldiers were lying in the open air and taking their rest, he went to the general's tent, expecting that nobody would prevent him from entering, as he was on terms of intimacy with Lucullus, and said that he was the bearer of some important news. And he would have entered the tent without any suspicion, if sleep, that has been the cause of the death of many generals, had not saved Lucullus; for he happened to be asleep, and Menedemus, one of his chamber-attendants, who was standing by the door, said that Olthakus had not come at a fit time, for Lucullus had just gone to rest himself after long wakefulness and many toils. As Olthakus did not go away when he was told, but said that he would go in, even should Menedemus attempt to prevent him, because he wished to communicate with Lucullus about a matter of emergency and importance, Menedemus began to get in a passion, and, saying that nothing was more urgent than the health of Lucullus, he shoved the man away with both his hands. Olthakus being alarmed stole out of the camp, and, mounting his horse, rode off to the army of Mithridates, without effecting his purpose. Thus, it appears, it is with actions just as it is with medicines—time and circumstance give to the scales that slight turn which saves alive, as well as that which kills.

XVII. After this Sornatius, with ten cohorts, was sent to get supplies of corn. Being pursued by Menander, one of the generals of Mithridates, Sornatius faced about and engaged the enemy, of whom he killed great numbers and put the rest to flight. Again, upon Adrianus being sent with a force, for the purpose of getting an abundant supply of corn for the army, Mithridates did not neglect the opportunity, but sent Menemachus and Myron at the head of a large body of cavalry and infantry. All this force, as it is said, was cut to pieces by the Romans, with the exception of two men. Mithridates concealed the loss, and pretended it was not so great as it really was, but a trifling loss owing to the unskilfulness of the commanders. However, Adrianus triumphantly passed by the camp of the enemy with many waggons loaded with corn and booty, which dispirited Mithridates, and caused irremediable confusion and alarm among his soldiers. Accordingly it was resolved not to stay there any longer. But, while the king's servants were quietly sending away their own property first, and endeavouring to hinder the rest, the soldiers, growing infuriated, pushed towards the passages that led out of the camp, and, attacking the king's servants, began to seize the luggage and massacre the men. In this confusion Dorylaus the general, who had nothing else about him but his purple dress, lost his life by reason of it, and Hermæus, the sacrificing priest, was trampled to death at the gates. The king himself, without attendant or groom to accompany him, fled from the camp mingled with the rest, and was not able to get even one of the royal horses, till at last the eunuch Ptolemæus, who was mounted, spied him as he was hurried along in the stream of fugitives, and leaping down from his horse gave it to the king. The Romans, who were following in pursuit, were now close upon the king, and so far as it was a matter of speed they were under no difficulty about taking him, and they came very near it; but greediness and mercenary motives snatched from the Romans the prey which they had so long followed up in many battles and great dangers, and robbed Lucullus of the crowning triumph to his victory; for the horse which was carrying Mithridates was just within reach of his pursuers, when it happened that one of the mules which was conveying the king's gold either fell into the hands of the enemy accidentally, or was purposely thrown in their way by the king's orders, and while the soldiers were plundering it and getting together the gold, and fighting with one another, they were left behind. And this was not the only loss that Lucullus sustained from their greediness; he had given his men orders to bring to him Kallistratus, who had the charge of all the king's secrets; but those who were taking him to Lucullus, finding that he had five hundred gold pieces in his girdle, put him to death. However, Lucullus allowed his men to plunder the camp.

XVIII. After taking Kabeira and most of the other forts Lucullus found in them great treasures, and also places of confinement, in which many Greeks and many kinsmen of the king were shut up; and, as they had long considered themselves as dead, they were indebted to the kindness of Lucullus, not for their rescue, but for restoration to life and a kind of second birth. A sister also of Mithridates, Nyssa, was captured, and so saved her life; but the women who were supposed to be the farthest from danger, and to be securely lodged at Phernakia, the sisters and wives of Mithridates, came to a sad end, pursuant to the order of Mithridates, which he sent Bacchides, a eunuch, to execute, when he was compelled to take to flight. Among many other women there were two sisters of the king, Roxana and Statira, each about forty years of age and unmarried; and two of his wives, Ionian women, one of them named Berenike from Chios, and the other Monime a Milesian. Monime was much talked of among the Greeks, and there was a story to this effect, that though the king tempted her with an offer of fifteen thousand gold pieces, she held out until a marriage contract was made, and he sent her a diadem with the title of queen. Now Monime hitherto was very unhappy, and bewailed that beauty which had given her a master instead of a husband, and a set of barbarians to watch over her instead of marriage and a family; and she lamented that she was removed from her native country, enjoying her anticipated happiness only in imagination, while she was deprived of all those real pleasures which she might have had at home. When Bacchides arrived, and told the women to die in such manner as they might judge easiest and least painful, Monime pulled the diadem from her head, and, fastening it round her neck, hung herself. As the diadem soon broke, "Cursed rag!" she exclaimed, "you won't even do me this service;" and, spitting on it, she tossed it from her, and presented her throat to Bacchides. Berenike took a cup of poison, and gave a part of it to her mother, who was present, at her own request. Together they drank it up; and the strength of the poison was sufficient for the weaker of the two, but it did not carry off Berenike, who had not drunk enough, and, as she was long in dying, she was strangled with the assistance of Bacchides. Of the two unmarried sisters of Mithridates it is said, that one of them, after uttering many imprecations on her brother and much abuse, drank up the poison. Statira did not utter a word of complaint, or anything unworthy of her noble birth; but she commended her brother for that he had not neglected them at a time when his own life was in danger, and had provided that they should die free and be secure against insult. All this gave pain to Lucullus, who was naturally of a mild and humane temper.

XIX. Lucullus advanced as far as Talaura, whence four days before Mithridates had fled into Armenia to Tigranes. From Talaura Lucullus took a different direction, and after subduing the Chaldæi and Tibareni, and taking possession of the Less Armenia, and reducing forts and cities, he sent

Appius to Tigranes to demand Mithridates; but he went himself to Amisus, which was still holding out against the siege. This was owing to Kallimachus the commander, who by his skill in mechanical contrivances, and his ingenuity in devising every resource which is available in a siege, gave the Romans great annoyance, for which he afterwards paid the penalty. Now, however, he was out-generailed by Lucullus, who, by making a sudden attack, just at that time of the day when he was used to lead his soldiers off and to give them rest, got possession of a small part of the wall, upon which Kallimachus quitted the city, having first set fire to it, either because he was unwilling that the Romans should get any advantage from their conquest, or with the view of facilitating his own escape. For no one paid any attention to those who were sailing out; but when the flames had sprung up with violence, and got hold of the walls, the soldiers were making ready to plunder. Lucullus, lamenting the danger in which the city was of being destroyed, attempted from the outside to help the citizens against the fire, and ordered it to be put out; yet nobody attended to him, and the soldiers called out for booty, and shouted and struck their armour, till at last Lucullus was compelled to let them have their way, expecting that he should thus save the city at least from the fire. But the soldiers did just the contrary; for, as they rummaged every place by the aid of torches, and carried about lights in all directions, they destroyed most of the houses themselves, so that Lucullus, who entered the city at daybreak, said to his friends with tears in his eyes, that he had often considered Sulla a fortunate man, but on this day of all others he admired the man's good fortune, in that when he chose to save Athens he had also the power; "but upon me," he said, "who have been emulous to imitate his example, the dæmon has instead brought the reputation of Mummius." However, as far as present circumstances allowed, he endeavoured to restore the city. The fire indeed was quenched by the rains that chanced to fall, as the deity would have it, at the time of the capture, and the greatest part of what had been destroyed Lucullus rebuilt while he stayed at Amisus; and he received into the city such of the Amisenes as had fled, and settled there any other Greeks who were willing to settle, and added to the limits of the territory a tract of one hundred and twenty stadia. Amisus was a colony of the Athenians, planted, as one might suppose, at that period in which their power was at its height and had the command of the sea. And this was the reason why many who wished to escape from the tyranny of Aristion sailed to the Euxine and settled at Amisus, where they became citizens; but it happened that by flying from misfortune at home they came in for a share of the misfortunes of others. Lucullus, however, clothed all of them who survived the capture of the city, and, after giving each two hundred drachmæ besides, he sent them back to their home. On this occasion, Tyrannio the grammarian was taken prisoner. Murena asked him for himself, and on getting Tyrannio set him free, wherein he made an illiberal use of the favour that he had received; for Lucullus did not think it fitting that a man who was esteemed for his learning should be made a slave first and then a freedman; for the giving him an apparent freedom was equivalent to the depriving him of his real freedom. But it was not in this instance only that Murena showed himself far inferior to his general in honourable feeling and conduct.

XX. Lucullus now turned to the cities of Asia, in order that while he had leisure from military operations he might pay some attention to justice and the law, which the province had now felt the want of for a long time, and the people had endured unspeakable and incredible calamities, being plundered and reduced to slavery by the Publicani and the money-lenders, so that individuals were compelled to sell their handsome sons and virgin daughters, and the cities to sell their sacred offerings, pictures and statues. The lot of the citizens was at last to be condemned to slavery themselves, but the sufferings which preceded were still worse—the fixing of ropes and barriers, and horses, and standing under the open sky, during the heat in the sun, and during the cold when they were forced into the mud or the ice; so that slavery was considered a relief from the burden of debt, and a blessing. Such evils as these Lucullus discovered in the cities, and in a short time he relieved the sufferers from all of them. In the first place, he declared that the rate of interest should be reckoned at the hundredth part, and no more; in the second, he cut off all the interest which exceeded the capital; thirdly, what was most important of all, he declared that the lender should receive the fourth part of the income of the debtor; but any lender who had tacked the interest to the principal was deprived of the whole: thus, in less than four years all the debts were paid, and their property was given back to them free from all encumbrance. Now the common debt originated in the twenty thousand talents which Sulla had laid on Asia as a contribution, and twice this amount was repaid to the lenders, though they had indeed now brought the debt up to the amount of one hundred and twenty thousand talents by means of the interest. The lenders, however, considered themselves very ill used, and they raised a great outcry against Lucullus at Rome, and they endeavoured to bribe some of the demagogues to attack him; for the lenders had great influence, and had among their debtors many of the men who were engaged in public life. But Lucullus gained the affection of the cities which had been favoured by him, and the other provinces also longed to see such a man over them, and felicitated those who had the good luck to have such a governor.

XXI. Appius Clodius, who was sent to Tigranes (now Clodius was the brother of the then wife of Lucullus), was at first conducted by the king's guides through the upper part of the country, by a route unnecessarily circuitous and roundabout, and one that required many days' journeying; but, as soon as the straight road was indicated to him by a freedman, a Syrian by nation, he quitted that tedious and tricky road, and, bidding his barbarian guides farewell, he crossed the Euphrates in a few days, and arrived at Antiocheia, near Daphne. There he waited for Tigranes, pursuant to the king's orders (for Tigranes was absent, and still engaged in reducing some of the Phœnician cities), and in the meantime he gained over many of the princes who paid the Armenian a hollow obedience, among whom was Zarbienus, King of Gordyene, and he promised aid from Lucullus to many of the enslaved cities, which secretly sent to him—bidding them, however, keep quiet for the present. Now the rule of the Armenians was not tolerable to the Greeks, but was harsh; and what was worse, the king's temper had become violent and exceedingly haughty in his great prosperity; for he had not only everything about him which the many covet and admire, but he seemed to think that everything was made for him. Beginning with expectations which were slight and contemptible, he had subdued many nations, and humbled the power of the Parthians as no man before him had done; and he filled Mesopotamia with Greeks, many from Cilicia and many from Cappadocia, whom he removed and settled. He also removed from their abodes the Skenite Arabians, and settled them near him, that he might with their aid have the benefit of commerce. Many were the kings who were in attendance on him; but there were four who were always about him, like attendants or guards, and when he mounted his horse they ran by his side in jackets; and when he was seated and transacting business, they stood by with their hands clasped together, which was considered to be of all attitudes the most expressive of servitude, as if they had sold their freedom, and were presenting their bodies to their master in a posture indicating readiness to suffer rather than to act. Appius, however, was not alarmed or startled at the tragedy show; but, as soon as he had an opportunity of addressing the king, he told him plainly that he was come to take back Mithridates, as one who belonged to the triumphs of Lucullus, or to denounce war against Tigranes. Though the king made an effort to preserve a tranquil mien, and affected a smile while he was listening to the address, he could not conceal from the bystanders that he was disconcerted by the bold speech of the youth, he who had not for near five-and-twenty years heard the voice of a free man; for so many years had he been king, or rather tyrant. However, he replied to Appius that he would not give up Mithridates, and that he would resist the Romans if they attacked him. He was angry with Lucullus because he addressed him in his letter by the title of King only, and not King of Kings, and, accordingly in his reply, Tigranes did not address Lucullus by the title of Imperator. But he sent splendid presents to Appius, and when they were refused he sent still more. Appius, not wishing to appear to reject the king's presents from any hostile feeling, selected from among them a goblet, and sent the rest back; and then with all speed set off to join the Imperator.

XXII. Now, up to this time, Tigranes had not deigned to see Mithridates, nor to speak to him, though Mithridates was allied to him by marriage, and had been ejected from so great a kingdom; but, in a degrading and insulting manner, he had allowed Mithridates to be far removed from him, and, in a manner, kept a prisoner in his abode, which was a marshy and unhealthy place. However, he now sent for him with demonstrations of respect and friendship. In a secret conference which took place in the palace, they endeavoured to allay their mutual suspicions, by turning the blame on their friends, to their ruin. One of them was Metrodorus of Skepsis, an agreeable speaker, and a man of great acquirements, who enjoyed so high a degree of favour with Mithridates that he got the name of the king's father. Metrodorus, as it seems, had once been sent on an embassy from Mithridates to Tigranes, to pray for aid against the Romans, on which occasion Tigranes asked him, "But you, Metrodorus, what do you advise me in this matter?" Metrodorus, either consulting the interests of Tigranes, or not wishing Mithridates to be maintained in his kingdom, replied, that, as ambassador, he requested him to send aid, but, in the capacity of adviser, he told him not to send any. Tigranes reported this to Mithridates, to whom he gave the information, not expecting that he would inflict any extreme punishment on Metrodorus. But Metrodorus was forthwith put to death, and Tigranes was sorry for what he had done, though he was not altogether the cause of the misfortune of Metrodorus: indeed what he had said merely served to turn the balance in the dislike of Mithridates towards Metrodorus; for Mithridates had for a long time disliked Metrodorus, and this was discovered from his private papers, that fell into the hands of the Romans, in which there were orders to put Metrodorus to death. Now, Tigranes interred the body with great pomp, sparing no expense on the man, when dead, whom he had betrayed when living. Amphikrates the rhetorician also lost his life at the court of Tigranes, if he too deserves mention for the sake of Athens. It is said that he fled to

Seleukeia, on the Tigris, and that when the citizens there asked him to give lectures on his art, he treated them with contempt, saying, in an arrogant way, that a dish would not hold a dolphin. Removing himself from Seleukeia, he betook himself to Kleopatra, who was the daughter of Mithridates, and the wife of Tigranes; but he soon fell under suspicion, and, being excluded from all communion with the Greeks, he starved himself to death. Amphikrates also received an honourable interment from Kleopatra, and his body lies at Sapha, a place in those parts so called.

XXIII. After conferring on Asia, the fulness of good administration and of peace, Lucullus did not neglect such things as would gratify the people and gain their favour; but during his stay at Ephesus he gained popularity in the Asiatic cities by processions and public festivals in commemoration of his victories, and by contests of athletes and gladiators. The cities on their side made a return by celebrating festivals, called after the name of Lucullus, to do honour to the man; and they manifested towards him what is more pleasing than demonstrations of respect, real affection. Now, when Appius had returned, and it appeared that there was to be war with Tigranes, Lucullus again advanced into Pontus, and, getting his troops together, he besieged Sinope, or rather the Cilicians of the king's party, who were in possession of the city; but the Cilicians made their escape by night, after massacring many of the Sinopians, and firing the city. Lucullus, who saw what was going on, made his way into the city, and slaughtered eight thousand of the Cilicians, who were left there; but he restored to the rest of the inhabitants their property, and provided for the interests of Sinope, mainly by reason of a vision of this sort: he dreamed that a man stood by him in his sleep, and said, "Advance a little, Lucullus; for Autolykus is come, and wishes to meet with you." On waking, Lucullus could not conjecture what was the meaning of the vision; but he took the city on that day, and, while pursuing the Cilicians, who were escaping in their ships, he saw a statue lying on the beach, which the Cilicians had not had time to put on board; and the statue was the work of Sthenis, one of his good performances. Now, somebody told Lucullus that it was the statue of Autolykus, the founder of Sinope. Autolykus is said to have been one of those who joined Herakles from Thessalia, in his expedition against the Amazons, and a son of Deimachus. In his voyage home, in company with Demoleon and Phlogius, he lost his ship, which was wrecked at the place called Pedalium, in the Chersonesus: but he escaped with his arms and companions to Sinope, which he took from the Syrians: for Sinope was in possession of the Syrians, who were descended from Syrus, the son of Apollo, according to the story, and Sinope, the daughter of Asopus. On hearing this, Lucullus called to mind the advice of Sulla, who in his 'Memoirs' advised to consider nothing so trustworthy and safe as that which is signified in dreams. Lucullus was now apprised that Mithridates and Tigranes were on the point of entering Lycaonia and Cilicia, with the intention of anticipating hostilities by an invasion of Asia, and he was surprised that the Armenian, if he really intended to attack the Romans, did not avail himself of the aid of Mithridates, in the war when he was at the height of his power, nor join his forces to those of Mithridates when he was strong but allowed him to be undone and crushed; and now began a war that offered only cold hopes, and throw himself on the ground to join those who were already there and unable to rise.

XXIV. Now, when Machares also, the son of Mithridates, who held the Bosporus, sent to Lucullus a crown worth one thousand gold pieces, and prayed to be acknowledged a friend and ally of the Romans, Lucullus, considering that the former war was at an end, left Sornatius in those parts to watch over the affairs of Pontus with six thousand soldiers. He set out himself with twelve thousand foot soldiers, and not quite three thousand horse, to commence a second campaign, wherein he seemed to be making a hazardous move, and one not resting on any safe calculation; for he was going to throw himself among warlike nations and many thousands of horsemen, and to enter a boundless tract, surrounded by deep rivers and by mountains covered with perpetual snow; so that his soldiers, who were generally not very obedient to discipline, followed unwillingly and made opposition: and at Rome the popular leaders raised a cry against him, and accused him of seeking one war after another, though the State required no wars, that he might never lay down his arms so long as he had command, and never stop making his private profit out of the public danger; and in course of time the demagogues at Rome accomplished their purpose. Lucullus, advancing by hard marches to the Euphrates, found the stream swollen and muddy, owing to the winter season, and he was vexed on considering that it would cause loss of time and some trouble if he had to get together boats to take his army across and to build rafts. However, in the evening the water began to subside, and it went on falling all through the night, and at daybreak the bed of the river was empty. The natives observing that some small islands in the river had become visible, and that the stream near them was still, made their obeisance to Lucullus; for this had very seldom happened before, and they considered it a token that the river had purposely made itself tame and gentle for Lucullus, and was offering him an easy and ready passage. Accordingly, Lucullus took advantage of the opportunity, and carried his troops over: and a favourable sign accompanied the passage of the army. Cows feed in that neighbourhood, which are sacred to Artemis Persia, a deity whom the barbarians on the farther side of the Euphrates venerate above all others; they use the cows only for sacrifice, which at other times ramble at liberty about the country, with a brand upon them, in the form of the torch of the goddess, and it is not very easy, nor without much trouble, that they can catch the cows when they want them. After the army had crossed the Euphrates one of these cows came to a rock, which is considered sacred to the goddess, and stood upon it, and there laying down its head, just as a cow does when it is held down tight by a rope, it offered itself to Lucullus to be sacrificed. Lucullus also sacrificed a bull to the Euphrates, as an acknowledgment for his passage over the river. He encamped there for that day, and on the next and the following days he advanced through Sophene without doing any harm to the people, who joined him and gladly received the soldiers; and when the soldiers were expressing a wish to take possession of a fortress, which was supposed to contain much wealth, "That is the fortress," said Lucullus, "which we must take first," pointing to the Taurus in the distance; "but this is reserved for the victors." He now continued his route by hard marches, and, crossing the Tigris, entered Armenia.

XXV. Now, as the first person who reported to Tigranes that Lucullus was in the country got nothing for his pains, but had his head cut off, nobody else would tell him, and Tigranes was sitting in ignorance while the fires of war were burning round him, and listening to flattering words, That Lucullus would be a great general if he should venture to stand against Tigranes at Ephesus, and should not flee forthwith from Asia, at the sight of so many tens of thousands. So true it is, that it is not every man who can bear much wine, nor is it any ordinary understanding that in great prosperity does not lose all sound judgment. The first of his friends who ventured to tell him the truth was Mithrobarzanes; and he, too, got no reward for his boldness in speaking; for he was sent forthwith against Lucullus, with three thousand horsemen and a very large body of infantry, with orders to bring the general alive, and to trample down his men. Now, part of the army of Lucullus was preparing to halt, and the rest was still advancing. When the scouts reported that the barbarian was coming upon them, Lucullus was afraid that the enemy would fall upon his troops while they were divided and not in battle order, and so put them into confusion. Lucullus himself set to work to superintend the encampment, and he sent Sextilius, one of his legati, with sixteen hundred horsemen, and hoplitæ and light-armed troops, a few more in number, with orders to approach close to the enemy, and wait till he should hear that the soldiers who were with him had made their encampment. Sextilius wished to follow his orders; but he was compelled to engage by Mithrobarzanes, who was confidently advancing against him. A battle ensued, in which Mithrobarzanes fell fighting; and the rest, taking to flight, were all cut to pieces with the exception of a few. Upon this Tigranes left Tigranocerta, a large city which he had founded, and retreated to the Taurus, and there began to get together his forces from all parts: but Lucullus, allowing him no time for preparation, sent Murena to harass and cut off those who were collecting to join Tigranes, and Sextilius on the other side to check a large body of Arabs, who were approaching to the king. It happened just at the same time that Sextilius fell on the Arabs as they were encamping and killed most of them, and Murena, following Tigranes, took the opportunity of attacking him as he was passing through a rough and narrow defile with his army in a long line. Tigranes fled, and left behind him all his baggage; and many of the Armenians were killed and still more taken prisoners.

XXVI. After this success Lucullus broke up his camp and marched against Tigranocerta, which he surrounded with his lines, and began to besiege. There were in the city many Greeks, a part of those who had been removed from Cilicia, and many barbarians who had fared the same way with the Greeks, Adiabeni, and Assyrians, and Gordyeni and Cappadocians, whose native cities Tigranes had digged down, and had removed the inhabitants and settled them there. The city was also filled with wealth and sacred offerings, for every private individual and prince, in order to please the king, contributed to the increase and ornament of the city. For this reason Lucullus pressed the siege, thinking that Tigranes would not endure this, but even contrary to his judgment, would come down in passion and fight a battle; and he was not mistaken. Now, Mithridates, both by messengers and letters, strongly advised Tigranes not to fight a battle, but to cut off the enemy's supplies by means of his cavalry; and Taxiles also, who had come from Mithridates to join Tigranes, earnestly entreated the king to keep on the defensive, and to avoid the arms of the Romans, as being invincible. Tigranes at first readily listened to this advice: but when the Armenians and Gordyeni had joined him with all their forces, and the kings were come, bringing with them all the power of the Medes and Adiabeni, and many Arabs had arrived from the sea that borders on Babylonia, and many Albanians from the Caspian, and Iberians, who are neighbours of the Albanians; and not a few of the tribes about the Araxes, who are not governed by kings, had come to join him, induced by solicitations and presents, and the banquets of the king were filled with hopes and confidence and barbaric threats, and his councils also,—Taxiles narrowly escaped death for opposing the design of fighting, and it was believed that Mithridates wished to divert Tigranes from obtaining a great victory, merely from envy. Accordingly, Tigranes would not even wait for Mithridates, for fear he should share in the glory; but he advanced with all his force, and greatly complained to his friends, it is said, that he would have to encounter Lucullus alone, and not all the Roman generals at once. And his confidence was not altogether madness nor without good grounds, when he looked upon so many nations and kings following him, and bodies of hoplitæ, and tens of thousands of horsemen; for he was at the head of twenty thousand bowmen and slingers and fifty-five thousand horsemen, of whom seventeen thousand were clothed in armour of mail, as Lucullus said in his letter to the Senate, and one hundred and fifty thousand hoplitæ, some of whom were drawn up in cohorts and others in phalanx; and of road-makers, bridge-makers, clearers of rivers, timber-cutters, and labourers for other necessary purposes, there were thirty-five thousand, who, being placed behind the fighting men, added to the imposing appearance and the strength of the army.

XXVII. When Tigranes had crossed the Taurus, and, showing himself with all his forces, looked down on the Roman army, which was encamped before Tigranocerta, the barbarians in the city hailed his appearance with shouts and clapping of hands, and from their walls with threats pointed to the Armenians. As Lucullus was considering about the battle, some advised him to give up the siege, and march against Tigranes; others urged him not to leave so many enemies in his rear, nor to give up the siege. Lucullus replied, that singly they did not advise well, but that taken both together the counsel was good; on which he divided his army. He left Murena with six thousand foot to maintain the siege; and himself taking twenty-four cohorts, among which there were not above ten thousand hoplitæ, with all his cavalry and slingers and bowmen, to the number of about one thousand, advanced against the enemy. Lucullus, encamping in a large plain by the bank of the river, appeared contemptible to Tigranes, and furnished matter for amusement to the king's flatterers. Some scoffed at him, and others, by way of amusement, cast lots for the spoil, and all the generals and kings severally applied to the king, and begged the matter might be intrusted to each of them singly, and that Tigranes would sit as a spectator. Tigranes also attempted to be witty, and, in a scoffing manner, he uttered the well-known saying, "If they have come as ambassadors, there are too many of them; if as soldiers, too few." Thus they amused themselves with sarcastic sayings and jokes. At daybreak Lucullus led out his troops under arms. Now the barbarian army was on the east side of the river; but, as the river makes a bend towards the west, at a part where it was easiest to ford, Lucullus led his troops out, and hurried in that direction, which led Tigranes to think that he was retreating; and calling Taxiles to him he said, with a laugh, "Don't you see that these invincible Roman warriors are flying?" Taxiles replied: "I should be pleased, O king, at any strange thing happening which should be lucky to you; but the Roman soldiers do not put on their splendid attire when they are on a march; nor have they then their shields cleaned, and their helmets bare, as they now have, by reason of having taken off the leathern coverings; but this brightness of their armour is a sign they are going to fight, and are now marching against their enemies." While Taxiles was still speaking the first eagle came in sight; for Lucullus had now faced about, and the cohorts were seen taking their position in manipuli for the purpose of crossing the river: on which Tigranes, as if he were hardly recovering from a drunken bout, called out two or three times, "What, are they coming against us?" and so, with much confusion, the enemy's soldiers set about getting into order, the king taking his position in the centre, and giving the left wing to the King of the Adiabeni, and the right to the Mede, on which wing also were the greater part of the soldiers, clad in mail, occupying the first ranks. As Lucullus was going to cross the river, some of the officers bade him beware of the day, which was one of the unlucky days which the Romans call black days; for on that day Cæpio and his army were destroyed in a battle with the Cimbri. Lucullus replied in these memorable words: "Well, I will make it a lucky day for the Romans." The day was the sixth of October.

XXVIII. Saying this, and bidding his men be of good cheer, Lucullus began to cross the river, and advanced against the enemy, at the head of his soldiers, with a breastplate of glittering scaly steel, and a cloak with a fringed border, and he just let it be seen that his sword was already bare, thereby indicating that they must forthwith come to close quarters with the enemy, who fought with missiles, and by the rapidity of the attack cut off the intervening space, within which the barbarians could use their bows. Observing that the mailed cavalry, which had a great reputation, were stationed under an eminence, crowned by a broad level space, and that the approach to it was only a distance of four stadia, and neither difficult nor rough, he ordered the Thracian cavalry and the Gauls who were in the army, to fall on them in the flank, and to beat aside their long spears with their swords. Now the mailed horsemen rely solely on their long spears, and they can do nothing else, either in their own defence or against the enemy, owing to the weight and rigidity of their armour, and they look like men who are walled up in it. Lucullus himself, with two cohorts, pushed on vigorously to the hill, followed by his men, who were encouraged by seeing him in his armour, enduring all the fatigue on foot, and pressing forwards. On reaching the summit, Lucullus stood on a conspicuous spot, and called out aloud: "We have got the victory! Fellow soldiers, we have got the victory!" With these words he led his men against the mailed horsemen, and ordered them not to use their javelins yet, but every man to hold them in both hands, and to thrust against the enemy's legs and thighs, which are the only parts of these mailed men that are bare. However, there was no occasion for this mode of fighting; for the enemy did not stand the attack of the Romans, but, setting up a shout and flying most disgracefully, they threw themselves and their horses, with all their weight, upon their own infantry, before the infantry had begun the battle, so that so many tens of thousands were defeated before a wound was felt or blood was drawn. Now the great slaughter began when the army turned to flight, or rather attempted to fly, for they could not really fly, owing to the closeness and depth of their ranks, which made them in the way of one another. Tigranes, riding off at the front, fled with a few attendants, and, seeing that his son was a partner in his misfortune, he took off the diadem from his head, and, with tears, presented it to him, at the same time telling him to save himself, as he best could, by taking some other direction. The youth would not venture to put the diadem on his head, but gave it to the most faithful of his slaves to keep. This slave, happening to be taken, was carried to Lucullus, and thus the diadem of Tigranes, with other booty, fell into the hands of the Romans. It is said that above one hundred thousand of the infantry perished, and very few of the cavalry escaped. On the side of the Romans, a hundred were wounded, and five killed. Antiochus the philosopher, who mentions this battle in his 'Treatise on the Gods,' says that the sun never saw a battle like it. Strabo, another philosopher, in his 'Historical Memoirs,' says that the Romans were ashamed, and laughed at one another, for requiring arms against such a set of slaves. And Livius observed that the Romans never engaged with an enemy with such inferiority of numbers on their side, for the victors were hardly the twentieth part of the defeated enemy, but somewhat less. The most skilful of the Roman generals, and those who had most military experience, commended Lucullus chiefly for this, that he had out-generalled the two most distinguished and powerful kings by two most opposite manœuvres, speed and slowness; for he wore out Mithridates, at the height of his power, by time and protracting the war; but he crushed Tigranes by his activity: and he was one of the very few commanders who ever employed delay when he was engaged in active operations, and bold measures when his safety was at stake.

XXIX. Mithridates made no haste to be present at the battle, because he supposed that Lucullus would carry on the campaign with his usual caution and delay; but he was advancing leisurely to join Tigranes. At first he fell in with a few Armenians on the road, who were retreating in great alarm and consternation, and he conjectured what had happened, but as he soon heard of the defeat from a large number whom he met, who had lost their arms and were wounded, he set out to seek Tigranes. Though he found Tigranes destitute of everything, and humbled, Mithridates did not retaliate for his former haughty behaviour, but he got down from his horse, and lamented with Tigranes their common misfortunes; he also gave Tigranes a royal train that was attending on him, and encouraged him to hope for the future. Accordingly, the two kings began to collect fresh forces. Now, in the city of Tigranocerta the Greeks had fallen to quarrelling with the barbarians, and were preparing to surrender the place to Lucullus, on which he assaulted and took it. Lucullus appropriated to himself the treasures in the city, but he gave up the city to be plundered by the soldiers, which contained eight thousand talents of coined money, with other valuable booty. Besides this, Lucullus gave to each man eight hundred drachmæ out of the produce of the spoils. Hearing that many actors had been taken in the city, whom Tigranes had collected from all quarters, with the view of opening the theatre which he had constructed, Lucullus employed them for the games and shows in celebration of the victory. The Greeks he sent to their homes, and supplied them with means for the journey, and in like manner those barbarians who had been compelled to settle there; the result of which was that the dissolution of one city was followed by the restoration of many others, which thus recovered their citizens, by whom Lucullus was beloved as a benefactor and a founder. Everything else also went on successfully and conformably to the merits of the general, who sought for the praise that is due to justice and humanity, and not the praise that follows success in war: for the success in war was due in no small degree, to the army and to fortune, but his justice and humanity proved that he had a mild and well-regulated temper; and it was by these means that Lucullus now subdued the barbarians without resorting to arms; for the kings of the Arabs came to him to surrender all that they had, and the Sopheni also came over to him. He also gained the affection of the Gordyeni so completely that they were ready to leave their cities, and to follow him, as volunteers, with their children and wives, the reason of which was as follows: Zarbienus, the King of the Gordyeni, as it has been already told, secretly communicated, through Appius, with Lucullus about an alliance, being oppressed by the tyranny of Tigranes; but his design was reported to Tigranes, and he was put to death, and his children and wife perished with him, before the Romans invaded Armenia. Lucullus did not forget all this; and, on entering Gordyene, he made a funeral for Zarbienus, and, ornamenting the pile with vests, and the king's gold, and the spoils got from Tigranes, he set fire to it himself, and poured libations on the pile, with the friends and kinsmen of the king, and gave him the name of friend and ally of the Roman people. He also ordered a monument to be erected to him at great cost; for a large quantity of gold and silver was found in the palace of Zarbienus, and there were stored up three million medimni of wheat, so that the soldiers were well supplied, and Lucullus was admired, that without receiving a drachma from the treasury, he made the war support itself.

XXX. While Lucullus was here, there came an embassy from the King of the Parthians also, who invited him to friendship and an alliance. This proposal was agreeable to Lucullus, and in return he sent ambassadors to the Parthian, who discovered that he was playing double and secretly asking Mesopotamia from Tigranes as the price of his alliance. On hearing this Lucullus determined to pass by Tigranes and Mithridates as exhausted antagonists, and to try the strength of the Parthians, and to march against them, thinking it a glorious thing, in one uninterrupted campaign, like an athlete, to give three kings in succession the throw, and to have made his way through three empires, the most powerful under the sun, unvanquished and victorious. Accordingly he sent orders to Sornatius and the other commanders in Pontus to conduct the army there to him, as he was intending to advance from Gordyene farther into Asia. These generals had already found that the soldiers were difficult to manage and mutinous; but now they made the ungovernable temper of the soldiers quite apparent, being unable by any means of persuasion or compulsion to move the soldiers, who, with solemn asseverations, declared aloud that they would not stay even where they were, but would go and leave Pontus undefended. Report of this being carried to the army of Lucullus effected the corruption of his soldiers also, who had been made inert towards military service by the wealth they had acquired and their luxurious living, and they wanted rest; and, when they heard of the bold words of the soldiers in Pontus, they said they were men, and their example ought to be followed, for they had done enough to entitle them to be released from military service, and to enjoy repose.

XXXI. Lucullus, becoming acquainted with these and other still more mutinous expressions, gave up the expedition against the Parthians, and marched a second time against Tigranes. It was now the height of summer; and Lucullus was dispirited after crossing the Taurus, to see that the fields were still green, so much later are the seasons, owing to the coldness of the air. However, he descended from the Taurus, and, after defeating the Armenians, who twice or thrice ventured to attack him, he plundered the villages without any fear; and, by seizing the corn which had been stored up by Tigranes, he reduced the enemy to the straits which he was apprehending himself. Lucullus challenged the Armenians to battle by surrounding their camp with his lines and ravaging the country before their eyes; but, as this did not make them move after their various defeats, he broke up and advanced against Artaxata, the royal residence of Tigranes, where his young children and wives were, thinking that Tigranes would not give them up without a battle. It is said that Hannibal the Carthaginian, after the defeat of Antiochus by the Romans, went to Artaxas the Armenian, to whose notice he introduced many useful things; and, observing a position which possessed great natural advantages and was very pleasant, though at that time unoccupied and neglected, he made the plan of a city on the ground, and, taking Artaxas there, showed it to him, and urged him to build up the place. The king, it is said, was pleased, and asked Hannibal to superintend the work; and thereupon a large and beautiful city sprung up, and, being named after the king, was declared to be the capital of Armenia. Tigranes did not let Lucullus quietly march against Artaxata, but, moving with his forces on the fourth day, he encamped opposite to the Romans, placing the river Arsanias between him and the enemy, which river the Romans must of necessity cross on their route to Artaxata. After sacrificing to the gods, Lucullus, considering that he had the victory in his hands, began to lead his army across the river, with twelve cohorts in the van, and the rest placed as a reserve to prevent the enemy from attacking his flank. There was a large body of picked cavalry opposed to the Romans, and in front of them Mardi mounted archers, and Iberians armed with spears, on whom Tigranes relied more than any of his mercenaries, as being the most warlike of all. However, they showed no gallant spirit; but, after a slight skirmish with the Roman cavalry, they did not venture to stand the attack of the infantry, and separating and taking to flight on both sides they drew after them the cavalry in the pursuit. At the moment when this part of the enemy was dispersed, the cavalry, which was about Tigranes, rode forward, and Lucullus was alarmed when he saw their brave appearance and numbers. He recalled the cavalry from the pursuit, and himself was the first to meet the Satrapeni, who were posted opposite to him with the king's chief officers; but before they came to close quarters, the enemy was panic-struck and turned to flight. Of three kings at the same time opposed to the Romans, Mithridates of Pontus appears to have fled most disgracefully; for he did not stay to hear even the shouts of the Romans. The pursuit was continued for a great distance and all night long, and the Romans were wearied with killing and taking prisoners, and getting valuables and booty. Livius says that in the former battle a greater number of the enemy, but in this more men of rank fell and were taken prisoners.

XXXII. Elated and encouraged by this victory, Lucullus was intending to advance farther into the country, and to subdue the barbarian; but contrary to what one would have expected at the season of the autumnal equinox, they were assailed by heavy storms, generally snow-storms, and, when the sky was clear, there was hoar-frost and ice, owing to which the horses could not well drink of the rivers, by reason of the excessive cold; and they were difficult to ford, because the ice broke, and the rough edges cut the horses' sinews. And as the greater part of the country was shaded and full of defiles and wooded, the soldiers were kept continually wet, being loaded with snow while they were marching, and spending the night uncomfortably in damp places. Accordingly, they had not followed Lucullus for many days after the battle when they began to offer resistance, at first making entreaties and also sending the tribunes to him, and then collecting in a tumultuous manner, with loud shouts in their tents by night, which is considered to be an indication that an army is in a state of mutiny. Yet Lucullus urged them strongly, and called on them to put endurance in their souls till they had taken and destroyed the Armenian Carthage, the work of their greatest enemy, meaning Hannibal. Not being able to prevail on them, he led them back by a different pass over the Taurus, and descended into the country called Mygdonike, which is fertile and warm, and contains a large and populous city, which the barbarians called Nisibis, but the Greeks Antiocha Mygdonike. The city was defended in name by Gouras, a brother of Tigranes, but in fact by the experience and mechanical skill of Kallimachus, who had given Lucullus great trouble in the siege of Amisus also. Lucullus seated himself before the city, and, by availing himself of every mode of pressing a siege, in a short time he took the city by storm. Gouras, who surrendered himself to Lucullus, was treated kindly; but he would not listen to Kallimachus, though he promised to discover concealed treasures of great value; and he ordered him to be brought in chains to be punished for the conflagration by which he destroyed Amisus and deprived Lucullus of the object of his ambition and an opportunity of displaying his friendly disposition to the Greeks.

XXXIII. So far one may say that fortune accompanied Lucullus and shared his campaigns: but from this time, just as if a wind had failed him, trying to force everything and always meeting with obstacles, he displayed indeed the courage and endurance of a good commander, but his undertakings produced him neither fame nor good opinion, and even the reputation that he had he came very near losing by his want of success and his fruitless disputes. Lucullus himself was in no small degree the cause of all this; for he was not a man who tried to gain the affection of the soldiery, and he considered everything that was done to please the men as a disparagement to the general's power, and as tending to destroy it. But, what was worst of all, he was not affable to the chief officers and those of the same rank as himself; he despised everybody, and thought no man had any merit compared with his own. These bad qualities, it is said, that Lucullus had, though he possessed many merits. He was tall and handsome, a powerful speaker, and equally prudent in the Forum and the camp. Now, Sallustius says that the soldiers were ill-disposed towards him at the very commencement of the war before Kyzikus, and again at Amisus, because they were compelled to spend two winters in succession in camp. They were also vexed about the other winters, for they either spent them in a hostile country, or encamped among the allies under the bare sky; for Lucullus never once entered a Greek and friendly city with his army. While the soldiers were in this humour, they received encouragement from the demagogues at Rome, who envied Lucullus, and charged him with protracting the war through love of power and avarice. They said that he all but held at once Cilicia, Asia, Bithynia, Paphlagonia, Galatia, Pontus, Armenia, and the parts as far as the Phasis, and that at last he had plundered even the palace of Tigranes, as if he had been sent to strip kings and not to conquer them. This, it is said, was urged by one of the prætors, Lucius Quintus, by whom they were mainly persuaded to pass a decree to send persons to supersede Lucullus in his province. They also decreed that many of the soldiers under Lucullus should be released from service.

XXXIV. To these causes, in themselves so weighty, there was added another that, most of all, ruined the measures of Lucullus; and this was Publius Clodius, a violent man, and full of arrogance and audacity. He was the brother of the wife of Lucullus, a woman of most dissolute habits, whom he was also accused of debauching. At this time he was serving with Lucullus, and he did not get all the distinction to which he thought himself entitled. In fact, he aspired to the first rank, and, as there were many preferred before him, in consequence of his character, he secretly endeavoured to win the favour of Fimbria's army, and to excite the soldiers against Lucullus, by circulating among them words well suited to those who were ready to hear them, and were not unaccustomed to be courted. These were the men whom Fimbria had persuaded to kill the consul Flaccus, and to choose himself for their general. Accordingly, they gladly listened to Clodius, and called him the soldier's friend, for he pretended to feel indignant at their treatment. "Was there never to be an end," he would say, "to so many wars and dangers, and were they to wear out their lives in fighting with every nation, and wandering over every country, and getting no equivalent for so much service, but, instead thereof, were they to convoy waggons and camels of Lucullus, loaded with cups of gold, set with precious stones, while the soldiers of Pompeius were now living as citizens, and with their wives and children were sitting quiet in the enjoyment of fertile lands and cities, though they had not driven Mithridates and Tigranes into uninhabited wildernesses, nor pulled down the palaces of Asia, but had fought with exiles in Iberia, and runaway slaves in Italy? Why, then, if there is never to be an end of our service, do we not reserve what remains of our bodies and our lives for a general who considers the wealth of the soldiers his chief glory?" By such causes as these the army of Lucullus was corrupted, and his soldiers refused to follow him either against Tigranes or against Mithridates, who immediately made an irruption from Armenia into Pontus, and endeavoured to recover his power; but alleging the winter as an excuse, the soldiers lingered in Gordyene, expecting every moment that Pompeius, or some other commander, would arrive to supersede Lucullus.

XXXV. But when news came that Mithridates had defeated Fabius, and was marching against Sornatius and Triarius, through very shame the soldiers followed Lucullus. Triarius, being ambitious to snatch the victory which he thought was in his grasp, before Lucullus, who was near, should arrive, was defeated in a great battle. It is said that above seven thousand Romans fell, among whom were a hundred and fifty centurions, and twenty-four tribunes; and Mithridates took the camp. Lucullus arrived a few days after, and secreted from the soldiers Triarius, whom in their passion, they wore looking for; and, as Mithridates was not willing to fight, but was waiting for Tigranes, who was already coming down with a large force, Lucullus determined to march back, and to fight with Tigranes before he and Mithridates could unite. As he was on his march the soldiers of Fimbria mutinied, and left their ranks, considering that they were released from service by the decree of the Senate, and that Lucullus had no longer any right to the command, now that the provinces were assigned to others. Upon this there was nothing, however inconsistent with his dignity, which Lucullus did not submit to do—supplicating the soldiers individually, and going about from tent to tent in humble manner, and with tears in his eyes, and sometimes even taking the soldiers by the hand. But they rejected his proffered hand, and threw down before him their empty purses, and told him to fight with the enemy himself, for he was the only person who knew how to get rich from them. However, at the request of the rest of the army, the soldiers of Fimbria were constrained, and agreed to stay to the end of summer, and if, in the meantime, no enemy should come down to fight them, they were then to be released. Lucullus was of necessity obliged to acquiesce in this, or else to be left alone, and give up the country to the barbarians. He therefore kept the soldiers together, without making any further attempt to force them, or lead them out to battle, for he was well content if they would stay with him, and he allowed Cappadocia to be ravaged by Tigranes, and Mithridates to resume his arrogance, as to whom he had written to the Senate, to inform them that he was completely subdued; and the commissioners were now with him who had been sent to settle the affairs of Pontus, on the supposition that the country was completely in the power of the Romans. Indeed, the commissioners were now witnesses that Lucullus was not his own master, but was treated with contumely and insult by the soldiers, who carried their audacity towards their commander so far, that, at the close of the summer, they put on their armour, and drawing their swords, challenged to battle the enemy who were no longer there, but had already moved off. After uttering the war shout, and flourishing their swords in the air, they left the camp, declaring that the time was up which they had agreed to stay with Lucullus. The rest of the soldiers were summoned by Pompeius by letter, for he had been appointed to the command in the war against Mithridates and Tigranes, by the favour of the people, and through the influence of the demagogues; though the Senate and the nobles thought that Lucullus was wronged, inasmuch as he was not superseded in a war, but in a triumph; and it was not the command, but the honours of the command that he was compelled to divest himself of, and to surrender to others.

XXXVI. But it appeared a still greater wrong to those who were with Lucullus in Asia, that Lucullus had not the power either to reward or punish for anything that was done in the war; nor did Pompeius allow any person to go to him, nor to pay any attention to the orders and regulations that he was making in concert with the ten commissioners, but he obstructed him by publishing counter edicts, and by the fear which he inspired from having a larger force. However, their friends agreed to bring them together, and they met in a village of Galatia, where they saluted one another in a friendly manner, and each congratulated the other on his victories. Lucullus was the elder, but Pompeius had the greater reputation, because he had oftener had the command, and enjoyed two triumphs. Fasces, wreathed with bay, were carried before both generals in token of their victories. But, as Pompeius had made a long march through a country without water and arid, the bays upon his fasces were withered, which the lictors of Lucullus observing, in a friendly manner gave them bays out of their own, which were fresh and green. And this the friends of Pompeius interpreted as a good omen; for, in fact, the exploits of Lucullus served to set off the command of Pompeius. But the conference resulted in no amicable arrangement, and they separated with increased aversion towards each other. Pompeius also annulled the regulations of Lucullus, and he took off with him all the soldiers with the exception of sixteen hundred, whom he left to Lucullus for his triumph; and even these did not follow him very willingly: so ill suited was the temper of Lucullus, or so unlucky was he in securing that which, of all things, is the chief and greatest in a general; for, if he had possessed this quality, with the other many and great virtues that he had, courage, activity, judgment, and justice, the Roman empire would not have had the Euphrates for its limit, but the remotest parts of Asia, and the Hyrkanian Sea; for all the other nations had already been defeated by Tigranes, and the Parthian power was not such as it afterwards showed itself to be in the campaign of Crassus, nor so well combined, but owing to intestine and neighbouring wars, was not even strong enough to repel the attacks of the Armenians. But it seems to me that the services of Lucullus to his country were less than the harm he did it in other things; for his trophies in Armenia, which were erected on the borders of Parthia, and Tigranocerta, and Nisibis, and the great wealth that was brought from these cities to Rome, and the display of the diadem of Tigranes in his triumph, urged Crassus to attack Asia, and to think that the barbarians were only spoil and booty, and nothing else. But Crassus soon felt the Parthian arrows, and so proved that Lucullus had got the advantage over the enemy, not through their want of skill or cowardice, but by his own courage and ability. This, however, happened afterwards.

XXXVII. When Lucullus returned to Rome, first of all he found that his brother Marcus was under prosecution by Caius Memmius, for what he had done in his quæstorship at the command of Sulla. Upon Marcus being acquitted, Memmius transferred his attack to Lucullus himself, and endeavoured to excite the people against him, and persuaded them not to give him a triumph, on the ground that he had appropriated to himself much of the spoils, and had prolonged the war. Now that Lucullus was involved in a great struggle, the first and most powerful men, mingling themselves among the tribes, by much entreaty and exertion with difficulty persuaded the people to allow Lucullus to have a triumph; not, however, like some, a triumph which was striking and bustling, from the length of the procession, and the quantity of things that were displayed, but he decorated the circus of Flaminius with the arms of the enemy, of which he had a great quantity, and with the royal engines of war; and it was a spectacle in itself far from being contemptible. In the procession a few of the mailed horsemen, and ten of the scythe-bearing chariots moved along, with sixty of the king's friends and generals, and a hundred and ten brazen-beaked ships of war also were carried in the procession, and a gold statue of Mithridates six feet high, and a shield ornamented with precious stones, and twenty litters loaded with silver vessels, and two-and-thirty loaded with golden cups, armour, and money. All this was carried on men's shoulders; but there were eight mules that bore golden couches, and fifty-six carried silver in bars, and a hundred and seven others carried silver coin to the amount of near two million seven hundred thousand pieces. There were also tablets, on which was written the amount of money that Lucullus had supplied Pompeius with for the pirates' war, and the amount that he had paid to those who had the care of the ærarium; and besides this, it was added that every soldier received nine hundred and fifty drachmæ. After this Lucullus feasted all the city in a splendid style, and the surrounding villages which the Romans call Vici.

XXXVIII. After Lucullus had divorced Clodia, who was a loose and unprincipled woman, he married Servilia, the sister of Cato, but neither was this a happy marriage; for he thus escaped only one of the misfortunes that resulted from his union with Clodia, the scandal about her brothers: in every other respect Servilia was as abominable as Clodia and a licentious woman, and yet Lucullus was obliged to bear with her from regard to Cato; but at last he put her away. Lucullus had raised the highest expectations in the Senate, who hoped to find in him a counterpoise to the overbearing conduct of Pompeius and a defender of the aristocracy, inasmuch as he had the advantage of great reputation and influence; but he disappointed these hopes and gave up political affairs, either because he saw that they were already in a difficult position and not in a healthy state, or, as some say, because he was satisfied with glory, and wished to fall back to an easy and luxurious life, after his many contests and dangers, which had not been followed by the most fortunate of results. Some commend him for making such a change, whereby he avoided what had befallen Marius, who, after his Cimbrian victories and that great and glorious success, did not choose to dedicate himself to honour so great and to be an object of admiration, but through insatiate desire of glory and power, though an old man, entered into political warfare with young men, and so ended his career in dreadful acts, and in sufferings more dreadful than acts; and they say that Cicero also would have had a better old age if he had withdrawn from public life after the affair of Catiline, and Scipio after he had added the conquest of Numantia to that of Carthage, if he had then stopped; for there is a close to a political period also, and political contests as well as those of athletes are censured when a man's vigour and prime have failed him. But Crassus and Pompeius sneered at Lucullus for giving himself up to pleasure and extravagant living, as if a luxurious life was not more unsuitable to persons of his age than affairs of state and military command.

XXXIX. Now in the life of Lucullus, as in an ancient comedy, we may read, in the first part, of political measures and military command, and, in the last part, of drinking and feasts, and hardly anything but revels, and torches, and all kinds of amusement; for I reckon among amusements, expensive buildings, and construction of ambulatories and baths, and still more paintings and statues, and eagerness about works of this kind, all which he got together at great cost, and to this end spent profusely the wealth which he had accumulated to a large and splendid amount in his military command; for, even now, when luxury of this kind has increased, the gardens of Lucullus are reckoned among the most sumptuous of the imperial gardens. But with respect to his works on the sea-coast and in the neighbourhood of Neapolis, where he suspended as it were hills by digging great tunnels, and threw around his dwelling-places circular pieces of sea-water and channels for the breeding of fish, and built houses in the sea, Tubero the Stoic, on seeing them, called him Xerxes in a toga. He had also country residences in the neighbourhood of Tusculum, and towers commanding prospects, and open apartments and ambulatories, which Pompeius on visiting found fault with Lucullus, that he had arranged his house in the best way for summer, but had made it unfit to live in during the winter. On which Lucullus said, with a smile, "You think, then, I have less sense than the cranes and storks, and do not change my residence according to the seasons." On one occasion, when a prætor was ambitious to signalize himself in the matter of a public spectacle, and asked of Lucullus some purple cloaks for the dress of a chorus, Lucullus replied, that he would see if he had any and would give them to him; and the day after he asked the prætor how many he wanted. The prætor said that a hundred would be enough, on which Lucullus told him to take twice as many;

in allusion to which the poet Flaccus has remarked, that he does not consider a man to be rich, if the property that he cares not for and knows nothing about is not more than that which he sees.

XL. The daily meals of Lucullus were accompanied with all the extravagance of newly-acquired wealth; for it was not only by dyed coverlets for his couches, and cups set with precious stones, and choruses and dramatic entertainments, but by abundance of all kinds of food and dainty dishes, curiously prepared, that he made himself an object of admiration to the uninstructed. Now Pompeius gained a good reputation in an illness that he had; for the physician had ordered him to eat a thrush, and, on his domestics telling him that a thrush could not be found in the summer season except at the house of Lucullus, where they were fed, Pompeius would not consent to have one got from there; but remarking to his physician, "What, if Lucullus were not so luxurious, could not Pompeius live?" bade them get for him something else that could be easily procured. Cato, who was his friend and connected with him by marriage, was so much annoyed at his life and habits that, on one occasion, when a young man had delivered in the senate a tedious and lengthy discourse, quite out of season, on frugality and temperance, Cato got up and said, "Won't you stop, you who are as rich as Crassus, and live like Lucullus, and speak like Cato?" Some say that a remark to this effect was made, but that it was not by Cato.

XLI. That Lucullus was not merely pleased with this mode of living, but prided himself upon it, appears from the anecdotes that are recorded. It is said, that he feasted for many days some Greeks who visited Rome, and that they, feeling as Greeks would do on the occasion, began to be ashamed and to decline the invitation, on the ground that he was daily incurring so much expense on their account; but Lucullus said to them with a smile, "It is true, Greeks, that this is partly done on your account, but mainly on the account of Lucullus." One day, when he was supping alone, a single course and a moderate repast had been prepared for him, at which he was angry, and called for the slave whose business it was to look after such matters. The slave said, that he did not suppose that he would want anything costly, as no guest was invited. "What sayest thou?" said Lucullus, "didst thou not know that to-day Lucullus sups with Lucullus?" Now, this matter being much talked of in the city, as one might expect, there came up to Lucullus, as he was idling in the Forum, Cicero and Pompeius, of whom Cicero was among his most intimate friends; but between Lucullus and Pompeius there was some difference, arising out of the affair of the command in the Mithridatic war, and yet they were accustomed to associate and talk together frequently in a friendly manner. Accordingly, Cicero saluted him, and asked him how he was disposed to receive visitors, to which Lucullus replied, "Exceedingly well," and invited them to pay him a visit. "We wish," said Cicero, "to sup with you to-day, just in the same way as if preparation were made for yourself only." Lucullus began to make some difficulty, and to ask them to allow him to name another day; but they said they would not, nor would they let him speak to his servants, that he might not have the opportunity of ordering anything more than what was preparing for himself. However, at his request, they allowed him just to tell one of his slaves in their presence, that he would sup on that day in the Apollo; for this was the name of one of his costly apartments. This trick of Lucullus was not understood by his guests; for it is said that to every banqueting-room there was assigned the cost of the feast there, and every room had its peculiar style of preparation and entertainment, so that when the slaves heard in which room their master intended to sup, they also knew what was to be the cost of the supper and the kind of decoration and arrangement. Now, Lucullus was accustomed to sup in the Apollo at the cost of fifty thousand drachmas, and this being the cost of the entertainment on the present occasion, Pompeius and Cicero were surprised at the rapidity with which the banquet had been got ready and the costliness of the entertainment. In this way, then, Lucullus used his wealth, capriciously, just as if it were a captive slave and a barbarian.

XLII. What he did as to his collection of books is worth notice and mention. He got together a great number of books which were well transcribed, and the mode in which they were used was more honourable to him than the acquisition of them; for the libraries were open to all, and the walking-places which surrounded them, and the reading rooms were accessible to the Greeks without any restriction, and they went there as to an abode of the Muses, and spent the day there in company with one another, gladly betaking themselves to the libraries from their other occupations. Lucullus himself often spent some time there with the visitors, walking about in the ambulatories, and he used to talk there with men engaged in public affairs on such matters as they might choose; and altogether his house was a home and a Greek prytaneum to those who came to Rome. He was fond of philosophy generally, and well disposed to every sect, and friendly to them all; but from the first he particularly admired and loved the Academy, not that which is called the New Academy, though the sect was then flourishing by the propagation of the doctrines of Karneades by Philo, but Old Academy, which at that time had for its head a persuasive man and a powerful speaker, Antiochus of Askalon, whom Lucullus eagerly sought for his friend and companion, and opposed to the followers of Philo, of whom Cicero also was one. Cicero wrote an excellent treatise upon the doctrines of this sect, in which he made Lucullus the speaker in favour of the doctrine of comprehension and himself the speaker on the opposite side. The book is entitled 'Lucullus.' Lucullus and Cicero were, as I have said, great friends, and associated in their political views, for Lucullus had not entirely withdrawn from public affairs, though he had immediately on his return to Rome surrendered to Crassus and Cato the ambition and the struggle to be the first man in the state and have the greatest power, considering that the struggle was not free from danger and great mortification; for those who looked with jealousy on the power of Pompeius put Crassus and Cato at the head of their party in the Senate, when Lucullus declined to take the lead, but Lucullus used to go to the Forum to support his friends, and to the Senate whenever it was necessary to put a check on any attempt or ambitious design of Pompeius. The arrangements which Pompeius made after his conquest of the kings, Lucullus contrived to nullify, and when Pompeius proposed a distribution of lands Lucullus with the assistance of Cato prevented it from being made, which drew Pompeius to seek the friendship of Crassus and Cæsar, or rather to enter into a combination with them, and by filling the city with arms and soldiers he got his measures ratified after driving out of the Forum the partisans of Cato and Lucullus. The nobles being indignant at these proceedings, the party of Pompeius produced one Vettius, whom, as they said, they had detected in a design on the life of Pompeius. When Vettius was examined before the Senate, he accused others, and before the popular assembly he named Lucullus as the person by whom he had been suborned to murder Pompeius. But nobody believed him, and it soon became clear that the man had been brought forward by the partisans of Pompeius to fabricate a false charge, and to criminate others, and the fraud was made still more apparent, when a few days after the dead body of Vettius was thrown out of the prison; for, though it was given out that he died a natural death there were marks of strangulation and violence on the body, and it was the opinion that he had been put to death by those who suborned him.

XLIII. This induced Lucullus still more to withdraw from public affairs; and when Cicero was banished from Rome, and Cato was sent to Cyprus, he retired altogether. Before he died, it is said that his understanding was disordered and gradually failed. Cornelius Nepos says that Lucullus did not die of old age nor of disease, but that his health was destroyed by potions given him by Callisthenes, one of his freedmen, and that the potions were given him by Callisthenes with the view of increasing his master's affection for him, a power which the potions were supposed to have, but they so far disturbed and destroyed his reason, that during his lifetime his brother managed his affairs. However, when Lucullus died, the people grieved just as much as if he had died at the height of his military distinction and his political career, and they flocked together and had his body carried to the Forum by the young men of the highest rank and were proceeding forcibly to have it interred in the Campus Martius where Sulla was interred; but, as nobody had expected this, and it was not easy to make the requisite preparations, the brother of Lucullus prayed and prevailed on the people to allow the funeral ceremony to take place on the estate at Tusculum, where preparations for it had been made. Nor did he long survive; but as in age and reputation he came a little after Lucullus, so he died shortly after him, a most affectionate brother.

# Comparison of Kimon and Lucullus.

Lucullus may be accounted especially fortunate in having died when he did, so that he did not witness the ruin of his country by the civil wars, but departed this life while Rome, though corrupt, was yet a free state. And in this he resembles Kimon more than in any other point; for Kimon also died while the Greeks were at the height of their prosperity, and before they had begun to fight against one another. Indeed, Kimon died in his camp, while acting as commander-in-chief of his country's forces, at the siege of Kitium in Cyprus; not retired home, as if worn out with hard service, nor yet indulging in feasting and wine-drinking, as though that were the end and reward of his military achievements; like that life of eternal drunkenness which Plato sneers at the Orphic school for promising to their disciples as their reward hereafter.

A peaceful retirement, and a life of literary leisure, is no doubt a great comfort to a man who has withdrawn himself from taking any active part in politics; but to perform notable exploits with no object in view except to obtain the means of enjoyment, and to pass from the command of armies and the conduct of great wars to a life of voluptuous indolence and luxury seems unworthy of a philosopher of the Academy, or of any who profess to follow the doctrine of Xenokrates, and to be rather fit for a disciple of Epikurus. It is a remarkable circumstance that the youth of Kimon seems to have been licentious and extravagant, while that of Lucullus was spent in a sober and virtuous fashion. Clearly he is the better man that changes for the better; for that nature must be the more excellent in which vice decays, and virtue gains strength. Moreover, both Kimon and Lucullus were wealthy; but they made a very different use of their wealth. We cannot compare the building of the south wall of the Acropolis of Athens, which was completed with the money won by Kimon in the wars, with the luxurious pavilions and villas washed by the sea which Lucullus erected in Neapolis with the spoils he had taken from the barbarian enemies of Rome. Still less can we compare the generous and popular hospitality of Kimon with the Eastern profusion and extravagance of Lucullus's table; for Kimon, at a small expense, fed many of his countrymen daily, while the other spent enormous sums to provide luxuries for a small circle of friends. Yet this difference in their habits may have been caused by the times in which they lived; and no one can tell whether Kimon, if he had returned home and spent an old age of indolence and unwarlike repose, might not have even exceeded Lucullus in riotous luxury; for he was fond of wine and of society, and, as has been told in his life, was greatly addicted to women. But success in war or in politics so delights ambitious natures that they have no time for pursuing minor pleasures. Had Lucullus died at the head of his army, I suppose that the most captious critic could scarcely have found anything to blame in his life. So much, then, for their mode of living.

II. Now with regard to their warlike operations, there can be no doubt that both proved themselves to be consummate commanders, both by land and by sea; yet, as we are accustomed to call those athletes who have in one day been successful both in wrestling and in the pankratium by the name of notable victors, so Kimon, who in one day won a victory both by sea and by land, thus gaining a double triumph for Greece, deserves to be given some place above all other generals. Moreover, Lucullus was given the chief command by his country, but Kimon won for his country the honour of commanding the other Greek states. Lucullus found his country in command of allies, and by their aid overthrew the enemy, but Kimon found his country acting under the command of others, and by his own force of character both made Athens the leading state in Greece and overcame the enemy, for he drove the Persians from the sea, and persuaded the Lacedæmonians to resign their claims to supremacy. If we are to believe it to be the greatest proof of ability in a general to be loved and willingly obeyed by his soldiers, then we see that Lucullus was despised by his soldiers, while Kimon was esteemed and looked up to by his allies, for the soldiers of Lucullus revolted from him, while the Greek states revolted from Sparta in order to join Kimon. Thus the former was sent out in chief command, and returned home deserted by his men, while the other, though sent out to act as a subordinate under the command of others, ended by returning as commander-in-chief of them all, having succeeded, in spite of the greatest difficulties, in obtaining three great advantages for his countrymen, namely, having delivered them from the fear of their enemies, having given them authority over their confederates, and established a lasting friendship between them and the Lacedæmonians. Both commanders attempted an enormous task, the conquest of Asia; and both were forced to leave their work unfinished. Kimon was prevented by death, for he died at the head of an army and in the full tide of success; while one cannot altogether think that Lucullus was not to blame for not having tried to satisfy the complaints of his soldiers, which caused them to hate him so bitterly. In this point Lucullus and Kimon are alike; for Kimon was often impeached by his countrymen, who at last banished him by ostracism, in order that, as Plato said, they might not hear his voice for ten years. It seldom happens that men born to command can please the people, or have anything in common with them; because they cause pain by their attempts to rule and reform them, just as the bandages of a surgeon cause pain to the patient, when by their means he is endeavouring to force back dislocated limbs into their proper position. For this reason, methinks, neither Kimon nor Lucullus deserve blame.

III. Lucullus accomplished by far the greater exploits of the two, as he marched beyond the Mount Taurus with an army, being the first Roman who ever did so, and also crossed the river Tigris, and took and burned the royal cities of Asia, Tigranocerta, Kabeira, Sinope, and Nisibis, in the sight of their kings. Towards the north, he went as far as the river Phasis; towards the east as far as Media; and southwards as far as the Red Sea and the kingdom of Arabia, subduing it all to the Roman Empire. He destroyed the power of two mighty kings, and left them in possession of nothing but their lives, forcing them to hide themselves like hunted beasts, in trackless wastes and impassable forests. A great proof of the completeness of Lucullus's success is to be found in the fact that the Persians soon after Kimon's death, attacked the Greeks as vigorously as if they had never been defeated by Kimon at all, and defeated a large Greek army in Egypt; while Tigranes and Mithridates never recovered from the overthrow they sustained from Lucullus. Mithridates was so crushed and broken in strength that he never dared to march out of his entrenchments and fight with Pompeius, but retired to Bosporus and died there; while Tigranes of his own accord came into the presence of Pompeius naked and unarmed, and cast down his royal diadem at his feet, not flattering him for the victories which he had won, but for those for which Lucullus had triumphed. He was well pleased to be allowed to resume the ensigns of royalty, and thereby admitted that he had before been deprived of them. He, therefore, is to be held the better general, as he is the better wrestler, who leaves his enemy weakest for his successor to deal with. Moreover, Kimon found the power of the Persians impaired, and their spirit broken by the series of defeats which they had sustained from Themistokles, Pausanias, and Leotychides, and was easily able to conquer men whose hearts were already vanquished: whereas Lucullus met Tigranes when he was full of courage, and in the midst of an unbroken career of victory. As for numbers, one cannot compare the multitudes who were opposed to Lucullus with the troops who were defeated by Kimon. Thus it appears that from whatever point of view we regard them, it is hard to say which was the better man, especially as heaven seems to have dealt so kindly with them both, in telling the one what to do, and the other what to avoid: so that it seems to appear by the testimony of the gods themselves, that they were both men of a noble and godlike nature.